Necessary Fraud

Legal History of North America

Legal History of North America

General Editor
  Gordon Morris Bakken, *California State University, Fullerton*

Associate Editors
  David J. Langum, *Samford University*
  John P. S. McLaren, *University of Victoria*
  John Phillip Reid, *New York University*

Necessary Fraud

Progressive Reform and Utah Coal

Nancy J. Taniguchi

University of Oklahoma Press : Norman and London

333.339
T16n

Library of Congress Cataloging-in-Publication Data

Taniguchi, Nancy J. (Nancy Jacobus), 1948–
    Necessary fraud : progressive reform and Utah coal / by Nancy J. Taniguchi.
        p.   cm.—(Legal history of North America ; v. 3)
    Includes bibliographical references and index.
    ISBN 0–8061–2818–6 (alk. paper)
    1. Coal leases—Utah—History—20th century. 2. Mining claims—Utah—History—20th century. 3. Railroad land grants—Utah—History—20th century. 4. Fraud—Utah—History—20th century. 5. Monopolies—Utah—History—20th century. 6. Public lands—United States—History—20th century. 7. Land reform—United States—History—20th century. 8. Antitrust law—United States.
    I. Title. II. Series.
    HD243.U8T36   1996
    333.33'9—dc20   95–53086
                                                                                        CIP

Necessary Fraud: Progressive Reform and Utah Coal is Volume 3 in the series Legal History of North America.

Text design by Debora Hackworth.

The paper in this book meets the guidelines for permanence and durability of the Committee on Production Guidelines for Book Longevity of the Council on Library Resources, Inc. ⊗

1   2   3   4   5   6   7   8   9   10

TO DASHIELL,
THE THIRD GENERATION BORN IN
CARBON COUNTY

Contents

Illustrations

ix

CHART

MAP

Acknowledgments

As a newcomer to Carbon County, Utah, in 1976, I attended a meeting of those interested in local history only to find out that the Utah State Historical Society was seeking a one-year intern, at a very modest salary, to work on nominating sites to the National Register of Historical Places. Thus began my career in history, leading eventually to graduate school and, now, a full-fledged teaching position. First of all, my thanks go to Allan Kent Powell and Philip F. Notarianni, who took on an unknown quantity and turned out a trained public historian. Second, as a starving graduate student, I was rescued by Dr. Floyd O'Neil, of the University of Utah's American West Center, who long ago realized the importance of this story and hired me to work on Utah coal. This study has grown far beyond that modest beginning, especially as it strayed into the realm of the law, where consistent help and advice has been forthcoming from Hugh A. Holub, an expert on the special problems of the West, and from Marcus A. Hollabaugh, a senior authority on the intricacies of federal antitrust prosecutions. Next, I need to thank my friends and colleagues who have shared information and given so much encouragement over the years: Helen Zeese Papanikolas; Frances Blackham Cunningham; Charles S. Peterson; Craig Fuller; Ronald Watt; Walter Jones; Linda Thatcher; Madge Tomsic and her nephew, Gary Tomsic; David Wetzel, and John Van Wagoner, who provided a family history with information I had been seeking for years. Carbon County officials (some of them now gone) expedited this study, including the county recorder, Ann O'Brien, and her ever-helpful staff; the former county clerk, the late Norman Pritchard; the county treasurer, Jessie Holdaway, and Ray Downard, former county assessor. Also thanks to Faye Torgerson, who (correctly) insisted that I needed to know word processing and taught me how to do it. In the remote corner of eastern Utah where most of this work was written, librarians were indispensible, especially Marge Sower, now retired from the Price City Library, and Lou Reinwand, formerly of the College of Eastern Utah.

A few people have been willing to read pieces of this manuscript, for which I am extremely grateful, especially to Carl Noggle, who read the entire first draft, and Hugh A. Holub (both former colleagues on the *bandersnatch*, the University of Arizona's off-campus newspaper that shocked the administration and forged such lasting friendships); and to Robert E. Jarvise, who helped clean up the final version. Vicki Eden graciously prepared the chart. To the staff and readers of the University of Oklahoma Press go thanks for their direction, especially to John Drayton and Mildred Logan, and to Gordon Bakken, and to Dennis Marshall for his efforts on my behalf.

All the study in the world does not create a true appreciation for coal. Only a visit to a mine can do that, and I am deeply grateful to Ricky Callor and to Dominic Guarascio, both of whom arranged separate tours to different mines, giving me a much firmer grasp of procedures, hardship, and coal-mining reality. To Sam Quigley, of Tower Resources, go thanks for a very practical view of the company side of coal mining. To the myriad residents and former residents of Carbon County, folk of that distinctive Heintz-57 background, thanks, too, for all the coal talk we've had over the years, often over a beer or a cup of coffee. If I've overlooked any of you, it's the sad consequence of my increasing age and forgetfulness.

My very warmest thanks go to the three Carbon County natives who have put up with the day-to-day realities of creating this book: to my husband Bob, and to our children, Dashiell and Darcy, who have grown up understanding that "Mommy needs to write." The errors here are all mine; the strengths derive from the help of others.

Introduction

The continuous miner roared as the drum edged upward, and sparks danced out as its teeth scraped against the rock of the mine ceiling. Quickly, the machine operator pulled the levers that lowered the drum from its too-high position where I had inexpertly raised it. Once again, it began to chew into the coal at the face, directly in front of me. Trying to keep the rotating drum, with its coal-gnashing teeth, running up and down the face, I simultaneously manipulated another lever that moved the chute at the back of the continuous miner in a wide, flat arc, dumping the newly mined coal evenly into the waiting mine car behind me. Another man at the rear of the mining machine moved the huge, rubber-covered electrical cables connected to all of this machinery out of the way of the moving parts. There, in the protection of the driver's cage, aided by two expert coal miners, I felt a profound respect for the skill and expertise needed to mine coal, perhaps especially in this modern, industrial age.

As our small group walked back out of the cold, damp mine, all the lights suddenly went off (a trick commonly played on neophytes, and planned as part of the excitement of the tour). Such blackness is beyond imagination, and the cliche about not seeing one's hand in front of one's face became awesomely real. Having stepped out of the continuous miner's protective cage, I remembered an old-timer's tales of a "bounce," when the weight of about two vertical miles of mountain above us had compacted the massive coal pillars that held up the mine ceiling. Huge chunks of coal had squirted out of the walls, killing or maiming those in the way. Sometimes the ceiling collapses, too, as roof bolts break away from the rock above. Wooden pillars then twist with the weight, and little wedges of wood placed at the top of the pillars shoot out to warn everyone to run. Occasionally, too, a spark, an explosion, or an electrical short can start a fire that consumes the coal around it, sucking all the oxygen out of the air. Memories leaped out of other interviews I had done, most recently with the only survivor of the Wilberg mine disaster of 1984. He had blindly felt his way out of the smoke-filled mine and finally arrived at the portal with enough carbon monoxide in his blood to kill an ordinary man. A full year later, when the last of the twenty-seven bodies was recovered, we were reminded that he had unknowingly groped past the forms of many of his dedicated coworkers. Like him, in the current blackness, we could see nothing.

Then the lights went on, and my fears vanished. Grinning, our guide led us back to the surface, where we removed our safety equipment. He also doffed his down vest; the rest of us had been shiveringly unprepared. For years I had heard about mining in Carbon County, driven past the portals, photographed mine buildings, and searched for documentation, but only this tour provided a personal feel for the coal.

In the years between 1976 and 1980, when I worked on-and-off for the preservation research section of the Utah State Historical Society, then under the expert direction of Allan Kent Powell and Philip Notarianni, I never wondered about the legal underpinnings of the area I studied. But in revising a now-ancient work for publication, I began to ask: "Why are all the best mines in Carbon County in private ownership, when the Mineral Leasing Act of 1920 demands that coal be leased?" Seeking a quick answer to this problem, and vaguely aware of some federal litigation, I went to the National Archives on a trip home to the Washington D.C. area to see my family. The archivists brought forth a "fat file," not once viewed by researchers since the Justice Department had deposited it there in the 1920s. The result is this book.

This story of fraud in the Utah coal lands provides a case study of the intricacies of American land law, specifically, of the Coal Land Act of 1873 and its application (and misapplication). The problems created by the limitations of this law, by its attempted enforcement, and by the litigation of several related cases based on the law itself, fills part of a very large gap in the history of America's mining West, and augments that of the Progressive Era.

Although the history of western mining has received significant attention, very little of this scholarship has been devoted to coal, and virtually none to coal's legal history. Exploring sample studies, one finds that mining in the West has been addressed by many major scholars, such as Gerald Nash, as part of his work on the twentieth-century American West; Thomas A. Rickard, in his still-classic study on American mining; and Duane Smith, the current dean of American mining historians.[1] Mining engineers and the funding of mining enterprises have been addressed by Clark Spence; mining men by Otis Young; mining entrepreneurs by Richard Peterson; mining law in general by Charles Wallace Miller; and land law in general in the massive work by Paul Wallace Gates with Robert W. Swenson.[2] Public-land policies have been lucidly discussed by E. Louise Peffer, William Wyant, Carl Mayer, and George Riley.[3] Robert H. Nelson has provided the sole work exclusively on federal policy regarding coal lands.[4] Much mining history is company-specific, such as works on Anaconda, Hecla, Colorado Fuel and Iron, and Bingham.[5] The study of copper mining, in particular, has lent itself to colorful personality profiles, such as those provided by Michael Malone and by C. L. Sonnichsen.[6] Uranium (including Utah uranium) has also found its historian, Raye C. Ringholtz.[7] Most of the work on coal has been devoted to issues of labor or safety. This includes books by the aforementioned Kent Powell (who wrote the only work specific to Utah coal), James Whiteside, Zeese Papanikolas, George S. McGovern, and Leonard F. Gutteridge.[8] Two fine regional coal mining studies—those of Lynne Bowen, on British Columbia, and of Dudley Gardner and Verla Flores, on Wyoming—mention litigation only briefly.[9]

This list is by no means exhaustive, but it serves to indicate what this book is not. It does not discuss a particular figure (either actual or archetypical), a particular company, or a specific event, such as a strike. It does not center on a general body of law or wide-ranging public policy. Nor does it deal with copper, uranium, or any of the other glamorous substances sought throughout the West. Gold and silver in particular are ignored, for the California gold rush alone generated much literature: even to review it would appreciably lengthen this introduction. Coal, instead, was always a handmaiden to other industries, especially to the railroads in the years before the advent of diesel engines. Consequently, the prosecution of coal-land fraud began as part of the antirailroad thrust of the Progressive Era.

The cases this book describes arose from the application of the Progressive reform impulse to the practical problems of industrial monopolies and their claims to public lands. In this context, the Progressive pursuit of twin goals—busting the trusts and transferring the public domain to the "right" people—caused internal contradictions that led to inconclusive results. As a bevy of historians has noted, Progressivism wallowed in contradictions, torn between its love of scientific efficiency and a desire to return to earlier American values.[10] If Progressive policymakers themselves could not agree on goals or means, what support could the front-line fighters—here, attorneys from the Justice Department—find for their task of bringing trusts to justice? Their job was made even more difficult by the legal maelstrom created as the three branches of the federal government simultaneously addressed the series of problems caused by an unrealistic law for coal lands.

In this story of scams and attempted retribution, the activities of various players, major and minor, are interwoven in a chronological tale of fraud, partial discovery, and belated resolution. In addition to the various branches of national government, the State of Utah and its dominant religious organization, the Church of Jesus Christ of Latter-day Saints (LDS), also had their roles. Commentary on the players and the passing scene comes largely from Utah newspapers, especially the organs of the coal district, and from the private correspondence of corporate officials and government attorneys. As the national significance of the Utah coal-land fraud cases emerges in this work, the reader is invited to consider who benefited from these activities, and if the benefit was worth the price.

PART I

Antirailroad, Antitrust

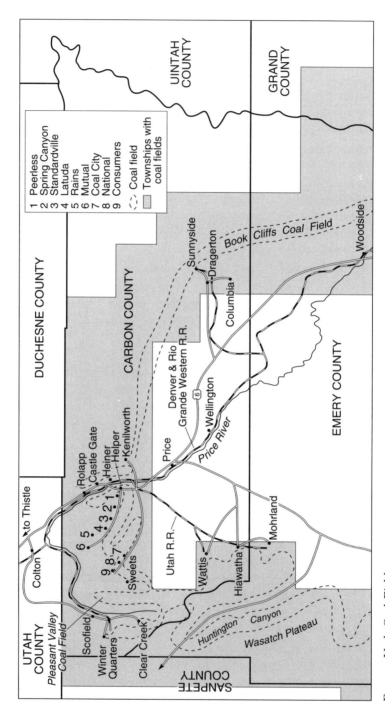

Eastern Utah Coal Fields

CHAPTER 1

Difficult Times— a Distinctive Place

Twenty-three-year-old Arthur A. Sweet caused problems. As he legally tried to claim some of Utah's richest coal land, he stepped right into the middle of a massive fraud. Other, more experienced mining men than he had already noted the rich subsurface wealth of Sunnyside, Utah. The coal deposits there would coke, and coking coal was in huge demand for the burgeoning western smelting industry. Only a commercial mine could fill this need, and a commercial mine required much more than the few hundred acres permitted under federal law. An expanding railroad/coal combination had sought to monopolize the area, and had already eliminated other competitors by various means. Sweet, too, had to be stopped.

What terrible thing had Sweet done? In 1902, he had filed a federal coal certificate for 160 acres at Sunnyside.[1] In so doing, he swore that the land was known to contain coal—a rarity in that locality, despite Sunnyside's known mineral riches. Why was this assertion so dangerous? Because most of Sunnyside's original claimants had received their land from the state, and no state could claim *known* coal land under its enabling act. In fact, the federal government had long claimed exclusive dominion over coal in the public domain, regulating its distribution under the Coal Land Act of 1873.[2] Yet the law was unrealistic. Among other defects, its limitations on allowable acreage—160 acres for an individual or 640 acres for an association with $5,000 invested—hamstrung those seeking to establish a commercial-size mine of two thousand acres or more. Not surprisingly, railroads and others had circumvented this requirement. Since flouting an unrealistic statute offered the only route to a commercial coal mine, all large-scale developers engaged in what they regarded as necessary fraud.

Railroads and coal were natural partners. Not only did coal transportation demand rails, but steam-driven locomotives needed coal for

3

fuel, especially in the largely treeless expanses of much of the West. Consequently, the first railroad to enter eastern Utah had already claimed more than 12,300 coal-bearing acres through various subterfuges.[3] Obviously, this amount was well in excess of the legal maximum. Sweet's federal claim became a serious threat to such clandestine activities.

Suddenly, armed thugs appeared on Sweet's Sunnyside land. Although he didn't know it, they were on the payroll of the Denver and Rio Grande Western Railway (D&RGW, or the Western), Utah's sister line of Colorado's Denver and Rio Grande (the D&RG). The gunmen's immediate objective was to protect the counterclaim of a Western "dummy," Charles Mostyn Owen, who had made a fraudulent filing through the State of Utah. Taking advantage of lax procedures at the land office, Owen had induced Utah officials to claim the disputed land as "grazing land" as a part of its statehood package. The state had originally been able to claim grazing land under the Utah Enabling Act, which had not only permitted Utah Territory to organize for statehood but had granted the new state four "school sections" per township, twice the usual amount.[4] This federally mandated largesse had then been manipulated to put coal land under Western railroad control.

If Sweet withdrew his federal coal claim, Owen could get title to his "grazing land" from the state at bargain-basement prices. If coal were later discovered on the property, Owen, or his legal successor, just got lucky. Partly by using a series of these so-called dummies, such as Owen, the Western had amassed its impressive holdings. Alerting the federal government to the existence of coal on the property might bring the whole house of cards tumbling down, especially where claims had not yet proceeded to patent.

In the late nineteenth century, federal administrations had generally ignored the details of the "land office business" of the West. The objective then had been to fulfill the dictates of Manifest Destiny, and development possibilities seemed limitless. All this changed in the early twentieth century, especially under the Progressive government of President Theodore Roosevelt.[5] As the federal government tightened its control over the diminishing public domain, increasingly the only way to get land was through the states. Utah residents, like others, were enmeshed in this situation. Despite Sweet's attempt to protect his claim through the judiciary, the restraining order granted him against the gunmen was ignored; the offending parties were never punished for contempt of court, and his injunction was dissolved in February 1903.[6]

Although, in a civil court action, Sweet eventually achieved ownership of half the disputed 160-acre tract, he could raise no capital for development of coal mining. Furthermore, he could get neither quotations on freight rates nor on a coal-car allowance from the Western—which was still publicly divorced from the Sunnyside fracas. In this instance the railroad relied on its transportation monopoly in an area where its control of coal mining was incomplete, but the result was almost the same. The railroad got Sweet's Sunnyside land, although it had to pay Sweet $4,000.[7]

Perhaps to keep an eye on Sweet, or to sweeten the deal, another Western-related corporation, the Pleasant Valley Coal Company (PVCC), then hired him as a telegraph operator. But when Sweet was instructed to copy all messages affecting the company from the wires of the Western Union, he reported this illegal practice. To combat the snooping, the telegraph company removed its wires from the PVCC office—but the Pleasant Valley company also removed Sweet from its employ.[8]

Thus frustrated, Arthur Sweet and one of his brothers, Frederick, a lawyer, apparently filed a complaint with the Department of Justice, alleging coal-land fraud in Utah. Fred Sweet later claimed that their signed affidavit reached the attention of the president himself; similar affidavits, he claimed, had reached the secretary of the interior and the commissioner of the General Land Office (the GLO).[9] Apparently, if the Sweets could not legally develop their own coal mine under the Coal Land Act of 1873, they would at least report those who scoffed at it.

Meanwhile, President Roosevelt was developing his own ideas regarding the unworkable Coal Land Act of 1873. As he reported to Congress on December 17, 1906: "The present coal law limiting the individual entry to 160 acres puts a premium on fraud. ... It is a scandal to maintain laws which sound well, but which make fraud the key without which great natural resources must remain closed." Thus noting the most obvious defect of the unrealistic act, he continued:

> The law should give individuals and corporations, under proper government regulation and control, (the details of which I shall not at present discuss) the right to work bodies of coal large enough for profitable development. My own belief is that there should be provision for leasing coal ... under proper [government] restrictions.[10]

The logic of this suggestion echoed the best of Progressive Era optimism. As a good progressive, Roosevelt had relied on the rational, expert advice of Senator Robert M. LaFollette, backed by Chief Forester Gifford Pinchot, in recently withdrawing millions of acres of coal land from further entry (i.e., availability for private ownership). Meanwhile, the attorney general had been trying to proceed against earlier fraud in coal lands. Ten days before Roosevelt's speech, federal attorneys Fred A. Maynard and Hiram E. Booth had cabled the attorney general from Utah:

> Grand jury returns indictment for conspiracy to defraud United States coal lands against Utah Fuel Co. ... Union Pacific Coal Company, allied railroad Companies and Officers are indicted for conspiracy under Inter-state Commerce law unlawful discrimination.[11]

The commissioner of the GLO promptly issued a warning about the pending litigation: "If final [land title] certificate issues and the Government then attacks the claim it must assume the burden of proof which is found to be a most difficult undertaking."[12] Obviously, speed in prosecution was essential.

By the 1900s, the United States in general felt a sense of urgency in regard to the public domain. Western lands, once thought to be limitless, were rapidly passing into private ownership, often that of so-called trusts. Traditional land hunger, still present, could not be assuaged in traditional ways. Many Easterners still wanted to "Go West!" The nation, on the verge of an industrial breakthrough, needed western resources for economic growth. Capitalists, uniting the two urges, sought to develop the West primarily for private gain. As land scarcity became apparent, the government had to mediate growing conflicts, tending toward the Progressive Era's goal of "the greatest good for the greatest number."[13]

Decisions about who deserved the shrinking public domain became, after 1900, a matter of hotly debated public policy. Under the administration of Theodore Roosevelt, national attention first turned to water, then to the forests, then to the extractive industries that dotted the West.[14] In the final phase, Roosevelt turned to coal. As he said in 1906: "The coal, like the forests, should be treated as the property of the public, and its disposal should be under conditions which would inure to the benefit of the public as a whole." Unfortunately, his plan to set up federal coal leases died in the House in

February 1907.[15] Consequently, the old, unsatisfactory Coal Land Act of 1873 remained in force. Developers, pressured by competitors and market operations alike, continued to commit what they regarded as necessary fraud. The government had to rely on the same old law to stop them.

The importance of coal at the turn of the century has now been forgotten. At the time, it fueled nearly all U.S. industrial growth, especially in the arid West, where, with few exceptions, water power and wood were unavailable. Coal fueled the railroads, ran the factories, and heated the homes of most western Americans. Therefore, the control of western coal land determined who could sway the nation. By the time the Progressives awoke to the disappearance of coal lands from the public domain, federal litigation provided the only chance to reclaim it. If court action was successful, trained public servants could then distribute it to the deserving, or preserve it to the nation by the leasing method recently suggested by the president.

Obviously, in this context, the federal government and the railroad/coal combinations inevitably clashed. Capitalists knew, as did the president, that the 1873 Coal Land Law was defective.[16] The developer of a coal mine could painfully amass a series of contiguous small parcels legally claimed by others, but this process was expensive and time consuming; consequently, many developers utilized the dummy system: they hired individuals who, for a price (usually $50 or $100), would begin the three-step process needed to secure ownership of public lands. In step one, dummies would claim (or file on, or enter on) land valuable for coal, asserting it was for their own use. While step two, verification of the land's "non-mineral" content, was in progress, dummies would "sell" their claims (not actual ownership) to the commercial developer. Step three transferred actual title, or ownership of the land, from the federal government to the owner of the claim—by this time, the commercial developer who had initially hired the dummies. This process, fast and cheap, was also illegal. Nonetheless, it was widely used, and became a popular target of Roosevelt's crusade for coal-land reform.

Spurred by Roosevelt's Progressive ideals and the need to begin litigation before final patents (denoting legal ownership) were issued, the Justice Department, on July 27, 1906, filed four hastily prepared bills in equity against the coal companies and selected employees connected with the Western, the Utah railway. Superficially, the suits appeared to fit in with the president's trust-busting crusade, one of his major claims to fame.[17] Yet the actions had been brought under the Coal Land Act of 1873, rather than an antitrust statute, despite the obvious union of railroads and coal.

Why use an admittedly bad law as the basis for an ambitious federal suit? The answer was simple: it was a matter of timing. The Hepburn Act, that would become the first truly enforceable antitrust statute, (and that explicitly forbade railroads to own their own coal mines) was still being debated in Congress when the magnitude of western coal-land fraud was discovered. Once passed, the Hepburn Act would probably be subjected to a constitutional challenge. If the Supreme Court overturned the act—a genuine possibility—any suit brought under its provisions would be voided. Why did the government not wait and see what happened? Because as of midsummer 1906 the Western's title to Sunnyside, the best coal land in Utah, would be forever unassailable, protected by a statute of limitations. If the government were to redress what appeared to be flagrant railroad fraud, if it were to restore coal lands to the public domain, if it were to take its best shot at setting an important legal precedent, it had to act immediately. Hence, the Justice Department had to assume the burden of proof that coal-land fraud had been committed without a satisfactory statute on which to base its case.[18]

The selection of Utah as a legal forum also came from pragmatic considerations. The current political tension between Progressives, Reform Republicans, the conservative wing of the Grand Old Party, and the Democrats[19] demanded a decisive federal victory. A state with a friendly federal bench and little political clout would minimize repurcussions. Utah offered both: the aptly-named federal district judge John Marshall (a strong advocate of federal power, as was his illustrious predecessor), and a state politically weakened by repeated accusations of theocracy and polygamy.

To some extent, Utah's political reputation was deserved. Its modern day settlement began with the entry of Mormons (or Saints, members of the Church of Jesus Christ of Latter-day Saints—LDS) into the Salt Lake Valley in 1847. Seeking to escape the country of their birth—the United States—they had carried with them ideas of a political theocracy and a cooperative economy totally foreign to the American mainstream. Their leaders also practiced polygamy (or, more specifically, polygyny, the taking of several wives by a single husband). Self-sufficient, proud, and highly defensive as a result of brutal attacks in the States, Mormons had long been a lightning rod for American preachers and politicians. Their general unpopularity, sometimes fanned by intentional misunderstandings, retarded Utah statehood for almost fifty years. In the meantime, various crusaders in the United States had launched efforts to control the Mormons, who, from their arrival in Utah, controlled the area.[20]

Utah was unique in another way. It was the only territory to have been attacked by the United States Army, and no one who had been alive during the so-called Utah War would ever forget it. Saints from northern Utah had fled south in the spring of 1858, many of them forced to camp for months in wagons, log huts, or dugouts carved in hillsides. They returned home only when commanding officers and church leaders assured them they were safe from atrocities by U.S. troops. No shots were fired in the war, but mistrust—and incidents that fueled it—remained.[21]

One of the ugliest ensuing altercations began over land. In August 1859, U.S. Army Sergeant Ralph Pike was shot and killed in broad daylight on the streets of Salt Lake City. He was walking back to his hotel (not to jail) from court where he was on trial for assaulting a Mormon boy, Howard Spencer. Spencer and Pike had differed violently over the ownership of some rich grazing land, needed for horses by Mormon ranchers and the army alike. Spencer had allegedly tried to defend his uncle's right to the land, and Pike had brutally attacked him. Despite an estimated hundred witnesses to Pike's death, the assailant, believed to be Spencer, was never apprehended. The Mormon-owned *Deseret News* characterized the attacker as "a brave, daring fellow";[22] predictably, the army newspaper disagreed, first inflating the number of soldiers killed and later villifying Mormons in general. The military organ complained of "the clemency shown to these (to use a very mild term) misguided individuals" and pointed to the presence of federal troops as a source of Mormon monetary profit.[23] The federal-territorial friction highlighted by this incident cast a long shadow over later relations between the U.S. government and Utah.

Certainly the years immediately following the Utah War saw no reduction in this animosity. For example, the first Republican presidential candidate, John C. Frémont, in 1856 campaigned on the promise to end "the dual relics of barbarism: slavery and polygamy." Republican ascendancy, begun four years later with Abraham Lincoln's election, led to increasingly punitive actions against the Mormons. The original army troops were withdrawn from the territory in 1861, but a fresh contingent arrived in 1862 and built a fort on the bench above Salt Lake City, where cannons could be kept trained on the Temple, the principal Mormon place of worship. Congress did its part, passing the anti-Mormon Morrill Act in 1862, the Poland Act in 1874, the Edmunds Act in 1882, and the Edmunds-Tucker Act in 1887. These increasingly harsh measures included the deputizing of "spotters" who pried into the intimate affairs of households alleged to be polygamous.[24] In addition, Mormons who were known to or believed to support polygamy, on election to Congress were challenged: Brigham H. Roberts was one, in 1898; Reed Smoot was another in 1903. After decades of this treatment, Utah's Mormons neither liked nor trusted federal interference in state affairs—including that involving Utah coal lands.

The coal situation in Utah was complicated by the arrival of the Denver and Rio Grande Western Railway in 1881. The line's founder, General William Jackson Palmer, had many qualities that endeared him to the Mormons. He was an experienced railroad man, held the Congressional Medal of Honor, and was a strong temperance advocate. This latter quality dovetailed with the Mormon stand on alcohol—a position that would eventually result in outright prohibition for the faithful.[25] Furthermore, Palmer's railroad offered the first competition to the exploitative Union Pacific and its companion coal company, which held a monopoly on Utah's commercial coal trade.

Despite Utah's welcome for Palmer and the Western, the territory of the Mormons was a pale second choice in Palmer's development schemes. He had originally pointed his rails toward Mexico; hence, the name of the line. Incorporated in Colorado in 1870 as the Denver and Rio Grande Railway (D&RG, or the Rio Grande), it was formed too late to take advantage of the alternate sections of federal land (usually in checkerboard bands, six miles wide, on either side of proposed trackage) accorded to earlier railroads. The Rio Grande instead had to content itself with "one hundred feet on each side of the central line" of its track, as granted by Congress in 1875.[26] Between 1870 and 1875, Palmer's crews slowly laid tracks southward until financial problems stalled construction just south of Pueblo, Colorado.[27]

Further extension demanded fresh capital. By 1875, Palmer had achieved a virtual coal monopoly in southern Colorado, which enhanced the railroad's potential. Palmer wrote to a possible investor, touting the economic power of coal at "the dead center of our driving wheel."[28] Rich deposits of gold and silver lay along the railroad's route, but it was coal that was the key to access and development.

In 1878, still heading southward, Palmer reincorporated his infant railroad under the laws of the Territory of New Mexico, in keeping with another provision of the 1875 railroad land-grant law that demanded a new corporation in each territory traversed.[29] He pressed toward the only feasible route between Colorado and New Mexico, Raton Pass, only to find the rival Atchison, Topeka and Santa Fe Railroad (AT&SF, or the Santa Fe) coveting the same route. Both lines armed their grading crews, whose posturing and potshots ended in a standoff. The railroads then took their case to court.[30]

After almost a year of litigation, the financially strapped Rio Grande leased its properties to the Santa Fe and sold a large block of stock to one of America's leading railroad magnates, Jay Gould. Then the U.S. Supreme Court granted the Rio Grande the right to the Raton Pass route. Palmer tried desperately to break the lease, capitulating only when Jay Gould, with his tremendous financial clout, forced an out-of-court settlement that defined separate territories for construction of the AT&SF and the D&RG. The Santa Fe wound up with the southern route through New Mexico and the Rio Grande therefore turned toward its second choice, through the land of Utah's Mormons.[31]

Still financially precarious, Palmer's company did what it could in Utah. In December 1880, the newly incorporated Sevier Valley Railway Company, formed by D&RG affiliates, secured rights-of-way from western-central Utah to the Colorado border. The following year, other friends of the Rio Grande incorporated another railroad to connect Salt Lake City with a coal deposit to the northeast. The system became unified in July 1881 with the formation of the Denver and Rio Grande Western Railway Company (the Western), under the laws of Utah Territory, and the D&RGW absorbed the first two roads. By December 1881, the Western had also secretly acquired the Mormon-built Utah and Pleasant Valley Railway (U&PVR) and its most valuable asset, coal.[32]

The Western's acquisition of the U&PVR and the Pleasant Valley mines must have been welcomed by the Mormons. The Pleasant Valley coal mine had limped along economically since its inception in 1875. Its rail link to northern Utah had been built by crews who accepted calico cloth as payment for their labor, giving the U&PVR a nickname, the Calico Road.[33]

While the Momons needed financial relief, the Western needed coal, and the company built on this powerful combination with the creation of additional Rio Grande-affiliated corporations.[34] Although its involvement in Pleasant Valley had not yet been made public, the *Salt Lake Herald* in May 1881 reported its version of the railroad's activities:

> The Denver and Rio Grande people induced some friends in this city [Salt Lake] to organize a company as required by the laws of Utah to secure a right of way for its line through this territory. All the money has been furnished by the Denver and Rio Grande, all the instructions have been given by Denver and Rio Grande people, Denver and Rio Grande engineers are doing the surveying in many parts of the territory, and the whole affair, save in the ostensible aspect, is in the hands of the Denver and Rio Grande, and will remain so as long as the company desires.[35]

The allegedly surreptitious method used in this initial expansion phase would shortly come to characterize Western involvement in Utah's coal lands.

The growth of the Rio Grande system—the entire network of rails and mines in Utah and Colorado—could not proceed without coal. Consequently, Ellis Clark, a geologist working for Western, sought the crucial mineral in advance of actual railroad construction. He found only one promising deposit in eastern Utah, "at the junction of Price River and Willow Creek [where] coal developments have been made." The land belonged to "the Brothers Black, contractors, Engineers Mellen and Kerr, the locations dating from June 1st, 1881" (possibly a prompt response to the *Herald* article, and a good reason for so much secrecy). Clark exhaustively described seven beds that had been opened in the area, beginning with the lowest, A, and working up through G. In his October 1881 recommendation to the Western he stated:

> The B and C beds are workable seams of coal, and together contain about 10,000,000 tons, one third of which can be mined . . . . None of the coal beds are large [although subsequent mining would prove them to be so], but their value to this company depends upon their close location to the line of railroad at a point (the heavy Price River Grade) where extra locomotive power will be required. The nearest coal at present known is Pleasant Valley, distance 44 miles, and Green River and Castle Valley 100 to 150 miles.
>
> I advise the immediate purchase and patenting of the property at the price of $4,000, thus saving the additional ten dollars an acre which it will cost from the government after the rails have been laid.[36]

Clark's report was passed to the Western's chief engineer, M. T. Burgess, for a final decision. Burgess had also been approached by Samuel Gilson, a local mining man, who was lobbying for tracks through more easterly Soldier Canyon to the Uintah Basin, citing Price Canyon's prohibitive steepness.[37]

Gilson had experienced a number of adventures in the West before his contact with Burgess. As a boy he went west with his brother during the California gold rush. Then they moved on to ranching in Nevada and Utah. By the 1870s, Gilson had joined those opposing the Mormons. He served as a deputy marshall in Utah antipolygamy raids and at the execution of John D. Lee, the scapegoat for the bloody Mountain Meadows Massacre, where Mormons killed passing travelers. By 1887, Gilson would be offering an $800 reward for the capture of the two chief leaders of the LDS Church, President John Taylor and his first counselor, George Q. Cannon. An enterpreneurial alliance with a non-Mormon railroad may have seemed natural to the ambitious Gilson.[38]

Nonetheless, Gilson did not tell railroad officials about his real reason for discounting the Price Canyon route. Steepness was not a factor; instead, Gilson had discovered an extremely rare hydrocarbon in the Uintah Basin that (with typical modesty) he called "gilsonite." This substance, then known only in the region of the Dead Sea, was selling for $160 a ton after it was hauled out by camel. Naturally, Gilson wanted a railroad to help him tap these riches, and he had no intention of sharing the wealth with a corporation that could claim one hundred feet on either side of its tracks or set freight rates at its pleasure.[39]

Knowing nothing of these gilsonite deposits, Burgess limited himself to a description of eastern Utah's coal in his annual report for 1881. As Burgess wrote: "The coal vein being worked west of Castle Valley [the Pleasant Valley mine] extends along the Book Cliffs north of the [proposed] lines from Upper Price Canon [sic] to and beyond the east end of this division. It may be reached through Salaratus Canon 15 miles east of Green River and at other points east."[40] With this report, Burgess laid out the location of coal deposits extending roughly one hundred miles along the proposed railroad route, an immense and tempting field.

Coal not only powered locomotives; as a transportable commodity it had to be hauled in bulk, generating lucrative freight changes. Industrialists preferred the hardest coal, anthracite, which burned the hottest, and dismissed lignite, the softest coal, as little more than peat. Utah's coals, all bituminous, fell in the midrange for heat and hardness; it was serviceable for industry and home heating alike. Furthermore, some of these bituminous coals might have the proper combination of water, volatile matter, fixed carbon, and ash to form coke, the best fuel for smelters. Knowing these facts, Palmer continued to stress coal's value to his London agent. He noted that Colorado coal values had risen from \$3 million to \$25 million between 1870 and 1880.[41] Utah coal might generate similar profits, if the land where it lay could be securely possessed.

To further this goal, in 1881, Palmer, together with railroad manager David C. Dodge and New York banker George Foster Peabody, incorporated the Rio Grande Western Construction Company in the Territory of Utah. This corporation, ostensibly chartered to build the railroad's necessary physical facilities, also became useful in securing necessary coal lands. To further complicate future coal-land titles, the Western Construction Company's charter contained a built-in life of twenty years, leading to its demise even before the federal government uncovered the coal-land frauds it had helped to perpetrate.[42]

The Western also acquired two other Utah railroads late in 1881. Its earlier acquisition of the Calico Road became public when the railroad and mine came under foreclosure on June 14, 1882. The new purchasers immediately passed the title to the Rio Grande Western Construction Company (not the railroad). [43] However, the construction company was a wholly owned subsidiary of the Western, a mere corporate link between mine and rails.

None of these industrial events took place in a political vacuum. The LDS church hierarchy, who had shepherded their people into the Great Basin to protect them from mob violence in the East, had worked hard to preserve local autonomy in their self-styled State of Deseret. Going back to January 1854, to provide for fuel in a relatively treeless area, the Utah legislature had offered a \$1,000 reward to anyone who could find a vein of coal eighteen inches thick or more within forty miles of Salt Lake City. Two men claimed the award in 1860, but they were refused it on the grounds that their mine was too far distant and that it produced inferior coal.[44] Nonetheless, coal remained a highly desirable part of plans for a self-sufficient Mormon domain.

In 1869 the Mormon hierarchy found themselves forced to deal with outside coal purveyors: transcontinental lines converged on their territory. While the railroads brought in new converts and provided job opportunities, the Union Pacific (UP) shortly held the Salt Lake Valley in the grip of a coal monopoly. It acquired most of the Mormon-built railroad lines in northern and central Utah and refused to ship Utah coal that had been mined at the end of some of these spurs, instead supplying the Salt Lake market with Wyoming coal from the Union Pacific Coal Company (UPCC). Under these circumstances,

Photo break during grading of a Rio Grande system railroad bed in the eastern Utah desert. Behind the crew is their equipment—horses, mules, and Fresno scrapers. Courtesy of the Western Mining and Railroad Museum, Helper, Utah.

the Mormon hierarchy eagerly welcomed Palmer's Denver and Rio Grande Western, assuming that its competition would end the monopoly.[45]

This chance for the coal trade suited the Western, which had overextended itself financially in the rush to reach Salt Lake City. The building spurt ended as the Western reached the Colorado border at the end of March 1883 and the first train rolled into Salt Lake City on a Sunday, April 8, to the horror of pious Mormons. Unconcerned, the Western pressed on toward Ogden, Utah's "northern gateway," and the transportation stronghold of the UP. The June linkage of the Western with the UP came only at the high price demanded by the UP, necessitating further Western moneymaking ventures.[46]

But the problems of the Western hardly ended there. Between 1882 and 1886 the Rio Grande system underwent a series of battles over control and company policy. In July 1886, it emerged as two corporations: the Denver and Rio Grande *Railroad*, replacing the old D&RG *Railway* (still called the D&RG, or the Rio Grande) and the Rio Grande Western (the Western, or RGW). Palmer, who had lost and then regained his seat as the Western president, had an even greater need to show that his Utah line could turn a profit.[47]

Palmer knew one way the Western could make money: in coal. He turned to his Pleasant Valley property to help recoup his finances. There he encountered his old rival, the Union Pacific. Under a subsidiary called the Utah Central, the UP had opened a new mine in the area but was shipping over the Western's Calico Road, which had just been widened to standard gauge to aid transshipment. In retaliation for the rough horsetrading at Ogden, Palmer began to squeeze his opponent's mine. The Western charged the Utah Central an exorbitant $1.25 per ton for shipping coal the sixty-seven miles to Salt Lake City, forcing the UP to continue to bring in Wyoming coal for its own Utah trains, at an actual cost of only $1.00 for a much greater distance.[48] As the UP had already learned with its earlier Salt Lake Valley rail monopoly, not only the coal could earn a pretty penny: the freight charges did, too.

In the 1880s, Utah was full of moneymaking enterprises, including hard-rock mining and its attendant smelters. By 1880, there were thirty-four smelters in Utah—and these were best run on coke, a coal derivative. As Utah ore production grew to an astonishing 20 percent of the national output by 1904, the demand for coal—especially coking coal—grew apace.[49]

Coking—the making of coke—to supply this demand had already been tried in Pleasant Valley, but proved unsuccessful because coal there lacked the proper chemical properties. No suitable coking coal was found until 1889, when officials of the Western's Pleasant Valley Coal Company discovered a new vein of coking coal at Castle Gate. At that time, the RGW made a concerted effort to lock up thousands of acres of Castle Gate coal lands. The most active agent in the deal, George Goss, was a director of the Sevier Railway Company, one of the organizations earlier acquired by the Western.[50]

This promising new Western foray into Castle Gate lands brought haunting results, the worst beginning on October 5, 1888. Stephen R. Marks, the initial claimant of a Castle Gate parcel, quit-claimed his claim to another man who turned it over to George Goss (for the Western's Pleasant Valley Coal Company) the very next day. By these means, the RGW acquired the *claim* to the "Marks Entry," but not the title (or actual ownership). The PVCC shortly made the Marks Entry, four contiguous quarter-sections in an inverted L-shape at the juncture of Willow Creek Canyon and Price River Canyon, the heart of its Castle Gate mine development. Goss added to this during the

A Denver and Rio Grande Western train steams up Price Canyon around 1885—behind it the famous Castle Gate rocks, emblem of eastern Utah. Wooden bridges, such as the one it is crossing, were frequently washed out by spring floods, increasing railroad expenses. Courtesy of the Utah State Historical Society, Salt Lake City, Utah.

years 1889 to 1891 by purchasing a number of other Castle Gate claims and, in a very unusual move, the corresponding dower rights of the owner's wives, for amounts of up to $3,700. In 1890 and again in 1892, Goss quit-claimed these to the Pleasant Valley Coal Company. That same year, Palmer, who had amassed an impressive collection of claims on his own, also deeded them to the PVCC. Only one cloud fell over this rosy picture of acquisitions: in 1891, Steven Marks proved up on his Castle Gate claim (meaning he fulfilled all ownership requirements). Ignoring his previous sale of the claim, he subsequently sold the land *title* to other parties.[51]

Unaware of Marks's machinations, the Western's PVCC had amassed approximately three thousand acres in the Castle Gate vicinity, the requisite amount for a commercial mine. A company geologist reported that Castle Gate's development would "directly stimulate the mining and smelting industries of Utah, ... increasing general prosperity and enlarging the miscellaneous railroad traffic."[52]

The Western's future seemed bright, but in other ways Utah fared less well. Its Mormons, politically under direct federal control due to Utah's territorial status, were suffering a renewed antipolygamy crusade. Under the authorization of the 1887 Edmunds-Tucker Act, the federal government appointed all territorial officials, limited Mormon service on juries, curtailed the monetary holdings of the LDS Church, and employed dozens of marshals (including Sam Gilson) as "spotters" to ferret out polygamous marriages. The marshals' techniques bordered on the criminal, as described by a contemporary:

> At night dark forms could be seen prowling about the premises of peaceable citizens, peering into windows. . . . Some of the hirelings were bold enough, or indecent enough, to thrust themselves into sickrooms and women's bed-chambers. . . . Twenty dollars per capita, for each polygamist arrested, was the ordinary price paid to these mercenaries.[53]

Tensions grew to the breaking point. From the Mormon standpoint, the only viable solution seemed to be statehood, which could permanently free Utah from such federal indignities.

Derailed statehood attempts had dotted Utah history since the first failure in 1849 to the latest disappointment in 1885. In a renewed effort to change matters, the First Presidency of the Mormon Church (the president and his two counsellors) decided to buy more favorable local and national press coverage. One particular critic, the hostile Associated Press corespondent at the Salt Lake *Tribune*, was soon replaced with the more congenial Byron Groo, who would later be involved with sensitive transfers of coal land.[54]

LDS leaders next contacted a national railroad lobby—one originally formed to agitate for favorable transportation legislation. One of the members of this lobby was the Gould forces, the same group that controlled the Rio Grande system. The Mormons, dog-tired of the spotters and other affronts, decided to ally themselves with some of the nation's foremost power brokers with little regard for the cost. This debt would later involve coal in its repayment.[55]

At first, the lobby was unsuccessful. The nation's two major political parties traded control of the presidency from 1885 to 1893, first bringing Democrat Grover Cleveland to the White House, then the Republican, Benjamin Harrison. These shifts stalled much legislation, and when an Omnibus Bill admitted the new states of Montana, Washington, and the two Dakotas (previously proposed as one) in 1889–1890, Roman Catholic New Mexico had been dropped from the original package: Mormon Utah was not even mentioned.[56]

Even more disheartening to the LDS faithful, in Utah the spotters' raids became still more frequent, and Congress readied yet more punitive antipolygamy legislation. Under intense pressure, Mormon President Wilford Woodruff received a revelation that the practice of polygamous marriage would be abandoned. This decision, privately read by the LDS First Presidency in June 1890, was publicly announced by President Woodruff the following September. Thus, the Woodruff Manifesto finally made Utah "acceptable" for statehood.[57]

Meanwhile, the Rio Grande system faced significant changes. The Castle Gate coal lands increased in value when the Western standard-gauged its lines in 1890, allowing easy transshipment of the best coal discovered to date in Utah. This freight went through Helper, two miles from Castle Gate, named for the "helper" engines that pulled the coal-laden trains up the steep Price Canyon grade. In Colorado, the D&RG became so overextended that it paid no dividend in 1891. The resulting fracas brought in a new president, Edward T. Jeffery, whose fiscally conservative policies destined him for long service and eventual involvement in the legal battle for western coal lands.[58]

Meanwhile, in Washington, D.C., Utah influence-peddlers, backed by the railroad lobby, readied a major statehood thrust for the winter of 1892/93. A relatively tolerant Democrat, Grover Cleveland, would be returning to the presidency in March after four years of Republican Harrison's intolerance toward Mormons. Yet the Republicans had maintained a majority in Congress, which had to pass an enabling act to be signed by the president to allow Utah to write a state constitution. Luckily for Utah, the statehood attempt became a political pawn in congressional maneuvers over Cleveland's Supreme Court appointments, and on July 16, 1894, the Utah Enabling Act was made law. (For political reasons, statehood itself was delayed until 1896.)[59]

At this juncture, the scene unwittingly became set for massive coal-land frauds throughout the future state. Joseph L. Rawlins, representing Utah Territory in the House, prided himself on "the liberal appropriations of public lands which, in the Enabling Act, I secured for Utah—the largest ever made for State purposes. Four sections out of each township were set aside as public lands. Prior to that time, no new state had been granted more than two."[60] Sale of these lands was supposed to finance public schools and other institutions. The large number of these "school sections" supposedly insured "that the public schools should be forever free from sectarian [LDS] domination."[61] In sponsoring this antisectarian provision, however, Rawlins delivered vast tracts of lands into the control of Utah's new state leaders. Faced with the combination of warring railroads, a burgeoning smelting industry, and a sizeable statehood lobby debt, they had to make hard choices concerning lands known to contain Utah's most valuable coal.

CHAPTER 2

Strife at Sunnyside

Utah approached statehood during the wrenching Panic of 1893. As the nation struggled to overcome the effects of economic collapse, the Denver and Rio Grande Western Railway survived largely through the sale of coal and coke, 80 percent of which was carried outside Utah at healthy freight rates. As a result, the railroad achieved "the best financial position it had known for years," in the assessment of its major chronicler.[1] Coal land therefore became more attractive than ever.

At the same time, some Utahns voiced alarm about such a strong railroad/coal combination. During the state constitutional convention in the spring of 1895, delegate Brigham H. Roberts spoke against "foreign corporations," which he feared would "place a destructive hand upon the industries of this new State and monopolize our magnificent resources to themselves." Another delegate promptly offered the example of railroads and coal.[2] Roberts's solution, that each company be limited to a single line of business, was rejected in the end as detrimental to capital investment. But Roberts made his point insofar that the constitution decreed that a corporation could engage only in the business authorized in its charter or articles of incorporation.[3] The strange usage of the Rio Grande Western Construction Company to acquire coal land could not legally happen again.

The disposal of Utah's munificent grant of public land also preoccupied the delegates. They considered a proposal to set the price of public school lands regardless of improvements, so that settlers (who would have priority purchase rights) should not have to pay twice for their own handiwork. Ensuing debate revealed that some settlers knew they were on school sections, and had been taking advantage of the situation by paying taxes only on the improvements for the last thirty-five years or so.[4] Speculators, too, obviously could have taken advantage of Utah's long territorial period and lack of a federal survey to enter on valuable property as "homeseekers," only later "discovering" coal. From the state's perspective, a high price on all state land would

21

benefit the school fund, but officials did not want to work hardship on bona fide settlers who had been farming for years. Unable to resolve this dilemma, the delegates approved a constitution that stated: "The public lands of the State ... shall be held in trust for the people, to be disposed of as may be provided by law,"[5] throwing the decisions into the lap of the new state government and its new state land board.

The Utah State Constitution finally received approval, and on January 4, 1896, President Cleveland signed the Utah Statehood Proclamation. The knowledge burst upon Salt Lake City with a shotgun blast fired by the Western Union Telegraph superintendent, when he received the news over the wires. Church and state harmony persisted in a predominantly Republican (and Mormon) legislature under Republican Governor Heber M. Wells. Latter-day Saints controlled the state house at better than three to one, and had almost a two-to-one margin in the senate.[6] On the national level, congressional seats split evenly between Mormons and non-Mormons, Republicans and Democrats. Joseph L. Rawlins, considered a "gentile" (or non-Mormon), was elected to the U.S. Senate on the Democratic ticket, paired with a Republican colleague. William H. King, who would later figure prominently in several coal-land fraud cases, went to the Democratic side of the House. A Republican won the other House seat, defeating the unsuccessful Democratic candidate, Brigham H. Roberts. Not only had Roberts, a delegate to the state constitutional convention, lost the election, his very candidacy had incurred the displeasure of the LDS Church, of which he was a very high-ranking member.[7]

Roberts had mounted his candidacy without consulting other Mormon leaders, earning their immediate disapproval. According to the Mormon Political Manifesto, accepted by all church members in 1896, a prospective political candidate had to consult higher church authorities to determine "whether he can, consistently with the obligations already entered into with the church upon assuming his office, take upon himself the added duties and labors and responsibilities of the new position."[8] Roberts had done no such thing. As a member of the First Council of the Seventy, he was expected to set an appropriate example in keeping with his high ecclesiastical post. Above him was the rest of the church leadership: the Quorum of Twelve Apostles and, above that, the First Presidency, composed of the president of the church (revered as a living prophet) and his first and second counselors. All these officials, together with the three-man presiding bishopric and one patriarch, comprised the LDS General Authorities, or church leaders.[9] Although defeated in the election, Roberts polled enough votes to make him a viable Demo-

cratic candidate in 1898. Thus would he revive the old bugaboo of polygamy, for Roberts remained consistent in his disregard of church procla-
mations. Despite the Woodruff Manifesto of 1890, Roberts remained a
practicing polygamist.

Many old issues remained alive in the new state. Considering that
Utah had achieved statehood under a Democratic president, some
observers questioned why Republicans should so dominate state government. Although a modern historian[10] cites party platforms, especially the Republican support of business and Cleveland's tariff cuts
and antisilver stance, a contemporary explanation presented a more
gritty view. LDS leader Joseph F. Smith, part of the First Presidency
throughout the 1890s and later church president, had published a
response to an 1892 call for Saints to be Democrats. Entitled *Another
Plain Talk: Reasons Why the People of Utah Should Be Republicans*,
it alluded to the Utah War, waged by the Democratic Buchanan
administration. Smith bitterly recalled:

> The sufferings of the people of Utah. . . . After a lapse of 34 years
> it chills my blood to think of them. Another exodus of the people
> . . . in the inclement spring of 1858—homes abandoned . . . men,
> women and children fleeing from an army whose threats of outrage
> and violence were borne to their ears by every breeze from the east.
> The recollection of the acts of mobs was then too recent. . . . Those
> who took part in those scenes, and yet live, cannot forget them.[11]

Smith also believed that the worst of the antipolygamy raids came
under the Democratic Cleveland administration: the people were
"made to feel the iron enter their souls . . . [and] hundreds . . . had
the leisure, within the walls of the penitentiary, to ponder upon the
insincerity and hollowness of Democratic professions."[12] Smith went
on to laud the Republicans for keeping the Union together in the
Civil War and noted that the Republican Party, with its avowal to
stamp out not just slavery but polygamy, too, had been "the open
opponent of the people of Utah. But it has never, while wearing the
mask of friendship, either struck or stabbed them."[13] To Smith and
others like him, principle meant as much as politics, and the memories
of long-ago federal intervention gave cause for constant vigilance.

Freedom from such interference—from the army, the spotters,
federally-appointed officials—had apparently been achieved with Utah
statehood. Despite this welcome outcome, however, the lobbying that
achieved it had come at an exorbitant price. Even the relatively easy
fights of the Omnibus states—the two Dakotas, Montana, and Wash-

ington—had cost an estimated $500,000: Utah's price tag, given its unique problems of polygamy, theocracy, and an original one-party system, was much higher, in direct proportion to its divergence from mainstream American values.[14]

A lobbyist for the Mormons spelled out the details. He regretted "the obligations that I ... have incurred from those who have helped us," which he outlined in a a nine-page, typewritten memorandum written in 1894, just after Cleveland had signed Utah's enabling act. As he reminded his readers: "All men in public affairs keep books. They render no service without expecting return." He closed by recalling how pro-Utah advocates "utilized their influences and friendships in politics" and emphasized "the great debt which we owe to them," a group headed by a powerful railroad lobby.[15]

Before Utah's leaders could pay this debt, they had to set up a working government, including the new state land board. Its members had formally to select the four school sections allowed per township, or to designate sections in lieu, if those granted by number were for some reason unsuitable (reasons ranged from prior habitation to general worthlessness; if they couldn't be sold, they were of no value to the state). Other problems accompanied this selection process. How much should be charged for these lands? How should the monies received be distributed? Correspondence, seeking advice, flowed from Utah to other land-grant states.[16] After reviewing the responses, the state land board forwarded its selection list to pro-Mormon Byron Groo, former *Herald* correspondent and now Register and Receiver of the United States Land Office in Utah. Late in 1896, Groo sent the request for over 1,800 acres, about three-fourths of which were coal and other mineral lands, to his superiors at the General Land Office in Washington, D.C.[17]

Groo performed this task with misgivings. He had already informed Utah's governor, Heber M. Wells, that, in his opinion, mineral lands could not pass to the state under its enabling act. Washington's response was clear, decisive, and agreed with Groo. The commissioner of the GLO emphatically stated that such lands could pass only "under the provision of the mineral land laws."[18] Yet the Utah Enabling Act was not specific on this point. Section 6, which enumerated the four sections that Utah could claim as school lands in each township, excepted only salt from the grant, remaining silent on other types of mineral land. This slight ambiguity gave state officials some room to dicker.[19]

Equitable allocation of the newly granted lands preoccupied the

Utah State Land Board throughout the summer of 1897. Many would-be claimants were hampered by the absence of a federal survey. In order to expedite matters, board members offered "that the state might select for individuals ... where the governor makes application to have the lands surveyed, there is a provision in law for the State to advance the money and they would order the survey done."[20] The State of Utah therefore became more firmly involved in transferring the public domain into private ownership. The specific process required appraisers, one of whom visited eastern Utah in October to view "the school lands of Price and Carbon County," with a view toward land transfer, not coal matters.[21]

Informal appraisals had been conducted for years. For example, George C. Whitmore had driven his cattle over from Sanpete County around 1880. By 1884, he was a squatter on the public domain, and later filed on a 320-acre homestead in Whitmore Canyon, named in his honor. His homestead lay about thirty miles east of Castle Gate, on the edge of the Book Cliffs that swung in an arc westward from Colorado down into south-central Utah. The area surrounding Whitmore Canyon soon became known as Sunnyside. Together with the peripatetic Sam (gilsonite) Gilson, Whitmore got local credit for first discovering Sunnyside's rich coal outcroppings. Gilson soon abandoned the area, locating coal lands further south. Whitmore stayed and ranched, leaving coal development to others.[22]

At about the same time, another small group settled about nineteen miles west of Whitmore Canyon, on flatlands earlier described as "valueless excepting for Indian hunters and to hold the earth together."[23] This grim description failed to daunt LDS President Brigham Young, who hoped to see Mormons inhabiting all of Utah before his death. In 1877, he had issued a "call" for pioneers to settle the desolate area, and Jefferson Tidwell responded. He explored "what is now Carbon, Emery and Wayne counties," and, when he returned to report to the failing president, Young promised him that "if he would settle on White river (now Price River) he would soon be on one of the great thoroughfares of the nation." Consequently, Tidwell, his wife, Sarah Seely Tidwell, and others arrived in October 1879 to found a new settlement. According to family history: "Some of the people wanted to name the town Jefferson in honor of her husband, but she wanted it named after her [favorite] brother," Wellington (Justus Wellington Seely II, who was known by his middle name).[24] She got her way. Soon, many of the extended Tidwell-Seely family would be involved in Sunnyside coal.

The Seelys were at least as prominent locally as the Tidwells. Like Tidwell, Orange Seely, Wellington's older brother, had devotedly answered the same settlement "call," taking his colonizing party to an area south of the Tidwells. Seely, already prominent in his former home, rose through a series of civil and ecclesiastical posts to become, in 1880, first counsellor of the Emery Stake (a position of religious importance), probate judge of Emery County from 1892 to 1896, and, in 1894, a Republican member of the territorial legislature. In his first term he participated in the formation of a new county carved out of the northern portion of Castle Valley, named Carbon for its greatest resource, where the town of Wellington lay. The southern part, where Seely resided, retained the name of Emery County. There, Orange's brother, Wellington Seely, was equally active in local Republican politics. Together the brothers founded a grist mill, which served several surrounding towns. The Seelys were becoming not only prominent but reasonably prosperous.[25]

The Tidwells, too, had some prospects for riches. In February 1890 they became part of an association of ten men who incorporated as the Tidwell-Rideout Mining District. They duly recorded their articles of incorporation, which included reference to their Sunnyside placer claims (which legally govern only hard rock mining, such as gold). The list of incorporators, led by George T. Holladay, included Daniel Rideout, Jefferson Tidwell, his sons William J. and John F., and five others. The key officer, who kept all the records and called subsequent meetings, was the recorder, William J. Tidwell, of the nearby town of Wellington.[26] This group was almost ready to mine coal.

Others found their way to the Sunnyside coal deposits, including mining engineer Robert Kirker around 1890. Although he later swore in court that he had fully complied with federal and state mining law, he equivocated.[27] Kirker had actually filed a certificate of intention to develop wax paraffin and asphalt lands (small quantities of these minerals are found in the Sunnyside area) but he made no mention of coal. Kirker, like others, had realized the shortcomings of the Coal Act of 1873 and found his own way around it, shortly thereafter joining Tidwell-Rideout Mining District.[28]

The group soon splintered. In 1897, Tidwell, Holladay, and others formed a new corporation, the Holladay Coal Company, to exploit the Sunnyside coal veins. Among the shareholders were six of the extended Tidwell family: father Jefferson, sons William J., John F., Hyrum, and Joseph R., and daughter Sarah (named after her mother), all of Wellington. Robert Kirker was not included.[29]

The Holladay Coal Company began competing with Kirker in developing the Sunnyside district. As they did so, they discovered that Sunnyside coal would coke. The state coal mine inspector announced this discovery in his 1897 report, noting that the company had acquired an astounding "one thousand acres of coal land [grossly in excess of the legal 640-acre limit], embracing an entire mountain, and are now engaged in mining coal for shipment to Salt Lake City. . . . [It] is the best for coking purposes that has yet been discovered."[30] Production levels remained a mystery, however; the space left for exact tonnage mined was left blank.[31]

Coking coal, with its promise of substantial profits, attracted agents of the Pleasant Valley Coal Company (PVCC). Holladay later testified that he was soon approached by Robert Forrester and W. J. Chipman, both of the PVCC, who "asked him to take a few hundred dollars for his interests" in Sunnyside. Holladay refused and they threatened that "unless he did he would pack his blankets out of the canyon without anything."[32]

This later recollection did not exactly match the originally reported offer. According to the local newspaper:

> G. T. Holladay of Salt Lake City, one of the owners of the Holladay-Tidwell coal properties in Whitmore canyon, stated . . . that they had been offered $10,000 for their properties by the P.V. Coal company. It is to be hoped that the owners will see their way clear to accept the proposition as the P.V. company [sic] will undoubtedly, should title pass to them, at once build a branch to the vein.[33]

By "P.V. company," of course, the newspaper meant the Western. The article revealed some of the complications that later clouded the Utah coal-land fraud cases. By the time government prosecutions started, a decade later, certain details were fading from memory. The railroad/coal corporate structure also took much effort to understand. Local confusion of the PVCC with the Western indicated the pervasive, basically accurate understanding that the two companies were virtually one and the same. Their interlocking directorates—in which some individuals served on the boards of related companies in the Rio Grande system in both Utah and Colorado—meant that legally separate corporations acted with a single direction and a single agenda, thus maintaining economic control. The fine points so crucial to a federal prosecution eluded most people outside the corporate structure.

The initial PVCC drive for Sunnyside coal relied on individual inclinations as much as legalistic maneuvers. As Holladay was considering his offer, his more pliant associates were also approached. Although they said they could make no binding agreement about the lands claimed by Holladay Coal, they did what they could to help the PVCC. In August 1897 and again in June 1898, two new "associations" filled out federal coal certificates, although they "never reduced to writing any association or agreement." Federal litigation listed their names. The first group included Joseph Seely, W. H. Tidwell, Joseph Tidwell, and Frands C. Grundvig; the second included John F. Evans, John F. Tidwell, William J. Tidwell, and Orange Seely. These documents were notarized by the PVCC's lawyer; other company officials, including a mine superintendent and the company doctor, witnessed them.[34]

The land claimed in this manner was contiguous with that of the Holladay Coal Company. As part of the legal requirements, the entrymen had to fill out forms that declared that these lands were for their own use, and that they had never before claimed any coal lands, a plausible story, since members of the Tidwell-Rideout Mining District had initially made their claims under placer (hard-rock) mining codes. Frands Grundvig, one of the new coal claimants, began selling the output in a small way. As reported in the local paper, coal from his "Wellington mine was being delivered at Price for $3.00 a ton."[35]

While these transactions took place, Holladay apparently was considering his options. He went to Salt Lake City to see William G. Sharp, superintendent of the Pleasant Valley Coal Company, demanding to know if the company had really sent Chipman and Forrester to his Sunnyside development. Sharp admitted that he had, although Holladay later alleged that Sharp also said that Forrester had been sent to erect conflicting claim notices as well. Yet Holladay's actions at the time indicated a more cordial understanding. When Sharp next offered Holladay a free railroad pass to Alaska, gateway to the fabulous Klondike gold rush of the day, Holladay took it. He got as far as Portland, Oregon, before he thought the better of his trip. News had allegedly reached him that "Kirker and others" had jumped his land and driven off his men. In April 1898, Holladay rushed back to Sunnyside, straight into a gun battle.[36]

According to Holladay's testimony during the Progressive Era prosecution:

> Kirker and his men came out of the cabin I had built and swore and cursed me. I had gone down there unarmed as I was ordered to do. Then Kirker came out with his gun and fired over my head. This irritated me and I tried to get my father's Winchester away

from him. I jumped off my horse and they all ran into the house like rats into a hole. I was not permitted to go on the land again until I was compelled to sell the land to the Pleasant Valley Coal Company.[37]

Interestingly, according to Holladay, Kirker's six companions in the Sunnyside shoot-out included not only W. J. Chipman, of the Pleasant Valley Coal Company, but Hyrum and John F. Tidwell, of the Holladay Coal Company; the Tidwell's brother, Orange, and Frank Tidwell, not a Holladay Coal Company member. The sixth was a stranger.[38]

Predictably, Kirker offered a different version of the incident when called to testify. Kirker claimed that he was part of a group of "straight, square, bona fide citizens of the United States," who located and developed their Sunnyside property "without any assistance from any coal company, railroad company or corporation or individual capitalist in Salt Lake" (an oblique reference to Holladay). Kirker continued that "Holliday [sic; his name is consistently misspelled throughout the article] and his crowd came . . . with guns to drive me off our property and the Tidwells adjoining." Allegedly, Holladay had located a conflicting claim that overlapped Kirker's, and tried to secure it by "jumping our cabin [and] using our tools." Kirker retook possession and used his own "45-70 Browning Winchester" to defend his property: "it was absolutely necessary to give Holliday and associates practical notice to vacate." He ended: "I was at Wellington before a Justice [of the Peace] Willson and discharged because it was clearly proven I shot in self-defense."[39]

In the same testimony, Kirker showed almost as much distaste for the Coal Land Act of 1873 as he did for Holladay, complaining that "it is absolutely necessary and of vital importance to have an area of thousands of acres instead of hundreds to guarantee . . . capital for the establishment, equipment of a coal plant and the operation of the same, and 160 acres here and there is of no consequence."[40]

Kirker was obviously well-acquainted with the risky, backbreaking, expensive work of developing a new coal mine. Once a vein was located, miners drove a tunnel into the earth, often miles under the mountain above (the overburden). They had to support the roof of their tunnel as they went along, using wooden pillars that were cut, shaped, and dragged in from the surrounding forest. Each of these had a wedge of wood placed between the top of the pillar and the roof: if the roof started to buckle, the pillars would twist with the pressure, the wedge would fall out, and the miners would know to run for their lives, not unlike the system still used today (see introduction to

Early coal mining demanded the use of horses and mules to haul coal carts within the mines—a big expense for mining companies. Here, around 1890, miners and Pleasant Valley Coal Company animals gather for a photo in front of the Castle Gate tipple, used to sort the coal. Courtesy of the Western Mining and Railroad Museum, Helper, Utah.

this book). As they drove the tunnel deeper, ventilation also had to be provided by the installation of a huge, expensive fan on the surface to circulate outside air. As side tunnels were driven, doors between them—generally operated by young boys, known as trappers—had to be opened and closed to insure a steady flow of air, at the same time allowing miners and coal carts, drawn by horses or mules, to pass in and out of the tunnels.

Miners loaded the carts at the face—the area deep inside the earth where the coal vein was exposed. Aside from the opening of a tunnel (with its initially unstable roof) coal mining itself was the most dangerous part of the work. Wearing lamps on their caps to illumine the otherwise deep blackness of the mine, miners would drill a hole in the face, plant a dynamite charge, tamp it in with a "dummy" (an earth-filled cylinder of cloth), run a fuse, light it, and retire to a safe distance while the explosive (known as giant powder) ripped chunks of coal off the face. Then they would fill a cart with coal. The sole basis of their pay, the load was weighed on a company scale by a company man.

Firing charges at the face could cause a "bounce," as the overburden settled, a process that often forced chunks of coal out of the walls or the face. Firing also raised highly flammable coal dust. This dust had to be settled by being sprinkled with water, lest an explosion result. The explosion could be ignited not only by the open flame of a miner's lamp but by the pipe or cigarette that he was then allowed to smoke in the mine. Sometimes the spark of a miner's pick hitting rock would set off an explosion; sometimes the blast would be caused by a missed charge (one that did not initially ignite), hit by the pick of a miner who didn't know it was there. In any such case, a thunderous explosion reverberated through the mine and any who were not killed by the initial blast or burned in the flames might survive just long enough to suffocate in carbon monoxide ("black damp") as the fire devoured all the available oxyen. Even today, some mines ignited in early times still smolder, since cracks in the earth allow oxygen to reach the "rock that burns."

The prevention of such accidents and production of profit-making coal tonnage required careful planning and a large initial expenditure. Not only did equipment have to be purchased for the mines (although the miners provided their own picks, lamps, and so on, usually bought at the company store) but a town had to be created to house the work force, miners and officials alike, which helped win back some of the wages paid, through the store and other amenities such as the company saloon. In addition, coal was sold by the ton (unlike gold, for example, which was sold by the ounce), necessitating efficient rail service if the mine were to pay. Under these circumstances, ownership of a sizeable, commercial quality coal field was an absolute necessity before a company would be willing to risk the high start-up costs of developing a commercial coal mine.

Knowing all these facts, Kirker, in his testimony, also turned on the unreasonable Coal Land Act of 1873. As he put it: "There is a lameness in the coal land laws, and we have a right to say so because we know it, experience in Utah has taught us, and much more than that." Then Kirker explained that his group had proceeded with complete legality, citing the mining statutes (for minerals other than coal) under which they had filed on a total of three thousand acres, considered near the minimum for a profitable commercial mine.[41]

While Kirker indeed described his true actions, their legality was dubious. As a federal investigator discovered years later, Kirker had filed for Sunnyside lands under placer-mining laws, which was excused by his "ignorance" in "not knowing anything about the coal-land law."[42] Given his own remarks, Kirker was obviously not so naive. Furthermore, for "$10,000. and some persuasion," he soon apparently threw in his lot with the PVCC, one of the few then-existing corporations with the necessary capital for coal-mine development.[43]

The Tidwells, too, had shifted their allegience from the Holladay Coal Company to the PVCC, for their own reasons. Holladay was not always an easy man to get on with: he frequently visited Price, where he owned a one-half interest in the Hotel Clarke. There he got into a kicking-and-flailing match with his partner that left him with a bad bruise in the groin and the other man with severe scalp lacerations, allegedly from blows from a sixshooter. Holladay readily paid the $25 fine assessed in the 1898 case, ostensibly because he did "not care to be detained by a small law suit that might cost him hundreds of dollars . . . in a business way." His revolver got him into trouble again on the train to Salt Lake City, where it fell out of his pocket, hit the floor, and discharged a bullet into his left arm, leaving injuries that were "painful but not serious."[44]

For whatever reason, the Tidwells had grown to dislike him, as emerged in court. As the *Deseret Evening News* reported, "there was much animosity existing between the company of which he [William J. Tidwell] was a member and Mr. Holliday, a coal mining operator." Or, as William's father, Jefferson Tidwell, put it, "Oh, Holliday? He never did anything as he agreed to in his life."[45]

Holladay, unable to force his way back onto the Sunnyside property, took the matter to court. In June 1898, the Holladay Coal Corporation (the vehicle used by Holladay) sued R. A. Kirker, Charles Kirker, and Frank Tidwell in the local district court for possession of the disputed Sunnyside property. Although most of the original documents are inexplicably missing, an index preserved at the Seventh District Court (Carbon County) gives an outline of the trial. Demurrers (legal documents alleging lack of evidence) stalled proceedings during the rest of 1898, giving the PVCC a chance to firm up the secret push for Sunnyside.[46]

Activities at this time have to be pieced together from local news. In October 1898, Robert Kirker was camped at Sunnyside, guarding the area and/or doing development work.[47] At the same time, the state land board sent two men to survey "Sections 14 and 15, in the eastern part of Carbon county . . . [which] adjoin and comprise an area about seventy two miles square. About 20 per cent of it is agricultural and the balance coal and asphaltum bearing." The foregoing information, reported in an article headlined "Lands Thrown Open," was in error

on three counts. First, the lands could not be legally opened: pending
a federal survey, their title was still vested in the United States and
not in the State of Utah. Second, each township (an area of thirty-six
square miles) included a section 14 and 15. The Sunnyside deposits,
the richest coal veins in Utah and the only high-grade coking coal,
lay right on the boundary of Township 14 South, Range 14 East, and
Township 14 South, Range 15 East, both in eastern Carbon County.
The entire area was being explored. Third, if 80 percent of the land
indeed contained coal, the lands could not pass to the state under any
circumstances, despite the fact that they were reportedly "thrown
open" for transfer from the state to private individuals. In retrospect,
the most important point made by this garbled article was that the
state land board probably realized that Sunnyside District was rich
in coal.[48]

In December 1898, events took another step forward as several
interested parties abruptly left Sunnyside. Robert Kirker and George
C. Whitmore abruptly leased their Sunnyside asphalt claims for $40,000
to Western agent Bernard R. McDonald, probably reasoning that
accepting this offer beat incurring the expense of commercial coal-
mine development in competition with the Western. Whitmore went
back to ranching. Kirker took his engineering expertise to the hard-
rock mining town of Mercur, in the southwestern part of the state.
Meanwhile, Robert Forrester, the geologist for the Pleasant Valley
Coal Company and one of Holladay's "visitors," started making regular
trips to Sunnyside.[49] A Price editorial crowed:

> Carbon county is rich in mineral wealth and with development will
> make a glorious record. The disposition of men with money to take
> hold and develop the great asphaltum and gilsonite beds of Whitmore
> Canyon shows that the eye of capital has turned towards us. There is
> going to be some great work done there within the next few months.[50]

The paper was right. A huge fraud was in the making.

CHAPTER 3

Monopoly in Coke

Sunnyside development lagged, pending a decision on Holladay's suit against Kirker. In February 1899, the local district court dismissed the case on the basis that Holladay had no grounds for his complaint. Two months later he filed an appeal with the Utah Supreme Court. On June 15, 1899, two weeks before the supreme court made its decision, the local newspaper glowingly reported another round of Sunnyside coal-land claims. The names of those involved had a familiar ring:

> Two miles square of coal land, or 1,280 acres, in Whittemore canyon have been located and recorded by the following named parties, who claim they will purchase the same from the government when it is surveyed and plat filed in the United States land office in Salt Lake City: John F. Evans and John F. Tidwell, 320 acres; Orange Seely and William A. Tidwell, 320 acres; Jefferson Tidwell and Joseph R. Tidwell, 320 acres; William S. Ronjue and Hyrum Tidwell, 320 acres.[1]

This time the men had apparently formed partnerships, rather than use a so-called association or individual entry, to get even more acreage under the limits of the Coal Land Act. The reason for repeated claims at Sunnyside was obvious, though the article spelled it out:

> *This is said to be the most valuable deposit of coking coal in the west* and lies adjoining that which has for some time been in the courts, but title to which is now quieted. Surveyors are at work on the property, and a plat will soon be ready for filing in the Salt Lake City Land office.[2]

The potential value of Sunnyside's coking coal grew apace with Utah's burgeoning hard-rock mining industries, and by the 1890s they were booming. One of the most productive areas, Bingham Canyon, lay just west of Salt Lake City. It had been opened in 1896 as a gold mine, but before entry work was completed, its owners had discovered that it contained one of the largest copper deposits in the world.

Refining the ore required a smelter. Construction began in September 1898 and finished nine months later, resulting in the first of many smokestacks to puncture the northern Utah skyline.[3]

Bingham's growth paralleled that of Utah coal. By the early 1900s, Bingham had been successfully developed, largely by the internationally famous Guggenheim syndicate, which later would create national problems in Alaskan coal. They added their own smelter under the auspices of the American Smelting and Refining Company, or ASARCO, which dominated the Utah smelter trade. Two other national giants entered the game: the International Smelting and Refining Company, and the United States Smelting, Refining, and Mining Company (USSR&M), the latter of which would later get into one of the most significant legal contests for Utah coal lands. All of these smelters ran on coke, promising riches to whomever owned coking coal.[4]

The Tidwell-Seely clan, with associates Evans and Ronjue, seemed poised for such wealth, thanks to their Sunnyside claims. The newspaper highlighted nearby development work involving "about fifteen men ... employed in two shifts."[5] Ostensibly, these men had claimed the land for their own benefit. The state coal mine inspector, Gomer Thomas, confirmed this fleeting fiction when he reported in 1899 that the mines were "the property of the original locators with Robert Forrester as agent." Since Forrester was the geologist of the PVCC, most local people were not fooled by this subterfuge. Furthermore, contradicting the newspaper account of a small-time development, Thomas reported Sunnyside production as a whole: 11,179 short tons of coal, employing seventy-two men, operated by "R. Forrester, Agent" and superintended by Joseph A. Sharp, formerly of the Pleasant Valley mine at Winter Quarters. A union of coal claims had occurred, in fact, if not in law. Until coke ovens could be built at Sunnyside, the coal was shipped to the PVCC coke ovens at Castle Gate for processing.[6]

The actual events at Sunnyside were later spelled out by a federal attorney.

> Forrester ... had his dummie entrymen appear at the Land Office and enter said lands and a lump sum of $45,055.20 furnished by order of [William Jackson] Palmer et al, was paid for the same, being the purchase price at that time required by the Government. Before even the patents issued, Forrester ... directed the entrymen to convey the lands that they had entered to one Royal C. Peabody of New York, brother of Geo. Foster Peabody [on the Board of the Western since 1892].[7]

Forrester later testified that he was simply "acting as agent for the [Sunnyside] locators." A disgusted federal prosecutor commented that "in the light of all the facts and documentary evidence . . . [this] is as ridiculous a claim as I ever heard made in the courts."[8]

Once again, essentially the same familiar group of men had per-jured themselves to claim some extremely valuable coal land, with the approval of the State of Utah. As Byron Groo, secretary of the state land board, later admitted, he had never checked up on any of the claims received. Groo had joined an expanded board in January 1898 after leaving his federal post as register and receiver of the local land office. Since statehood, he had been involved in the paperwork transferring Utah's lands into private hands. Abandoning his earlier cautious, advisory approach, Groo and other members on the state land board simply relied on the word of the claimants regarding the legality of their claims and forwarded the documents to Washington.[9]

After the time and expense incurred in buying up Castle Gate lands, the PVCC and the associated Western railroad had every reason to sue the more expeditious, inexpensive dummy system at Sunnyside. The rail line was completed, stockholders and bondholders clamored for regular payments, and the growth of Utah's smelting industry left no room for a gradual approach to Utah's best coking coal. Under these circumstances, the actions of Forrester made perfect sense. But what about the Mormons? Why would these proven faithful, who had established a religious beachhead in one of the most desolate parts of Utah, want to help a "foreign," non-Mormon, railroad?

Answers might vary with the individual. The Tidwells may have needed the money. In 1898, Wellington's delinquent tax list included all three Tidwells associated with the Tidwell-Rideout Mining District, William J., John F., and Jefferson. Patriarch Jefferson owed the most, a sum of $31.40, explaining the lure of the $50 they were reputedly offered to make dummy claims. More affluent Orange Seely needed other motivation: even before moving to Castle Valley he had owned five thousand head of sheep, and part interest in a sawmill, cooperative store, tannery, and other businesses. In Emery County, he became coowner, with Wellington, of the Seely Brothers grist mill, and by his own testimony owned "fine farms in the county." But if the Sunnyside coal venture were truly his investment, as he testified, why sell his claim to the Western for a rumored $50? Why lie about obtaining the land for his own use, and jeopardize his self-proclaimed status (in a vanity publication issued in 1898) as "a most representative and respected citizen?"[10]

The Tidwell family erected this cabin and accompanying tent at Sunnyside in order to claim coal-rich land. Classified as "grazing land," such properties became the subjects of the first Progressive Era federal suits. The woman (far left) is probably Sarah Seely Tidwell and the man at center (without hat) is probably Jefferson Tidwell. Courtesy of the Western Mining and Railroad Museum, Helper, Utah.

Frands Grundvig, the claimant who was selling "Wellington coal" in Price, provided the most likely answer for all the Saints involved. According to a family history written by his grandson:

> About 1899 a few Mormons Honesteaded in Whitmore Canyon *to secure coal land for the Church.* My Grandpa and Uncle Hyrum Tidwell were among them. I heard them explain to Father the details of the deal. Hyrum's brother William J. had helped Bob Forrester survey the land for the Utah Fuel Company [*sic*; this was the corporate successor to the PVCC] which was already operating at least three coal mines in the Bookclift Range.[11]

Records that would definitively confirm or disprove this assertion remain locked in the vaults of the LDS Historical Department, unavailable to researchers.[12] But Grundvig's recollection has a reasonable ring. The men involved in the Sunnyside coal-land fraud were dedicated members of the LDS Church. They had proved their devotion by leading colonizing parties into desolate Castle Valley, an area long avoided because of its marginal agricultural worth. If the LDS Church were to command that there be land transactions, these faithful men of eastern Utah would be the likely agents.

But why would the Mormon Church sanction such an illegal deed? In fact, given its long-standing desire to retain economic self-sufficiency and no great love for the Western, why help the railroad at all? Why to such a generous extent?

If, in 1899, the LDS Church did indeed order some of its members to become dummy entrants on Utah's richest coal deposit, the most likely reason seems to be the statehood lobbying debt. LDS leaders, with their long memories and deeply held principles, had not forgotten what they owed to the railroad lobby that had finally won Utah statehood, and, with it, Mormon freedom from federal persecution. At the time, the First Presidency had bemoaned: "Promises that have been made so lavishly to accomplish the end in view—statehood— [are such] that we cannot, as we view it at present fulfill them in the manner that is desired." By the end of 1896, LDS President Wilford Woodruff lamented:

> We the Presidency of the Church are so overwhelmed in financial matters it seems as though we should never get through with it. Unless the Lord opens the way in a marvelous manner, it looks as though we should never pay our debts.[13]

Their creditors included the Gould interests, now involved in the Rio Grande system. Perhaps the Sunnyside coal-land transfer, accomplished by Saints long-proven faithful, was just the answer they sought.

This cooperative arrangement would also explain why the Western would be willing to spend so lavishly to secure claims and begin development on land it could not legally own until the completion of a federal survey. If no one of importance in Utah were to raise questions about the legality of these land transactions, the likelihood of Washington agencies so doing were remote indeed: the General Land Office had long been known for its corruption.[14] Once Utah authorities approved these transactions, the claimants were safe. Or so it must have seemed in 1899.

Besides, in 1899, Utah was again in national disgrace, for reasons far more titillating than coal. The polygamist Brigham H. Roberts, in his history of the LDS Church, later described "a very remarkable arousement [sic] of public sentiment against what was called a reversion to polygamy," beginning in May and June 1898.[15] Roberts himself was the major cause. Running that year against Judge Henry H. Rolapp, a monogamous Mormon then sitting in judgment on *Holladay v. Kirker*, Roberts won the Democratic nomination. During the subsequent campaign, the fact became widely known that "Mr. Roberts was involved in the 'Mormon' church institution of plural marriage; for he had been forced into exile during the polygamy crusade of 1886–1888 . . . and had returned to Utah and served a term of imprisonment for the minor violation of the Edmunds law."[16]

The Roberts candidacy rent LDS solidarity, further weakening Utah politically. Several prominent Mormons publically deplored Roberts's actions. Governor Heber M. Wells proclaimed that "a vote for Roberts is a vote against Utah." George Q. Cannon, who as of September 1898 served as first counselor to the new LDS Church president, Lorenzo Snow,—and who had himself served time in the penitentiary for plural marriages—said that "any man who cohabits with his plural wives violates the law."[17]

Roberts did exactly that: his second wife had recently borne twins, providing ample fuel for his accusers. Ironically, however, in the political imbroglio of the 1898 election, the anti-Roberts campaign by LDS leaders only heightened commitment by non-Mormons (who usually voted Democratic) to his cause. Roberts won by more than five thousand votes, and later claimed that he had carried every non-Mormon stronghold in the state.[18] So he went to Washington.

Roberts's reception there was another story. When he appeared for the swearing-in ceremony at the House of Representatives in December 1899, amid the new antipolygamy crusade, he was refused his seat pending an investigation. Back in Utah, a seemingly unlikely agent participated in his undoing: Charles Mostyn Owen, a civil engineer who had appeared in Price in late February 1899 giving court testimony as "an expert on irrigation," soon turned to other work. By September, Owen was "spotting" against five polygamous husbands in south-central Utah. Two weeks later Spotter Owen caused a sensation by filing the first of his affidavits alleging unlawful cohabitation (that is, continuing polygamous relations) against Lorenzo Snow, the new president of the LDS Church. Owen would make similar allegations in the early 1900s, as the federal government began its legal proceedings against Utah coal-land fraud, but for the moment, he found a different target. In mid-October, just six weeks before the new Congress was to convene, Owen swore out an affidavit of adultery against Utah's newly elected Democratic representative, Brigham H. Roberts.[19]

The House debated the pros and cons of seating a practicing polygamist. Roberts first had to confront a " 'monster petition,' " allegedly containing seven million signatures demanding his exclusion, although many were shortly shown to be duplications or those of young persons collected in Sunday schools. No one questioned the fact that Roberts had been duly and legally elected, or that his presence in the House fulfilled the will of the Utah electorate. Instead, the Ministerial Association of Salt Lake City, fanning anti-Roberts flames, construed the issue to be "a violation of the 'covenant' made between the Mormon leaders and the government when Utah was admitted to statehood"—referring to the alleged agreement that polygamy would be abandoned.[20]

Joseph Rawlins, who had originally sponsored the Utah Enabling Act with its lavish school section grants, now sat in the Senate on his state's behalf. He answered the charge that, by electing a polygamist to office, Utah had broken faith with the United States by saying that Mormon officials had indeed forbidden all future polygamous marriages, and that polygamy was outlawed in the Utah constitution. He continued: "During the past year the state has been raked in search of cases of polygamy with which to feed this new modern sensation, but no complaint has been presented against any man charging him with this offense. Some cases of unlawful cohabitation have been prosecuted and punished. So far Utah has sacredly kept the compact."[21]

In fact, the local district courts dismissed Owen's cases against the five rural Saints and President Snow for insufficient evidence, putting Owen "in a swearing mood." In November 1899, however, based on Owen's testimony, the court swore out a warrant for Roberts's arrest on his return to Utah. Roberts, fighting for his congressional seat, remained in Washington until January 1900. At that time, the House voted 268 to 50, with 36 not voting, to exclude Roberts.[22] Utahns suffered the ignominy of a repeated failure to meet national "standards," and an accompanying political debility on the national scene. Their hatred of repressive federal actions smoldered.

The refusal to seat Roberts was hardly an isolated event in the Progressive Congresses of the early twentieth century, although the reason was unique. The same Congress had to deal with another sort of "unsuitable:" a senator who had literally bought his seat. Copper king William Andrews Clark went before the Senate Committee on Privileges and Elections early in 1900 as a result of two typically western events: a bitter rivalry with another capitalist (in his case, Marcus Daly) and fantastic wealth derived from the recently acquired public domain. The committee heard fanciful lies, uncovered fabulous bribes, and forced Clark to resign. Unchastened, he returned to Montana and waited until the hostile governor had left the state. Then he got the friendly lieutenant governor (and acting governor) to appoint him to fill the vacancy created by his own resignation. The governor, having returned, balked, appointed his own man, and, before anyone could decide which man really represented Montana, the Senate adjourned. Clark therefore ran again (at far less expense) in 1900, winning the coveted Senate Seat, holding it until 1907, a glaring example of what western land money could buy.[23] (While in the Senate, Clark also promoted the San Pedro, Salt Lake and Los Angeles Railroad, a crucial piece in the growing puzzle of Utah coal.)[24]

In Utah, meantime, coal mining was expanding rapidly, with even greater production apparently just over the horizon. The state coal mine inspector reported in 1899 after his mid-year inspection tour through eastern Utah's coal fields: "The time has come to open up the coal fields of Castle Valley. ... All that is needed to make these fields superior to others is organized capital to operate them on a large scale."[25] He neglected to mention that large-scale landholding was most difficult to achieve under the parsimonious strictures of the Coal Land Act of 1873.

Sunnyside, seemingly a patchwork of tiny, "individual" claims, was finally ready for sizeable commercial development, thanks to the decision rendered on *Holladay v. Kirker* at the end of June 1899. The Utah Supreme Court had reversed the finding of the lower court. The supreme court's decision, written by Judge Henry H. Rolapp, granted Holladay "the highest form of possession" because he "had men ... working upon the property in question at the time of the forcible entry." The association was granted the legal maximum allowable acreage under the Coal Land Act of 1873, 640 acres. Specific descriptions included mention of "Tidwell's opening." A final statement of the law specified that, as long as the legal limit on acreage was not exceeded, preference right of entry would extend to those actually working the land when the federal survey was completed. The occupant was also extended protection from forcible removal by others. Still, Holladay did not secure title to the property, which still resided in the United States, pending the federal survey.[26] Even more unfortunately for Holladay, the work force that had assured Holladay's success in claiming Sunnyside was now working for someone else.

Robert Forrester, the key agent in this change, was sent to negotiate for Holladay's claim. He was certainly well suited for evaluating the worth of Holladay's coal land. A native of Scotland, he had received an education in geology at the University of Edinburgh before emigrating to America in 1887. Two years later he had arrived in Utah and served as United States inspector of mines for Utah Territory in 1892. His activities as mine inspector enhanced his knowledge of coal deposits both in Utah and Wyoming, where he had explored contiguous coal deposits outside his official jurisdiction. After leaving this territorial position, he became chief geologist for the Pleasant Valley Coal Company.[27]

Negotiations proceeded erratically. Reportedly, Forrester originally offered Holladay $10,000, but was rebuffed when stockholders demanded more. The ensuing talks led to a mutual understanding between both sides, obliquely referred to in later years as "the Conference ... Under 'Bill' Tidwell's Old Pigeon Coop." Finally, the Holladay Coal Company shareholders agreed to sell the Sunnyside claims for $22,000.[28]

The Western wanted to bury its connection with this coal-land acquisition as deeply as possible in a quagmire of legal minutiae. The Western Construction Company, due to expire in 1901, was therefore named as the original owner of record of the Sunnyside lands.[29] Pending the demise of the construction company, the railroad legal department could take a couple of years to develop other ownership plans.

Robert Forrester dropped some hints about the cooperative nature of Sunnyside development. Fielding questions about a possible conflict between his role as PVCC geologist and "agent" for a "new" Sunnyside company, he announced that his new employer "will not antagonize the interests of the Pleasant Valley Coal company, and that it will receive the support of the Rio Grande Western Railway company."[30]

The Western and PVCC indeed gave generous support to the new venture. More than $45,000 had already been spent just in securing the land claims. The state coal mine inspector in 1899 reported new improvements that signified further lavish expenditures:

> two steam hoists and two boilers, two 15-foot fans and buildings, one dynamo producing 600 lights, and the company has built one barn with room enough for seventy-five horses, two oilhouses, one large hotel that will accomodate 100 men. The hotel is furnished with electric lights and baths; also twenty miners' cottages with electric lights, and one large store.[31]

Forrester got to display his handiwork to his true employers in November 1899, when he escorted the leading officials of the Denver and Rio Grande Western around Sunnyside. General William Jackson Palmer, president, and Colonel D. C. Dodge, vice president and general manager, together with their guides and guests, steamed into town in Palmer's private car, Nomad, and Dodge's, named simply A. The rails they traveled belonged to the Carbon County Railway, a new Western subsidiary that had just completed the spur line to Sunnyside. Palmer took the occasion to announce an extensive building program that would add one hundred miles of Rio Grande track in Utah, Colorado, Nevada, and California.[32]

Sunnyside was a worthy setting for such a pronouncement. In acquiring it, the Western had achieved a true monopoly in Utah's coking coal.[33] The timing was perfect. In 1899, "the most successful year in the history of the coal mine industry in Utah," almost a million dollars worth of coal and coke came out of Carbon County. All of the coke, and almost 90 percent of the coal, came from Western-connected mines.[34]

Such a moneymaking proposition spurred others to risk coal-mine development. By 1899, several small ventures had opened along a roughly north-south line in eastern Utah. They began with Clear

Coking coal, extremely valuable for the smelting trade, was made from coal by slow roasting in brick ovens. The ovens pictured here were under construction about 1902 at Sunnyside, location of Utah's best coking coal. Sunnyside production was monopolized by the Rio Grande system. Courtesy of the Western Mining and Railroad Museum, Helper, Utah.

Creek Mine, opened by the PVCC just south of Winter Quarters. About five miles southwest of Pleasant Valley, over a high ridge, two new mines sprang up in Huntington Canyon, including the Bear Canyon Mine, operated by Don Robbins, who would later find himself entangled in federal coal-land litigation. Roughly fifteen miles southeast of Bear Canyon, the Cedar Creek Mine opened in northern Emery County. This wagon mine, begun for local trade, would eventually point toward another area of Utah coal-land fraud.[35]

At the turn of the century, however, the federal government cared little about fraud and instead actively promoted private land ownership. On July 2, 1900 the federal survey of Utah was finally completed, allowing long-standing claimants on federal lands to achieve title.[36] The Western moved quickly, not just to gain title to coal lands but to obscure the means used for their original acquisition. The Western Construction Company, which had "bought" the Sunnyside land from its claimants through Robert Forrester, their "agent," did not long survive the federal survey. Its imminent demise, slated by charter for 1901, forced the Western to address the formation of the "new company" Forrester now supposedly served.

Given the frauds that had led to Western ownership (through the PVCC), as mentioned in passing earlier in this chapter, the railroad had to bury its Sunnyside landholdings deep in legalistic paperwork. To this end, corporate attorneys devised a masterwork of legal intracacies. They began in October 1900 with the incorporation of the Utah Coal and Coke Company in New Jersey, a state known, for good reason, as the Mother of Trusts. The ostensible directors of Utah Coal and Coke were actually friends and relatives of the owners of the Denver and Rio Grande Railroad, the parent company incorporated in Colorado. They were also involved with the eastern banking houses of Kuhn, Loeb and Company, the Goulds's backer, and Spencer, Trask and Company, the banking house associated with Palmer's Western. These men, led by brothers Royal C. and George Foster Peabody, required General Palmer to promise that he would refrain from further coal or railroad development within Colorado and Utah for the next ten years. In the meantime, a "sale" of Sunnyside coal lands took place to this series of dummy directors. As one of them later testified:

> At the request of my Cousin, Mr. Peabody, I was asked if I would allow my name to be used as an incorporator. ... It was a very short time that I was an officer. I had no pecuniary interest in the company.[37]

Twelve days after its formation, the new corporation changed its name to the Utah Fuel Company, probably because a different Utah Coal and Coke Company had already incorporated in Utah in 1899. All the dummy directors then deeded their interest to Royal C. Peabody, who in turn "sold" the stake to his brother George. In the course of these transactions, the company's capital rose from $10,000 to $10,000,000. As the process was later unravelled by federal investigators:

> Palmer, Peabody and others having in this manner organized a corporation with an authorized capital large enough to pay for the Utah holdings ... entered into an agreement, nominally between the [Rio Grande Western] Construction Company and the Utah Fuel Co., but in truth and in fact among themselves.[38]

In a further series of deals, the Western Construction Company, prior to its demise, sold its long-held Pleasant Valley capital stock to the newly created Utah Fuel Company. In turn, Western Construction acquired the stock of Utah Fuel, which had just subsumed the PVCC. As the Western Construction Company neared its chartered end, it signed a series of agreements, between November 1900 and July 1901, whereby the Rio Grande Western Railroad obtained all the Utah Fuel stock, and its subsidiary, the PVCC. The long-perceived union of railroad and coal mines achieved actual corporate structure, and Utah's finest coal properties were cemented to the Rio Grande system.[39]

This connection was enhanced as the Colorado and Utah branches of the Rio Grande system underwent their own, simultaneous, transformation in 1901. Beginning in January, George Gould became a board member of Colorado's D&RG. A month later, the banking house of Kuhn, Loeb and Company, representing Gould, negotiated a contract with Palmer's financial associates, Spencer, Trask and Company. In April, while these negotiations were underway, Gould moved up to president of the D&RG board of directors. His control became obvious at the May 15 D&RG stockholders' meeting, when the pending deal with Palmer's Western reached fruition. The Denver and Rio Grande obtained controlling interest in the common and preferred stock of the Western; Gould backed Edward T. Jeffery as the Western's new president (duplicating the position Jeffery held on the D&RG); Gould became chairman of Western's board, and William Jackson Palmer was ushered completely out of the line he had founded.[40] In effect, the two lines—the Colorado D&RG and the Utah Western—were now united under the same management, but the bonds and securities consummating this union were not yet transferred. The two lines continued to operate as separate corporations until 1908. Throughout this process, the Rio Grande system was strengthening its grip on Utah coal land.

This surge to secure Utah lands had its counterpart all over the West, clogging federal channels. The General Land Office, in the Interior Department was so glutted with land contests that Congress was forced to act. On March 3, 1901, a bill passed mandating a six-year statute of limitations on contesting land patents to reduce the huge backlog. Even land obtained by fraud could not then be challenged.[41] When, in 1906, the Justice Department finally realized the magnitude of Utah coal-land fraud, time for a federal case had almost run out.

CHAPTER 4

Polygamy, Politics, and Public Policy

Congressional interest in tightening up public-land policy suited the new president of the United States, Theodore Roosevelt. Previously exiled to the vice presidency, in an attempt to curb his reforming influence, Roosevelt entered the White House on September 14, 1901 on the wings of an assassin's bullet. He soon began implementing his own Progressive agenda for the United States. He outlined his vision, in a casual way, on July 4, 1886, voicing his love for "big things; big prairies, big forests and mountains, big wheat fields, railroads." But he added that "each one must do his part if we wish to show that the nation is worthy of its good fortune."[1] Roosevelt's love of bigness also extended to government, where he did his own part. In his new position, he began by saving forests under the prodding of his chief forester, Gifford Pinchot.

Pinchot was born among the well-to-do, and had gone to Phillips Exeter and Yale. His formal qualification as America's first trained forester had been won in Europe, in thirteen months of study after his Yale graduation. He entered government service in the 1890s, when the Department of Agriculture supervised the nation's few foresters but the Interior Department managed the national forests. A proposed Division of Forestry had to be housed in one of the two agencies, and Agriculture eventually became its home.[2]

Shortly after Pinchot won appointment as chief forester, under the Department of Agriculture, in 1898, he began a drive to transfer the nation's trees from Interior into Agriculture. Interior Secretary Ethan Allen Hitchcock supported Pinchot, although the secretary's job hardly permitted the same singleness of purpose. Hitchcock already had his hands full supervising various agencies, including the General Land Office, which transferred most public lands into private hands.[3] These divergent federal roles created an obvious source of friction in Roosevelt's administration.

47

The conservation of forests led to later concern with coal. As Roosevelt wrote: "In its administration of the national forests, the forest service found that valuable coal-lands were in danger of passing into private ownership without adequate money return to the government and without safeguard against monopoly; and that existing legislation was insufficient to prevent this."[4] Attempts to correct that situation soon involved not only the executive but the judicial and legislative branches as well.

Personality conflicts militated against easy solutions. Despite a superficial agreement on goals between Pinchot and Hitchcock, the two never developed a rapport. Pinchot, a member of Roosevelt's so-called Tennis Cabinet, used his influence to further his own agenda, such as wresting "his" precious forests from Interior's grip. He had a rather dim view of Secretary Hitchcock, as he later reported: "Ethan Allen Hitchcock ... was a high-minded gentleman with the very best intentions in the world. If you knew him you had to respect him. But he was far from a Heaven-born executive. ... Government work ... was not his forte."[5] The incipient conflict between the chief forester and the Interior Department would break into the open in 1911, in a dispute over coal.

President Roosevelt, meanwhile, pursued other reforms in addition to public-land conservation. Returning to his beloved big railroads, he discovered they had become "trusts." He proposed the remedy of "the State [that] not only has the right to control them, but it is duty bound to control them wherever the need of such control is shown."[6] Consequently, the president called for legislation—or possibly a Constitutional amendment—to allow federal supervision of corporate activities despite their legal existence as creatures of the states where they were incorporated. But he eschewed an excessive exercise of federal power, including "too stringent legislation."[7] Hence, Progressive reform began in a haze of contradictions.

Furthermore, presidential recommendations did not guarantee congressional action. One stumbling block was the composition of Congress; for example, Wyoming Senator Clarence Don Clark was the brother of Dyer O. Clark, manager of Wyoming's Union Pacific Coal Company. The Wyoming senator (no relation to Senator William Andrews Clark, of Montana) began congressional service in 1895 and was returned for three more terms. By 1905, he had been appointed to positions that had the power to give the UP some protection. He chaired the Senate Judiciary Committee and held positions on the Committees on Railroads and on Public Lands and Surveys.[8]

Despite such connections, however, Congress began enacting a reform package. It began in 1903 with the Elkins Act, which mandated enforcement of existing railroad rate structures and abolished imprisonment for convicted offenders in the hope of increasing convictions. Congress also established the Bureau of Corporations, but its immediate effects were not apparent.[9]

Another part of the Progressive agenda, public land law reform, met with less success. Western senators reacted unenthusiastically, exemplified by Wyoming's Senator Clark, who complained: "I am not ready to believe, nor am I ready to acknowledge, that our Western States are engaged in one sole operation of stealing the land of the United States from the public domain."[10] Despite this disclaimer, a major coal-land scam was in progress in the West, even as Clark spoke.

In December 1900, Stanley B. Milner had appeared before the Utah State Land Board with his application for "grazing lands" on the escarpment that looped east from Castle Gate to Sunnyside in Carbon County. Like the Utah Fuel Company, he sought state selections, although Milner's claims were replacement sections (technically, *in lieu* sections, not part of the original school land grant of Sections 2, 16, 32, and 36 in each township, but sections replacing unsuitable lands). The board approved his application the following day. Utah's governor, Heber M. Wells, as president of the state land board, and Byron Groo, as secretary, added Milner's lands to those being requested by the new state under the provisions of its enabling act. They forwarded the list to the U.S. General Land Office in Washington, D.C. with the approval of the register and the receiver of the United States land office in Salt Lake City. The following June, the GLO confirmed the state's request. Milner, lacking the cash flow of an interstate railroad network, paid off a portion of the lands and began making payment on the rest. Final patent awaited his payment in full.[11]

To develop his new mine, Milner tapped both economic and political expertise. In 1901, he hired that well-known mining man, Sam Gilson, the gilsonite king, to manage his holdings twelve miles northeast of Price. Gilson by this time had long abandoned his career as U.S. marshal, which he had pursued in heat of the anti-Mormon campaigns of the 1870s and 1880s. Together, the two men began experimenting with the production of that great moneymaker, coke. They also organized the Carbon County Land Company and enlisted one of Utah's rising elite on the board of directors: Hiram Booth, future federal prosecutor for Utah, became president of the Carbon County Land Company in 1903, with the backing of George

Sutherland, Utah's junior U.S. senator and later U.S. Supreme Court justice. Booth may have been chosen for his ignorance of the specifics of the company's land filings, an amazing occurrence in light of the vituperative litigation of his brief tenure; or, he may have perjured himself when he later claimed that he simply accepted Milner's offer to serve as company president and attorney for 1903, subscribing "for ten shares of stock at ten cents a share. . . . While I was connected with the company there was no crooked work going on."[12]

In fact, according to records of the Utah State Land Board, Stanley Milner, acting as agent for Harley O. Milner, applied for school sections as "grazing land" in March 1903, and the application was approved by the board and by the local federal land office later that month. In December of the same year, Sam Gilson applied for and received approval of similar claims on other, nearby, tracts. These parcels, obtained for the Carbon County Land Company, were added to others acquired between 1901 and 1904 by Gilson and the Milners, including Stanley's wife, Truth. Therefore, with federal approval, by December 1904, Utah had agreed to deed these individuals (actually a business association), more than five thousand acres of coal-rich "grazing land," much of it in in-lieu sections on Utah's Book Cliffs coal belt. Financial backing for mine development came through the good offices of Peter Campbell, Boston banker and Milner's uncle.[13]

The year 1903 was also made memorable for the Carbon County Land Company by the one serious wrinkle in its otherwise smooth mine development scheme. One key quarter section had an adverse claimant. The steep canyon entry offering access to Milner's vast coal claims had already been filed on under the Coal Land Act of 1873 by another Price resident, John B. Millburn.

Millburn had led a life of adventure before settling in Price. As a young man, he had shipped out of his native Maine for the life of a sailor. Tiring of that, he tried farming in Iowa and then freighting in Colorado and Utah, being drawn away briefly by the Klondike gold rush of 1897–1898. Returning to Price, he had opened a saloon, which gave him unlimited access to the alcohol that made him mean and angry. In 1903, he challenged Stanley Milner over 160 acres that both men claimed, at the strategic canyon opening to the rich coal lands beyond.[14]

The protest was sent to the commissioner of the General Land Office in Washington, D.C., who directed that a hearing be held before the register and receiver of the Salt Lake branch of the federal land office. There, Milner asserted, he had legally purchased this particular quarter section from the government as soon as the federal survey was completed on March 17, 1903, and that he had been in continuous possession of the area since December 18, 1900. He pointed to the five hundred-foot tunnel he had dug, and claimed to have spent "$10,000 in valuable and lasting improvements upon the ground."[15]

Millburn countered that he had held a claim since 1894, an assertion brought forward by his attorney, E. W. Senior, a man with his own connections to Utah coal. In the course of the testimony it was revealed that, until approximately 1902, Millburn had been joined in ownership of his quarter section by the Utah secretary of state. The outcome hinged on whether or not Millburn had established bona fide occupation of the disputed coal land. If Millburn's claim held, Milner and Gilson could never hope to ship from their proposed mine.[16]

While this contest was pending, in the summer of 1903, President Roosevelt decided to see the beleaguered West again for himself. His tour took him to Salt Lake City, where Sam Gilson ingratiated himself with Roosevelt, currying favor for possible assistance in the consortium's battle for Utah coal. Milner presented the well-known outdoorsman with a hand-carved walking cane. Made of red cedar and fashioned with only a penknife, the cane sported animal heads carved into each of its many knots, including "deer, coyotes, a horned toad, a lynx, lizard, mountain lion, sheep, bear, rabbit and a snake," crowned with an eagle's head protruding from a band, half gold, half silver, marked respectively East and West. T. R. probably loved it.[17]

As events transpired, violence, not politics, brought the conclusion to the Milner-Millburn coal-land fight. First, in October 1903, the registrar and receiver of the Salt Lake Land Office awarded the land to John Millburn, regretting the loss of investment Milner had sustained but noting that "he could by small expenditure and a little exploration, have readily determined the quarter section involved."[18] Consequently, John Millburn received a federal patent for 120 acres of coal land in 1904, but he didn't keep it long. In 1905, Millburn drunkenly confronted the Price deputy sheriff, against whom he had a grudge, pulled out his rifle, and was shot dead on the spot. Most of Milner's immediate development problems died with Millburn.[19] Utah Fuel/PVCC geologist Robert Forrester promptly noted that "Mr. Milner ... owns practically all the coal frontage between our Castle Gate property and our Sunnyside Property—a distance of about twenty miles."[20] A new competition seemed in the offing.

By 1905, Utahns's preoccupation with coal development had diminished proportionally with a new anti-Mormon crusade. Again, hue and cry had arisen in Salt Lake City against that recurring Mormon shibboleth, polygamy. The first whispers of this new political controversy began on May 14, 1902, when Mormon apostle Reed Smoot first announced his candidacy for one of Utah's two U.S. Senate seats. Smoot had been ordained an apostle of the LDS Church in 1900, making him a member of the Council of the Twelve, those dozen men closest to the First Presidency, as the Mormon Church's president and his two counselors are known. Smoot, a Republican, was the highest-ranking member of the LDS Church ever to run for public office, and his candidacy caused an immediate stir. By the end of November 1902, the Salt Lake Ministerial Association, which had successful galvanized the anti–B. H. Roberts campaign, was attempting to arouse the nation against Smoot.[21]

With Smoot as its candidate, the Republican Party came in for close scrutiny. Thomas Kearns, a gentile (non-Mormon) already representing Utah in the Senate under the Republican banner, undermined party solidarity by using his newspaper, the *Salt Lake Tribune,* to fan the campaign against Smoot. Kearns, interested in furthering the fortunes of a fellow gentile over the Mormon apostle despite sharing the same political affiliation, thereby earned great animosity from other Republican Party members. Another newspaper opined: "It looks as if a coalition had been arranged between Smoot and [George] Sutherland by which the former is to be elected to the Senate this time, while two years from now Sutherland will step into the place left vacant by Kearns."[22] This succession took place as predicted: Republican Sutherland won the 1904 Senate election.

First, however, Smoot's impact on the Republican Party was brought to the attention of its highest-ranking national member, President Roosevelt. Senator Kearns called on Roosevelt and reported that the president advised "against the election of any [Mormon] Apostle to the United States Senatorship."[23] Meanwhile, pro-Smoot forces, aroused by a congressional attempt to forbid polygamy and unlawful cohabitation nationwide, also lobbied Roosevelt.[24] Two of Smoot's brother apostles and a gentile mining man, called separately. The latter specifically reassured the president that Smoot was not a polygamist and that Mormons were dedicated U.S. citizens.[25]

Despite this controversy, the Utah legislature elected Smoot to the Senate seat on January 21, 1903, defeating incumbent Senator Joseph Rawlins and Utah Governor Heber M. Wells, both fellow Republicans. Formal protest of Smoot's election began five days later, specifically alleging that the election results indicated a theocracy in Utah that existed solely to perpetuate polygamy.[26]

Once again, Utah was accused of "breaking faith" with the national government, specifically over polygamy. What truth lay in this allegation? Recent research reveals its accuracy. Utahns generally were aware that Mormon plural marriages continued to be performed by some of the high-ranking members of the LDS Church. Some prominent Mormons publicly repudiated the practice, however, one such being Governor Wells, who was born into a polygamous family. Yet Wells's refusal (in 1901) to sign a bill nullifying Utah's criminal statute against unlawful cohabitation may have resulted in his defeat for the Senate seat a year later. Furthermore, several Mormons continued to live in plural marriages already contracted, and polygamous First Counselor George Q. Cannon had recently spoken in favor of both polygamous families and plural marriages in foreign lands.[27] A new church president, Joseph F. Smith, had been ordained in 1901, and his views on polygamy initially remained somewhat obscure. Reed Smoot, a member of the church leadership, was seen either to condone polygamy or, at least, to wink at its practice.

Accordingly, when Smoot was sworn in as United States senator on March 5, 1903, Smoot's adversaries readied their arsenal. Spotter Owen now took up Smoot's trail on behalf of the Utah-based Protestants' Committee and the Salt Lake Ministerial Association. Owen had passed part of the interval between polygamy crusades in dummying coal lands for the Western's coal subsidiaries, an activity he continued on the side. Soon, several senators demanded Smoot's expulsion, and the Smoot hearings began on March 2, 1904. The power of senatorial committees was not lost on Utah's freshman senator, and he learned potentially useful lessons from his baptism by fire.[28] But first, he had to fight for his political life.

The first witness subpoenaed by the Senate Committee on Privileges and Elections was LDS Church President Smith. His views on polygamy were rapidly clarified when he admitted that he had continued to live with his plural wives since the 1890 Manifesto and had fathered children by all five since then. Smith professed an unbelievable ignorance of the marriage practices of others, however, even his closest church associates. His testimony, recently assessed as "one of the most damaging of the entire investigation," contributed to the perception of a Mormon political "betrayal" and the mobilization of powerful national reform organizations, such as the Women's Christian Temperance Union, in a renewed antipolygamy crusade.[29]

Haunted by the memories of past conflicts, many Mormons felt compelled to restore the reputation of their church. Smoot himself went so far as to write to President Smith, revered as a living prophet, to suggest that he publicly renounce polygamy once and for all.[30] Smith used the April 1904 Conference of the LDS Church (a gathering of Saints from all over the world, held regularly in Salt Lake City) to address this painful issue. There he offered a Second Manifesto to the faithful for their sustaining vote. He referred to the Woodruff Manifesto of 1890 and reaffirmed the LDS Church's prohibition of any new plural marriages. He also stated that those transgressing would be excommunicated, subject to church judicial procedure. The faithful assembled sustained this measure in a powerful, if typical, show of solidarity. Recent analysis, however, indicates that this document did nothing to change the official church stance from what it had been in 1890, stating that it "simply refuted rumors and ratified Smith's testimony in Washington."[31]

In Washington, the first Smoot hearings concluded on May 2, 1904, after focusing on a series of points, described here from the national standpoint. First, the LDS Church had allegedly continued polygamy, which exposed the 1890 Woodruff Manifesto as a political sham. Second, plural marriage was believed to be sanctioned by church leaders, including Smoot, who must have known it persisted. Third, the LDS Church had allegedly controlled the political machinery in Utah and in other states with large Mormon populations in order spread the practice and keep it alive. The conclusions were that Mormon polygamy was a great moral evil, that Smoot represented a deviant group, and that he was therefore unfit to sit in the U.S. Senate.[32]

One of the obvious concerns of these hearings was the marital status of Smoot himself. Consequently, the colorful cowboy detective Charlie Siringo was hired (evidently by a "Mr. Cannon") to investigate. As Siringo noted in his book, in a chapter entitled in part, "Working on United States Senator Smoot":

> I had been instructed to run down a certain young lady of Provo [Utah], who was supposed to have married this citizen and was living in one of the church colonies in Old Mexico as one of this man's plural wives. ... I found out all about the young plural wife of Mr.———. She was then in Logan, Utah, finishing her education. ... [I]f he had other than his lawful wife, I failed to discover it.[33]

This convoluted wording resulted from Siringo's disenchantment with his former employer, the Pinkerton Detective Agency, prompting him to reveal as much as possible without incurring retribution. "Mr. Cannon" he noted was probably Frank J. Cannon, editor of the anti-Mormon Salt Lake *Tribune,* then involved in an in-state political challenge against Smoot's Regular Republicans. Despite such efforts, Smoot was indeed proved monogamous. He so testified on his own behalf and presented sympathetic witnesses in 1905. But the Senate committee still refused to report.[34]

The Smoot hearings took place just a few blocks from ongoing attempts at federal land reforms. President Roosevelt's 1903 tour of the West had filled him with fight for the vanishing public domain, which resulted in the impaneling of the second Public Lands Commission that October. Not surprisingly, Gifford Pinchot was one of its advocates and acted as commission secretary. Other members were W. A. Richards of Wyoming, chairman (who had succeeded Binger Hermann as commissioner of the GLO), and F. H. Newell.[35]

Pinchot had desired to create this body not only to preserve the public domain for home seekers, but to see the nation's forests transferred from "the Department of the Interior, where they were thoroughly mishandled, to the Department of Agriculture, where I was confident we [the Division of Forestry, which he headed] could do a good job." His fixation on changing the administrative home of the Division of Forestry blunted his crusade for preserving public lands. Even more detrimental to coal lands, which were rapidly being privatized, Pinchot's regarded forests as "the most valuable lands still in public ownership."[36]

The Public Lands Commission issued two partial reports, in March 1904 and February 1905. Together, they demanded that mineral deposits should bring the government at least that remuneration fixed by law, and that "the public lands should be saved for the homemaker," not railroads or major coal developers. Further, the reports lamented that current statutes tended "to bring about land monopoly" in which, "almost without exception, collusion or evasion of the letter and spirit of the land laws was involved."[37] The Coal Land Act of 1873 certainly offered a good example of the problem.

Yet the commission offered no concrete solutions and never submitted a full report. Pinchot busied himself with his division, renamed the Forest Service, created just five days before the second partial report appeared. He had achieved his major goal, control of the nation's forests, and this probably dimmed his ardor for other types of western land.[38] Others would have to carry on the fight.

The first, resultant, land battle came in Oregon, where the second

Public Lands Commission had uncovered irregularities in timber land transactions. Subsequent prosecution led to the conviction of Oregon's senator, John H. Mitchell, for fraud. Binger Hermann, commissioner of the General Land Office, was also forced to resign, although his constituents shortly returned him to the House, where he served on the Public Lands Commission. As Pinchot noted: "What all this [investigation] came to was that while many of the public-land laws were more or less defective, their administration by the Interior Department [home of the GLO] was horrible. And this belief was confirmed and strengthened by the Oregon land-fraud cases, and by much besides."[39]

In fact, the Oregon timber cases led directly to Utah coal. In 1904, while in Oregon to prosecute the timber cases, the newly appointed special assistant to the attorney general, Marsden C. Burch, was collared by a reporter who told Burch of rumors of even more flagrant fraud in Utah. In his thorough manner, Burch traced the source of the reporter's rumor to a bragging, self-educated mine developer, himself allegedly knee-deep in Utah coal-land scams. As Burch later noted (referring to himself in the third person):

> Having satisfied himself that his information was authentic with the consent of the Attorney General he [Burch] conferred with Secretary [of the Interior Ethan Allen] Hitchcock upon the subject. The latter declared that he never had before heard of any coal land frauds but that if there was something there that Burch should fire away at it and he would stand by him.[40]

So fire away he did.

CHAPTER 5

A Legal Watershed

A year before Burch's involvement, in October 1903, the government had unsuccessfully tried to reclaim more than five thousand acres of Utah coal land using a civil, administrative procedure. This first Utah litigation was part of a frenzy of national public-lands reform that had made its first concrete appearance with the debate over the passage of the Newlands Reclamation Act in 1901 and 1902. The scandal of the Oregon timber frauds that aired the following year strengthened this crusade. This initial phase of public-lands policy reform culminated in the appointment of the second Public Lands Commission on October 22, 1903, simultaneously with the first foray into coal-land fraud investigations in Utah.[1] Movement on so many fronts, however, meant fewer resources to devote to each.

Consequently, the government lurched into a complex situation minimally prepared. Seeking a quick resolution, federal attorneys had brought nine actions in the United States Land Office in Salt Lake City against the Western, the UP-related Clark family, and the State of Utah. In retrospect, the case against the state, based on the Utah Enabling Act, attacked the most significant issue. Specifically, it addressed the ambiguity regarding which lands might pass to the state under the school selections process. Section 6 of the Utah Enabling Act, silent in regard to mineral lands, granted four school sections in place in each township. Section 8, however, allowed Utah to select salt lands, in contradiction to current mineral statutes.[2] The state therefore contended that the inclusion of salt lands in the act meant that the Congress had intended that other-mineral lands, including coal lands, should also pass to the state. Federal prosecutors, of course, disagreed. However, this belief on the part of state officials lay at the center of most coal-land frauds, as Utah simply tried to dispose of "its" land for its own purposes.

Several specific problems hamstrung this initial federal prosecution. First, evidence collection gained public exposure when the Price paper reported the arrival of "H. V. A. Ferguson, a special agent of the department of the Interior" and his investigation of the five thousand acres of school sections in Carbon, Emery, and Sevier Counties. Second, there was a problem with witnesses. A coal expert slated to appear for the prosecution was instead called to testify for the defense, where he ably averred that the land in controversy was indeed fine for grazing and could be known to contain coal only by driving a long tunnel. The government, with no other witnesses to call, lost the case. A Utah newspaper promptly predicted that, in an appeal to the General Land Office in Washington, D.C., the commissioner would no doubt find for the defendant, "as the government has failed to show by a single witness that coal either existed upon or in the ground." The paper was right; the government lost again.[3]

Although this first prosecution effort failed, it occurred during a transformation in Utah's legal climate. The transfer of the Sunnyside deposits to the Utah Fuel Company had apparently marked a watershed in state-railroad relations, exemplified by the behavior of Byron Groo. He had begun his tenure on the state land board in 1896 by warning of the illegality of acquiring mineral lands from the federal government as state selections, but by 1900 he turned a blind eye to one fraudulent claim after another. Five years later, however, he had grown intractable to his railroad-employed claimants. In February 1905, Utah Fuel Attorney William Bird repeatedly called on Byron Groo, still the Board's secretary, asking him to submit the chosen "grazing" property to the federal land office in Salt Lake City. A disgruntled letter from Bird complained: "nothing has been done by Mr. Groo although he has made to[o] many promises. His excuse today is that the Board of Land Commissioners has been in session every day ... and he can do nothing until they get through."[4]

What events had caused this change? A hundred years after the instance, one cannot say with certainty, but significant events came in annual procession beginning right after the turn of the century. In 1901, the new Utah Fuel Company and the Pleasant Valley Coal Company sought even more lands from the state, perhaps appearing increasingly insatiable. From the corporate standpoint, however, the Gould-Harriman "war," which broke into the open in 1902, absolutely demanded the utmost in economic power and control. Such capitalistic wrangling, typical though it was, opened the crack in corporate armor that first excited federal interest—and then litigation, beginning in Utah in 1903. In addition, in 1904 the first "independent" coal-mine developers (those not associated with a railroad) began work in eastern Utah. This new group assumed the mantle of "healthy competition" that had been previously bestowed upon the Rio Grande system when it confronted the monopolistic Union Pacific during the nineteenth century. A further straw in the changing wind was the activity of Spotter Charles Mostyn Owen, a frequent dummy of the Rio Grande system. Owen hit a new low, posing in Mormon temple garments for photographs that ran on the front page of the *Washington Times* in December 1904. These photos, judged utterly tasteless at the time, even in 1992 were considered "inappropriate" for publication in a scholarly work on Mormon polygamy.[5] As Owen fanned the crusade against Smoot when congressional sessions resumed in early 1905, any corporation that employed him no doubt lost all vestige of Mormon support.

This series of events was not what the railroad had originally anticipated. Instead of viewing the Sunnyside acquisition as some sort of conclusion, corporate officials regarded it as part of an ambitious expansion program. The full extent of these plans was outlined in a 1901 letter from Henry Gordon Williams, then leaving the Castle Gate general superintendency for a new position as general manager for Utah Fuel. He wrote to the PVCC president with some preliminary estimates for opening an extension of the Castle Gate mine in Willow Creek Canyon, just east of the original mine portal. He projected an output of 25,000 to 30,000 tons of coal, noted the existence of springs to sprinkle the volatile coal dust, and itemized the prices of requisite equipment. He also mentioned one drawback: the PVCC did not own the land.[6]

Williams, however, was prepared to deal with that difficulty. Noting "considerable lands being held under coal filings and . . . some land contests pending which will require considerable expenditure" in addition to those bought as "grazing land" from the state, Williams gave specific acreage and prices for tracts at Sunnyside, Huntington Canyon, Castle Gate, Winter Quarters, Clear Creek, and Mud Creek (also in Pleasant Valley). He summarized: "The total of both the Utah Fuel Co. and P. V. Coal Co. in process of being secured and on which the State is liable to call on us for payment is 12,359–98/100 acres, on which is due $21,426.73. [The balance of $2 per acre.]"[7] The Rio Grande subsidiaries, he wrote, also held some coal land under federal filings. The companies would soon have to pay $20 an acre for these lands, but visible coal outcroppings (the current federal definition for coal land) necessitated paying the higher price. Some of the total Williams identified could be let go—they had been filed on only to forestall the claims of others. Williams concluded:

Others of these lands (a small amount) can be relinquished as coal filings and taken up as State selections at a much less cost. As an off-set to the above, however, it will undoubtedly be necessary for the proper protection of the company to take up a few pieces of coal lands in these districts which are not yet filed upon. . . .

The total acreage [of these] . . . is 1560 acres requiring $24,650. to complete purchase.

Williams then added a section on "contested lands" and a grand total of $52,826.73 required for 14,319.98 acres.[8]

In one, thoughtful, letter, Williams had neatly encapsulated actions that would take years for the company to complete, and even longer for federal agents to unravel. He had targeted tracts in Carbon, Emery, Sanpete, and Sevier counties, all known to contain commercial quality coal. Later, a team headed by the Justice Department would try to sort out matters relating to this dark-veined complex of lands. Some of them they would never illuminate.

A few days after sending this letter, Williams applied his general recommendations to a specific situation: that of the proposed Willow Creek mine, adjoining Castle Gate, which he had earlier described. He discussed the current market for the coal: a contract with the Southern Pacific Railroad, which might not be renewed. He then noted the on-the-ground completion of the requisite federal survey, lamenting lack of final approval. Despite claims to nearby parcels by local citizens, competition was slight and "the bulk of them [the lands] can be secured under State selections . . . [so the price] will be very small in comparison with the value of the lands."[9]

This exhaustive report shortly circulated through a hard-pressed railroad hierarchy. After George Gould's 1901 buyout of Palmer's Rio Grande Western and the de facto consolidation of the Western with Colorado's D&RG, Gould got control of the industrially compatible Colorado Fuel and Iron Company. His main competition, E. H. Harriman, of Union Pacific, simultaneously forced Senator William Clark, of Montana, into a minority position on the San Pedro, Los Angeles and Salt Lake Railroad, giving Harriman control of a route publicly coveted by Gould. The UP thereby gained control of another route to the Pacific, while Gould, who had just secured railroads on the East Coast, was still seeking a West Coast connection. The two expanding railroad giants headed for a clash, and it came in 1902 as the Ogden Gateway, the juncture of the UP and Western, slammed shut. As a result, the Rio Grande system could no longer transship its goods at the UP-controlled Ogden station, which effectively cut off the Gould lines from the Pacific.[10]

Gould fought back, deciding to build his own line westward. Surprisingly, the coveted construction contract went to the obscure Utah Construction Company, which previously had built only a few small railroad lines. This company, begun by brothers William H. and Edmund O. Wattis and Edmund's in-laws in 1887, had foundered during the Panic of 1893. William Wattis then appealed to a fellow Mormon, David Eccles, for emergency funding. Eccles's First National Bank of Ogden provided financing on a series of Wattis-conducted jobs over the next few years. According to Eccles's biographer, this Mormon banker—Utah's first millionaire—sensed management problems in this series of requests, but he continued his support of Wattis with his personal fortune. When the Wattis family company reorganized in 1900 under the new title of the Utah Construction Company, Eccles received a third of the stock; two Eccles associates split another third, and the Wattis brothers obtained the remainder. Edmund's in-laws were then "moved into less critical positions."[11]

This fledgling business acquaintanceship between Eccles and the Wattis brothers would later blossom into a new consortium for developing eastern Utah coal and other major enterprises. In the meantime, however, the Utah Construction Company had won "the largest railroad contract ever let west of Chicago ... [when] Eccles used his personal reputation" in helping the virtually unknown Wattis team secure the Gould railroad job.[12]

Utah Construction employees then devoted themselves to building the Pacific railroad required by the Gould-Harriman fight. Official incorporation of the new line took place on March 6, 1903, at the prompting of George Gould. Although he kept his involvement secret until 1905 somewhat to mitigate the feud with Harriman, Gould's new Western Pacific Railway Company (WP) was financed by a $50 million loan backed by the resources of the two Rio Grandes. Three contracts spelled out the details of this agreement. Contract A involved Rio Grande purchase of WP second-mortgage bonds. Contract C outlined reciprocal traffic agreements among the various Gould lines. But, according to a modern historian, "Contract B ... presented the Western Pacific with a signed, blank check to be honored by the Rio Grande companies."[13] From its inception, the WP sucked the financial life blood of the Rio Grande. The railroad system, in turn, put an increasing premium on expanding its lucrative western coal-land holdings.

Such expansion took place through both action and reaction. Moving ahead in Colorado, the Rio Grande utilized the services of the everreliable Emery County surveyor William J. Tidwell to secure yet more coal land. In 1902, he and another man supported the fraudulent land claims of the railroad's rising star, Alexander H. Cowie, in Delta County, before going on to witness numerous other dummy claims in Colorado.[14] The entry of A. H. Cowie into the Rio Grande hierarchy presaged the swelling power of the Jeffery faction. The two men, first associated in Colorado, would increasingly concern themselves with Utah affairs, leading to a direct clash with the Utah hierarchy as the two lines became ever more closely linked.

Meanwhile, Western officials had other problems on their minds. They had to react to encroaching economic competitors in Utah before they could concern themselves with the ambitions of Cowie, Jeffery, and others in the Colorado office. New prospective developers increasingly probed the rich coal land of Castle Valley, filing claims on veins already tapped by Western-controlled mines.

Sunnyside, the best of Utah coal, was then the main preoccupation. This prize seam could not long go unnoticed by others. In 1902, as foreshadowed at the opening of chapter 1, optimistic, youthful Arthur A. Sweet (he was only twenty-three) had challenged Utah Fuel dummy Charles Mostyn Owen to his Sunnyside "grazing land" claim. A resident of Utah since age fifteen, Sweet had demonstrated a business precocity denied to his three elder brothers. A later tribute noted that "he recognized the value of business situations and utilized his opportunities to the best advantage."[15] This spirit had prompted Arthur, with the help of his brother Frederick, a trained attorney, and a partner to file a federal coal-land claim to 160 Sunnyside acres "for the purpose of occupying, prospecting, and developing the same as coal lands." A legal filing under the Coal Land Act of 1873 availed him little when two gunmen showed up on the land. As Sweet later testified in court, they first fired over his head and "asked him if he would go 'at his pleasure' or by force. He consented to go 'at his pleasure.'" He and Frederick then got a court injunction against such physical intimidation and filed a civil complaint in the local district court challenging Owen's allegedly fraudulent acquisition of known coal lands as grazing lands. Sweet also lodged a complaint with the General Land Office in Washington, D.C., alleging that the State of Utah had, at Owen's instigation, illegally claimed coal lands under its enabling act, a point that would be long debated. Meanwhile, during these interchanges, despite the injunction, the gunmen maintained a constant vigil to prevent Sweet from reentering the Sunnyside area.[16]

Sweet received a federal patent for 80 of the 160 acres in June 1903, despite the fact that his injunction had been ignored and dissolved the preceding February. There his luck stopped. Owen got a larger, surrounding tract from the state the following December, isolating Sweet's parcel. Sweet soon sold out for $4,000 to a Western agent and took a job as telegraph operator for the PVCC. This employment ended with his being fired when he refused to copy Western Union messages for his employer and reported the illegal practice. Next, Arthur and Frederick Sweet allegedly renewed their complaints about Utah coal-land fraud to the Department of Justice as well as the Interior Department, apparently hastening a federal investigation.[17]

Concurrently, the PVCC and the Utah Fuel Company experienced a bitter miners' strike during the winter of 1903/04. Some of the events of the strike clearly indicated the support that the Western and its subsidiaries enjoyed from the State of Utah. For example, at the request of Utah Fuel officials, the governor obligingly sent the National Guard to help protect the railroad-owned mines from the strikers. The miners, backed by the United Mine Workers of America (UMWA) and the legendary Mother Jones, had demanded union recognition and a series of work-related improvements. The National Guard, supported by the state government and most leaders of the Mormon Church, arrested and deported the organizers, usually following a trial.[18]

Cases heard in Castle Valley had a kangaroo-court flavor, revealing the power of Utah Fuel over the local judiciary. For example, in December 1903, during the trial of A. B. Edler, the UMWA organizer and attorney, his counsel, William H. King, had to face the local Utah Fuel lawyer, Mark Braffet, who was supposedly "assisting the County Attorney." Braffet had been active in Carbon County politics since the 1890s, when he served as county clerk, the county's first. A lifelong friend of several eastern Utah outlaws, Braffet relied for protection during the strike on his bodyguard, C. L. "Gunplay" Maxwell. This convict had just received a timely governor's pardon from the state penitentiary, where he had been serving five years for bank robbery and homicide.[19]

During Edler's trial, when King branded a Utah Fuel statement as an outright lie, Braffet angrily shouted: "You shut up! You make a few statements like that and there will be real trouble here." In a courtroom packed with Utah Fuel guards (for example, Maxwell) and company officials, the defense pleaded for an end to such intimidation. After Edler's conviction, King declared: "I have never seen a place where the desire to railroad a man through to jail is so manifest. . . . There is not another place where an attorney for a corporation is supreme to the court."[20]

The sorry state of justice in Castle Valley was not lost on the greater-Utah press. A cartoon published in a Salt Lake newspaper just days after this farcical trial depicted members of the jury and the bailiff in hats labeled "Utah Fuel Company"; the judge carried pistols with the same inscription, and all others in the courtroom were portrayed as gun-toting outlaws, with the exception of the witness and the terrified defendant. Such blatant company excesses, causing mirth and derision in the Salt Lake press, underscored some of the difficulties of imposing legal controls on the Rio Grande system within Utah.[21]

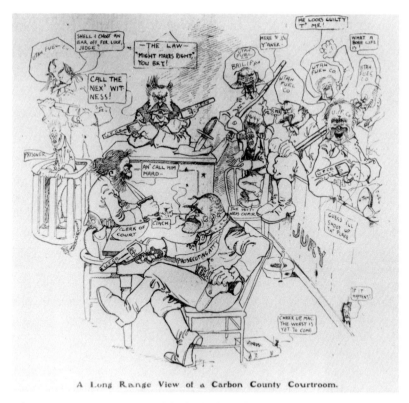

A Long Range View of a Carbon County Courtroom.

This 1903 cartoon was printed by both the Salt Lake *Herald* and the *Eastern Utah Advocate*. It gives a fairly accurate portrayal of the Utah Fuel Company's control over the Carbon County judiciary.

Railroad power did not deter Arthur or Frederick Sweet. Unlike Milner and Gilson, the other local entrepreneurial pair, who stuck to development, the Sweets used a double-barreled attack on the railroad/coal combination. While they continued explorations for their own coal mine, they also recognized the power of litigation to weaken or distract their opponents. In February 1904, the Sweets turned to the U.S. Land Office in Salt Lake City, backing coal-land claimant Albert Simmons in his suit against Owen L. Davies that alleged coal-land fraud. Davies, a Salt Lake City cigar broker, had claimed land in Salina Canyon in March 1903, supposedly for his own use. Simmons asserted that Davies had repeatedly used this ploy to dummy lands for the Utah Fuel Company. Three other counterclaimants to the tract now in dispute had already withdrawn their suits, at an estimated cost to Davies of $25,000, which included funds spent in out-of-court settlements. Either cigars were selling extremely well, or Davies indeed had a corporate backer. A later newspaper article asserted that *Simmons v. Davies* was the case "that started the investigation into the alleged fraudulent practices by the Utah Fuel company."[22]

Indeed, federal interest in Utah coal-land fraud seemed to have been piqued. A March 1904, newspaper article had just reported forthcoming suits supposedly resulting from "a clash of railroad interests [presumably Gould and Harriman]. . . . The cases are now being prepared, and will be filed in a few days in both the United States Land Office and the United States district court."[23] These allegedly grew out of the earlier Land Office hearings, where sufficient evidence was developed "to invalidate the [Utah Fuel] company's titles to most of its lands at Clear Creek, Scofield, Sunnyside and elsewhere throughout Eastern Utah."[24]

While the press thus speculated, the hearing on *Simmons v. Davies* was suspended, pending a decision on the entryman's right of appeal by the commissioner of the General Land Office in Washington, D.C. In February 1905, the commissioner denied an appeal, ordering the hearing to proceed. A trial was set for the following July. Meanwhile, government agents were unearthing considerable evidence of fraud. At their request, the case was continued again and again, not going to trial until January 1906.[25]

Concurrently, Arthur Sweet continued the search for his own mine. He hiked along the Book Cliffs, west from Sunnywide, toward Castle Gate. About twenty miles later, two miles short of Castle Gate, he came upon the little Mormon farming community of Spring Glen. There, Sweet saw that some of the residents, in carving out nearby coal seams to heat their homes, had stumbled on a rich coal deposit in Bull Hollow, just west of the Aberdeen Mine recently opened by the Price Trading Company.[26] Sweet saw it as a possible new approach to the coal wealth denied him at Sunnyside.

In order to secure his own mine in this area, Sweet had to follow several steps: determine the extent of local coal deposits, control sufficient acreage for a commercial mine, and obtain capital for development. This time Sweet asked his father-in-law, Henry Wade, to help him get started. Together, the two men began making local contacts in December 1904. Among those who agreed to help them was Heber J. Stowell, a farmer who had had his own problems acquiring land and hanging on to it.[27] Farming, especially in eastern Utah, never made much money, and Stowell was still scrabbling for a living ten years after he had settled in Spring Glen. Sweet and Wade shortly made him an offer that he couldn't refuse. He later alleged that they promised him $1,000 if he would help them locate coal in the mountains above Spring Glen and secure the title for the coal land thus located. A similar offer was accepted, too, by other Spring Glenners. Sweet and Wade had found the right place for their mine.[28]

Their efforts did not go unnoticed in this usually sleepy area. Soon the news reached officials at Castle Gate, and communications flew back and forth between the camp and corporate headquarters. Worried company officials wired: "Try to find out what Wade and three men are doing and keep watch on them." Then the bad news arrived: "Mr. Crow found out that the men who went up Gentile Canyon [included] Henry Wade, A. A. Sweet, (Wade's son-in-law) who jumped some land at Sunnyside, which the company was obliged to buy ot [sic] him."[29]

Despite the earlier problems with Sweet, the railroad's greatest fear was not small-fry developers but other competing railroads, thanks to the ongoing Gould-Harriman war. A later corporate report speculated: "If the San Pedro people are actually investigating this country, it is very important that we should have absolute proof of it at the earliest possible date."[30]

Was the San Pedro really involved? This line, known in full as the San Pedro, Los Angeles, and Salt Lake Railroad, had celebrated its first run between Salt Lake City and California (at Riverside) on March 12, 1904. On January 30, 1905, its last spike was driven to extend the line all the way to Los Angeles. It was originally backed by Senator William Andrews Clark (Montana), the copper king. Known as the Midas of the West, Clark had planned to increase his fortune by linking Utah's burgeoning industries and farms with

California's shipping facilities. His alleged connection with the Sweets was apparently part of a plan to locate fuel and shippers for his new railroad. He succeeded dramatically in Utah, also earning the cooperation of Reed Smoot, the Mormon businessman and United States senator then battling for his seat. Clark's railroad became a bone of contention in the contemporary standoff between the UP and the Rio Grande, as wrangling commenced in the courts and on the ground. Judicial decisions finally gave half of the control to each line, although Harriman interests in fact dominated (they eventually bought the line outright in 1921). Thus, Sweet and Wade, in allying themselves with the San Pedro, were apparently joining the UP against Sweet's old enemy, the Rio Grande.[31]

Sweet and Wade had already suggested the benefits of such an alliance to their local coal-mine locators. One of them, Price resident William H. Lawley, later testified about the details of the deal. The new entrepreneurs had offered him "one-fourth interest in certain [company] store privileges on certain land . . . near Spring Glen, Utah, in case a sale of said lands is made to the San Pedro Railroad Company, or to its representative."[32] Considering the high-stakes atmosphere of eastern Utah coal-land development and the risks run by all those contemplating fraud, it did no harm to promise fat returns.

Flamboyant Utah Fuel lawyer Mark Braffet also had his say in the Sweet-Wade development. When Braffet wrote confirming the interest of the San Pedro Railroad, he also noted that Sweet was then in Salt Lake City to determine if the land he wanted had already been claimed. Braffet warned: "His coal locations . . . would be in the vicinity of Willow Creek [the new Castle Gate Mine No. 2] an[d] in the absence of any filings in the United States Land Office [I] think it would be well to watch future movements of these people."[33] Braffet was also well aware of Sweet's probable reliance on federal coal-land law. Not only might Sweet acquire territory contiguous with Castle Gate, but he might alert federal watchdogs to irregularities in the titles of adjacent lands claimed through the state. In later years, Braffet would recall this concern when he sought ways to harass his former employers.

Ignorant of the stir they had caused, the Sweet consortium began basic development work at Bull Hollow, relying on laborers clearly hostile to the Western and its subsidiaries. The ugly coal miners' strike of 1903–1904 had left a legacy of animosity and a willing pool of fired workers. As another spy's report noted: "The twelve men working in this [Bull Hollow] mine are Italians from Strike Town and as soon

as they [Wade and Sweet] can work them to advantage they are going
to put on forty men and have promised the strikers jobs." He reiterated
the probable backing of the San Pedro or of Senator Clark for the
Bull Hollow development. The Italian strikers, much pleased with
the chance to earn an income, "will fight Utah Fuel to the finish."[34]

Meanwhile, as Braffet had predicted, the Sweet-backed consortium
was duly and legally trying to gain ownership of this new coal area.
In December 1904 and January 1905, an association composed of Spring
Glen residents, with Arthur A. Sweet holding power of attorney, filed
papers entitled "Declaration of Intention to Purchase Coal Land" with
the U.S. Land Office in Salt Lake City. The documents were notarized
by another Spring Glenner, J. W. Warf, who immediately took an
interest in these promising local developments. In February 1905,
probably with the blessing of the Sweets, Warf wrote to the officers
of the Colorado Fuel and Iron Company, affiliated with the UP,
regarding "propositions that I think ought to interest you. . . . I have
discovered one of the best veins of coal yet found in the West. . . .
This coal is upon unsurveyed land and we hold some 3,000 acres of
it by right of discovery and occupation." This letter came into the
possession of Robert Forrester, who worriedly wrote to the vice president of the entire Rio Grande system that the property in question
was "that land including and also adjoining the lands we have decided
to acquire" that lay, as Forrester indicated on an accompanying map,
directly between the Castle Gate tract and the lands claimed by Stanley
Milner. An adjacent quarter section also appearing on the map was
labeled: "Land owned by Price Trading Company [the Aberdeen
Mine]."[35]

Forrester, usually the local troubleshooter for coal-land competition, had entered this fray rather belatedly. His tardiness resulted from
his absence, in New Mexico, when the Sweets first moved into Bull
Hollow in December 1904. At that time, Forrester had been resident
in San Juan County, New Mexico, where he had rounded up a group
of willing dummies to obtain more coal land for the Rio Grande.
Accompanied by William Bird, a Utah Fuel attorney, this group had
begun paperwork that concluded in August 1905. In a similar scheme
to that of the cigar-selling Davies, the New Mexico dummies claimed
known coal lands, but each swore he was "in the actual possession of
the coal mines . . . and made the entry for his own use and benefit,
and not . . . for the use or benefit of any other party." The notary
public who witnessed two of these fraudulent affidavits then swore
out his own, similar, claim. On August 18, 1905, this group filed their

separate affidavits with the United States Land Office for the Territory of New Mexico, each alleging a desire to purchase the legal maximum of 160 acres. As a result, Bird and Forrester, acting for the Utah Fuel Company, locked up the better part of four coal-rich sections (because of control of adjacent land) on which mines were already opened.[36]

Bird had rushed back to Utah from New Mexico Territory as the Bull Hollow spies' reports came in, leaving Forrester to complete the deal. Emulating earlier success against Sweet at Sunnyside, Bird decided to contact an alternate claimant, to file on Sweet's new federal coal-land entries under state law. If all went as planned, a new "non-mineral" state selection would accrue to the Utah Fuel company before Sweet could get his federal coal-land claim through the clogged U.S. General Land Office.

To implement this plan, in January 1905 Bird wrote to prospective dummy Bernard R. McDonald. Bird first outlined the Sweet-Wade filing attempts to obtain the Bull Hollow land. He explained that two associations were involved: the first, Sweet and other capitalists; the second, Spring Glen homesteaders. Both associations had claimed the largest possible acreage under the coal-land law (640 acres each), and each claimed to have already expended thousands of dollars in development. Bird questioned these expenditures. He suggested that first the obliging surveyor William J. Tidwell be enlisted to disprove the existence of the requisite $5,000 improvements, thereby invalidating the declarations by which 640 acres could be obtained. If this maneuver were successful, Bird further suggested, McDonald could move in using the proven abuse of the state selections system. "You purchase the land from the State of Utah, having them select the same for you ... [then] the State will be required to protest these two coal declaratory statements, and that will be done in your name ... [but] I do not want to get you into a scrap that we cannot win." The actual existence of coal on these lands was never in doubt. Bird simply pointed out that the expenditures claimed by the Sweets were inflated. Furthermore, Bird noted, the extent of the coal beds could be known only through the use of a prohibitively expensive diamond drill. According to standing definition, only land showing coal on every forty-acre subdivision could officially be classified as coal land. McDonald's non-mineral affidavit might succeed on the basis of definition alone.[37] But this time, as already noted, when a railroad dummy appeared with a fraudulent claim, the state land board stalled.[38]

CHAPTER 6

On Your Mark . . .

A series of events beginning in 1904 opened the way for federal prosecution of Utah coal-land frauds. In Utah's entwined affairs of church and state, then being scrutinized in the Smoot hearings, both ecclesiastical and political actions had profound political results. To recapitulate the significant events, the Smoot hearings began on January 16, 1904, to investigate allegations that he and fellow leaders of the LDS Church had sanctioned polygamous marriage in the years since the 1890 Woodruff Manifesto. Taking of testimony began on March 2, with LDS President Joseph F. Smith's damaging assertions. The April General Conference of the church, at which Smith issued a formal statement of the position on polygamy, failed to convince the nation of the Saints' sincerity and integrity.[1] Consequently, Utah's credibility fell to a new low.

The Smoot hearings concluded for the year in May 1904, and charges that the LDS Church had broken faith with the United States government had political repercussions that fall. Specifically, in November, Utah Senator Thomas Kearns, a wealthy gentile mining magnate, split from the Republicans and fostered the formation of the anti-Mormon American Party. His goal: to become the dominant political power in Utah. The Mormon issue also affected the presidential elections that year, when Theodore Roosevelt was returned to the presidency, this time winning the election in his own right. Roosevelt carried Utah by 62,446 votes to 33,413, largely through partisan Republican support, marshaled for him by Senator Reed Smoot. In January 1905, as the Smoot hearings reopened, Roosevelt tried to remove one of Smoot's chief detractors by offering the prosecuting counsel a lifetime position on the Ohio federal bench. The Committee on Elections and Privileges, thus thrown into confusion, persuaded the attorney to continue with the Smoot hearings, "though by doing so he came as dangerously near to being unethical in accepting the appointment as the president was in making it," according to Brigham H. Roberts, Mormon historian and practicing polygamist.[2]

At this point, on January 7, 1905, George Moyer, an attorney and state land board member, apparently wrote directly to the United States attorney general about land frauds in Utah, breaking decades of official silence. This letter has been lost, but Moyer referred to it in a later communication of June 1905. He also mentioned a meeting with Marsden C. Burch, the special assistant to the attorney general who, while investigating Oregon timber frauds, had heard allegations that drew him to Utah.

In the interval between Moyer's first and second letters to the attorney general, many events of political significance to Utah had transpired. Resumption of the Smoot hearings began on January 11 and continued until January 28, when they closed with "what were expected to be the final arguments made by the attorneys."[4] According to historian Roberts, who had himself been denied his congressional seat because of his continuing practice of polygamy, the Smoot case had reached "the height of its development [in] January, 1905," with LDS notoriety compounded by the nonappearance of six "missing witnesses," four of whom were absent because of alleged ill health or absence from the country. The most damaging to the Smoot case, however, were two of his fellow apostles, John W. Taylor and Mathias F. Cowley, who simply refused to appear. Smoot, forced to deal with the white-hot rage of fellow senators on this account, nonetheless was still advising LDS President Smith to keep Taylor and Cowie out of the reach of the investigating committee some eighteen months later. Although Smoot had initially offered to resign his Senate seat in April 1904, rather than embarass his church, by the following year the battle was clearly joined.[5] Once again, as with the statehood thrust, the LDS Church and the State of Utah had to muster whatever forces they could to maintain the position of their apostle-senator, Reed Smoot.

By March 1905, changes were clearly in progress. That month brought a new state administration and a changing of the guard, including the dismissal of the old state land board. New commissioners were appointed under the directorship of W. D. Candland, and Byron Groo, who had served so faithfully, left the office of land board secretary. As a result, the Rio Grande system could no longer rely on a sympathetic cadre of officials to approve their land requests.

Simultaneously, the *Salt Lake Herald* published specific details of the Utah coal-land fraud. On March 12, 1905, the lead article announced: "Light Cast On Methods Used to Grab Coal Lands"; the report was subtitled: "Following Indictments in Oregon for Timber Frauds, Government Officials Investigate in Utah." Cautiously citing the efforts of "special agents whose identity has been kept secret," the paper reported that federal investigations had revealed that "hundreds of thousands of acres of valuable coal lands have been acquired for corporations in devious ways and by questionable methods." It revealed the familiar "grazing land" scheme, claiming that "in a majority of cases it would be difficult for a mountain sheep to find sustenance on a thousand acre tract." It then alleged that these state selections had "since passed into the hands of the Utah Fuel company, which is seeking to control all the coal of Utah."[6]

In these transactions that transferred land from the United States to Utah to private owners (often Utah Fuel), completion of the process meant that the land had proceeded to patent; in other words, that the dummy or coal company had acquired legal title. In such cases, the federal government then bore the burden of proving fraud. Even widespread knowledge of coal-land illegalities did not guarantee an easy federal prosecution, however. One of the main problems the Justice Department faced was that of faulty law—the root of many land scams in the first place. In this instance, no federal statute existed that clearly outlawed the complexities of the dummy system, involving corporations, real persons (because the corporation is also a person in law), and the state. Each of these issues would have to be addressed in what proved to be decades of litigation.

Unconcerned with such technicalities, the newspaper continued with its juicy scoop. The article alleged that "more than 2,000 of these [individual] coal entries have been made in the local [state] land office, and not more than one in fifty of the persons who made the filings has completed the purchase."[7] In other words, dummies could also be used to "lock up" prospective coal-land acquisitions so that further company prospecting could be conducted at leisure. Counterclaimants, of course, had recourse to trying to file a federal coal claim, the method attempted by the Sweets, but this method had major, obvious drawbacks. Meanwhile, if the coal vein did not extend into the land, or was cut off by geological faulting, the company dummy would fail to pay up, and forfeit the claim. If, on the other hand, the land held sufficient accessible coal, or offered a "gateway" to other coal-rich parcels, the Utah State Land Board would find another "individual" claimant at its door. In this instance, the federal counterclaimant had to be persuaded to drop his claim by any one of several methods already mentioned. This system, while occasionally risky, had nonetheless allowed the Rio Grande system to acquire ownership of thousands of acres of Utah coal land quickly and cheaply, circumventing a federal law that mandated a 640-acre maximum.

As the article further noted, Robert Forrester, on behalf of the Utah Fuel Company, had acted as the agent for at least sixty dummy entrants, many of whom were named in the article (not included, however, were the Sunnyside dummies, nor Forrester's own family members). Allusion to the Oregon timber frauds implied the probable fate of the dummies, as did the reference to Binger Hermann, late of the General Land Office. Bringing the story home, mention was made of Owen Davies's ongoing hearing and Utah Fuel's lavish developments at Sunnyside and Castle Gate. Finally, after noting that coal had to be exposed on every forty-acre tract for a property to be considered "coal land," the article printed a summary of the Coal Land Act of 1873.[8] An article published the following day predicted a grand jury probe: "The special agents of the government are reported to be only at the beginning of their work."[9]

Polygamy ranged alongside coal-land fraud as front page news. A separate story in the March 12 *Salt Lake Herald*, headlined "Mothers Congress and Mormonism," explained why the National Congress of Mothers opposed the senatorship of Reed Smoot. As an apostle of the Mormon Church, Smoot allegedly supported a system that degraded womanhood and embodied "false ideas of home and marriage."[10] The juxtaposition of these two reports was probably no accident: they emphasized the internal and external political pressures being applied against Utah.

Obviously, these pressures were felt by the Mormon Church and its chief lightning rod, Reed Smoot. In April 1905, Smoot absented himself from the general conference of the LDS Church by reason of a pressing trip to San Francisco. At a subsequent conference in October, he refused to sustain apostles Taylor and Cowie, two of the "missing witnesses," as members of the Quorum of the Twelve. In a church characterized by outward harmony and consensus, such actions approached mutiny.[11] At the very least, they marked significant internal turmoil.

On the corporate front, the Western railroad faced increasing pressure of its own. Dogged by a growing pack of would-be competitors, it simultaneously spied on the opposition and tried to corral more of eastern Utah's coal. Utah Fuel geologist Robert Forrester wrote to Charles H. Schlacks, second vice president of the Utah Fuel Company, on March 8, noting a coal proposition made by Price resident J. W.

Warf to the Colorado Fuel and Iron Company. Forrester enclosed
Warf's letter, describing a bed of coal "from 18 to 28 feet thick and
of the best coking quality . . . only about 10 miles from the D & R G
Ry [Railway], and a nice grade and of easy access . . . upon unsurveyed
land." It lay between Utah Fuel's patented lands and those claimed
by Stanley Milner. Marked on the map Forrester drew and enclosed
was a single quarter section owned by Price Trading Company, a
mercantile institution including and partially funded by James M.
Whitmore, a Price banker and brother of George Whitmore, the first
homesteader at Sunnyside.[12] As Forrester well knew, the Whitmores
were no friends of the Western. In fact, the Utah Fuel Company was
then engaged in protracted litigation with George Whitmore over
Sunnyside water.

The progress of the Whitmore water case illustrated many of the
pitfalls later evident in coal-land fraud prosecutions. First of all, the
Western and its related companies would go to great lengths to protect
their investment in Sunnyside coal. Utah Fuel, like other coal companies, needed water to sprinkle the volatile coal dust within the mines
and to supply their company towns. George C. Whitmore needed it
for his stock, his crops, and for personal use. He had been using it
since the 1870s, when he homesteaded along Grassy Trail Creek in
Whitmore Canyon, where he ranched with his brother, James M.
"Tobe" Whitmore. Both brothers went into banking, together found-
ing the First National Bank at Price in 1901, and George, returning
to their original home in Sanpete County, later founded his own bank
there. George Whitemore was now also heavily involved in railroad
deals with the San Pedro on the Sanpete side of the Wasatch Plateau,
according to spies McDonald and Tidwell. This was another affront
to the Western.[13]

In 1901, George Whitmore had sued the Utah Fuel Company and
the Western in the Seventh Judicial District Court at Price, claiming
that they were stealing his water. He alleged that the two companies
had drained local springs and lowered the water table through construction of their coal mines, which had diverted some underground
springs, and through drawing water for their town of Sunnyside. A
decision the following year favored the railroad, but in 1903 the state
supreme court upheld Whitmore on two of three counts on appeal.
In September 1905, Whitmore had the case reopened to determine
the quantity of the water illegally taken by the railroad companies in
the earlier case, and to assess damages for the water so taken.[14]

Whitmore won his case but was unable to collect damages, so he returned to the courts in 1913. The court record by that time amounted to more than 1,500 typewritten pages of evidence, indicating how hard the railroad system had fought the suit. Finally, on July 22, 1914, Whitmore signed a "Satisfaction of Judgment," indicating his receipt of $12,500 won through thirteen years of litigation.[15] His experience indicated how long and hard the Rio Grande system would fight to keep the assets it needed for its coal-mine development.

The Whitmore water case also provided evidence of the Rio Grande system's continuing national political involvement. As the litigation unfolded, Robert Forrester, the Utah Fuel troubleshooter, realized that his company might have to go elsewhere for the necessary water, so he explored Range Creek, east of Grassy Trail Creek. In a series of letters to the general manager he noted sections already acquired by others, those open to purchase from the state, and those advised for company purchase, "but which cannot be entered until May 29th, 1905," pending completion of the federal survey. Forrester distinguished between sections absolutely required (a total of more than 1,300 acres) and those recommended for purchase (nearly another 3,000 acres), all in the still unsurveyed public domain.[16] Forrester added that he had already filed Range Creek water applications with the state engineer in the name of the Utah Fuel Company.[17] Copies of all these letters were forwarded to Charles H. Schlacks, vice president of the Rio Grande system, who was also informed of the ease of getting the Tidwells' local water rights and the amount needed to buy the claims of a local rancher: "a maximum of $5,000.oo . . . if they could catch him in the proper mood." After this payment and the completion of the federal survey, the Fuel Company could make an application for the land and accompanying water rights, which "would also insure us against a possible much larger expenditure. . . . Both Mr. Sutherland and Mr. Braffet think this procedure in acquiring these lands is very desirable."[18]

George Sutherland's continuing involvement with the legal office of the Utah Fuel Company came as something of a shock, since he had just been elected to the United States Senate. In November 1904 he had joined the beleaguered Reed Smoot in representing Utah. Sutherland's continuing involvement with the Rio Grande system, including efforts to acquire still more of the public domain, did not bode well for federal prosecutors trying to stop Utah coal-land fraud. Furthermore, Sutherland and Smoot, who had been classmates at Brigham Young Academy, would be the ones to consult for the many patronage jobs then open.[19] The divergent views of a Roosevelt Republican and a lawyer working for a coal company presaged more political conflict for Utah.

None of these considerations had any immediate bearing on the Rio Grande system's problem of obtaining land from the public domain. In discussing Sunnyside developments, general manager H. G. Williams noted that "only a small portion of the State Selections (about 8%) are still remaining, . . . [that could be secured] before all the $1.50 lands were disposed of by the State."[20] The days of bargain-basement land purchases were largely over. The public domain was almost gone—unless some of it could be restored through federal litigation.

The work of the state land board lightened: it had to deal with only the few remaining school sections and in lieu lands. Members of the Milner consortium appeared in May 1905 with a request, backed by a nonmineral affidavit, for one of the in lieu sections, although the land actually contained coal. Robert Forrester promptly learned about this transaction as the two companies wrangled over Utah's last cheap coal lands.[21]

In the subsequent lull, state land board member George Moyer again wrote directly to the U.S. attorney general, referring to his communication of January 7 that apparently had elicited little response. Citing the recent "pleasure of meeting your able assistant Marsden C. Burch," Moyer continued: "It was deemed advisable to hold up all proceedings in the departments pertaining to patents or titles to these [coal] lands," pending changes in sensitive political positions affecting the transfer of lands. Moyer then got to the heart of his complaint:

> I feel warranted in saying that the extent or value of the [Utah coal] lands fraudlently taken far exceed that of any other state in the West. I think it is safe to say that over five million dollars are actually involved in these lands. I can see no reason to doubt the power of your department to reclaim these lands.[22]

Even without knowing of this communication, competitors for Utah coal felt a new urgency. Reports flew from the field to the office of the Rio Grande system. A mid-July mailgram announced: "Engineers surveying along the main line . . . [with] 8 men in the gang . . . they will not give out any information." The worried recipient of his information queried: "Are they U.S. Government?"[23] The reply, in the negative, was accompanied by the explanation that "this surveying party is making for Mr. Milner the coal speculator." The head office responded: "Kindly say who Mr. Milner the coal speculator is and what is his financial capacity, etc."[24] Robert Forrester ultimately received this request to "dictate a brief 'biography' of our friend S[.] B[.] Milner, and state off-hand about where his lands in Utah are located—about how many acres approximately. . . . You have got it all in your mind or at your fingers end."[25]

While Forrester resolved the mystery of "Mr. Milner the coal speculator" and sent the information on up the corporate line, other spies sent word of different competitors in Huntington Canyon. Even before the creation of the Utah Fuel Company in 1901, the Western and the PVCC had learned of coal in this canyon, south over the ridge from Pleasant Valley. Employees of the PVCC had purchased some of the land from the estate of a recently deceased local resident, who held a valid patent. In 1902, the PVCC had expanded its holdings there by buying the Huntington Canyon Mine, thus effectively blocking a similar maneuver being considered by the Union Pacific. The UP had even had the benefit of a Huntington Canyon survey performed in 1893 by none other than Robert Forrester, before he had entered Rio Grande employ. At that time, however, the two great railroads were still working harmoniously, so neither felt the pressure to follow up on Forrester's report. Huntington Canyon, while underlain with valuable coal, had then seemed too far from an existing railroad to be worth developing.[26]

The construction of Clark's San Pedro had changed all that. Completed in 1905, it cut within striking distance of eastern Utah and had been captured by UP forces, now a threat to the Rio Grande system. Coupled with the disposal of eastern Utah's last coal-bearing school sections, sufficient reason existed for the Western to move into Huntington Canyon.

On June 30, Forrester had wired Utah Fuel manager H. G. Williams that he was sending William Tidwell over to Huntington Canyon to snoop about, if he could "be spared from Range Creek . . . for two weeks."[27] Giving up work related to the Whitmore water litigation, Tidwell followed up on the report of another Utah Fuel spy and sometime dummy, Bernard R. McDonald.

On July 3, McDonald sent the alarming intelligence that one of the men claiming Huntington Canyon land had declared that "the San Pedro people was after Huntington coal land and that they had virtually closed the deal with the exceptions to what Don Robbins was holding and. . . . If Don did not get in line why they were going to jump all of his land." McDonald was also told that George Miller, an Emery County politician, "had the papers in his pocket authorizing him to get said coal lands from different parties leaving Robbins out."[28]

Don Robbins had become a stumbling block in part through his success. A Utah native, Robbins was born in Salt Lake City in 1852. By the turn of the century he had become well known as a self-taught coal expert, with extensive hands-on experience. Recently he had founded a company in Emery County to mine Huntington Canyon coal. By 1902, this company was in control of an estimated 25,000 acres of Huntington Canyon coal land, on which it had opened approximately twenty prospects. One of these, the Bear Canyon Mine, was already in operation, offering "some of the finest coal in the country," according to the state coal mine inspector. By 1905, two other small mines were in production, both under Robbins's management, selling coal to local farmers. However, Robbins did not hold title to all the land he controlled. Some had been filed on (though not yet patented) by others, notably the Freed family and their in-law, Walter Filer. Other acres were locked in behind their property by steep mountain topography. As it later developed, Robbins lacked the financial means to buy all of this strategically located land legally. His relatively modest wealth (compared with that of a Clark, Gould, or Harriman) therefore invited a buyout, and competing vultures circled for the kill.[29]

Forrester explained the significance of these lands to Utah Fuel's general manager, H. G. Williams. First, he noted that Miller had the backing of "[George C.] Whitmore and others ... in doing what they can to get Huntington coal land" for sale to the San Pedro. As Forrester pointed out, control of Huntington Canyon was crucial, not just for the coal itself but for a possible railroad route. He continued: "The activity of surveyors trying to get a pass over the Wasatch Mountains from San Pete Valley, and the report of Craig and Ashton [Whitmore's companions] going up through Castle Valley from Price, I believe is all in line with that same matter." By building up over the top of Huntington Canyon, the new railroad could tap the struggling Union Pacific coal mine in Pleasant Valley, then drop back, "get down Huntington Canyon to the coal beds claimed by Don Robbins," and link up with Clark's new railroad to the Pacific. As Forrester observed:

> If they decide to do so, this will put the Union Pacific in excellent shape to provide the San Pedro with all the coal which they will need along their line ... even into Southern California, with the advantage that Harriman, through his Union Pacific Coal Company, is shipping over his own rails as against our shipping over competing lines.[30]

Forrester said there were two ways to block this possibility: either extend into Huntington Canyon the D&RGW line currently serving Pleasant Valley, or try "acquiring the holdings of Don Robbins in Huntington Canyon in advance of the San Pedro interests." He favored the former.[31]

Forrester then returned to an earlier theme: the threat of local competition. "I believe the San Pete Valley Ry. is a very menacing condition confronting us today, because with the purchase of that road by the San Pedro" they would have control over important rights-of-way in western Utah. "Mr. [George C.] Whitmore, a banker in Nephi, has had for some time an option upon the San Pete Valley Ry. for the sum of $250,000.oo. This option has now run out ... so I think it might be a good idea to ... consider seriously the acquisition of the road." He concluded: "Perhaps this information is not of much if any vallue, but I am constrained to write to you as fully as I have done because of the activity of survey corps in the field and the movement to obtain control of the lower Huntington Canyon coal field."[32]

A copy of this letter went to C. H. Schlacks, who forwarded the information to his superiors. He also wrote back to Forrester that he was "pleased to have you keep a good weather eye on the opposition. We must rely upon you to investigate and get information ... and devise and communicate to us the procedure you would recommend to protect our interests." The effects of Forrester's opinion filtered through the Rio Grande hierarchy, maturing in 1907 when the Western acquired the San Pete Valley Railway for a reported $1 million, and replaced the former officers with a slate headed by the same C. H. Schlacks.[33]

Adding a new railroad to the Rio Grande system increased the necessity to get coal land along its route. Only then could locomotive fuel be easily and cheaply obtained. Consequently, William Tidwell sent more reports from Emery and Sanpete Counties. First, he discovered that "two men representing E. H. Harriman ... called upon George Miller, ... and placed $10,000.oo to Miller's credit with [banker] George C. Whitmore provided he could get the people who had filed upon lands for ... Robbins to quit claim to them." While these negotiations were in progress, Tidwell continued, "Don [Robbins] put men on his claims and told them to hold claims if they had to kill to do it. He sent word to them that the U.P.R.R. wanted the coal and had offered $40,000.oo for it." Tidwell gave it as his opinion that a deal appeared to be in the works, and "Miller will be left out and will be a good man for us to use in fighting Whitmore's gang." He proposed to go look for the surveying team at the head of Huntington Canyon, meanwhile arranging for Miller to be "watched all the time on this side."[34]

Tidwell indeed encountered the surveyors, and reported his findings on July 17, writing to Forrester:

> Dear Friend, I have been through Huntington Canyon, Joes Valley and Fish Creek Canyons and find a party of Surveyors five in number camped in Cottonwood Canyon ... getting a line from Hilltop to Gooseberry Valley. [T]hey were very mute and told nothing in regard to who or what interests they represented.[35]

Tidwell also noted the presence of "C. S. [Gunplay] Maxwell, representing to be in our interests through M. P. Braffet," adding that "[C. W.] Shores hired H. Frandsen to locate Coal in or near Straight Canon. I had Orange Seely send message to you." Tidwell requested "a code so I would be able to communicate with you direct."[36] The involvement of these individuals in these transactions underscored continuing loyalty (as with Seely), but it would also spell later lawsuits for the Rio Grande system when cordiality ceased.

A week later, not having received a code and apparently feeling miffed, Tidwell wrote Forrester a more formal letter:

> Dear Sir.—I ... find That unknown parties have been to the Coal outcrop at four different times ... [and] they have surveyed a road from end of the San Pete Valley Rail Road to the Coal and claim they will finish the road in Nine Months from date they made survey in June 1905.[37]

Their destination he reported as the "San Pedro and Los Angeles" and added that local parties interested in nearby Ferron Canyon coal had "not sold to anybody but think they will soon." Reporting even worse news for Forrester, Tidwell continued: "W. D. Candland [head of the state land board] says the State will cancel all contracts made in Carbon Co. ... and the United States will contest" coal land already paid for. Further, Candland had connected "R. G. Miller's Frandsen Bros. with Utah Fuel Co., and say[s] the President of the Land Board and State Mine Inspector will accompany him to investigate lands now selected." Tidwell ended plaintively, "they wish me to go with them soon."[38]

Despite the increasing possibility of being found out, the direct economic threat of the San Pedro forced Utah Fuel officials to act quickly in their bid to lock up the last of Utah's commercial coal. Almost simultaneously with Tidwell's missives, manager H. G. Williams wrote to the company's New York offices confirming "some conversation I had with Mr. Don Robbins, who is at least the most prominent of the parties" involved with Huntington Canyon land. In the discussion, Robbins claimed he had gone to Chicago in mid-1905 to try raising capital. He then hoped to:

> buy the land outright so he would be in [a] position to offer the land upon the terms which I told him were the only ones that would be considered ... that the land was already patented and that there could be no possible question as far as the Government was concerned regarding the title.[39]

Williams's views resulted partly from information received from Tidwell, who had made a synopsis of his reports for Forrester in a July 20 letter to the Utah Fuel manager. Tidwell included the news— also relayed to Forrester—that he had overheard a conversation between Whitmore and associates at "the Whitmore trial in Price" that had led him to believe that Miller would be excluded.[40] The plethora of competitors for Utah's shrinking public domain increased the opportunity for a policy of divide and conquer.

Forrester meanwhile prepared the requested biography of Stanley Milner to add to the growing corporate pile of paper on the fate of Utah coal land. In a typewritten report, he noted that Milner "is in a good position to carry out any projects upon which he may enter." But a handwritten note was added: "He is also very cautious in taking up a new enterprise." Forrester attached local newspaper clippings: "New Railroad Planned in Northeastern Utah" and "New Railroad to Carry Coal." Also keeping an eye on this project, Utah Fuel's H. G. Williams scanned the local papers. He wrote to his immediate superior, Charles Schlacks, second vice president of Utah Fuel, enclosing an article entitled "Road From Coal Fields." The circle was complete when Forrester wrote to Williams on October 13, 1905, enclosing "Milner to Build Railway" and "Colonel Milner Files Maps of his Proposed Road into this County." The latter report included information that the proposed eighty-nine-mile line would connect with the San Pedro, Los Angeles and Salt Lake Railroad, an outcome long feared by the D&RG. In the Rio Grande's worst-case scenario, the San Pedro might get coal land through Robbins, Sweet, *and* Milner.[41]

As Rio Grande system officials well knew, the Sweet family was

still actively developing its Utah coal land. Like the Huntington Canyon group, the Sweets had been counting on the San Pedro, but
subsequent events almost killed off their company. Their prospects
had seemed rosy when, in April 1905, the Sweet-Wade consortium
officially incorporated as the Western Coal and Coke Company—not
to be confused with the Western railroad. By July, however, this
association was dead, slain over money. Henry Wade had sued his
son-in-law, Arthur A. Sweet, for $81,200. Wade alleged that he had
lost the money in two separate stock transactions. In the first instance,
some of Wade's stock had apparently been tendered to a third party
on option. When he reneged on the purchase, the stock had reverted
to Sweet, not Wade, and Sweet persistently refused to relinquish it.
The second batch of stock Wade had allegedly lent to Sweet to enable
Sweet to take an option on the company's property. In Wade's view,
the land's value derived largely from overtures to Senator Clark's San
Pedro line. When Sweet decided to forego a Clark alliance, Wade
wanted his stock back. Sweet again refused. The ensuing litigation split
the company's board of directors, and all mine development stopped.[42]

In these shifting circumstances, federal prosecutors were trying to
build a case they could win. Soon—very soon—the pressure of time
would become the deciding factor in the onset of major litigation.

CHAPTER 7

Get Set . . .

As Western-affiliated officials and independent entrepreneurs frantically tried to lock up Utah's remaining coal land, federal investigators did what they could to combat this takeover. In August 1905, a disturbing tidbit emerged in Tidwell's report to Utah Fuel's general manager, H. G. Williams:

> Mr. Milner is building the road and is determined to build it at once. Mr. Gilson also says Two Geologists have been to his camps and made Geological Sections of the country and asked for information in regard to Utah Fuel Co. lands at Sunnyside. . . . He says they are at Sunnyside now.[1]

Gilson was right about the government surveyors (although wrong about their most recent location). A new cadre of federal agents was on the prowl in Utah.

On August 11, 1905, Joseph A. Taff, of the U.S. Geological Survey, had initiated a sweeping study of eastern Utah, trying once and for all to pin down which forty-acre parcels contained coal. Only then would the General Land Office know which of Utah's requests to approve and which to deny, on the basis that the state could not claim coal land under its enabling act. (However, even that assumption would later have to be tested in court.)

Taff's field notes began with descriptions of the coal occurring at Price Trading Company's Aberdeen Mine, followed by a tour of the Wade-Sweet development, "with H. Wade and W. H. Lawley." The Sweet company rift had been healed (the court action dropped). By August 16, Taff was at Castle Gate, where he "interviewed . . . Genl. Supr. [General Superintendent] of Utah Fuel Co. . . . [and] Examined mine maps."[2] Taff's work exhaustively continued west to Spring Canyon, then south into Emery County, and eventually east along the Book Cliffs, reaching Sunnyside in the early fall. An assistant geologist inspected the Sunnyside coal mines, taking samples for analysis, without questioning the mechanism by which the company had obtained this lucrative area. Then the U.S.G.S. survey team moved on. By October, Taff was back in Emery County, in the company of George Hair of the Salt Lake branch of the General Land Office.[3] Even the search for coal had to bow to the weather, however. Taff had to recall his crew when heavy snow fell in the Book Cliffs in November 1905. Milner, too, building his road, had to pull in his workers. Eastern Utah's mountains would be locked in until the following April.

In one of his first reports to the director of the U.S.G.S., Taff described a major stumbling block to the successful prosecution of a federal case: the so-called forty-acre rule. This decision by the secretary of the interior had decreed that coal had to be exposed on each forty-acre parcel for such an area to be designated "coal land." As Taff explained:

> Under the existing conditions of the coal deposits as I find them, such a ruling prevents the proper classification of coal lands, prevents the sale of such lands desired by honest would-be purchasers in tracts of sufficient size to warrant profitable exploitation, has caused large tracts of very valuable coal lands to be classed as grazing land, and sold at $1.50 per acre, and will cause the continued sale of such lands if it remains in force.[4]

Taff suggested a new definition of coal occurence "in legal subdivisions as established by United States surveys to distance of 1 mile beneath the surface" of commercial coal outcrops.[5] His suggestion was ignored. Taff's call for change would swell to a veritable chorus before the federal prosecution team could get a favorable definition of "coal land." Meanwhile, the truly bad Coal Land Act of 1873, with its crippling administrative interpretations (such as the forty-acre definition) remained on the books.

In the summer of 1905, while Taff was exploring coal on the ground, moves toward federal prosecution were finally getting underway. On August 30, special assistant attorney J. Harwood Graves wrote to the U.S. attorney general, officially noting "a matter of general information in Utah that the Utah Fuel Company, which is the creature of the Denver and Rio Grande Railroad, has, largely by means believed to be fraudulent, obtained a virtual monopoly in coal lands in that State." Graves then acknowledged the power of the local press: "This has been openly charged in the newspapers of the State, and names and dates unhesitatingly given." Under these circumstances, Graves's charge had been to find "some specific instances which might serve as the basis ... of an investigation before a grand jury."[6]

Graves's letter enclosed the most lucid, damning evidence so far: the affidavit of C. D. Sudbury. This statement outlined the Salina Canyon coal-land scam in explicit detail. Sudbury swore he and thirteen other dummies had accompanied Utah Fuel employees on an all-expense-paid trip about ten miles up Salina Canyon, where the party had viewed some "coal holes" approximately eight feet high, five feet wide, and from twelve to twenty feet long. No surveyor's marks were in evidence; nonetheless, upon returning to the Utah Fuel offices in Salt Lake City, the dummies found land deeds with proper legal descriptions drawn up for their signatures. Sudbury signed a claim for the land, but balked at signing the mortgage, saying that "signing such might result in a deficiency judgment against him." The Utah Fuel attorney, Major William Bird, assured him that this was a technicality. Two days later, Sudbury returned to the Utah Fuel office, where, in the company of Bird and attorney William Foster, he signed a blank quit-claim deed. Sudbury continued to make a fuss about the mortgage, upon which another Utah Fuel employee placed $1,600 on Bird's desk, enough to cover the full amount of the mortgage. Bird offered Sudbury $115 for his land, with the understanding that $50 of it should be returned to the Utah Fuel employee who had initiated the transaction. Sudbury protested the kickback and eventually received the amount he demanded. Sudbury had to return to the Utah Fuel offices one more time to sign a new quit-claim deed, with F. A. Calkins indicated as the grantee. The former document, with the grantee's name left blank, was destroyed.[7]

In his letter, Graves reported that several of the fourteen men in the Sudbury group had "become alarmed at rumors of prosecution, . . . and have expressed a willingness to tell all they know if called upon to do so, hoping thereby to shield themselves." He continued:

> The operations of this [Utah Fuel] Company, however, have not been confined to this means of securing title to coal lands. Through its principal geologist and confidential agent, Robert Forrester, it has secured large tracts of coal land at a very low price, by having the same selected as State land valuable only for grazing purposes, and then purchased the same at an appraised value of $1.50 per acre.[8]

As Graves correctly explained the system, dummy entrants would make application to the state for targeted land, and Robert Forrester would appear on their behalf before the state land board to testify, as a trained geologist, that coal was not present. Utah officials would claim it from the federal government as school sections; that is, grazing land. When the government relinquished the coal-rich "grazing land" from the public domain, the new owners would deed it to second parties and, as Graves said, "title to them [the lands] would eventually be found in the Utah Fuel Company."[9]

Graves noted that "it would be a comparatively easy matter to secure the conviction of Robert Forrester . . . for perjury." He thought additional litigation would "possibly result in the restoration to the Government of large tracts of land of great value," and quoted from the March 13 *Salt Lake Herald* article in support of the extent of the frauds. Graves continued:

> It seems clear that the title to some of this land, at least, is still vested in the United States, for it was notoriously known to be coal land prior to the admission of Utah to statehood and therefore, under decisions of the Supreme Court, did not pass to the state as school land.[10]

In support of this contention, Graves cited a single section that "had been filed on as coal land since 1876 by more than forty persons," but that passed to Laura J. Bird (daughter of Utah Fuel's Major Bird) as a state selection after Robert Forrester himself swore that it was valuable chiefly for grazing land. He made this statement despite the fact that, in 1901, in support of a federal coal filing, he had also sworn before William Bird, notary public, that Forrester "had opened a valuable coal mine in this particular land." Graves also noted "instances, notably near Castle Gate, Utah, where the Utah Fuel Company . . . have actually opened up veins of coal and run tunnels, and then had the same closed," and obtained the land as grazing land through the usual dummy method or through the state selections process.[11]

The result of these actions, according to Graves, was that an individual entryman, without railroad affiliation, could not hope to obtain the legal 160 acres of coal land. If an entryman were to attempt to do so, Utah Fuel would enter a protest. The ensuing taking of testimony (in which "the ordinary rules of evidence do not apply") would be drawn out to such an extent "as to make the costs ruinous to a person of moderate means."[12] (The ongoing Whitmore water case was proof in point.) In this manner, the Utah Fuel Company, and, through it, the Rio Grande system, had long assured their virtual monopoly in Utah coal.

Thanks to the efforts of special assistant Graves and others, the U.S. attorney general now had clear information on the machinations used in Utah coal-land fraud. In Utah, however, new state officials seemed to lag behind in their understanding. The incoming secretary of the state land board, John DeGrey Dixon, was apparently ignorant of the system outlined by Graves that had been in such common usage before his tenure. In mid-September 1905, Dixon wrote to the Utah State coal mine inspector asking his help to examine "certain coal lands." He then wrote to the special agent for Iowa asking about the laws by which states had obtained federal lands under their respective enabling acts. The response explained the process and complained that "the interested states will never get their dues until they combine their efforts," revealing a certain frustration with federal authorities. Dixon also wrote to the General Land Office in Washington, D.C., trying to clarify his predecessors' actions. The response, penned by William A. Richards, explained how so much western land fraud had transpired.[13]

Dixon's respondent, Richards (of Wyoming) had been commissioner of the General Land Office since 1903. Prior to that, he had served on the second Commission on Public Lands, alongside Gifford Pinchot. After three years of experience on the cutting edge, during a time of change, of federal public-land policy, he was well suited to answer Dixon's queries. He responded with an explanation of what had been the state selection process, and admitted that, *after* certain Utah lands had been released for individual purchase, an examination by the state coal mine inspector and land board members revealed "large deposits of mineral wax and asphaltum." Although the lands apparently held more value for coal-related minerals than for grazing, the General Land Office had hesitated to request their relinquishment, uncertain of its legal standing. The question, said Richards, was still in doubt, but he referred to "an examination now in process by an agent of this office." Richards further deplored the inaction of Utah's U.S. district attorney in pursuing fraud, which retarded release of disputed properties. To forestall new frauds, Richards suspended all further state selections in Utah as of September 1905, a precursor of Roosevelt's later coal land withdrawals. While these suspensions were in effect—affecting more than five million acres of public lands in Utah alone—Dixon's state land board had the unpleasant duty of informing citizens that their applications were pending indefinitely.[14]

Even while these investigations were wearing on, economically motivated Rio Grande dummying continued in Salina Canyon. Hasty telegrams flew back and forth between the system's officials. On November 25, A. H. Cowie wired: "General Manager [H. G. Williams] advises party cannot provide thirty two hundred and further they have only till Monday November 27th to secure Salina land will arrange for loan from Denver [the Rio Grande headquarters] today." He continued by inquiring why the land should cost $20 an acre rather than $10, "inasmuch as railroad is not operating. Answer quick as must arrange matter this afternoon."[15]

Robert Forrester responded immediately by cipher telegram (conveniently translated in handwritten notes made by the recipient). He stated that the targeted property in Salina Canyon was "hundred sixty and sixty three hundredths acres, price ten dollars an acre. Amount needed sixteen hundred six dollars thirty cents." He continued with the financial arrangements:

> Think entryman should be able to borrow this amount from caffey his brotherinlaw and caffey should be willing to loan this amount on account of business privilege. Papers have all been filed in land office and nothing further necessary than entryman to take up money to land office and receive final receipt.[16]

The entryman in question was clearly filing for a legal parcel of coal land. Even more clearly, he was illegally doing so as a dummy for the Western.

The Gould system was hardly alone in these fraudulent activities. The Rio Grande's persistent rival, Harriman's Union Pacific, was making its own arrangements to lock up coveted Utah coal. At the end of December 1905, Walter G. Filer, of Salt Lake City, signed an agreement with D. O. Clark, vice president and general manager of the Union Pacific Coal Company, and brother of Wyoming's U.S. Senator Clark. While the Rio Grande had been pursuing Salina Canyon coal claims and wooing Don Robbins in Huntington Canyon, the UP was moving into the latter area through Walter Filer.[17]

This formal option between Clark and Filer listed the full details of the transaction. Thirteen thousand acres of Huntington Canyon coal land were specifically described. The UP Coal Company was willing to buy all of it for $75 an acre. Filer had to produce clear title, as would be indicated by a receipt from the U.S. Land Office in Salt Lake City. This transaction was to take place in stages. First, four thousand acres of frontage land on both sides of the canyon was demanded. Then, at least six thousand acres of the more remote hinterlands had to be transferred. Several "understandings" were spelled out, including:

> It is understood that the said Filer has not at the present time in himself or under his control the title to the said lands but is proceeding

to acquire title to the same from the present owners and locators thereof. ...

It is understood that this option is to remain open for acceptance until and including the 1st day of March, 1906.[18]

Filer understood these terms, but the others he involved probably did not. Realizing that he could not legally acquire all of the land himself, Filer had decided to involve others in sidestepping the Coal Land Act of 1873, which would have limited him to 640 acres for an association. He turned to his father-in-law, Charles M. Freed, the head of a family of would-be locators. By mid-February 1906, he had rounded up twenty-five other people, almost a third of whom bore the surname Freed. They all submitted federal "Applications to Purchase Coal Land" to the U.S. Land Office in Salt Lake City—ostensibly land for their own use. The agent for all of them was Don C. Robbins. Filer and Robbins had found each other, and the UP had found the pair of them.[19]

But their applications, like those of others at this time, were threatened by the investigations of the state land board and the General Land Office. Meanwhile, Western officials learned of Sudbury's defection. By December, Sudbury and others were being called to testify in a hearing in the General Land Office branch in Salt Lake City. As related to A. H. Cowie in a cipher telegram:

> Sudbury and Wolf gave details about Carpenters connection and receiving your check for fifty. Sudbury went on and gave all particulars connected with his case and testified that Manager's [Williams's] Secretary handled money and Geologist's [Forrester's] Secretary did part of business and that both were employed by Coal Company.[20]

The telegram concluded with the news that the men would have to appear on January 3.[21]

Other witnesses were already testifying. Western reports on the land office hearing flew in a series of cipher telegrams, which were quickly decoded by the recipients, who again provided handwritten translations of key terms. For example, on December 29, Cowie was informed: "Tell Geologist [Robert Forrester] wade and sweet on stand wade giving all particulars concerning Sunnyside land."[22] Federal investigators appeared to be probing the entire spectrum of Rio Grande–related coal-land frauds.

As word of the investigation spread, a worried William Foster, Utah Fuel attorney and Forrester's secretary, wrote to his sister, Marsena. She had been one of the dummies in the Salina Canyon scheme, and William was afraid she might be subponeaed as a witness. He pleaded with her to "please call on Major Bird for instructions before going on the stand." Then he reassured her: "There is no way in which it can be shown that you took up this land in the interest of any one other than yourself." Foster went on to outline an expedient perjury:

> You heard about this coal land from some one—who don't remember who now—and thought it might turn out to be a good investment. ... Not having the money yourself, you borrowed it from your father.... Shortly after you had paid the Land Office the Government price for the land, ... a man from the east by the name of Calkins made you a proposition for your land. ... You could place your profit at about $250.00. ... [I] think this would be your only course if you were called as a witness. It would also be best not to say any more about it than you have to, but of course you understand that part of it.

Foster concluded: "Hoping you are well, and having lots of good times, I remain, Your brother, Will"[23]—but despite his wishes, the good times for fraudulent coal-land claimants seemed about over.

Understanding how the Utah coal-land scam worked was just the first step in stopping the fraud. In order to halt the easy flow of land from public to private ownership, key officials had to be replaced. This action, while mandated by the enormity of the coal-land frauds so far uncovered (which only hinted at their true extent) nonetheless had to be accomplished through regular channels—some of which were staffed by men tainted by the very frauds in question. A difficult and delicate process began.

In part, federal success depended on Utah's internal politics. One consideration as the strength of the Regular Republican Party, led by Reed Smoot—still Utah's senior senator. The defection of Thomas Kearns late in 1904 and his formation of the American Party certainly weakened the Republicans numerically, although it allegedly also made it easier for Smoot to control the Republican Party by attracting those hostile to Kearns. On the other hand, Smoot's standing in the LDS Church was not enhanced by his nonconsensual behavior in the October 1905 General Conference. In the midst of these tides of church and state, Smoot's allies went down in defeat in November 1905, as the American Party won the Salt Lake mayoral race, gaining a political control that would last for another six years. Smoot consequently turned even more strongly toward federal politicians for support, confiding to LDS Church President Smith shortly after the election: "I am in hopes that he [President Roosevelt] will be as friendly as ever, for without his friendship, I am positive it will be impossible for me to win out."[24]

Roosevelt showed some measure of regard for Smoot when, at the end of January, he appointed two men that Smoot recommended: the Mormon William Spry, as U.S. marshal, and non-Mormon Hiram E. Booth, as United States attorney for Utah. By the end of the year, however, when the Utah coal-land frauds—and Booth's connection with the Milner consortium—gradually unfolded, the president apparently regretted the choice of Booth. Another factor in the president's subsequent coolness might have been the report of the Senate Committee on Privileges and Elections. In June, the committee voted seven to five to expel Smoot , and the fight went to the Senate floor.[25] Thus, both men on Utah's Senate delegation were living under very cloudy skies—one laboring under official accusations and the other, a Western consultant, liable soon to face his own Armageddon.

Senator George Sutherland, Utah's Junior senator, also a Republican, had lingering corporate connections that raised suspicions about his committment to Roosevelt's public-lands crusade. Sutherland and Smoot publicly split over federal patronage appointments of register and receiver of the U.S. Land Office in Salt Lake City when the president sought their advice in March 1906. George Moyer, the whistle-blowing state land board member, had already outlined major concerns about Sutherland in letters to the Justice Department. He pointed out that Sutherland remained a counsel for the Colorado Fuel Company, a Rio Grande system affiliate. Moyer also alleged that one of Sutherland's client companies was trying to acquire coal land worth more than $3 million, an effort being resisted by the incumbent Utah register, Frank Hobbs. Moyer claimed that Hobbs had provided twelve years of faithful service and should be retained, so that "the Coal Companies by their Agents and Attornies, do not dictate the appointment of officials whose duties are of such importance." While stopping short of a direct accusation of Senator Sutherland, Moyer again called for a federal investigation to achieve this end.[26]

Other people questioned the candidates whom Sutherland favored. George Albert Smith, a fellow apostle of Reed Smoot and receiver of the Salt Lake City branch of the General Land Office, gave Smoot an insider's view of the problems:

> It is my firm conviction that the coal corporations are taking a hand
> in this. . . . They have indicated their intention of making it warm
> for some of the Government employees who have tried to do their
> duty, by preventing fraud. But for Mr. Hobbs, thousands of acres
> of coal land would have fallen into the hands of the coal company,
> as grazing land.[27]

Smith then outlined what he knew of the abuses regarding state-land
selection: "The State was led into selecting much of such land too
and turned it over to the same parties at grazing land prices, thus
losing thousands of dollars to the State."[28]

Smith was particularly perturbed that his own office might once
again become a vehicle for fraud:

> It there is not something in my surmise, why is it that they [the coal
> company supporters] are insisting on the end of the office where the
> coal people can be favored, instead of my end, where they could
> not? Why is it that they are determined to have the end where the
> most work is required instead of the easy end, when they both pay
> the same salary? . . . With a new man in the other end of the office
> it would not take long to reduce the standing of this office to what
> it was when I first came in. But with Mr. Hobbs in the Register's
> end he would be able to keep things in fair shape.[29]

Although, apparently, Smoot reprimanded Smith for impugning the
character of Sutherland's favorite, Smith's opinion carried the day.
Hobbs was retained as registrar and, in a compromise measure, E. D. R.
Thompson, the man favored by Sutherland, was appointed to the less-
sensitive receiver's post.[30]

This early skirmish over control of Utah coal land presaged a
full-scale conflict over public lands. The battle had already been joined,
in a sense, in the dispute pitting Sweet-backed Albert Simmons against
cigar-selling Owen Davies in the same U.S. Land Office in Salt Lake
City. The case was called early in January 1906, and the decision was
rendered a month later. The register and receiver found unequivocally
that Davies had committed fraud, and further stated that testimony
with no direct bearing on this particular case "was allowed to go into
the record as tending to prove that the methods alleged to have been
adopted in the case . . . has [sic] been in vogue for years past by the
company or companies named." The decision invited further attention
be given to these practices, "in order that such [legal] action might
be taken . . . as to other entires."[31] Once again, the federal government
was explicitly being invited to investigate Utah coal-land fraud.

Favorable timing facilitated federal litigation: the U.S. Congress was also increasingly interested in allegations about collusion between railroads and coal companies. On March 7, 1906, after lengthy hearings, the Senate and House issued a joint resolution on "the subject of railroad discriminations and monopolies in coal and oil." The document—the Tillman-Gillespie Resolution—instructed the Interstate Commerce Commission to make periodic reports to Congress, or to the president when Congress was not in session, based on ongoing investigations into reported abuses. The resolution specifically demanded information on, among other matters, inequitable distribution of railroad cars, monopoly in the carrier trade or in mine operations, and the effect of monopolies on independent operators. The Interstate Commerce Commission was directed to recommend remedies for these abuses, and to accomplish these tasks "as soon as it can be done consistent with the performance of its public duty." This directive would soon help to uncover further evidence of the gigantic scope of western coal-land fraud.[32]

One month later, in April 1906, Washington bureaucrats also acted to halt the continuing transfer of suspected coal lands in the West. W. A. Richards, commissioner of the General Land Office, wrote to his superior, Interior Secretary Hitchcock, confirming a directive to "pass no coal entires in the State of Utah to patent until your further orders." As of September 1905, he reminded the secretary, he had also halted action on "all State selections in the State of Utah pending the conclusion of investigations then being prosecuted." In May, Richards wrote again, noting arrangements "for a complete investigation in Utah and Colorado by that Department [Justice] of coal entries alleged to have been unlawfully made, and state selections alleged to have been made for lands solely valuable for coal deposits." Richards also outlined the proposed departmental split in jurisdictions: the General Land Office of the Department of the Interior would deal with pending entries or selections; the Justice Department would prosecute "patented or certified lands which had passed beyond the jurisdiction of this office." in either civil or criminal suits. Commissioner Richards elaborated on the problem of "deficiencies in appropriations" experienced by his department, which could not afford to keep men at their regular work while they were simultaneously being pulled away to support the Attorney General's investigation.[33] Perhaps this communication helped heal the breach reported by the eastern Utah press in March, when it noted: "Friction between the two [departments] may cause abandonment of the [coal lands] investigation."[34] This article may have given some small comfort to those still competing for Utah coal.

While Washington bureaucrats wrestled over political turf, other interested parties were exploring the terrain of eastern Utah. As soon as the snow there slushed into mud, coal experts of all sorts slogged back to work. The *Advocate* reported in April 1906 on the expected arrival of William G. Sharp, former general manager of Utah Fuel and now president and managing director of the United States Smelting, Refining and Mining Company (USSR&M). Sharp not only represented his new New York–based concern, he intended to visit the mine run by his brother, David, near Helper, and look into the "acquirement of stone lands by certain parties to the east and south of Helper"— an oblique reference to the use of the Timber and Stone Act to acquire other probably coal lands in definace of the Coal Land Act of 1873. The entry of a new corporation, albeit one led by an old acquaintance, presaged a future twist to Utah coal-land ownership.[35]

Geologist Joseph Taff, too, resumed his laborious survey. In 1906, however, his carefully titled field notes, labeled "U.S. Geological Survey," bore the additional heading: "Department Justice" As the Secretary of the Interior explained a year later, Taff had been detailed to the Justice Department at its request. He led a corps of special agents who were "not detectives and are not so used, although it may be at times necessary for them ... to use the means necessary to discover the fraud and the criminal."[36]

"The means necessary" sometimes involved simply staying alive. Taff's counterparts, J. Broderick, Henry Bushnell, and two others, were simultaneously working west from Colorado to Sunnyside. The mule carrying the party's water ran away somewhere near the Utah-Colorado border. The men began walking north to try to intersect the line of the D&RGW. Their lips and tongues swelled with thirst until they could no longer speak. On the second day, Bushnell became delirious and grabbed handfuls of sand, which he ground between his teeth. When he collapsed, his companions dragged him to a spot about four miles from Green River, Utah. Fortunately, a sheepherder found them that evening. From his hospital bed, Broderick agonized: "Even now I cannot sleep from the recollection of that awful sound. I doze off for a few minutes and then am awakened by the sound of trickling water or of sand being ground between Bushnell's teeth." Shortly thereafter, Broderick left the survey.[37]

Faced with this sort of difficulty, the survey parties did not immediately apprehend the economic importance of Sunnyside to the Rio

Grande system, although they headed straight for that area when their work resumed in April 1906. On April 20 they explored "Tidwell Canyon" (in Range 14 S. 14 E.) and reported taking photographs ("Kodaks") of the Sunnyside camp and coke ovens, symbols of its rich deposits.[38]

While Taff's party was making its painstaking way through approximately ninety townships in the Book Cliffs range, other investigators were scrutinizing Utah's land records. Special Agent Percy Sowers of the Department of the Interior coordinated with George Hair of the General Land Office in Salt Lake City to ascertain whether state selections claimed by ASARCO (the American Smelting and Refining Company, one of the "smelting trusts") were mineral in nature, "having been suspected of being more valuable for coal than for any other purpose."[39] Possibly through this investigation of ASARCO, the crucial economic role of Sunnyside coke—the Western's true monopoly—in the growing smelting industry of the West dawned on federal agents. By restoring Sunnyside coal lands to the public domain, they would also be achieving a measure of control on Utah's smelting industry.

Coal-land fraud continued, often just ahead of prosecution, the *Eastern Utah Advocate* reporting the allegations of irregularity. While investigators were amassing evidence on land fraud by the Western's affiliates in Utah, Robert Forrester was apparently increasing the Rio Grande's holdings outside the state. According to newspaper reports, early in 1906 Forrester had found more coal in Colorado. However, he was not alone in this discovery. Reports claimed that Forrester's attempt to buy patented coal land near Durango was being contested by an agent of the Southern Pacific, a UP affiliate. Eventually, Forrester succeeded in acquiring the disputed tract—about 22,000 acres. He moved in a team of company men from Castle Gate to open the mine. By May, this enterprise had been organized as the Calumet Fuel Company, a new subsidiary of the D&RG. From this valuable base, Rio Grande officials expanded their holdings in Colorado's San Juan River coal region, which greatly augmented coal production from the original mines further east. The Rio Grande was entering the most prosperous coal-mining year in its history.[40]

As western coal land disappeared into private ownership with startling rapidity, an associate of the Sweet-Wade consortium tried to lock up another promising tract. Lucius Curtis, supported by the testimony of both Arthur Sweet and Henry Wade, filed for land just east of Castle Gate in April 1906 under the Timber and Stone Act. Contending that the land was valuable only for building stone, Curtis neglected to mention that its rocky appearance did nothing to distinguish it from the rest of eastern Utah, where stone was the main crop. His allegation of its content was corroborated by Special Agent George E. Hair, of the General Land Office. Hair wrote:

> [These] lands [were] investigated by me Sept. 4, 1905, while examining within twps [townships] for coal. Entire tract lies far below and from one and one-half mile to two miles distant from nearest coal lands.[41]

As it turned out, Hair was right, and Curtis had obtained a virtually worthless tract. More significantly, however, Hair's affidavit sounded a new note in land transfers. No more would a claimant's statement be sufficient "proof" that a property was nonmineral. A federal agent had to corroborate claimants' statements before ownership could be awarded.

Under this combination of circumstances, more and more federal operatives entered Utah. Justice Department attorney Marsden C. Burch strove to weld his team together from disparate agencies. First, a Justice Department colleague, Fred A. Maynard, received a special appointment covering Utah and Colorado to uncover the unlawful actions of the Rio Grande. Taff, of the U.S.G.S., and Land Office agents Hair and Sowers ferreted out the actual content of Utah lands. Another Interior investigator, Isaac Lamoreaux, who had been in eastern Utah since early 1906, brought his knowledge of land titles on file in local courthouses to the team. Burch, with the others, had to synthesize these reports and draw the shape of the fast-paced story of Utah coal-land frauds.

Early in July 1906, Burch's team stopped short. They realized that some of the lands under investigation would be beyond litigation in only a few days. No reliable statute existed on which to build a case, so Burch opted for bills in equity based on the Coal Land Act of 1873, which had never before sustained a criminal charge. At home in Rochester, Michigan (trying to recover from a "temporary illness"— possibly bleeding ulcers), Burch urgently wired the attorney general on July 3: "Maynard wires statutes limitations one case coal [*sic*] entry pleasant valley coal company expires July 8th and he has prepared a bill in equity to recover." Burch requested Maynard be given the authority to do so.[42]

Permission was granted, and the Salt Lake *Tribune* reported on 10 July regarding "an action ... begun by the Department of Justice in the federal court against one of the leading coal companies in

Utah,"—as yet unnamed. The details could not be made public until the company attorney was served papers in the case, but the eastern Utah newspaper speculated that the Utah Fuel Company might be the corporation involved.[43] On 13 July, the attorney general received another pressing wire from Burch, requesting specific permission to file five bills in equity: two each against the Pleasant Valley Coal Company and the Utah Fuel Company in Utah, and one against the Union Pacific Coal Company in Wyoming, all of them citing coal-land fraud within Utah. The same day that the attorney general granted his permission, July 19, the *Eastern Utah Advocate* broke the story with a headline; "Booth Removes Coal Land Lid." A subheading providing oblique reference to Sutherland announced: "United States Senator May Be Drawn into Net."[44]

As Burch prompted the filing of these first bills in equity against the railroad-affiliated coal companies, he wrote to the solicitor general outlining his goals and the sum of his efforts to date. He particularly wanted to win the cooperation of Interior Secretary Hitchcock, who, despite Burch's efforts, had remained unconcerned about the size of the theft underway. Burch referred to President Roosevelt's recent withdrawal of some of the coal-bearing West, but felt "sick and sore . . . that he did not simply withdraw the whole of the coal land region from sale for re-classification."[45] Such an action would protect the coal-bearing public domain in the interim before Congress acted, as Burch felt they must. With cautious optimism, he added:

> [We must] . . . depend upon the popular voice to compel congress to repeal the Coal Land Act altogether, and thus save all these lands. That may come later. Indeed, it will come, if Congress can be once made alive by the force of public opinion to the wasteful and,—if it had been intentional,—wicked disposition of the . . . lands of the government.[46]

CHAPTER 8

A Wonder Indictments Stopped Where They Did

Newspaper reports of the federal coal-land fraud cases called forth some hurried responses. Those rumored to be implicated in the fraud rushed to defend themselves in print. Byron Groo, former Utah State Land Board secretary, explicitly denied any collusion between the coal companies and the old state land board. Utah's former governor, Heber Wells, ex officio chair of the land board, issued a written report that, with an ethnic slur, claimed the accusations stemmed from "politics worked in by the fine Italian hand of the democratic organ." The federal district attorney for Utah, Hiram E. Booth, anticipated further accusations as he clarified his connection with the Milner company. Booth admitted that Stanley Milner may have acquired extensive holdings of his own, but—as reported in the *Eastern Utah Advocate*—said: "Whether Colonel Milner transferred any land to the company I do not know, and I have no knowledge of the extent of his holdings in Carbon County."[1] The newspaper article, which appeared on the eve of the actual filing, was just the first sprinkle of comment in what would soon become a deluge.

Federal litigation of coal-land fraud perpetrated by the Rio Grande system formally began with four bills of complaint in equity filed on July 27, 1906, in the United States District Court of Utah. (A related case against the Union Pacific Coal Company was prosecuted separately.) Two virtually identical pairs of bills alleged similar abuses by the Pleasant Valley Coal Company and the Utah Fuel Company. The first of each pair attacked the dummy-entry system as a fraudulent conspiracy to defraud in violation of the Coal Land Act of 1873. It alleged that agents of the companies had hired certain dummies to obtain federal coal certificates through the General Land Office by fraudulently asserting that the desired lands were for individual use and that no other coal cash entries (sections acknowledged to contain coal that were immediately purchased for cash) had been made by the same individual. The agents made a list of familiar names: Robert Forrester and William H. Bird were listed for both companies; in addition, William F. Colton, president and general manager of the PVCC, was named, as were Henry G. Williams and Royal C. Peabody, for Utah Fuel. The dummies' names, too, had a familiar ring: Charles Mostyn Owen, for the Pleasant Valley Coal Company; Hyrum, Joseph R., John F., William J., and Jefferson Tidwell, Orange Seely, William S. Ronjue, Frands Grundvig, and others for the Utah Fuel Company. The scams at Pleasant Valley and at Sunnyside had been fairly thoroughly uncovered.[2]

The second bill each filed against Utah Fuel and Pleasant Valley Coal alleged abuses of the state selections system. After stating that the only way known coal lands could legally be obtained was through the provisions of the Coal Land Act of 1873, the complaint averred that, instead, the defendants had gone through the State of Utah and obtained known coal land as grazing land through the Utah Enabling Act. The state itself was not made a party to the suit, but those accused reflected the same old crowd. Again, Robert Forrester topped the list, this time for fraudulently acquiring land in his own name for both companies. Others cited in both cases included other company officials (such as Charles Mostyn Owen) and Forrester's relatives (including May Kimball, who had shortly thereafter become his wife). Through these actions, allegedly close to thirty thousand acres, worth then between $5 million and $6 million, had been bought for $1.50 an acre, instead of the $10 to $20 they should have commanded.[3] With these suits, the courts became the vehicle for the federal attempt to forestall future coal-land fraud and to reclaim lands almost irretrievably lost from the public domain.

Three days after the filing, Burch, newly recovered, sat down to type a ten-page letter, explaining the intracacies of all the western coal-land cases to the solicitor general. Burch reported that he had reached Salt Lake City on 8 July, finding "matters in as satisfactory a condition as could be expected. Mr. Maynard, as usual, has been indefatigable in his researches," a zealousness that, although valuable to date, would later lead the federal government into some difficulty. Burch lamented that the evidence so far amassed was not "in as satisfactory a condition as I would like," but added: "I became strongly impressed with the idea that we must act soon, or serious consequences and complications might arise."[4]

He then gave the good news: the team had discovered that the actual coal acreage obtained by fraud probably amounted to only 10 percent of the land suspected to contain coal, because the "land grafters" had only claimed the "mountain 'fronts,' " thereby controlling the lands behind them without any actual or pretended ownership. On the other hand, what the front lands lacked in acreage "they make up in value; some of the land being of enormous richness, and capable of furnishing an amount of coal which can hardly be conceived of," according to the "researches of our entirely safe geologist, Mr. Taff."[5]

Filing of the Utah bills in equity had been delayed until the last minute because of concerns with "the Dailey [*sic*: Daly] or Bitter Root cases in Montana," which had pulled Burch away for a few days. He predicted success there, partly because "they have wisely selected cases in which the Marcus Daily estate was not particularly concerned," and partly because "the old trouble of frosty atmosphere and an adverse jury would not likely recur here."[6]

This problem of an antifederal "frosty atmosphere" would later color some of the Utah coal-land cases, but first Burch had to explain the details of these suits. In conference with his Utah investigative team and Colorado's Assistant Attorney Long, Burch had gone over the points of law. To the solicitor general, he explained in more detail the contents of the bills in equity: one each regarding coal-cash entries (the dummy system) and another regarding state-selections abuses, filed against the PVCC and Utah Fuel. Since the latter was chartered in New Jersey, a problem of jurisdiction arose, but Burch relied on recent circuit court decisions in deciding to file in Utah. Because of a recent progovernment Supreme Court decision on a demurrer in *U.S. v. Trinidad Coal and Coke Company*, a Colorado case, Burch had a model for his bills against the dummies, for their alleged evasion of the federal Coal Land Act of 1873. "But," he added, "the State Land Selection cases were full of new points and difficult considerations."[7] Despite this early awareness, the State of Utah was not enjoined in any of these cases until much later.

The Roosevelt Progressive program operated largely at a national level, with Big Government attempting to control Big Business, particularly railroad "trusts." The support of the states (specifically, of western members of Congress) was crucial to much of the success of Progressive legislation. The states, therefore—even Utah—presented a far less appealing target for litigation than did the railroads, at least from the political standpoint. From the perspective of obtaining legal precedent in order effectively to stop the rapid loss of western coal land from the public domain, however, the states *had* to be enjoined in litigation as much as did interstate businesses. A large part of the coal-land loss went through state, not federal, channels (that is, more was lost as fictive "grazing land" in state school sections than under dummied federal coal certificates, largely because of their relative expense). Thus, although the original antirailroad thrust of the Utah coal-land fraud cases fit well with the national Progressive program, in the long run it served the government poorly as a vehicle for setting court precedents.[8] As a result, resolving the intricacies of Utah coal-land fraud was going to take a long, long time.

In keeping with the priorities of the moment, of course, the Justice Department pursued its cases. As Burch explained: "Maynard had prepared the facts in a rough draft of the bill," which was thrown aside as "we worked step by step, paragraph by paragraph for several days before finishing one of them. I think I must have labored fourteen or fifteen hours a day, ... [as] the hot west winds that pour in from the Nevada and Utah deserts" enervated the litigation team. When the first state selections bill was finished, since the next would be "substantially like it," Burch felt he could turn his attention to problems in Wyoming.[9]

There, Burch continued, Isaac Lamoreaux had ferreted out abuses using "Additional Soldiers' Homestead Scrip" (a slightly different scam) by the Union Pacific Coal Company, the Kemmerer Coal Company, and the Anaconda Copper Mining Company, involving coal deposits "of exceeding fine quality [that] could hardly be excelled in the United States." There, too, Burch had been fearful of a six-year statute of limitations, but Lamoreaux had discovered that patent had not been issued until February 1901, allowing the prosecution team time in which to construct a case. Despite this favorable timing in Wyoming, however, Burch explained that the political conditions made Utah a better venue for the "landmark" federal case:

> The manager of this company [the Union Pacific Coal Company] is the brother of Senator Clark of Wyoming, chairman of the Senate Judiciary Committee. The Union Pacific Coal Company is simply an auxiliary of the Union Pacific Railroad Company, which has held all the region ... in a stern grasp for years past, not merely upon the basis "of all the traffic will bear," but upon the theory that no one else had a right to traffic in coal along its line but itself.[10]

Antagonizing Senator Clark might create future difficulties for federal prosecutions because the Senate Judiciary Committee had to approve all federal judges. On the other hand, Utah, with its public notoriety for polygamy, theocracy, and alleged complicity in fraud, made a much safer political target.

The Smoot hearings, continuing into 1906, underscored Burch's point. Spotter Owen, peripetatic dummy for the Rio Grande system, arrived in Washington with a new list of purported polygamists that spring. Unlike at the earlier Brigham H. Roberts hearing, however, the list did not include Smoot's name. Even the snooping of highly skilled professionals like Charlie Siringo had been unable to uncover any plural wives in Smoot's household. Nonetheless, when, in June, the Senate committee voted on the resolution to expel Smoot, it passed seven to five. Smoot thus had to take his fight to the Senate floor.[11]

Burch, in his letter outlining the western public-lands crusade, continued: "Conditions are not as favorable in Wyoming for litigation by us as in Utah. . . . I do not think the court looks upon the government with as much favor as Judge Marshal[l] in the same circuit over in Utah."[12] This district judge, John Marshall, would indeed become a key figure in the fate of the coal-land cases.

Although Utah appeared to be the best forum for litigating western coal-land frauds, the hidden activities of the LDS Church and the state government may have made it the most complex. For one thing, the chances for uncovering earlier cooperation between Utah's leaders and the perpetrators of Utah coal-land fraud diminished as federal pressures grew. As the Senate threatened Utah's elected representative through the humiliating Smoot hearings, Utah officials took a self-protective stance. Divisions rent both the Utah Republican Party—still under American Party fire—and the LDS Church itself in the wake of the fallout from the Smoot hearings. In Washington, Mormons struggled to redeem the reputation of their church and establish Utah's equality in the Union, rather than continue as a perennial political stepchild perpetually forced to battle accusations of polygamy and theocracy. Finding the necessary fundamental cooperation with federal prosecutors, the on-site representatives of an apparently antagonistic federal government, seemed unlikely. Growing federal-state friction diminished the possibility of a quick legal resolution.[13] Perhaps fortunately, Roosevelt's focus on non-Mormon, outside-affiliated "combinations of capital" as the likely wrongdoers skirted this volatile cauldron for the moment.

Ignorant of the magnitude of historical church-federal animosity and its influence on the current cases, Burch concluded his views on the bills in equity and devoted the rest of his missive to problems in Washington. He was particularly disappointed that both the solicitor general and Interior Secretary Hitchcock would be on vacation by the time he could get to the capital. The greatest problem so far encountered, according to Burch, was Interior's ruling that coal had to be identified in commercial quantity on each forty-acre parcel to be classified as "coal land." Because of this legal definition, "grafters have simply begun to run away with fine coal lands under the Stone & Timber Act ... and [they] can transfer the lands from one party to another with rapidity, so as to hide themselves behind the recent Detroit Timber Co. case, and the Clark case." Only the secretary of the interior could easily change this ruling, which he had declined to do. Burch lamented:

> The honest truth is that somebody down there in his Department is deceiving him, and this he can learn from any honest and sincere Register and Receiver of the Land Office in states where there are coal lands. ... We must manage to make him more fully alive to the situation, or else in filing bills and attempting to recover coal lands already gone, we are saving at the spigot, which he, in allowing these rulings to remain unreviewed and unrevoked, is wasting at the bung hole.

In order to stop this "wasting at the bung hole," Burch felt "almost emboldened to go to the President himself,"[14] where he might have received a more sympathetic audience. But to step outside the established hierarchy was not Burch's nature. He did not go to Roosevelt. In this matter, his actions differed widely from steps later taken by Gifford Pinchot, who even went right over the head of the president in publicly alleging coal-land fraud.

In the meantime, Pinchot's influence could be seen in the withdrawal of six million acres of public land (of a total of fifty-six million acres believed to contain coal) that Burch had seen announced in the morning paper. Although this limited withdrawal raised an immediate public and congressional outcry, Burch felt "sick and sore to think that he [President Roosevelt] did not simply withdraw the whole of the coal land region from sale for re-classification, as he might easily have done, and then depend upon the popular voice to compel congress to repeal the Coal Land Act altogether, and thus save all these lands."[15] This obvious legislative solution to the defective Coal Land Act of 1873 would take many more years to realize. In the meantime, the best solution to the problem of coal-land fraud seemed to lie in the courts.

Ordinary citizens apparently welcomed federal prosecution in Utah. The *Advocate*, the coal district newspaper, jubilantly reported the involvement of Attorney General Moody, Special Assistant Attorney General Fred A. Maynard, and District Attorney Hiram E. Booth, and skimmed lightly over Booth's involvement in the Milner-Gilson coal company activities. The article continued with an emphasis on federal solidarity and ability:

> The name attached to the complaint shows that Secretary of the Interior Hitchcock and Attorney General Moody, backed by President Roosevelt, mean business. It is that of M. C. Burch, one of the ablest lawyers in the department of justice.[16]

Meanwhile, state officials publicly denied rumors of complicity. According to a former member of the land board, Fisher Harris, the old board "followed the law, both state and national, with the most scrupulous care, and watched the interests of the state of Utah with intelligence and fidelity." It also had had "literally" to "bring order out of what was chaos" through means of a "practically untried law." Harris was referring to the school sections granted to Utah in its enabling act. He elaborated on the administrative function of the board in interpreting the grant, choosing, appraising, and selling the state lands "in order that the state should have the proper benefit from the government's generosity."[17] Thus the knotty problem of the state-selections abuses, in some ways secondary to the federal campaign for a workable coal-land law and control of the "trusts," quickly swept to the forefront in the Utah press.

In the same newspaper article, Harris was quoted as noting that Byron Groo, criticized for his actions as secretary, had been the board's unanimous choice for that position. Board members asserted that a thorough investigation of all state selections would have cost more than the value of the land itself. Consequently, land board officials had had to rely on the affidavits of those claiming parcels, although the land office quickly became widely known as " 'a place where men went when they wanted to swear a lie.' " Turning on the General Land Office of the United States, Harris declared that, as final arbiter of the state selections, it bore ultimate responsibility for any fraud. He concluded:

> The old land board of whose methods I have been speaking ... drew their inconsequential salaries and rendered faithful service to the state. They were not clairvoyants, nor geologists, nor could they locate hidden water with a peach tree switch, but they brought to the discharge of their duties such ability as they had.[18]

Not only was Harris protecting his own reputation, but the battle lines between state and federal governments, supposedly united in prosecuting coal-land fraud by business combinations, suddenly hardened.

This desire to blame the federal government for coal-land problems struck a responsive chord in much of Utah. It also presaged friction at a much higher level. One link in this federal-state-business conundrum, Senator Sutherland, promptly and vociferously disclaimed all knowledge of coal-land frauds. He admitted that "upon one single occasion some years ago . . . I personally went before the registrar and receiver [of the Salt Lake land office] in response to a subpoena which had been served upon an officer of the P.V. Coal company," but was otherwise uninvolved. A few days later he resigned as senior partner in the firm that had been representing the Rio Grande system and that also had supplied a partner to help defend Reed Smoot. In a more forgiving tone, an *Advocate* editorial commented: "Such associations by such officials may be merely the misfortunes of our complex civilization."[19] Sutherland, professionally unscathed, would one day rise to judgment of the last of the ongoing Utah coal-land cases—involving state selections—finally to be resolved in the U.S. Supreme Court.

Other immediate responses at the federal level boded ill for the prosecution of the Utah coal-land suits. When, in August, Burch formally requested a conference with vacationing Interior Secretary Hitchcock to discuss the litigation, a snippy reply went to the solicitor general. It referred to "an obvious refutation of statements made by Mr. Burch . . . in so far as he intimates that the Secretary is not already fully advised as to the proper construction and application of the statutes governing the disposition of coal lands." Secretary Hitchcock was described as "considerably fagged," and could not agree to the conference proposed by "Mr. Burch, whose apprehensions as to the administration of the public land laws are shown to be without foundation."[20]

Three days later, an infuriated Justice Department attorney, H. W. Hoyt, complained:

> The Interior Dept. . . . evidently think[s] he [Burch] is mistaken and unduly alarmed and even if he is precisely right and thieves are running away with all the public lands, we can do nothing as long as the Secretary [of the Interior] doesn't think so. . . . There is no purpose in Mr. Burch submitting these matters to me if they are not to go on to Mr. Hitchcock. . . . [A]nd I, for one, have been snubbed sufficiently.[21]

Burch was himself becoming considerably fagged under the dual pressures of interdepartmental conflict and judicial prosecution. His

September letters were handwritten, not typed, and he was away from
his desk, at home in his native Michigan, trying to recuperate. As he
explained: "My trip west during the extreme hot weather of early
August following very severe exertions to keep up with the business
has brought on one of my attacks of bleeding." Despite his ill health,
he reiterated the importance of the Utah coal-land litigation:

> The cases involve very valuable property now held by a powerful
> corporation who have the strongest counsel money can procure east
> and west. The effect of these suits has already been very great all
> over the west in the coal bearing regions, and the struggle to defeat
> the United States will be great and prolonged.[22]

Unfortunately for his department this last assertion was correct.

As Burch had predicted, Rio Grande system attorneys rushed to
court to try to derail the suits. First, they insisted that the only proper
venue for the cases was New Jersey, where Utah Fuel had been
incorporated. Burch, citing what he called "the western phrase to
'catch them going and coming,' " requested approval from the attorney
general to file in a second jurisdiction. His request was granted, and
the papers reached the New Jersey district attorney shortly before
September 12, 1906, when the statute of limitations would take effect.[23]
So far, the federal attorneys had beaten all statutory deadlines through
hard work and hastily written bills of complaint.

As the legal process continued, state and national newspapers reported a far more titillating Utah story: ongoing polygamy in the LDS
Church. C. M. Owen, indicted as a D&RG dummy and performing as
a sometime spotter, had resumed his attack on the Mormon hierarchy. In
September 1906, he accused LDS President Joseph F. Smith of adultery,
based on the birth of a child to Smith's plural wife the previous June.
Smith was then in Europe on church business, but Owen—quoted in a
Salt Lake City evening paper—promised "to have the warrant served
upon Mr. Smith when he returns home." Owen's action was seen by
Smith's friends and supporters as politically motivated. One wrote:
"There never was a time when the feeling of the public was so intense
[against us] as at present," a view echoed by Reed Smoot. Smith returned
home and faced the "charge made by C. Mostyn Owen—one of the
meanest and vilest creatures on earth"—words used by Smith's son,
Joseph Fielding Smith. Joseph Fielding went with his father when he
paid the $300 fine levied "on complaint of C. M. Owen, a devil incar-
nate."[24] Whether or not anyone realized Owen's concurrent function as
a Rio Grande dummy and recruiter of other dummies is unclear. It is

obvious, however, that cooperation between the railroad and the state's chief ecclesiastical leaders, such as had occurred in the later 1890s, had come to a vicious end.

The interesting timing of these polygamy accusations and the progress of the federal coal-land suits does seem to point to possible political motivation, although it has so far been impossible to document this. It appears likely that the polygamy issue was being fanned to manipulate Utah's leadership. Obviously, any action that discredited the Mormon hierarchy would tend to reflect not only on Utah as a predominately Mormon state but on Reed Smoot, the LDS apostle, then fighting for his political life. Not only could Utah's American Party thereby reap political benefits, as in its control of the Salt Lake City government, but, as Smoot's star faded in the congressional heaven, that of Utah's junior senator, George Sutherland, would, by comparison, shine more brightly. The developing congressional controversy over public lands increasingly pitted Smoot against Sutherland, as well as against Wyoming's Senator Clark (the brother of the UP coal company manager) and others. Although a recent historian has ascribed these differences to divergent philosophies on conservation,[25] further scholarly consideration needs to be given to other types of motivation, both practical and political, including the contemporary battle over coal lands.

Political forces bearing on Utah increased as the Interstate Commerce Commission (ICC), newly empowered by the Tillman-Gillespie Resolution, also began a series of hearings in Colorado and Utah. A visiting commissioner inquired into price-fixing in violation of the Hepburn Act by the Union Pacific and the Rio Grande. Utah subpoenas were served in late September, leading a local reporter to speculate that if railroads could not carry coal out of the state where it was mined, great changes would come to Utah. First, "it means that the Denver and Rio Grande will be in a position to supply fuel to the state of Utah to the exclusion of the Harriman lines." Second, newer mines in eastern Utah (such as those of the Sweets and Milner) would be "on the same footing" as the Rio Grande, or the Gould system, as it was called in the press.[26]

In early October, the ICC commissioner in charge of the hearing arrived from Denver, where he had just chaired a similar tribunal that had uncovered not only price-fixing but "great infraction of both the land laws and the anti-trust act" by the Union Pacific. As a headline put it, "Union Pacific Wanted Everything On The Map: Utah Fuel Company Amateurish in the Business Compared to Other Concerns."

Collusion by the UP and the Gould system in establishing freight charges in Utah was indisputably established. The fairness of these rates (or lack of it), and alleged discrimination in providing coal cars to competing mines, had to await a second hearing in November.[27]

Meanwhile, as Burch recovered his health, he again headed west to contribute to the various federal investigations. In a rare public pronouncement, he spoke about the Utah cases as he passed through Salt Lake City on his way to Montana in October 1906. He noted that the industrial growth of the nation, and especially the use of coal for locomotive fuel, had led to a series of railroad/coal combinations that "apparently have crowded out all others in getting coal lands. To do this on a large scale it has been necessary to evade the law ... and to resort to the perversion of the coal land act itself in acquiring large tracts." Burch continued with the significance of Utah litigation: "The discovery of what was doing in Utah was made earlier than in other states, and hence Utah takes precedence in coal land litigation." Thus, Burch disingenuously sidestepped all the issues of a friendly federal bench, the statute of limitations, the antipolygamy crusade, congressional power blocks, and the myriad other factors that had colored the government's choice of venue. He concluded the interview with the hope that the Coal Land Act of 1873 would shortly be changed, and that the land now withdrawn throughout the West would be sold or leased under new legislation.[28]

Burch's Utah cases were then in the federal court of Judge John A. Marshall, where the Rio Grande coal companies had filed demurrers. Arguments centered on the state-selections cases, as John M. Waldron, aided by Waldemar Van Cott (Smoot's attorney and one of Sutherland's former partners), Mark Braffet, and others, argued that the Utah Enabling Act had "specially favored" the state, and that the decisions of the secretary of the interior confirming the grants were unassailable in court. Furthermore, arguing from a constitutional standpoint, Waldron held that if the judiciary were to invalidate the transfer of these coal-bearing school sections to the state, it would be contravening the will of the Congress that had passed the enabling act. The courts, in such an event, would be grossly violating the constitutional separation of powers. One of Waldron's main supporting arguments reiterated the definition of "known coal land" (forty acres; exposed coal). An attorney for the ICC listened as Maynard, Booth, and E. B. Critchlow countered these arguments for the government. The case was taken under advisement.[29]

The *Advocate*, the coal district paper, in an article accompanying the report of the court hearing, noted that subpoenas had been served by U.S. deputy marshals, and speculated that "the federal grand jury is about to take cognizance of the coal cases." This investigation, indeed, the involvement of the grand jury itself, sprang from the ICC hearing, during which David J. Sharp, brother of William Sharp (who by that time was with USSR&M), had claimed he was driven out of business by price-fixing on the part of the Union Pacific Coal company. He had testified that when he cut retail prices in Salt Lake City the UPCC had refused to deliver any more coal wholesale to him and he was "cut off from a supply by all the coal mining companies in this territory." A pending prosecution under the antitrust law was postulated. Accusations of monopolizing of coal land through the dummy system, the subject of the federal complaints already filed, had also allegedly surfaced in the ICC hearings. The article repeated the speculation that "the grand jury may take cognizance of these and investigate their criminal aspects."[30] All the weapons in the federal arsenal were being leveled against the railroad coal-land fraud.

The grand jury proceedings could not be reported, of course, but the local *Advocate* made some very astute guesses based on the parade of witnesses called to appear. The newspaper speculated that the two-hour testimony of the Utah Fuel auditor was "probably the most important ... acquainted as he is with the minutest details of the Utah Fuel company's business," not only in coal but in "the railroad end of the coal business." The ICC hearing had also reconvened, and had been exploring not only violations of commerce law but also fraudulent land entries.[31]

While these hearings took place, the Interior Department continued its withdrawals of western lands, pending a determination of their mineral content. This effectively halted any new coal-mine development. These withdrawals, done by Interior Secretary Hitchcock at the urging of President Roosevelt, included 18,000 acres in Utah alone. Someone had apparently gone over Hitchcock's head in alerting other federal officials to the continuation of coal-land fraud. The public attention to the problem that resulted focused on the General Land Office, where most transfer decisions took place. The commissioner, Wyoming's William A. Richards, sat at the eye of the storm. Although he had chaired the second Public Lands Commission (the first federal watchdog to challenge claims to the public domain) he was still implicated in the long-standing Land Office irregularities. Richards, accused of aiding land fraud throughout the West, submitted his resignation in November 1906.[32]

Meanwhile, in Utah, where the grand jury remained closeted, the concurrent ICC hearing produced fascinating testimony that revealed a variety of dubious or illegal practices. For example, according to the *Advocate* newspaper, the former chief clerk at Sunnyside had revealed special freight rates that had been granted to the Wasatch Store Company, another subsidiary of the Rio Grande. Utah Fuel auditor W. O. Williams confirmed this testimony, adding that no dividends had been paid on stock of the Rio Grande system companies, since all the profits "went to pay off interest on outstanding bonds," presumably the result of the onerous Contract B. (As discussed in chapter 5, this contract enabled the Western Pacific to sap Rio Grande assets in payment of WP debts.) On the land fraud itself, Byron Groo failed to recall how the railroad had gotten its hands on all those valuable coal lands. George T. Holladay recounted his shootout with Robert Kirker and the Tidwells at Sunnyside, after which he was allegedly forced to sell his claim to the Rio Grande for $22,600. Arthur A. Sweet, telling of his rivalry with Utah Fuel dummy, spotter Owen, described being driven off a nearby parcel by armed men. George Whitmore corroborated the Holladay-Kirker shootout and added that he had never mined the coal on his own land "because the railroad company demanded three dollars a ton for hauling it to market"; the company claimed its subsidiaries could sell him coal more cheaply in Salt Lake City. Agent Percy Sowers, of the Interior Department, described the workings of the dummy system, uncovered by his research. The last word on intent to defraud belonged to geology professor Marcus E. Jones. He testified that he had worked for the Rio Grande system, investigating coal lands in Utah and Colorado. In response to questions, he exhaustively described the veins in Carbon County and Salina Canyon, stating finally that "a man of ordinary intelligence would know that all the district was underlaid with coal."[33]

The day after the detailed article reporting this ICC testimony appeared, Maynard and Booth jubilantly wired the attorney general: "Grand Jury returns indictment." This indictment appreciably strengthened the government's case in federal court. United States attorneys had succeeded in front of the grand jury on the grounds of conspiracy to defraud the nation of its coal lands, and of perjury. Those individuals now facing criminal indictments were H. G. Williams, general manager of the Utah Fuel Company, William R. Foster, Robert Forrester's private secretary, Alexander H. Cowie, Utah Fuel vice president and president of the railroad's Wasatch Store Company, Elroy N. Clark, Utah Fuel attorney, and two other men associated with the Oregon Short Line and the Union Pacific Coal Company. All their associated companies were also indicted. The grand jury had also uncovered the exact workings of the dummy system in Salina Canyon, which had led to multiple deedings of the property, first from the dummies to Clark's father-in-law, and thence to a local coal man acting for Utah Fuel. The newspaper, reporting on this, declared this scam "only a small part of a monster conspiracy," much of which the government had yet to uncover.[34]

Similar results emerged from the concurrent ICC hearing in Denver. There, too, the commissioner found evidence of freight discrimination by railroad/coal combinations, although he refused to rule on coal-land fraud. Nonetheless, testimony revealed that in 1902 Robert Forrester had located coal land for the Rio Grande in the vicinity of Somerset, in the west-central part of Colorado. Forrester had tendered more than $30,000 for it to the receiver of the local U.S. Land Office at Gunnison. He had then turned the land over to the D&RG, which had awarded these coal companies the very best freight rates.[35]

Reaction to these legal developments varied widely. An editorial in the *Eastern Utah Advocate* stated: "Knowing many of the witnesses appearing before the federal grand jury and their hatred of the Utah Fuel company and even the individuals identified with it, the great wonder is that indictments stopped where they did."[36] However, the people indicted were apparently unrepentant. The same newspaper described "a jocund throng of railroad and coal company officials" arriving to post their bonds and joking with federal officials:

> "If you would put coal down to $3.50 [a ton] I would feel like letting you go," said the commissioner as soon as the men were seated.
> "We will have to put it up to $7.50 to get even," was the quick response of Attorney [Mark] Braffet.[37]

Then those indicted left to await a trial the following March.

The state land board also had its say in these new developments. It had recently received notice from the General Land Office of the withdrawal of suspected coal land based on the doctrine being pursued in federal litigation that the state could not claim coal land under its enabling act. Board members stated that anyone who wished to fight the federal government over withdrawals alleged to be coal land could do so in the name of the state. However, Utah could provide neither money nor other support.[38]

Enraged citizens whose claims had been stymied wrote their congressmen, who turned on President Roosevelt for an explanation.

Addressing Congress in early December, the president stated that he did not intend that these lands be permanently closed to entry. Instead, he explained: "It is not wise that the nation should alienate its remaining coal lands." All of those believed to contain coal had been withdrawn only temporarily, until the manner of administering them "can be properly settled by . . . legislation." Then he got to the heart of his plan to withdraw

> these lands from sale or from entry, save in certain especial circumstances. The ownership would then remain in the United States, which should . . . permit them to be worked by private individuals under a royalty system, the government keeping such control as to permit it to see that no excessive price was charged consumers.[39]

Although Roosevelt favored a leasing system for coal land, western Congressmen eager to promote development hesitated to implement this suggestion. But the heat was on for change.[40]

While Congress bickered with him, Roosevelt turned to officials in his Interior Department for more ammunition. Secretary Hitchcock wrote a twelve-page letter to the president explaining his reasons for the coal-land withdrawals, which had still not reached the extent favored by the prosecutor, Burch. Chief Forrester Gifford Pinchot provided Roosevelt with a seven-page rebuttal. According to the chief forester, in July 1906, Hitchcock withdrew 10 million acres of land "from all disposal under public land laws, to protect the public interest in the coal which it was supposed to contain." In September, the Forest Service discovered a land rush in progress on "forest reserve land containing coal," up to 20 million acres of it. Pinchot accused Hitchcock of serious confusion in determining which lands were inside and outside forest reserves. The two men also differed over whether "withdrawals should be *from coal entry*' or were lands " 'officially known to contain coal.' " According to Pinchot, protecting all lands from coal entry had been agreed upon. When Hitchcock had later included the forest lands, he had protected only those lands officially known to have coal. Since Hitchcock steadfastly maintained that coal had to be exposed on every forty-acre subdivision to quality as official coal land, much of the coal-bearing public domain was still slipping away. The president had apparently only discovered this fact in conference with Congressman Mondell, of Wyoming, an opponent of the current withdrawals. In his heavily marked-up memo, Pinchot revealed much interagency strife:

The mistake of the Secretary of the Interior was due to extreme carelessness on the part of somebody, and since it is now corrected would not merit such detailed remarks as the above if it were not for the Secretary's surprising [previous word crossed out] effort to shift the burden of the mistake from the shoulders where it belongs to those of the President by clouding the issue with twelve pages of specious arguments. [41]

A colleague had appended a marginal comment to this section: "Perhaps too 'straight from the shoulder.' "

As Pinchot concluded, coal in the public domain had to be protected until "Congress saw fit to act."[42] That time had not yet come. The unworkable Coal Land Act of 1873, which had necessitated fraud in the first place, remained the law of the land.

PART II

Second Thoughts, Different Targets

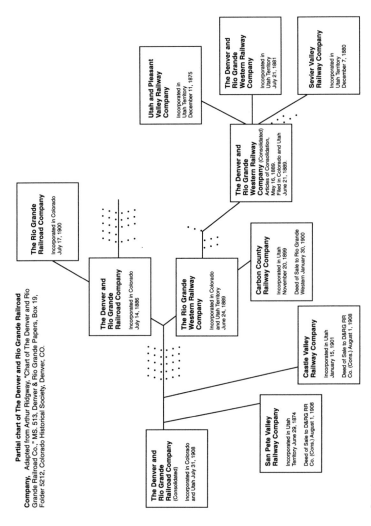

Partial chart of The Denver and Rio Grande Railroad Company, Adapted from Arthur Ridgway, "Chart of The Denver and Rio Grande Railroad Co.," MS. 513, Denver & Rio Grande Papers, Box 19, Folder 5212, Colorado Historical Society, Denver, CO.

The Rio Grande Railroad Company
Incorporated in Colorado July 17, 1900

The Denver and Rio Grande Railroad Company
Incorporated in Colorado July 14, 1886

The Rio Grande Western Railway Company
Incorporated in Colorado and Utah Territory June 24, 1889

The Denver and Rio Grande Railroad Company (Consolidated)
Incorporated in Colorado and Utah July 31, 1908

San Pete Valley Railway Company
Incorporated in Utah Territory June 29, 1874
Deed of Sale to D&RG RR Co. (Cons.) August 1, 1908

Castle Valley Railway Company
Incorporated in Utah January 15, 1901
Deed of Sale to D&RG RR Co. (Cons.) August 1, 1908

Carbon County Railway Company
Incorporated in Utah November 20, 1889
Deed of Sale to Rio Grande Western January 30, 1900

The Denver and Rio Grande Western Railway Company (Consolidated) Articles of Consolidation, May 16, 1889. Filed in Colorado and Utah June 21, 1889.

Utah and Pleasant Valley Railway Company
Incorporated in Utah Territory December 11, 1875

The Denver and Rio Grande Western Railway Company
Incorporated in Utah Territory July 21, 1881

Sevier Valley Railway Company
Incorporated in Utah Territory December 7, 1880

Dotted lines represent the addition of various other companies.

CHAPTER 9

Success in the West?

The infighting at the federal level diminished in the winter of 1906/07, when the president revamped the two federal departments directly involved, Justice and Interior. First, the Justice Department received a new head: in December 1906, Roosevelt plucked Charles J. Bonaparte from his Cabinet position as secretary of the navy to serve as attorney general. Interior remained under Secretary Hitchcock, who attempted a crucial procedural change in response to Roosevelt's urging. On January 18, 1907, Hitchcock complied with a presidential directive to protect the coal-bearing public domain from fraudulent acquisition by requiring an on-site examination of each forty-acre tract (in accordance with the standing definition) before patent would issue. Regrettably, this decision failed to yield the desired effect, since Congress failed to appropriate sufficient funds to employ the number of special agents demanded by the directive.[1] The problem of the forty-acre definition of coal land still hampered federal prosecutors.

Congress followed its own agenda in other areas as well. For example, Representative Frank Mondell (Wyoming) expressed the views of most western states when he said that Roosevelt's coal-lands withdrawals had violated the constitutional separation of powers by rendering inoperable the Coal Land Act of 1873. Mondell likewise objected to the federal coal-leasing proposal as an unlawful exercise of federal power.

The fight over public lands gained another interested participant when, on February 20, 1907, the Senate voted forty-two to twenty-eight on Reed Smoot's membership, falling short of the two-thirds majority needed for expulsion. In explaining the vote, a fellow senator reportedly remarked: "I don't see why we can't get along just as well with a polygamist who doesn't polyg as we do with a lot of monogamists who don't monog."[2] Smoot, originally also opposed to the presidential leasing system, would later lead the way to its adoption. But, for the

117

meantime, the Congress adjourned that March without any action on leasing.[3]

Meanwhile, life was going badly for Interior Secretary Hitchcock. Plagued by underfunding, his administrative decisions eroded in the Owens Valley water controversy in southern California, Hitchcock tired of his work. He submitted his letter of resignation on March 1, 1907, and with him went his land office commissioner.[4]

The new interior secretary, James R. Garfield, tried to continue the fight to protect the public domain from acquisition through fraud. He, too, struggled with the limitations imposed by insufficient congressional appropriations, resulting from the withdrawals battle. Roosevelt advised Garfield to use all available agents to "enforce the existing laws, and protect the bona fide settlement of public lands by homeseekers." The president also suggested that lands already examined should be released if nonmineral, and that some 28 million acres containing coal "shall be open to coal entry as soon as you shall classify such lands and promulgate rules and regulations for making entry." Other lands had to remain withdrawn pending "proper examination" by the USGS.[5]

Much of this work passed through the office of the new commissioner of the General Land Office, Richard Achilles Ballinger, who shortly turned out to be an obstacle, not an asset, to the Roosevelt antifraud campaign. Ballinger's appointment on March 5, 1907, capped a career that had already included the mayoralty of Seattle and a successful private law practice. In this profession, Ballinger had made many wealthy friends in the Pacific Northwest, some of whom now clamored for unallocated public lands. Gifford Pinchot later claimed that Ballinger's attitude "would determine the [Public Land] Commission's future action on the one major subject upon which it had not yet reported—mineral lands, and especially coal."[6]

These changes at the top had no immediate effect on the prosecutions in Utah, where matters seemed to be going well for the government. First, in January 1907, the Utah federal judge, John Marshall, denied the Rio Grande system's demurrers, sending the cases to trial. Marshall based his ruling on the principle that Utah has no right to take known coal lands as state selections under its enabling act. Furthermore, he decided, if minerals were subsequently found on these lands, the putative owners had to return them to the public domain.[7]

Also beginning in January 1907, Justice Department attorneys shifted their sights to independent developers, the economic rivals of railroad "monopolies." These operators, too, allegedly had circumvented the unrealistic Coal Land Act of 1873, and consistency demanded federal prosecution. The first of these indictments returned by the grand jury elicited strong local disapproval, expressed in the headline, "Four More Are Nailed to the Cross." It emphasized shifting sentiments toward land fraud in Utah's coal district depending on who were the defendants; in this case, the popular Huntington Canyon coal-land owners Don C. Robbins, E. W. Senior, Walter G. Filer, and Lester M. Freed. They were charged with conspiracy to defraud the United States, a crime that carried a maximum penalty of $10,000 fine or up to two years imprisonment, or both. They had allegedly committed this fraud by swearing false affidavits claiming coal land as grazing land and swearing it was for their own use.[8]

The Robbins-Freed consortium filed their own demurrer contesting the same points of law as those disputed by the Rio Grande system. In April, Burch reviewed the government cases against both groups of coal-land fraud defendants for the new attorney general, Bonaparte. Burch admitted that the government probably could not win a conviction for perjury against the Robbins-Freed group because Congress had not ordered the perjured affidavits and "the action of the Secretary of the Interior in requiring them, . . . was extra legislative." Burch was therefore forced once again to rely on the "very loosely drawn" Coal Land Act of 1873 in prosecuting a criminal conspiracy to obtain more than the legally mandated 640 acres.[9] If Marshall's court were to reject the ability of this law to sustain a criminal indictment, the issue would go to the U.S. Supreme Court, where Burch felt the government would lose. If, on the other hand, the Robbins-Freed consortium were convicted in Marshall's Utah district court, they would probably bring an appeal to the eighth circuit court, where the decision would probably favor the government. Burch weighed the difficulties ahead and concluded:

> From one point of view it would seem unfortunate to obtain a large number of indictments for conspiracies of this character in different states, and have them overturned in the Supreme Court thereafter, but I do not feel at liberty, under all the circumstances which surround me, to withhold action.[10]

He ended: "It is difficult from this standpoint and at this time to state whether these criminal cases [against the Robbins consortium] or our suits in equity [against the Rio Grande subsidiaries] will prove most valuable to the Government in our work."[11] Concurring with Burch's assessment, the Justice Department approved Burch's plan of attack in the hope of winning at least one series of suits.[12]

Other federal cases filed that January drove to the heart of the state selections problem, also involved in the suits against the PVCC and Utah Fuel Company. A second federal suit against independents began on January 18, 1907. Federal attorneys brought a suit in equity against Arthur A. Sweet for illegally acquiring coal lands as state selections. (Ironically, only five years earlier Sweet had accused the State of Utah of obtaining known coal lands as grazing lands at Sunnyside, intending to sell them to Spotter Owen.)[13] Now, the Sweets were developing Bull Hollow under the auspices of the Independent Coal and Coke Company (IC&C), originally chartered in Wyoming in October 1906, excluding the feuding in-laws, Sweet and Wade, from

The main portal of the Kenilworth mine, owned by the Independent Coal and Coke Company, the first "independent" developer (i.e., not a railroad) commercially to mine coal in Carbon County. When this photograph was taken (December 1, 1907) the mine was shipping about 150 tons of coal daily. Three men in business suits—probably the Sweet brothers—pose above and to the right of the portal. Courtesy of the Utah State Historical Society, Salt Lake City, Utah.

The steeply inclined Kenilworth tramway transported coal from the portal, high on the mountain, to the tipple (foreground). Coal was tipped out of the cars, through the hole, onto shaking screens, where it was sorted by size. Photo (1907) courtesy of the Utah State Historical Society, Salt Lake City, Utah.

its incorporators. When the pair later made up, they were included on the board of directors. By 1907, the company seemed to be flourishing, reporting one hundred employees at work, the purchase of a Shea locomotive, and projecting one hundred tons a day from the newly named Kenilworth mine by the middle of that September.[14]

The case against the Sweets horrified Utah State Land Board members. Despite their earlier announced intention to remain aloof from any federal litigation, they apparently felt compelled to back the first independent economically to challenge the Western. Arthur Sweet was something of a local hero, refusing to bow to railroad pressures after the fracus at Sunnyside and successfully opening a competing commercial line. Ultimately, his efforts seemed to offer the best chance for lower coal prices for all the people of Utah.[15] Consequently, the land board decided to back Sweet in fighting the federal suit. On February 2, 1907, its members appropriated $5,000 toward Sweet's expenses in litigation against the United States, specifying the tract thus covered: the IC&C's Bull Hollow development, now called Kenilworth.[16]

The state had apparently failed to check the specifics of the suit. The land cited in the federal case actually lay about twenty miles further southwest, on the Black Hawk coal vein that straddled the Carbon-Emery county line. This was uninhabited territory, far from a railroad and the promise of easy development. Yet once the land board members realized their mistake, they had little recourse but to continue. They had locked the state into a case that would eventually set the national precendent for mineral lands selections in land-grant states.[17]

A third federal case against independent developers was filed in March 1907 against the Milner-Gilson group. Col. Stanley Milner and his partner, gilsonite king and former federal marshal Sam Gilson, had amassed more than 5,500 acres of coal-bearing in lieu sections between 1900 and 1903, claiming them as grazing land from the state. Milner and Gilson had created the Carbon County Land Company in 1903 to manage this property, and had selected Hiram E. Booth, now U.S. district attorney for Utah, to serve the first year as company attorney and president. The land had not yet proceeded to patent, and Milner's untimely death in 1906 had transferred his estate to his widow and executrix, Truth A. Milner, who had also filed on some of the land. In March 1907 the attorney general's office began civil proceedings against this group in Judge Marshall's U.S. district court, alleging that the property was known to contain coal when Utah obtained it as in lieu sections under the 1895 enabling act.[18]

At the time these proceedings were formulated, federal attorney Fred A. Maynard did what he could to establish good working relationships in Utah, where a deep suspicion of federal intentions still prevailed. He told the state land board that Utah would not be made party to the Milner case, despite the abuse of the state-selections process. Maynard allegedly declared that "it was not the intention of the government to contest the state's rights to these lands, but rather to protect the state against the improper disposition of the same." In other words, although Utah could not have valid title and the claim of the Milners was likewise null and void, only the Milners were being charged with fraud. The land board and its successors interpreted this statement broadly, taking it to mean that Utah was immune from all federal coal-land fraud prosecution involving lands granted under its enabling act.[19] This conciliatory federal stance extended to Hiram E. Booth, connected with both the Milner group and the federal prosecution. He was not forced to resign his position as district attorney, although, for the Milner-Gilson case, his assistant district attorney signed the actual bill of complaint.[20] Thus, long-lived Mormon fears of federal persecution, dating from the Utah War and the more recent antipolygamy crusades, were somewhat calmed.

The federal prosecution team also redoubled their efforts to ferret out fraud on the part of the Gould system. Investigators followed the tracks of Robert Forrester, and on March 18, 1907, a grand jury in the Territory of New Mexico returned four counts of perjury and two of conspiracy against a coterie of coal-land dummies headed by this peripatetic agent. Forrester and the late William Bird had contacted the group in 1904 to acquire control of most of four sections of coal land in northern New Mexico. In June 1907 Forrester was again indicted, this time for land fraud committed in Colorado. In response to this news, Utahns hailed with pride the significance of their *own*, Utah railroad coal-land cases, claiming that theirs would "determine what other investigations shall be made by the government. ... Utah was considered the best state in which to carry on an investigation which will be used as a criterion for the other districts to follow."[21]

The first real pause in this federal prosecution came because of limited congressional funding. In April 1907, Interior Secretary Garfield issued an order directing special agents Hair and Sowers to concentrate their efforts solely on Utah. Justice Department investigations in other western public-land states were to be ignored. Citing a "limited appropriation," Garfield complained that "the [basic] field work, especially in the State of Utah, has been neglected and is now in arrears." Investigations of coal-land fraud had retarded the process of examining new land claims. The land withdrawn by Roosevelt could be restored to entry only if examination were completed, and westerners' patience was wearing thin.[22]

Accordingly, Garfield took two important steps to streamline his workload. On April 12, he issued an order abrogating all rules and regulations regarding coal lands in states, territories, and Alaska (always a special case), and promulgated a whole new set of rules. Secondly, he reclaimed his agents from the command of the Justice

Department, placing them under his own field division chief for Utah and Colorado. Unfortunately, this latter action slowed prosecution. The attorney general's staff now had to make specific requests to Interior officials, who would then "extend to them such assistance as may be deemed necessary." A few months later, Garfield visited Utah, found conditions "satisfactory," and authorized the sale of 160,000 acres of nonmineral state selections from the public domain.[23]

Then, in Wyoming, in mid-April, the government achieved its first coal-land fraud success through litigation. Smarting under indictments there and in Utah and Colorado for railroad rate-fixing and illegal acquisition of coal lands, the Union Pacific Coal Company capitulated rather than, as the Gould system had decided to do, appeal and face a trial. In May, the UP restored more than 260,000 acres of Wyoming coal lands to the public domain, relinquishing a sizeable investment in exchange for an end to all federal criminal charges.[24]

Meanwhile, much known coal land returned to the nation for redistribution under the Coal Land Act of 1873. Like others before him, Interior Secretary Garfield addressed the deficiencies of this law when he filed his first annual report in June 1907:

> The purpose of the public land law is not to get rid of the public land, but to provide a method under which lands may be obtained by those who intend to use them legally and honestly. The highest use of lands is the making of homes. . . .
>
> . . . to develop a [coal] mine profitably . . . a much larger acreage is necessary [than allowed under existing law]. . . .
>
> [T]he best possible method of accomplishing these [desired] results is for the Government to retain the title to the coal, and to lease under proper regulations which will induce development when needed, prevent waste, and prevent monopoly.[25]

Once again, Congress, fearful of the loss of state control over lands, their content, and the wealth they generated, ignored this appeal for a federal leasing system.

Simultaneously, almost imperceptibly, the federal coal-land crusade began shifting focus. President Roosevelt had initiated litigation against railroad coal fraud as part of his antimonopoly crusade. Yet ongoing federal investigations had revealed similar offenses by independent coal developers, the local heroes in the economic war against railroad monopoly. Since heroes as well as villains were at fault, the coal-land law itself was becoming increasingly suspect, at least in the executive branch. This transformation resulted in a contradictory government stance. At the same time that the Justice Department was alleging the strength of the Coal Land Act of 1873 in bearing a criminal charge, the Interior Department (and, in private, Justice, too) was increasingly emphasizing its obvious weaknesses. As this process continued, the center could not hold.

Some Utah officials, like their federal counterparts, were beginning to see the coal-land law in a new light. In midsummer 1907, a time of year when coal production usually reached its nadir, a disturbing letter confronted the commissioners of the Utah State Land Board. Utah's governor wrote to predict a winter coal shortage. He asked that the Land Board request the secretary of the interior to release the state's withdrawn coal lands for sale, and added: "The coal lands should be placed in one compact body, and worked in the way that may be determined as the most practical."[26] Indirectly, the governor was also calling for a change in the defective law. Development needs were starting to supersede concerns about fraud in originally obtaining coal land.

Other pressures bore on Roosevelt to soften his view on alleged railroad monopolies, the most touted coal-land fraud targets. In November 1907, prompted by an analysis of the Sherman Anti-Trust Act, Attorney General Bonaparte sent the president his views: "Consolidations of enterprise may result in actual economy in production and thus promote healthy competition." The only exception to this rule was a single giant trust, which would provide "no adequate protection against extortion."[27] The villainous "combinations of capital" excoriated by the president in 1903 were taking on a new mien.

Expectations of a quick and successful end to litigation soothed fears of monopoly. The Robbins-Freed group seemed headed for conviction when, in September 1907, Judge Marshall ruled that the Coal Land Act of 1873 was broad enough to sustain a criminal indictment. The friendly eighth circuit court was expected to uphold his ruling. Consequently, Attorney General Bonaparte urged a speedy trial.[28]

At the same time, Maynard requested permission to examine personally the Utah coal land in litigation, accompanied by Booth, Hair, and Lamoreaux, using "saddle horses, a cook, provisions and a tent." Thus, more fully informed, he was ready when the trial against Utah Fuel and Pleasant Valley Coal began in Marshall's court in November.[29]

During the Utah Fuel–PVCC trial, the government called an

impressive parade of witnesses to support its contentions that Sunnyside was known for its coal. Supplementing his testimony, USGS Geologist Taff, used the relatively new technique of showing photographs of the area, which elicited "universally favorable" comments, according to Burch. The local newspaper, ever partisan, praised the testimony of all the government witnesses, despite "severe crossfire" and "searching cross examination" by the companies' lawyers.[30]

Two events squelched these optimistic views. First, in December, Judge Robert E. Lewis, of the district court of Colorado, ruled in companion suits against the Rio Grande and the Union Pacific coal companies and their employees that the Coal Land Act of 1873 could not sustain a criminal suit. This opinion went exactly counter to that of Judge Marshall of Utah, throwing the issue into the United States Supreme Court, where Burch feared an adverse decision. One week later, Judge Lewis quashed indictments against sixty individuals accused of Colorado coal-land frauds. Luckily for the prosecution, the federal government had just won the right of appeal in cases where a jury was not involved. Yet conditions for federal success seemed to be deteriorating. Under the circumstances, while the Justice Department publicly began preparing to continue the coal-land cases, its attorneys privately began considering other arrangements.[31]

CHAPTER 10

Panic and Politics

On the last day of 1907, the United States attorney for Utah, Hiram Booth, typed a letter to Attorney General Bonaparte summarizing progress in the Utah coal-land cases. He focused on two clusters of the pending suits generated by Roosevelt's original antirailroad crusade: those involving the Rio Grande subsidiaries and those against Union Pacific alleged dummies, Robbins, Freed, et al. Booth reported that the cases against the latter group, under Fred Maynard's direct supervision, had been delayed pending a hearing on the Rio Grande cases, since they involved the same questions of law. Booth continued: "It is the opinion of Mr. Maynard and myself that the Government has a much stronger case against the Utah Fuel Company et al than in the Robbins-Filer-Freed-Senior case, and we deem it best to try that case first."[1]

The government further strengthened its position by slapping Utah Fuel with a new suit in Colorado to recover a reported 19,450 acres of coal land in Gunnison County. The formerly adamant Gould system grew more ready to consider settling out of court. Early in January 1908, the Utah Fuel Company's chief counsel, Joel F. Vaile, contacted Burch and the U.S. attorney general proposing a possible general compromise of both the civil and criminal suits in equity against the corporation and against individual dummies. Vaile offered to go to Washington if necessary, citing "the public interest" as motivation.[2]

Burch, too, conferred by letter with the attorney general, describing his own conference with Vaile. Burch felt that the Gould system had been driven to this conciliatory stance by "the determined attitude of the President and yourself [the attorney general] to appeal from Lewis' decisions, . . . [which] has had the same effect that a decision by Judge Lewis in our favor would have had." Burch discussed the pros and cons of such a settlement: future frauds would be forestalled by the federal determination to date; some public outcry could be expected if fines were imposed, rather than a prison sentence; the government could insist that the coal lands be restored to the public domain, but it could also give the defendant companies preference rights to purchase at fairer, higher prices. He suggested a conference between the attorney general and the secretary of the interior to hammer out uniform treatment toward Harriman's Union Pacific and Gould's Rio Grande. Perhaps sensitive to shifts in public policy, but more likely just speaking his mind, he added:

> In conclusion permit me to say, on the one hand, while I have always been full of fight against these people, the spectacle of an end of the war has many attractions for me. Yet I should earnestly oppose any peace which did not insure the absolute sovereignty of the law and the supremacy of the Government and of this Administration in the premises; and I think it goes without saying that if it is not the will of my superiors that this matter be seriously considered, I will carry on the struggle as long as the authorities are willing to sustain me.[3]

As Burch sensed, the federal coal-land fraud crusade was winding down.

Later in January, Attorney General Bonaparte, Burch, Interior Secretary Garfield, and Rio Grande attorney Vaile met to begin the compromise procedure. Afterwards, the secretaries recalled special agents from the field, directing them to devote their time to taking depositions from key figures in the coal-land frauds, such as Royal Peabody of New York, member of the board of directors of the Rio Grande. The prosecution team was charged with working out the specifics of the compromise.[4]

Burch met with his assistants, Booth and Maynard, at his offices in Denver. Attorney Vaile joined them for further discussions, and then Booth and Maynard returned to Utah. A series of letters from Denver and Salt Lake City, outlining compromise suggestions, started arriving on the attorney general's desk, beginning in mid-February. After reporting some differences on details, the prosecuting team adopted Burch's suggestions that the railroad should relinquish absolutely the lands involved in the litigation, as well as the money paid for them, and that the Utah Fuel Company and the individuals still facing indictment should plead guilty and accept a fine, after which the case could be dismissed. Yet all agreed with Burch, who believed that "no action in the case ... [should] be taken until the Supreme Court shall have passed upon the appeals from the decisions of Judge Lewis, so far as to determine finally whether the coal land law will support any indictment whatsoever."[5] As always, the very heart of the federal case, the unrealistic Coal Land Act of 1873, remained highly problematic. For their own part, Maynard and Booth stressed that, assuming the Supreme Court construed the coal act as able to support criminal charges, "all of said cases [should] be prosecuted to the end."[6]

The government's final offer modified these suggestions somewhat. Federal officials adamantly insisted that any land fraudulently obtained should be returned to the public domain, and the monies paid for it forfeited. Regarding the charges against individuals, they would have to plead guilty and pay a fine. No action would be taken in the criminal cases until the Supreme Court rendered a decision on the applicability of the Coal Land Law of 1873 to a criminal prosecution.[7]

As the Justice Department contemplated the impact of the pending Supreme Court decision, the Gould system had some time to mull over the compromise offer. Not until April 13 would the Utah Federal District Court reconvene, at which time the prosecutors had to proceed on charges of a criminal conspiracy in violation of the Coal Land Act of 1873, or ask that the case be continued.[8] Meanwhile, the system found its assets dwindling due to the effects of the Panic of 1907. In the grim months of late 1907 and early 1908, the loss of coke revenue was particularly damaging, dropping by a full 60 percent. After the panic, Gould was known as the Sick Man of Wall Street and the corporations he owned suffered with him.[9]

The federal government could not ignore the panic's effects. For one thing, federal prosecutors increasingly had to justify their expenses. Not only did the Justice Department have to pay the regular salaries of those pursuing coal-land frauds, it had been paying the expenses of a number of witnesses, a photographer, surveyors, stenographers, and others. Costs multiplied with the number of states in which litigation was pending. As Burch counselled the attorney general in April 1908: "I am now satisfied that all these defendant [Gould] companies, whether in Wyoming, Colorado, Utah or New Mexico, will band together to break the Government down." He continued: "If it were not for the effect of such a course upon the public in this region, I would almost advocate letting them keep the land and we save the good money we are forced to put out in carrying on the litigation." As the effects of the panic deepened that spring, this concern with adverse public reaction to a compromise diminished considerably.[10]

Trying to economize without abandoning the suits, Attorney

General Bonaparte commanded the Utah prosecutors to keep expenses as low as possible. They responded that they had exactly the same desire, but complained:

> The whole power of the millions behind the Gould system has been employed, and is now being employed to defeat the Government in its efforts to undo the frauds by which title to thousands of acres of immensely valuable coal lands were obtained from the United States. ... We have never known of a case where money and cost seem to be of so little concern; but, on the contrary anything and everything that the ingenuity of counsel can conceive has been and will be employed with apparently no regard for expense.[11]

Gould, despite his growing reputation for financial debility, had evidently decided that his coal-land holdings were well worth the high price of continuing litigation.

Even President Roosevelt became embroiled in the discussion over the expense of federal suits. After a meeting that included Bonaparte, business representatives, and labor leader Samuel Gompers, he received these "personal and confidential" suggestions from his attorney general:

> The practical effects of the suggested change in the [anti-trust] law deserve very careful attention. ... [The current law is] attended by a preposterous amount of delay and expense to the Government. It is true that this [Justice] Department has had a very fair measure of success in prosecutions under the Anti-Trust law, but this has been because every case has been investigated almost without regard to the cost and trouble involved.[12]

Unfortunately, not even the difficult-to-manage antitrust statute supported the current coal-land fraud cases, even though they had originally been aimed at separating railroads from coal lands. Cases brought under the untried Coal Land Act of 1873 seemed even less likely to justify the cost of their prosecution.

Bonaparte's letter continued with his expression of shock at the suggestion of a "general 'amnesty' " for the trusts. He asked the president to consider

> the effect which would be produced upon public opinion by the recommendation of immunity to all the Trusts for all their past offenses not involved in pending prosecutions, especially if made just at this time.[13]

Bonaparte did not explain this reference. However, Roosevelt had recently made a very unpopular decision regarding the J. P. Morgan syndicate and coal.

The president's actions in dealing with the Morgan interests indicated a level of tolerance for the concentration of coal companies in the hands of a "trust." In this instance, according to Roosevelt himself, the Panic of 1907 had forced his decision. As he explained in his *Autobiography*, he had had to turn to "the so-called Morgan interests [owners of U.S. Steel . . . the only interests which retained a full hold on the confidence of the people of New York . . . [and] strengthen them, in order that the situation [lack of confidence due to the Panic] might be saved." Roosevelt therefore allowed the Morgan group to acquire the Tennessee Coal and Iron Company, to "substitute . . . [U.S. Steel] securities of great and immediate value for [Tennessee Coal and Iron] securities which at the moment were of no value." Roosevelt calculated that this move "would only increase the proportion of the Steel Company's holdings by about 4 percent, making them about 62 percent instead of about 58 percent of the total value in the country"— although at the time he communicated to his attorney general that the acquisition "will not raise it's portion] above sixty per cent." Roosevelt justified his decision on a good Progressive belief: "The action was emphatically for the general good. It offered the only chance for arresting the panic."[14] Perhaps he was right, but his attempt at economic stabilization also undermined the Justice Department's position in opposition to coal "monopolies."

Despite such widespread fiscal anxiety, the panic had no immediate effect on the coal-land fraud cases. The taking of testimony continued during March and April 1908, pending the Supreme Court decision on the applicability of the Coal Land Act of 1873. People alleged to be dummies were called to the stand, including seventy-three-year-old Jefferson Tidwell, who was allowed to tell his story in his own fashion because he had never been in a courtroom before. Spinning his yarn about Sunnyside coal, he testified:

> It stuck out six or seven feet high and rods across, and in the sun of a bright morning it glittered like silver. I was poor; we were all poor, so it looked awfully good to us. We dug and drilled and worked until we were out of food, and our feet were out of our shoes. We did the best we knew how. We were on unsurveyed ground so held it by work.[15]

Tidwell admitted that Robert Forrester had acted as his family's agent, but disparagingly dismissed George Holladay as a shyster. Although a few important points emerged, Tidwell's testimony, punctuated with laughter from all in attendance, was largely inconsequential.

It culminated in his description of a government surveyor's wife. She had accompanied her husband to Sunnyside, he said, and "My, she had white arms. They glistened in the sun. I saw them one day. I saw them from behind a bunch of brush." With that fascinating tidbit, his testimony ended.[16]

Tidwell was followed by his sons and associates, who offered far less humor and not much, if any, more in the way of enlightenment regarding the alleged frauds. In testimony typical of the dummies, some Scofield residents "were not certain" if Mr. and Mrs. Charles Mostyn Owen had suggested land deals to them. However, they had each been credited with paying $3,200 (that they had never seen) for some valuable coal property. Another witness had been liberally plied with alcohol before he was asked to sign coal-land papers.[17]

Despite consistently poor memories, Utah's hostile entrymen did establish a few facts for the government. For example, the prosecuting team learned that more than $50,000 had been spent on developing the lands prior to entry. All of the land allegedly obtained by fraud was ultimately deeded to Royal C. Peabody, for which the dummies received a uniform $160 each. The late William Bird had paid for the land for each of the dummies at the General Land Office with a cashier's check. The only remaining question involving money was its ultimate source, believed to be George Foster Peabody, or the banking firm of Spencer, Trask and Company, with which he usually dealt. As Fred Maynard noted: "We are satisfied ... that we know the exact facts of this case and that the Utah Fuel Company ... was one of a number of agencies" used by Peabody, Palmer and Dodge to acquire coal land they then deeded to the Gould system. To strengthen the government's case, Maynard requested permission from the attorney general to travel east to take depositions from Peabody and others. He also wanted to examine the books of the Pleasant Valley Coal Company and the Rio Grande Western Construction Company (books that actually contained what he was looking for). His request was granted, with the plea that a specific list of expenses be provided as soon as possible. The government was still counting its pennies.[18]

The hearings on the criminal bills of complaint continued, and the newspapers kept local interest alive, reporting: "The Utah cases are the most important of their kind brought in the West."[19] The taking of testimony ended in November, with the calling of May Kimball Forrester, Robert Forrester's wife, to the stand. She emphatically denied purchasing lands for her husband's employer, insisting instead that she had earned the payment price through her employment as the Scofield school teacher. Despite her protestations of innocence, public opinion seemed to favor a government victory.[20]

In the face of these myriad pressures, the Rio Grande system underwent corporate reorganization. On July 31, 1908 Utah's Western and Colorado's Rio Grande were finally consolidated into a single entity, known as the Denver and Rio Grande or D&RG. The following day, a number of other companies were officially acquired, including the Carbon County Railway (which had built the spurs to the Sunnyside and Pleasant Valley Districts), and the San Pete Valley Railway and Sevier Railway, which had built the lines on the western side of Salina Canyon and had offered the promise of marketing its coal. The *Advocate* newspaper had earlier described the bonds to be issued to refund the combined companies and support completion of the Western Pacific from Salt Lake City to Oakland. In May, it noted that, with the completion of the WP, "Gould will have over seventeen thousand miles of railroad, traversing twenty-three states." This prospect particularly alarmed his rival, E. H. Harriman, who, together with Otto Kahn, of Kuhn, Loeb and Company, the UP's banking house, had garnered seats on the board of the Equitable Trust Company. In July, this company absorbed the Bowling Green Trust Company, which held the mortgage on the D&RG. Despite this incipient financial threat to his holdings, Gould displayed confidence as he showily toured eastern Utah in the company of Forrester a month later.[21]

Gould's confidence seemed to have been reasonable: in October 1908 the pressures on his coal and transportation network were reported to have eased somewhat. The *Advocate* reported: "Ogden Gateway Opened to Carbon County Coal," following a three-year blockage of shipping over the Harriman-controlled Oregon Short Line. An accompanying article noted that the Gould system's Utah coal would still cost more than the competing UPCC product from Wyoming, but it would be cheaper than that mined by independents, due to preferential Rio Grande freight rates. By the following spring, the news leaked out that the Rio Grande had agreed to keep its Utah freight rates high so that UPCC coal could retain competitive pricing in the Utah market, presumably in exchange for the right to pass through Ogden.[22] The differences in freight rates, with their severe impact on Utah's independents, would lead to further accusations against the Gould system by the Sweet family—accusations that paralleled, and colored, ongoing litigation over coal-land fraud.

Meanwhile, public interest shifted from state to state throughout the fall, as related coal land cases received press coverage. In *U.S. v. Diamond Coal and Coke*, the Diamond company's use of soldiers' scrip (certificates issued to soldiers, redeemable in public lands) to purchase five thousand acres of coal land in Uintah County, Wyoming, was being defended by Mark Braffet and John M. Zane (also lawyers for Utah Fuel). The lands themselves had been prospected by Robert Forrester, the company, incorporated in Salt Lake City.[23] Some Utahns accordingly felt that this was one of "their" cases and followed its progress. In Colorado, a week after the Wyoming case began, the government forged an out-of-court settlement with the D&RG's Ute Coal Company, of Gunnison, another of Forrester's acquisitions, a case that had been in the courts since 1906. Originally, Judge Lewis had awarded the government only $5,125 for land it claimed was worth $630,000. On appeal, federal officials settled for $40,000. A second Colorado case ended in October when the attorney general's special assistant for Colorado, Frank K. Hall, asked permission to dismiss another suit against the Utah Fuel Company, pending since June 1907. Hall reported that a man accused of being a dummy was the county attorney of Delta County and "reputed to be worth upwards of $50,000," giving credence to the contention that he had bought the coal land for speculative purposes for a proposed railroad right-of-way that was no longer needed. While the secretary of the interior was being consulted, Hall dismissed the case, only to find the following February, new evidence that seemed to support the allegation of fraud.[24] Hall's premature dismissal of this Colorado case increased the importance of the Utah coal-land cases for government prosecutors.

By the fall of 1908, public interest had shifted to the upcoming presidential contest. In the local papers, news of the November election soon eclipsed that of the coal-land suits. As President Roosevelt had hoped, William Howard Taft, his chosen Republican successor, emerged victorious. However, Roosevelt still had four months left to serve until Taft's inauguration the following March.

A change in administration presaged a possible change in public-lands policy. Accordingly, many people began jockeying for a favorable position based on their own interests in the public domain. Among others, members of Roosevelt's Tennis Cabinet tried to make contingency plans for the assumption that they might stay, even though the Bull Moose would be gone. Gifford Pinchot described a new tenor in his habitual walks with the president, usually accompanied by Interior Secretary Garfield and others.

Until then [the Taft election] we had talked of our work, cabbages and kings, and all sorts of cheerful matters. Now the talk ran mainly to the coming Administration, and what we could possibly do to protect the T. R. policies. We were angry and indignant, and no wonder.

There was, indeed, grave reason for anxiety about the public resources. At the end of T. R.'s Administration large numbers of . . . [acres] had been withdrawn by his order from threatened appropriation by private interests, but they were not yet permanently safe. A President who chose could still turn them over [to Big Business]. . . .

This was also true of rich coal lands.[25]

So Roosevelt's adherents began trying to "safeguard and secure every natural resource that belonged to and ought to remain in the hands of the people of the United States." These worries about the Taft administration presaged a growing split at the highest federal levels. The Roosevelt-Taft differences would eventually break out in the open—over coal.[26]

As Roosevelt completed his last few months in office, the government strengthened its hold on the public domain, first through the judiciary. On December 14, the Supreme Court issued its decision on the Coal Land Act of 1873. Surprisingly (given Burch's predictions to the contrary), the justices ruled that the Coal Land Act could indeed support a criminal charge, sustaining the ruling of Utah's Judge Marshall and reversing that of Denver's Judge Lewis. Federal attorneys were free to continue their prosecutions of intention to defraud by associations that had acquired more than the legal maximum of 640 acres. Although the local newspaper remained surprisingly silent on this event, some astute Utah businessmen evidently took note.[27]

The first of these, LeRoy Eccles, together with an associate, filed a federal coal claim on a contested, state-conveyed school section on December 15, the day after the Supreme Court ruling. Eccles, from a family long active in Utah business circles, realized that if coal land titles obtained from the state were voided by federal litigation, the property in question would have to be legally repurchased from the federal government. Furthermore, coal-mine development ran in his family. Eccles's father, millionaire David Eccles, had already formed his own Utah coal company, in 1907. Originally incorporated as the Wyoming Coal Company, its officers included David Eccles, president, fellow Ogden businessman M. S. Browing, vice president, and Judge Henry H. Rolapp (who had adjudicated the Sunnyside coal-land case,

Holladay v. Kirker, secretary and treasurer. Following in these footsteps, LeRoy Eccles's new interest in the contested "Sweet section," patented by the State of Utah to Arthur A. Sweet the previous July, grew with the possibility of a federal victory. The Sweet school-section case was still pending at the district court level, awaiting action on the Rio Grande suits that involved the same point of law. If the court ruled that Utah had legally achieved ownership, the Sweets had clear title. If not, and the state's—and the Sweets'—ownership were overturned,[28] Eccles wanted to make sure he stood first in line.

The second man to gamble on a federal victory in the Utah coal-land fraud cases, Charles W. Reese, submitted a federal filing on the Huntington Canyon holdings of Walter G. Filer. Most members of the Freed-Robbins-Filer consortium commanded considerable local respect, but not Filer. He had signed the promissory note with the Union Pacific that had led to federal litigation for conspiracy to commit fraud. Even the reserved Burch later described him as a "scalawag." As Charles Freed's son-on-law, he had been part of the family group, but his increasing unpopularity—and, quite possibly, knowledge of his deal with the UP—evidently made his property fair game. The land of the other members of the consortium, however, remained unchallenged.[29]

Meanwhile, the Justice Department made its own adjustments to passing events. In December, the prosecutors in the Utah civil suits rested their case. The court recessed and defense testimony had to wait until the court resumed in March. In the interim, federal attorney Maynard decided to zero in on the Morton Trust Company as the holders of the Pleasant Valley Coal Company bonds. He went to New York to take depositions of its officers for the continuation of the trial.[30] Maynard shortly discovered that Morton Trust officials had put up $2 million for the PVCC. This bank had then sold the bonds to buyers worldwide, who had made their investments believing that the coal company held legal land patents. The bond sale put a new wrinkle in the government's case. If the state patents were set aside, the nation might have to reimburse those who had loaned money for the bonds; alternatively, the government might have to purchase the bonds outright. At the very least, the Justice Department could expect more lengthy, expensive litigation. The financial exigencies of the Panic of 1907 had cut deep. Furthermore, the Roosevelt administration, which had begun these "landmark" cases, would not be in office to conclude them.[31]

Attorney General Bonaparte also reacted to the forthcoming

changing of the guard. In January 1909, he wrote to President Roosevelt explaining the practical difficulties of hiring and paying special anti-fraud investigators to protect the public domain. The Justice Department had so far received no specific enabling legislation from Congress, which made continuity of the investigation teams under the Taft Administration problematical. Nonetheless, as Bonaparte explained, "if it [this group] is maintained by my successor ... it will develop [into] a highly efficient and trustworthy detective agency, maintained at a comparatively moderate cost."[32]

Other concerns about public lands reached the desks of the outgoing administration, many spurred by Roosevelt's sizeable withdrawals. The Utah Board of Land Commissioners, among others, wrote requesting that coal-bearing lands needed for grazing be released, reserving the subsurface coal to the nation. Congress agreed with this view and three weeks later passed a provision to free some of the public domain by an act named for Roosevelt's frequent opponent on many public lands issues, Representative Frank Mondell, of Wyoming.[33]

Signed into law on March 3, 1909, the last day of the Roosevelt administration, the Mondell Act mandated the separation of surface and mineral rights on agricultural land that was later found to contain coal. In such cases, the owner could either relinquish the subsurface rights to the federal government or face litigation in which the government bore the burden of proof that fraud had been committed. In eastern Utah, the Carbon County Land Company and estate of the late Stanley Milner commenced a survey of their lands with an eye toward returning coal rights to the government, after which they could be repurchased at new, higher prices. The local newspaper erroneously speculated that pending federal suits against them would be dropped.[34]

The paper, the *Advocate*, was more accurate in its recapitulation of the significant changes in coal-land pricing to date. First, it noted, the price had been set by distance from the railroad, at either $10 or $20 an acre. Next, after the Roosevelt withdrawals, more than 66 million acres were reopened for sale at a maximum price of $100 per acre. Most recently, as of April 1909, the price had risen to a maximum $300 an acre, based on available tonnage and its valuation. The article labeled this amount "conservative, especially in the Utah district because of the thickness of the beds."[35] Nonetheless, these soaring prices were hardly an incentive for honesty in reporting the presence of coal on "agricultural" lands. The Taft administration would still have to deal with problems of coal-land fraud.

On March 4, 1909, the awaited transfer of power took place, Roosevelt leaving the Oval Office to William Howard Taft. The same day, Taft took the first step that would lead to his rift with Roosevelt: he installed Richard Achilles Ballinger as secretary of the interior, after a year's hiatus in Ballinger's federal service. The selection of Seattle's Ballinger for interior secretary did not bode well for the prosecution of coal-land fraud, nor, ultimately, for the Taft administration. In fact, under Taft, the union of antitrust goals with public-land policy faded rapidly, as can be seen in a 1910 speech given by Taft's new director of the Geological Survey. Speaking to a gathering at the University of Chicago, C. W. Hayes pointed to a "confusion in the minds of certain advocates of conservation ... [that has] confused conservation with the destruction of the trusts." In sharp contrast, he continued, "the logical conservator of our natural resources is the trust."[36]

A measured shift in policy had emerged shortly after Taft's inauguration. As Taft entered office in March 1909, he also replaced Attorney General Bonaparte with George Wickersham. Almost immediately, Wickersham sought a compromise with the Rio Grande's chief attorney for all of the cases then pending against the Utah Fuel Company and the Pleasant Valley Coal Company, implementing plans long under consideration. Concurring in this decision were special attorney Maynard (speaking for himself), the U.S. district attorney for Utah, Hiram Booth, and the local Interior official. The terms mirrored almost exactly the year-old recommendations of chief prosecutor Burch.[37] In waiting for this changing of the guard, the Republicans evaded the charge of compromise with the trusts in an election year. In addition, the action of the Justice Department under Taft left Roosevelt's trust-busting reputation intact.

To smooth the way for the new administration, Burch wrote to Attorney General Wickersham explaining the background of the coal-land cases: ·

> I have thrown in a little historical matter and generally arranged in such a way to make the settlement appear to have been a proper one upon the part of the Secretary [of the Interior] and yourself, and at the same time have it the least worrisome to the defendants that is possible consistent with any newspaper account.[38]

In keeping with political and legal realities, Burch wrote that, under the compromise, the government would be receiving $55 per acre, an amount "more than the price placed upon the same lands by the

Land Department after examination by the Geological Bureau." He supported the company's contention, which he had so recently been fighting in court, that

> while its [the Gould syndicate's] present owners had not been guilty of fraud themselves, they had purchased the entire stock of the company from the parties who originally were alleged to have been guilty . . . [but they were] not morally culpable, and that they would prefer to pay all that the Government asked . . . than have the honesty of their own intentions continued to be litigated in the Federal Court.[39]

After further negotiation, representatives for both sides reached an agreement in April 1909. The Utah Fuel Company paid a total of $200,000 to the federal government: $8,000 of this was in fines for fraud and $192,000 was in damage claims for coal illegally extracted from public lands before completion of the federal survey. The cases in New Jersey and those against individual dummies were dismissed. This action gave the Rio Grande system clear title to all the coal land in litigation, with one exception. The Gould system agreed to reconvey 1,440 acres of undeveloped coal land in Salina Canyon, where its fraud had first been discovered. The company was also required to forfeit the $14,400 paid for this property. With these agreements, the Progressives' so-called landmark Utah coal-land fraud cases ended.[40]

Not all Utah litigation was over, however, just the showy antirailroad suits. The cases against independent developers remained in the courts for years to come. Through these, federal attorneys doggedly pursued local heroes in an attempt to address the abuses of the defective Coal Land Act of 1873.

CHAPTER 11

What Next?

Almost palpable public fury greeted the government's announcement of an out-of-court settlement with the Rio Grande. Utah newspapers reacted as if the trusts had won. Leading the cry, local reporters did their own historical assessment of the coal-land fraud prosecutions in the spring of 1909. First, they faulted the Department of the Interior for allowing patents for coal land to pass as grazing lands. Second, they castigated the attorney general's office for failure to prosecute until the last minute, when only a weak case could be constructed. Finally, they looked at finances. A Salt Lake newspaper published an intriguing balance sheet, claiming: "The figures tell the story of who won the victory." An accompanying table read:

Cost to Uncle Sam

Paid special examiner		$8,000
Paid Special Attorney Maynard		15,000
Paid Special Attorney Burch		15,000
Paid travelling expenses		3,000
Paid special agents		6,000
Paid witnesses		2,000
Paid other expenses		10,000
	Total	59,000
Lands given coal company		5,000,000
	Total	$5,059,000

What Fuel Company Paid

Fine	$8,000
Paid the government	192,000
Land returned government	14,400
Total	$214,400

Balance in favor of coal company $4,844,600.[1]

The same article that reported this uneven exchange and the estoppal of all other criminal prosecutions against the railroad, coal subsidiaries criticised specific government prosecutors. Hiram E. Booth, U.S. attorney for Utah, was singled out as he reportedly made a "hasty departure" for Washington, D.C. There he would allegedly confer with Utah's senators, Smoot and Sutherland, to request their help in further delaying the case against Milner's Carbon County Land Company, with which he had been associated. The newspaper also lashed out at others and the system that employed them:

> These special attorneys from Washington are nearing the end of salary, for the Taft administration appears to be different from that of Roosevelt. ... Ofttimes such failures are wholly to be laid at the hands of the "special assistant" attorney [Maynard], but they are more far reaching. The system [of bringing in such outside attorneys] is bad and the departments at Washington should find a remedy.[2]

Although not noted at the time, Fred Maynard, too, had created unusual expectations in members of the Utah land board, apparently to win their support for the antirailroad cases. Whether or not this understanding would ultimately benefit the state would be decided more than twenty years later.

In the meantime, as Marsden Burch had previously suggested, the Justice Department used its own press connections to report the settlement with Utah Fuel. A laudatory article using a press release and touting "Victory for Local Men" began:

> Through Colonel Hiram E. Booth, United States district attorney for Utah, and Fred A. Maynard, special assistant to the attorney general of the United States, a great victory was won for Uncle Sam yesterday when the criminal and civil suits, known as the Utah Fuel Coal Fraud cases, were settled. Their work nets the government about $315,000.[3]

The article continued that the criminal charges against individuals, including Robert Forrester, had been dropped. The Salina Canyon lands were incorrectly valued at $15,400, although the other figures remained the same. After outlining the history of the litigation, the article incorrectly added that "one coal case remains on the docket in Utah—United States against Don C. Robbins, Walter G. Filer, Charles M. Freed and Edwin W. Senior." The Milner (Carbon County Land Company) case, which had occasioned so much Utah comment, and the Sweet case, also pending, were completely overlooked. In conclusion, the flattering article referred to more than eleven thousand typewritten pages of evidence alone, exemplifying the years of hard work performed by government attorneys:

So well have the cases been prepared that unconditional surrender was the only possible course for the accused company and its officials. The state and the nation are richer for the victory. And men who seek to acquire government land fraudulently have received another sermon on the text: "Don't!"[4]

That account sounded wonderful. The truth differed.

Privately, federal officials must have been rattled by the virulent public outcry over the negotiated settlement of these Utah coal land cases. Almost immediately, some individuals began considering new litigation. In mid-April, a short two weeks after his optimistic press release, Burch received a thought-provoking letter from Maynard. In reviewing notes left by Interior Agent Lamoreaux, Maynard had noted that, although the out-of-court settlement had effectively estopped further litigation against cited lands held by the accused firms, individual dummies were still liable to prosecution. Furthermore, since the Utah Fuel Company had neglected to request that the negotiated settlement cover all its coal lands in Utah, new indictments could also be filed on unlitigated parcels. But again, a statute of limitations loomed: certain suspect lands would pass beyond litigation the following month. At least, Maynard concluded, he had the old bills in equity to use as precedents, should Burch and his superiors approve renewed prosecution.[5]

Burch wanted to stay out of the fray. He forwarded Maynard's letter to the new attorney general, Wickersham, who concurred with Maynard. However, Wickersham specifically stated his "desire to recover the lands, if possible, without suit, and, so far as may be, without publicity." No one in federal circles wanted to admit publicly that the original coal-land cases were not a complete government victory.[6]

Lacking knowledge of a federal reevaluation, the Rio Grande system turned to internal housecleaning, with emphasis on the previously expanded legal department. Company officials, obeying an "expressed desire to curtail expenses," promoted seven-year veteran Utah Fuel attorney Mark Braffet to general counsel for Utah and Colorado. His new duties, listed in an April 1909 company directive, included overseeing

all matters in relation to lands, water rights, etc. in Utah . . . [maintaining] the more or less intimate relations necessarily existing between [Carbon] County officials and the Legal Department of the Company . . . [and] looking after the political interests of the Company in Carbon County . . . [including] aiding such County officials in regulating such liquor traffic in and about the Company's camps.[7]

In a single move, Braffet had become virtually king of Carbon County, heart of eastern Utah's coal district. His arrogant abuse of power would only increase the number of the railroad's enemies—and his own.[8]

First, Braffet had to help head off new, unexpected, federal suits. Shortly after his promotion he had to answer the latest charges quietly brought by the federal government against alleged dummy entries done for Pleasant Valley Coal and Utah Fuel. In April and May 1909, the government prepared two more bills in equity against the Utah Fuel Company and the Morton Trust Company, seeking reconveyance of fraudulently obtained coal land. Responding to letters from Maynard and Burch, the attorney general had approved these bills, embracing 1441.57 acres claimed by dummy entrants at $20 an acre, but now valued at over $72,000. After the bills were filed, Lamoreaux uncovered further abuse of the dummy system, exemplified by the actions of Fannie C. Bird (now Mrs. Sterling), a daughter of the late William Bird, formerly "Land Attorney of the Utah Fuel Company." She had claimed school sections near Castle Gate now valued at over $81,000, and had apparently never transferred them to another, although the Utah Fuel records indicated they were company property subject to taxation. Bird's wife had also obtained two nearby school sections: these she had subsequently conveyed to other parties, who transferred one to the Utah Fuel Company and the other to PVCC. (As Maynard noted, Utah Fuel owned all the stock in the PVCC.) Maynard had also demanded the reconveyance of these lands, noting: "So far as the School Section lands are concerned we shall of course encounter the legal question peculiar to said lands."[9] Although the Justice Department was still emphasizing litigation brought under the Coal Land Act of 1873, charging a criminal conspiracy to defraud the government to obtain less than its legally mandated maximum acreage, the knotty problem of the school lands and its attendant difficulties of federal-state relations quietly festered.

Maynard noted another body of unlitigated lands near Sunnyside, comprising 2044.98 acres and valued at more than $102,000 by the Taff survey. Forrester had been deeded these lands by another daughter of William Bird, and by his own mother, and he insisted they were his private property. Maynard discounted this view, saying: "It does not seem likely that the company would allow such a large tract of valuable coal lands to be purchased by Forrester, nor that Forrester would buy them, when he knew that the only practical way ... [to work them] would be through the [Utah Fuel] company's tunnels." Maynard recommended commencing a suit if Forrester refused to reconvey them to the government, stating it should list both Forrester and Utah Fuel as defendants. Maynard concluded that Lamoreaux felt he had now uncovered all of the coal-land fraud perpetrated by the Rio Grande system within the period covered by the statute of limitations.[10]

The threat of these new federal suits came as a surprise to Utah Fuel. The company's chief counsel, Joel Vaile, had gone to Europe. His substitute, John Zane, "threw up his hands [at the notice of alleged fraud] and suggested settlement, saying that they desired to close out every kind of trouble of that kind in which the company is or might be involved." Burch, alerted by Maynard to the possibilities for new federal litigation, submitted his own, detailed "memorandum for the Attorney General." In it, he asserted that the discoveries already detailed by Maynard were "probably the limit in that State [Utah]." He was wrong. Braffet knew this all too well, and later, with his insider's knowledge of unlitigated parcels, he would make things very hot for the Rio Grande system. For the moment, though, Burch concluded his report. He felt that Interior Secretary Ballinger would be invited to the proceedings, "although that Department has in no sense been connected with these discoveries . . . and could only claim such right [to be present] by reason of their supervisory control of the public lands."[11] The earlier interagency friction had apparently survived the change of presidential administration.

In replying to these new allegations of coal-land fraud, Zane and Braffet, acting for both Utah Fuel and the PVCC, contended that the lands in question could not be proven to contain coal, therefore the legality or illegality of their sale as school sections would be the subject of long litigation. They offered to reconvey to the United States specific plots totaling eight hundred acres not under mortgage, and pay half the current assessed valuation, or $73,000, for the rest. They also explicitly requested clear title to "a few scattered tracts of small dimensions" also owned by the two companies, thus ending once and for all litigation on Utah coal lands. The government rejected this last request and began preparing suits against dummies for these "isolated" parcels, including Forrester's wife, his mother, and Owen. At the same time, Forrester himself, along with six others, was bound over for trial for coal-land fraud in Colorado.[12]

A few days after his latest proposal, Maynard discovered yet another chink in the armor of the Rio Grande system. Referring to his earlier examination of witnesses and of the pertinent law, Maynard reported: "I have reached the conclusion that the United States had a legal claim against the predecessors in the interest of the Utah Fuel

Company, namely, George Foster Peabody, Royal C. Peabody, D. C. Dodge, the estate of William J. Palmer, deceased, William G. Sharp, William F. Colton, and others." He requested a special appointment from the attorney general to prosecute this claim. He was after bigger fish than the individual dummy claimants of Utah's state selections.[13]

In response, Attorney General Wickersham offered Maynard the desired official appointment as his special assistant. Maynard was empowered to draw up bills in equity against all the officials he had identified. Yet the complications of earlier litigation and the still unclear nature of the public-land laws in general, and the Coal Land Act of 1873 in particular, meant that constructing a case would take some time. Fortunately, this time, no statute of limitations hung over the proceedings. The government enjoyed the luxury of being able to go at a deliberate pace, so sorely lacking in the original Utah coal-land suits.[14]

A day later, on June 30, Wickersham wrote to Maynard empowering him to institute—and promptly settle—the proposed suit in equity against the kin of Forrester, Bird, and others. When the Utah Federal District Court met on July 26, Maynard carried out these instructions to the letter. Within fifteen minutes, at the request Maynard's colleague, Utah federal district attorney Hiram Booth, Judge Marshall issued a dismissal. Booth accepted a check for $73,000 from the attorneys for Utah Fuel, the exact sum proposed a month earlier by Braffet and Zane. Two other suits against individual dummies were concurrently dismissed by order of Attorney General Wickersham, who reiterated that

> there will be no prejudice in bringing other suits to recover title to lands, to compel the company to pay the government for coal extracted or in criminal actions, which may result in the cases of any other lands held or claimed by the government.[15]

A few months later, these reconveyed lands were resold by the national government for an additional $5 an acre, bringing far less than their supposed valuation. Nonetheless, the Justice Department enjoyed an improved reputation.[16]

The results of coal-land litigation in Utah contrasted dramatically with federal fortunes in Wyoming. There, in 1907, the Justice Department had successfully achieved reconveyance of lands claimed by the Union Pacific without a trial due to the UP's reluctance to enter into a court action. In July 1909, the sale of these coal lands on the open market brought more than $7.5 million into the federal treasury.[17]

Also that July, Utah journalists published an expose of "two factions after prospective lands between Castle Gate and Sunnyside"—the Rio Grande system and the Milner-Gilson consortium. Although the Milner case was being continued for another term of the court, local sentiment, antirailroad but proindependent, clearly favored a dismissal.[18] The federal government seemed destined for few future successes in Utah.

Another Utah coal-land contest, of seminal importance, ended in October 1909. The confrontation that had allegedly started federal investigation of Utah Fuel's dummying, *Albert L. Simons v. Owen L. Davies*, reached final settlement in a civil hearing at the Interior Department. After four years of controversy, the Secretary of the Interior upheld Simons's contention that Davies was a Rio Grande dummy, and canceled his entry.[19] This additional available acreage in Salina Canyon excited few people, however. No railroad existed to tap the deposits, and they were virtually worthless without one. Since the Rio Grande system had just reconveyed the rest of its Salina Canyon lands, it would not build a line there; neither would Harriman, now controlling the fortunes of the WP and San Pedro, which competed with his own Union Pacific. For a long time, these once-coveted lands remained undeveloped.

Still contemplating new ways to attack the Rio Grande system, Maynard wrote to Burch: "I have been daily expecting to hear from you . . . concerning the proposed suit of the United States vs. the Palmer Estate et al." In the meantime, Maynard had also been reviewing "the conspiracy case of the United States vs. Filer, Freed, Senior and Robbins." Noting that the case was due to go to trial in November, he was "most reluctantly forced to the conclusion that this case should be *nolle prossed* [prosecuted no further] solely on the ground of our inability to establish the conspiracy charge in the indictment."[20] Once again, government attorneys were seeking a remedy under the unworkable Coal Land Act of 1873, which had engendered so much fraud in the first place. And, once again, a legal precedent from a successful prosecution seemed to be eluding them.

Continuing his explanation, Maynard bleakly admitted: "Not one person have we been able to find who will give direct testimony tending to show the formation of the conspiracy. All of the witnesses who know of the transaction would be unwilling, adverse, and hostile." Yet since these lands had not yet proceeded to patent, the government could achieve their reconveyance and a forfeiture of the purchase price with a civil process through the General Land Office and the secretary of the interior. A lengthy, expensive, and probably futile court procedure could thus be avoided.[21]

The standard of success was still the Utah Fuel Company cases. As Maynard explained, by following the civil procedure "we could thereby obtain practically all that we obtained in the cases against the Utah Fuel Company, that is so far as the individual defendants were concerned." Furthermore, "having recently dismissed the indictment[s] against the individual defendants in the Utah Fuel Company case, who were all prominent and some of them rich men, . . . we would continually be confronted with the question, 'Why does the Government release rich individual defendants and insist upon prosecuting a poor broken down man like Robbins, or . . . Senior who were [sic] only connected with the case in a professional way[?']" He was very concerned that the government have "a good case to present to the public and in no way weaken the profound respect that the people generally now have for the laws relating to coal lands," which he had worked so hard to uphold despite their numerous admitted flaws. Others in the Justice Department concurred in Maynard's assessment, and the criminal case against the Freed consortium was dismissed at the same time the proposed civil action was begun.[22]

These changes elicited a sigh of relief from Burch. He began an interoffice memorandum by saying, "I was never quite satisfied with the indictments in the case," and he went on to cite his reasons: First, the suit had begun when there was "great zeal upon the part of both the Interior Department and the White House for the prosecution of such offenses" which tended to sway grand juries. Second, there had never been any chance of convicting Robbins and Senior. Most importantly, Burch admitted, "it was through Mr. Robbins' statements to a newspaper man and that man's statements to me that the first [Utah] coal land frauds were discovered and pushed, which has led to the final saving . . . of the coal lands of the United States to the Government and all the good results which we have seen." Furthermore, attorney Senior had encouraged Burch, offered him "warm sympathy," and even provided him with a brief at a time when "everything was nebulous and uncertain as to result." Filer, on the other hand, was a "scalawag who got his father-in-law, Freed, a wealthy Jew, and the various members of his family" involved. The only regret Burch had regarding the dismissal was "a fusillade of venom [which] will be indulged in by the Salt Lake Tribune," which would have equally condemned the government for unjust prosecution had the case been allowed to continue. Yet Burch resignedly suggested acceptance, in advance, of this probable tirade. Once again, government officials remained acutely conscious of public opinion as expressed in the press.[23]

The decision to substitute a civil hearing for a criminal action brought a howl from Don Robbins. He caustically observed in the local press that Maynard was simply trying to bolster his own image, so tarnished by the outcome of the Utah Fuel cases. Robbins intimated that pursuing hapless independents was just a political ploy, a view that seemed justified when the government lost in the initial hearing in 1911 and was forced to appeal the case to the commissioners of the General Land Office.[24]

Additional difficulties faced by the Justice Department resulted from a new, formal procedure instituted under Taft. For example, Interior Secretary Ballinger had to write to Attorney General Wickersham stating that—although the two men had been professionally associated for years—Interior's agent, George Hair, had requested the assistance of Maynard, of the Justice Department, in prosecuting the Freed-Robbins case. Ballinger added, in a tremendous understatement: "Mr. Maynard has expressed willingness to appear as attorney for the government in the hearings before the local land office and render assistance to Chief of Field Division Hair." The close, informal intra-agency cooperation of the Utah Fuel cases disintegrated as agency heads instituted more and more red tape.[25]

Hair needed Maynard's assistance to deal with the Utah Board of Land Commissioners. In December, the board president wrote to Hair explicitly reiterating his refusal to reconvey to the nation some mineral land already sold by the state. He relied for his authority on Maynard's remarks:

> The conditions under which this land was selected and sold are the same as governing the land included in the agreement entered into between the [former] State Board of Land Commissioners and Attorney Maynard for the United States, and it will be necessary for the United States to institute proper proceedings to determine the allegation that the land was known to be mineral land, more valuable for mineral than agricultural purposes, before the State acquired title thereto.[26]

This was the most forceful statement to date of the state's position on the federal-state conflict over who would control mineral-bearing school sections. More than two decades would pass before this issue was ultimately decided.

Maynard himself was apparently unaware of the difficulties he had caused in his first attempt to get Utah's cooperation in prosecuting the Rio Grande system. He continued with his new plans against railroad officials, bringing them to completion in December 1909. Working at leisure on proposed indictments, he reviewed litigation to date for his new Justice Department superior, Assistant Attorney General Ernest Knaebel, now head of the Division of Land Fraud. Still unwilling to give up on the Rio Grande, Maynard explained the basis for another new suit. First, he had to outline the complex corporate network used by the Rio Grande system to acquire western coal lands, including the interlocking directorates of the railroad, the Rio Grande Western Construction Company, and the Utah coal subsidiaries. The Gould interests, as the ultimate purchasers of the Rio Grande system, had been the object of earlier suits. Maynard contended that the initial owners of the D&RG Railway—Palmer, Dodge, et al—had not been affected by the suits against the Goulds. Second, he asserted that it was since the incorporation of the Utah Fuel Company, in 1900, that the original bills in equity had provided corporate indemnity for coal taken from the lands. He believed that the government could still go to court over the money owed it for coal illegally mined before that date. Third, the PVCC could also be made party to a new federal suit, because illegally mined coal from Sunnyside had been mingled with its Winter Quarters production. The size of this theft particularly bothered Maynard. As he wrote to Knaebel:

> At present I have no proof before me of the exact number of tons of coal extracted during these years [before federal survey], but have good reason to believe that the exact tonnage appears in the books of the Pleasant Valley Coal Co., and that it will appear there that 352,000 tons were taken from said lands while they were unsurveyed public lands of the United States, and were mingled with the coal produced from their other mines, operated under the name of the Pleasant Valley Coal Company.[27]

In this instance, Maynard insisted, the statute of limitations had no bearing, for it applied only to land titles and not to coal removed from the land. After citing his success in recently obtaining $73,000 for the government and several similar suits as precedents, Maynard stated: "The conclusion I have reached [is] that the suit above authorized by the Attorney General should be commenced at once."[28]

By a coincidence, Burch, formerly the senior prosecutor of the western coal-land cases, was in Knaebel's office when Maynard's letter arrived. He tried to fill in some details of the Utah coal-land cases, but Knaebel still remained unclear as to whether the Construction Company, dissolved in 1901 by its incorporating agreement, or the PVCC was to blame for illegal coal removal. Knaebel wrote back to Maynard, who replied that the Construction Company had first owned all the stock in the Pleasant Valley Coal Company, which was later acquired by Utah Fuel, and that "the Palmer, Peabody crowd managed and controlled both companies and actively, as individuals, directed all of the movements of both and participated in the spoils." In other words, according to Maynard, the PVCC, or the old Western, or both, could be liable.[29]

Despite Maynard's assurances, others at the federal level harbored doubts. Maynard received a letter fully a month later expressing concerns with his proposed suits. Beginning with an apology for the delayed reply, the writer (supposed by Maynard to be Knaebel) stated:

> Judge Burch and I, after full consideration, agreed that it would not do to join the Pleasant Valley Coal Company in the proposed litigation, and this, without any question, is the attitude the Attorney-General has expressed.[30]

Maynard replied that, given this decision, PVCC officers Sharp and Colton could not be considered for prosecution. This apparent agreement dissolved with a sharp rebuke administered by Knaebel, who wrote: "I do not know [why] ... Sharp and Colton were not to be prosecuted. ... It would seem to me ... that there could be no objection raised under the [earlier] compromise agreement to the prosecution of these men." Maynard then defended his position by citing recently received correspondence, including the paragraph quoted above, discussing the concurrence of Judge Burch and the attorney general. However, since Knaebel had not signed the letter, and denied initialling it (as Maynard thought he did), his support was indeed in doubt.[31]

In a conciliatory vein, Maynard continued his letter with a discussion of pending federal cases in Colorado (against the late William Jackson Palmer and David C. Dodge) and in New York (against George Foster Peabody), officers of the first Denver and Rio Grande corporation, based in Colorado. He ended: if "you still think suits should be brought against Sharp and Colton, they can be brought at any time, and I shall of course comply with your wishes." Despite this friendly tone, confusion reigned at the Justice Department over the coal-land fraud cases.[32]

CHAPTER 12

Questions of Culpability

Throughout the fall of 1909, Fred Maynard may have wondered about the confused reception that his ideas for new Rio Grande system prosecutions were receiving in the Justice Department. The fact was, the attorney general was distracted: Wickersham was caught up in the greatest scandal to so far hit the Taft administration—the alleged Alaskan coal-land fraud.

A familiar scenario began as well-heeled businessmen zeroed in on Alaska's extensive Cunningham coal-land claims. Atypically, however, these transactions had allegedly been facilitated by Richard Ballinger, once a Seattle attorney and now secretary of the interior. The chief of the General Land Office field agents, Louis R. Glavis, publicized the event when the original consortium allegedly offered the Cunningham claims to the huge Morgan-Guggenheim "trust." During the summer of 1909, Glavis contacted unresponsive Interior Secretary Ballinger; then he turned to Gifford Pinchot on the basis that these lands might be more valuable as a national forest. Glavis also prepared a report for President Taft, who discussed it with Ballinger and Justice Department officials, including Attorney General Wickersham. In September, Taft publicly exonerated Ballinger and authorized the firing of Glavis, on the basis of "unjustly impeaching the official integrity of his superior officers." Had it not been for publicity, the issue might have ended there. In November 1909, however, *Collier's* magazine published Glavis's report under a front-page cartoon of Ballinger in the grasp of the Guggenheims. Enraged, the public nationally demanded a thorough congressional investigation.[1]

Under these circumstances, Attorney General Wickersham paid scant attention to Maynard's work on the newest Rio Grande coal-land cases. Worsening overall communications and the increasing distractedness of the attorney general colored further letters Maynard received. In January 1910, as the congressional investigation into the Cunningham claims began, Wickersham rejected Colorado as a forum for further anti–D&RG cases, suggesting instead that the suits "will

lie only in the respective districts where the defendents reside." As
Maynard already knew, however, this reasoning meant that the cases
would be heard in Colorado.[2]

As Maynard had originally conceived the case, perhaps trying for
another hearing before the friendly Judge John Marshall, the complaint
of theft of illegally mined Sunnyside coal would have included the
assertion that it had been mingled with the production of the legally
acquired Pleasant Valley Coal Company. Then, both former PVCC
manager William Sharp and former PVCC president William F.
Colton would have been included among the defendants.[3] At the
attorney general's suggestion, however, allegations involving the
PVCC, Sharp, and Colton had been eliminated from the case, and
with them the possibility of a Utah venue. All the other defendants—
Palmer, Peabody, and Dodge—lived outside Utah, in New York or,
regrettably, in Colorado.

Federal attorneys took a dim view of the Colorado courts. As
one lamented:

> I do feel that to try the case there [Colorado] would be unfortunate
> if not suicidal; leaving out of consideration the attitude which Judge
> Lewis has so often showed towards prosecutions concerning the
> public lands, . . . [there are problems with the County of Denver.
> The jury there] may be constituted of independent farmers; but
> frequently they are drawn from among 'business men,' and you
> know what that means in Colorado.[4]

Amid these difficulties, federal officials doggedly constructed their
case. Maynard wrote to Ernest Knaebel with news of their progress.
A possible witness had offered Maynard the PVCC account books for
$10,000 and protection from having to testify—an offer Maynard
rejected. He felt that he already had most of the facts and, considering
that the attorney general himself earned only $12,000 annually, must
have been happy to forego the expense. Maynard also reported to
Knaebel the possibility of a compromise in the Palmer-Peabody cases,
ending "Ever Your Friend."[5]

Similar investigations in Colorado uncovered much Utah Fuel
Company land fraud there. Special agents had identified twenty
dummy entries, totaling 3,040 acres, worth more than $3 million,
along the north fork of the Gunnison River, where the Rio Grande
system had beaten out John D. Rockefeller's Colorado Fuel and Iron
Company by buying out a dummy association. As in Utah, the dummies had deeded the land to Robert Forrester, who had passed it

on to the Utah Fuel Company. Although the agents recommended prosecution, action had to await the approval of the attorney general, who was out of the office testifying on the Alaskan coal-land frauds.[6]

Not only did the Alaskan scandal slow the work of the Justice Department, it profoundly affected Congress. In the House, a revolt against the Speaker, Joe Cannon, resulted when insurgent Republican George Norris (Nebraska) insisted that members of the joint congressional investigating committee be elected, not appointed by the Speaker. As a result, no subsequent Speaker has equaled Cannon's early strength. In the Senate, Utah's George Sutherland's star rose as he chaired the joint congressional investigating committee. His strong partisan support for the Republican Taft administration would result in later political rewards—specifically, an appointment to the Supreme Court.[7]

Congressional action failed to allay the fears of those convinced of the administration's complicity in the Cunningham claims scandal. Gifford Pinchot, for one, felt compelled to attack Interior Secretary Ballinger in print. President Taft had already warned Pinchot of possible repercussions. When Taft first exonerated Ballinger, he wrote to Pinchot "to urge that you do not make Glavis's case yours." Taft, concerned that Pinchot's "hasty action" on behalf of Glavis or his objection to Ballinger's continuance in office might lead to his "withdrawing from the public service," added: "I should consider it one of the greatest losses my administration could sustain if you were to leave it."[8] But Taft would brook no insubordination.

Taft had been aware of Pinchot's views at least as far back as 1909, when the editor of the influential *Outlook* magazine told him in a letter: "Gifford Pinchot [spoke] to me the other day concerning Dick Ballinger: "I couldn't work with him as I have with Jim [Interior Secretary Garfield]. . . . Ballinger and I might clash."[9] When Pinchot published his opinions at the height of the Cunningham claims outcry, their differences became unreconcilable. So Taft fired him, opening an unbridgeable gulf between himself and Roosevelt, the former president. The Republican Party, the political home of both men, would never be the same.[10]

In retrospect, this controversy also affected public-land policies in general. A later historian asserted that "there was something frenzied and pathetic in Pinchot's anger. . . . [The conflict] had, in effect, relegated conservation a position secondary to revenge upon Interior."[11] Pinchot's grudge endured for more than a quarter of a century, surfacing again when a new Interior Secretary, Harold Ickes, described his predecessor as "not guilty."[12] In this vituperative atmosphere, federal prosecution of state and corporate coal-land fraud was vitiated.

Despite the difficulties arising for future trust-busting litigation, the past federal coal-land cases figured prominently in the Alaskan investigation. Congress subpoenaed all of the papers in the Utah Fuel Company cases, but when informed of the immense volume of material involved, allowed attorneys to winnow the pile. This material fueled questioning by Louis Brandeis, Glavis's attorney and later Supreme Court justice. Brandeis eventually implied not only Ballinger's involvement, but that of Attorney General Wickersham and President Taft as well. For some members of Congress, this insinuation went too far. Utah's Senator George Sutherland lashed out: "To inquire into this is an insult to the President, and I, for one, do not propose to be a party to it." In the final Senate committee vote of June 1910, a partisan tally sustained Ballinger's innocence, seven to five, yet failed to resolve permanently the larger land-fraud issues raised.[13]

Congress, now free of the investigation, began to address head-on the dual problem of monopolistic carriers and coal-land ownership. Each arm of this western coal-land stranglehold was soon more closely regulated. First, on June 18, 1910, Congress passed the Mann-Elkins Act, extending the powers granted to the Interstate Commerce Commission under the Hepburn Act. It established a commerce court to review infractions of the body of interstate commerce law, and reemphasized that no railroad company could transport "any article or commodity, other than timber and the manufactured products thereof, manufactured, mined, or produced by it." Violations carried the threat of fines and imprisonment. Additionally, the new commerce court possessed the power to set railroad rates—discretion that could deprive the Rio Grande—among other railroads—of its most lucrative role in coal development.[14] In areas where railroads held a transportation monopoly, such as in eastern Utah's coal district, they could literally charge all that the traffic would bear.

Two days later, Congress passed an act that provided for exclusively agricultural entries on coal lands. This solved some of the problems caused by federal withdrawal of mineral land desired by ranchers, but was far from the promulgation of a national mineral-land statute. Furthermore, the exorbitant coal-land price went untouched. Newly reclassified coal land in Utah, relinquished by the Rio Grande, jumped in price from $50 to $300 and acre by June 1910. Under these circumstances, only large corporations could afford to buy it. In Carbon County, an immediate response to these changes came in an editorial:

"The chances for a poor man to own a coal mine has [*sic*] just about passed." Furthermore, even wealthy capitalists had to band together to claim enough federal acreage for a commercial venture, as the unrealistic 640-acre limitation set by the Coal Land Act of 1873 remained in effect. Thus, the standing statute still invited fraud.[15]

Congress refused to consider further reform, even as members of the executive branch struggled with the administration of the defective coal-land law. The beleaguered Ballinger wrote to President Taft in June 1910 in support of the congressional restoration of agricultural, coal-bearing land. At the same time, he drew the president's attention to the persistent problem of overlapping jurisdiction in administrative law agencies and the national judicial system: "Inasmuch as action by the courts is not taken in some cases until long after the decision of the department has been rendered, unusual hardship frequently results in those cases where the decision of the department is not upheld by the courts."[16] Ballinger proposed a logical solution: congressional intervention: "Legislation [requested would] . . . in a few years establish a system of public land law, backed by a court of recognized standing."[17] As sensible as this proposition may have seemed, the desired cooperation long failed to materialize.

Meanwhile, death resolved some ongoing western coal-land suits. At the end of December, a newspaper headline announced: "Robert Forrester Dead." The Rio Grande geologist, target of a number of federal actions, had succumbed to stomach cancer at his home in Seattle. His wife and Dr. Andrew Dowd, long-time Sunnyside physician, were with him. A number of lengthy obituaries eulogized him: "one of the best known geologists in the United States" and "a very bright man." The impressive list of his coal-mine developments included the Sunnyside, Somerset, Castle Gate, Clear Creek and Winter Quarters mines of the Utah Fuel Company, the Diamond Coal and Coke Company of Wyoming, the Morrison mine of the Sterling Coal and Coke Company, Perrin Peak mine of the Calumet Fuel Company, and the Home Fuel mine at Coalville.[18] In death, Forrester's method in obtaining these mines—his frequent role as "agent" for company dummies—was tactfully overlooked. With his demise, a number of federal cases, including the only one filed against Rio Grande operatives in the Territory of New Mexico, abruptly ended.

A few months earlier, in July 1910, Arthur A. Sweet had also died. A later publication eulogized his "progressive spirit . . . and . . . constructive character, far-reaching and resultant." It also claimed his demise was due to "a nervous breakdown occasioned by unremitting attention to his many and complex business interests,"[19] not the least of which was fending off a federal coal-land fraud indictment.

One of Arthur's older brothers, attorney Frederick A. Sweet, then assumed control of the family companies, not only their legal affairs. Some doubt apparently existed about Fred's business acumen, as reported in the press when the senior family members toured the works at Hiawatha.

> Both [parents] realize that the undertaking was a big one for him to handle; but F.A. is the right kind of a man to handle big propositions. He will bring the investment phase of the company out well, not only for himself, but for other members of the company.[20]

To contrast with the New Mexico case of *United States v. Forrester*, where an individual had allegedly acted alone, Arthur A. Sweet had had business associates. Consequently, the suit against Arthur Sweet was converted into one against the administrator of his estate, his

Sizeable spread of equipment at Hiawatha, Utah, represents a considerable capital investment and helps explain the prevalence of coal-land fraud under the Coal Land Act of 1873. This complex was the second commercial coal development of the Sweet family, done under the names of Consolidated Fuel Company and Southern Utah Railroad Company. In the background can be seen the tipple and high tramway. Courtesy of the Western Mining and Railroad Museum, Helper, Utah.

brother and partner, Frederick. Perhaps acting under the assumption that only widespread litigation could resolve the linked problems of coal-land exploitation and freight discrimination, attorney Fred Sweet, backed by his two remaining brothers, decided to file his own complaint. He shortly took on the entire western railroad network.

Fred Sweet's challenge to the West's transportation giants grew out of his holdings on the Black Hawk coal vein, along Miller Creek, including the school section still disputed in federal courts. There, the Sweets' company town of Hiawatha and its attendant mines in the Black Hawk vein were run by the Consolidated Fuel Company, a second Sweet enterprise begun after they sold out of Kenilworth in 1908. The development, due to its remoteness, suffered heavily from the Rio Grande's rail transportation monopoly in eastern Utah. Not only did independents like the Sweets pay more for haulage than the railroad's own mines, but the D&RG always made sure its own mines got sufficient cars before supplying any to its competitors, virtually controlling its opponents' production. The Rio Grande also refused to establish through rates from the mines on the Black Hawk vein, instead charging for transshipping at Price. The impending completion of a new D&RG affiliate, the Western Pacific, could only heighten this competition.[21]

But the Sweets had a new statute to work with: the recently passed Mann-Elkins Act. Consequently, in January 1911, Fred Sweet, on behalf of his family's Consolidated Fuel Company, filed a complaint with the Interstate Commerce Commission against the D&RG and twenty-five other railroads. Nearby Castle Valley Coal Company joined the complaint, alleging that, although they had invested large sums in coal-mine development and had reached sizeable commercial production quotas, railroad shipping agreements had created an unfair rate structure. Carrying charges favored Wyoming coal, which effectively eliminated Utah shippers from much of the natural market territory in the West. Specifically, they complained that "the present established freight rates on all classes of coal from said Utah Mining District . . . to the cities, towns and stations in California and Nevada, . . . which provides for a higher charge that $5.15 per ton of 2,000 lbs., are unjust, unlawful, unreasonable and discriminatory."[22]

Within eighteen months, a large number of western shippers had joined this suit. The first of these, joining in the spring of 1911, were the League of Southern Idaho Commercial Clubs and the Hay Dealers' Association of Los Angeles, California. That fall, the Sweets' former company, Independent Coal and Coke, added its name, followed by the Compton Coal Company of Idaho in June 1912. As an undated, handwritten memo at the end of the docket reported: "This is what you might call 'A Haymaker.' . . . If it only don't rain and we ever get it in the Barn."[23]

This suit helped enhance the Sweets' business reputation in Utah. Further accolades came in March 1911, when Orem's *Weekly Bulletin* (published simultaneously in Salt Lake City and Boston) issued two consecutive issues featuring the Consolidated Fuel Company and its town of Hiawatha. Next, Will C. Higgins, editor of the *Salt Lake Mining Review*, published the "Success of the Consolidated Fuel Company" in April 1911. The following month, the same journal reported a visit to Hiawatha by more than sixty Salt Lake businessmen, including Utah's former governor, Heber M. Wells, editor Higgins, and directors of Utah's banks and major industries, including an associate of the Eccles interests.[24] All of this publicity had a distinctly promotional flavor.

The economic potential of the Black Hawk district proved increasingly alluring, especially if fairly priced rail transportation could be secured as a result of the Sweet's suit against the Rio Grande. As ICC hearings began on alleged freight-rate discrimination, other entrepreneurs swept onto the Black Hawk vein. For example, in May 1911, a new company, Black Hawk Coal, incorporated under Daniel Heiner, president, and a board of directors that included Ogden capitalists M. S. Browning, Judge H. H. Rolapp (who had presided over the *Holladay v. Kirker* case), and David Eccles, all former coal-development associates. A second consortium, the Castle Valley Coal Company (one of the plaintiffs in the ICC case), built the town of Mohrland to the south, just over the Emery County line. The town name came from the owners' initials, M O H R—James H. Mays; A. J. Orem; Moroni Heiner (son of Daniel); and Windsor V. Rice. They also had been previously associated with Ogden businessmen Browning and Eccles. By June, both Orem's *Bulletin* and the *Salt Lake Mining Review* lauded Mohrland and the Castle Valley Coal Company with praise similar to that accorded Consolidated Fuel.[25] However, these articles delicately circled the details of coal-land acquisitions.

A new emphasis on the law colored the usual promotional praise in these articles. For example, one extended "thanks to the inter-state commerce law" for allowing independents to enter Utah's coalfields— presumably by weakening the Rio Grande's transportation monopoly. In regard to coal-land acquisition, the articles seemed disingenuous. Since both the Castle Valley and Mohrland companies had obtained their land from the state, it was essential to establish that these lands were not known to contain coal at statehood. Consequently, one article stressed "real red blood," "the spirit of sport," and the ideals of Rudyard Kipling in explaining why former mining associates had entered on this vein. Ignoring the nearby Bear Canyon Mine (described by none other than Robert Forrester when he served as U.S. Mine Inspector for Utah Territory in 1892), the article claimed that the Castle Valley holdings had been discovered by "two twentieth century sports enthusiasts who penetrated the wilds of Cedar Creek in quest of big game ... James H. Mays and Moroni Heiner."[26] The Bear Canyon mine was thus transformed into the animal itself. The Coal Land Act of 1873, or its probable enforcement, apparently commanded new respect.

The Secretary of the Interior, too, showed an increased interest in this old law. In a public policy statement presented to Congress in mid-1910, he responded to a protest by Frank Mondell (Wyoming), who had charged that "prices fixed by the government [on coal land] were prohibitive, that they paralyzed the coal industry in the West, resulted in increasing the cost of coal for the consumer ... and created a monopoly." Disagreeing, the secretary argued that the current high price of coal acreage was designed "to prevent monopoly by making it unprofitable to purchase large areas for indefinite holding without development." Echoing a more and more common refrain, he also suggested a federal leasing law, such as those once adopted by Australia, New Zealand, and Canada's Yukon Territory.[27] Western congressmen, fearful of federal control over their land, wealth, and resources, again ignored this suggestion.

Federal power increased in another way, however—in prosecution of land fraud. Justice Department attorney Fred Maynard and others now had more time to proceed against coal-land fraud, thanks to a reinterpretation of the six-year statute of limitations on prosecution. Earlier, the six years had begun to run when the fraud was committed, forcing the haste so detrimental to the original Utah coal-land cases. Now, the statute was ruled to take effect from the time the fraud was discovered, prolonging the time allowed to proceed against Palmer, Peabody, Dodge, et al., among others.[28]

The beginning of 1911 brought a new flurry of interest in coal-land fraud. Pinchot decided once more to speak for the record, urging Congress to action on public-land reform.[29] Collier's also published renewed attacks against Interior Secretary Ballinger, leading to his resignation on March 7, 1911. He was replaced by Walter L. Fisher, hailed by Pinchot as "actively against Ballinger's attacks on the Conservation policy." The following June 26, newspapers reported that Alaska's coal-land claims had been denied the Guggenheim-Morgan syndicate, easing tensions in Washington and once again diminishing interest in coal-land fraud.[30]

Concurrently, national exchange on another sensitive Utah issue highlighted the importance of respectability in the Mormon state. In February 1911, *Collier's* published a letter from Theodore Roosevelt in support of Reed Smoot in response to earlier published allegations of collusion between the former president and the leaders of the Mormon Church. Roosevelt countered the claim that the Mormons had "agreed to deliver to Roosevelt the electoral votes of Utah, Wyoming and Idaho, in return for three things"—an end to pressure for a constitutional amendment mandating federal regulation of marriage, defense for Reed Smoot in his Senate seat fight, and patronage positions for Mormons, especially Smoot supporters, in the three states. Roosevelt absolutely denied the allegations, not only on his own behalf, but that of President Taft and all other official leaders of the Republican Party. He stated that he had consulted both of Utah's senators for patronage positions, meaning the non-Mormon Sutherland as well as Mormon Smoot. Admitting that he "found Senator Smoot more favorable to the cause of conservation than the majority of his colleagues in the Senate," Roosevelt found no other reasons for favoritism. Roosevelt had left the enforcement of the ban on polygamy up to the Mormons themselves. He concluded by praising the Mormons' large, healthy families; abstemious ways, and support not only "for the best interests of the Mormon Church, but . . . [for] the highest duties of American citizenship." With this letter, Mormons felt they had finally achieved respectability in the national public arena. This publication of Roosevelt's remarks was still being listed in a church almanac as a historic event more than eighty years later.[31]

Meanwhile, the Justice Department was focusing on its Utah coalland concerns. In April, Fred Maynard and his associates appeared in the Denver court of Judge Lewis, where they filed an amended complaint covering "the whole period of time in which the Palmer-Peabody crowd had control of the [Sunnyside] lands and extracted coal therefrom," reasoning that, since the land had been obtained by fraud, so, ever since the land was acquired, had the coal.[32] When the defense attorneys countered that, because the patents had issued, the government could make no collateral attack, Maynard stressed that he was after the value of the coal itself, not the land conveyed in the patents. A colleague assured Maynard that "Judge Lewis . . . was surely impressed by the force of the reasoning."[33]

Maynard reported this progress to the attorney general and continued with news of the related suit against Peabody, on trial in New York. As the alleged mastermind behind the layered Rio Grande ownership of the Utah and Colorado coal lands, Peabody was likely to appeal if he lost, to protect the family's "reputation for philanthropy." Hoping for success, Maynard stated: "Most of our case has been developed from what took place in the Utah Fuel cases."[34]

In the same correspondence, Maynard reported on two other Utah coal-land fraud cases, both pending since 1907. The first, *U.S. v. Truth A. Milner, executrix of the estate of Stanley B. Milner, Samuel Gilson et al.*, slated to be heard the following June, involved in lieu sections held by Milner's Carbon County Land Company. Maynard had purposely not enjoined the state in this suit, supposedly to protect Utah as an unwitting participant in fraud. As a result, the disputed in lieu lands would not automatically be returned to the public domain— although Utah officials did believe that the disputed sections, if lost to the Carbon County Land Company, would accrue to the state. Second, the Sweet case was coming up. Apparently in a quid pro quo trade-off, Utah's attorney general had agreed to "cause the appearance of the State to be entered [in the Sweet case] . . . so that when a decree is finally rendered it will . . . settle for all time the question as to whether School Section lands, known to contain coal prior to statehood, belong to the United States or to the State." Maynard felt "confident of obtaining a decree favorable to the Government," thus validating the four years he had already spent on similar litigation. Although the Sweets' defense attorneys had allegedly "thrown up their hands and have admitted to me that we have an absolute case," Maynard pursued formal adjudication to set a precedent. He felt "that in this way [we] will better satisfy the people of Utah," who had been gravely disappointed by the original compromise with the Rio Grande.[35]

This sensitivity to earlier antirailroad opinion had influenced the conversion of the Sweet case, originally filed for simple consistency, into the vehicle for Progressive reform. The popular antirailroad coal-land fraud cases had proved unwinnable due to a whole string of circumstances. When the state, through error, had joined in the Sweet case, its impact took on a new significance.

Meanwhile, Maynard's relationship with the Justice Department was deteriorating. A May 1911 letter addressed to "My dear Mr.

Maynard," while silent on the cases involving Utah independents, asserted: "You have (inadvertently, of course) departed from the instruction of the Attorney General" in litigating against the Palmer-Peabody group. Later that month, Assistant Attorney General Ernest Knaebel confessed to the attorney general that Maynard had been acting unsupervised: "The fact is (though it is hard for me now to give a reasonable explanation of the existence of the fact) that I had not classed Mr. Maynard with those over who[m] I was expected to exercise supervision."[36] As a result, Maynard had apparently been charging enthusiastically ahead while policy in Washington was hardening. Nationally, Progressive trust-busting was on the wane.

Unaware of this background, Maynard doggedly tried to keep the attorney general informed of his progress. He had to explain further his reasons for filing an amended complaint in the Palmer-Peabody case on trial in Colorado. Beginning with the assumption "that you will recall all the facts and circumstances leading up to that [original] settlement," he jumped to "the main fact, namely, that you [the attorney general] was confronted with certain decisions of the Solicitor of the Treasury to the effect that no one but himself had the power to settle any suits, and that his power was limited to suits in which a money claim was involved." While this decision "was not the law," the Justice Department had acquiesced, although no proof then existed as to the value of the coal taken from the lands in litigation, for which the defendants had paid a fine. Maynard reminded the attorney general the result of subsequent litigation: a $73,000 fine paid to the government. The present litigation against Peabody, Palmer, et al. allegedly promised the collection of additional fines. Yet Peabody's answer to the complaint had forced the government to address the issue of the legality of the land patents, resulting in an amended federal complaint. Maynard believed that his amended complaint had been approved by Knaebel, and he stressed that the ownership of the coal mined, not the coal land itself, was still the major issue at law. After dwelling on the falsity and fraud of the entire coal-lands acquisitions process, Maynard referred to "the doctrine of relationship" (now the doctrine of relation). In essence, he asserted that this doctrine, which would provide immunity from further federal prosecution to former owners of the land litigated from 1906 to 1909, did not apply.[37] This point would prove crucial to the outcome of the case.

While the attorney general digested this new information, in July the Freed case came up for a hearing. The defendants, the sixteen-member Freed-Filer group, were fighting for their reputations as much as their four thousand acres of Huntington Canyon coal land. Their standing in the community had emerged when Maynard had first brought this case in court but could find no witnesses sympathetic to the federal government. In fact, he had described witnesses as "unwilling, adverse and hostile. They are all tied together by ties of blood or business."[38] Consequently, in 1909 the government had requested a dismissal at federal district court level, and Maynard had been forced to pursue the suit before the register and receiver of the Salt Lake Land Office, utilizing the executive branch of the government, rather than the judicial. This time, he predicted, the prosecution would succeed, "notwithstanding the local land officers, under the hypnotic spell of the local conditions and their personal relations with influential defendants." Although patriarch Charles Freed had died on March 23, 1910, the same day the register and receiver had finally posted the notice of contest, his heirs and business associates continued as the defendants.[39]

In the hearing, the government relied heavily on the Clark deposition, in which Dyer O. Clark, manager of the Union Pacific Coal Company, described a 1905 agreement with Walter Filer, son-in-law of Charles Freed. In the accompanying written "understanding," Filer agreed to accept $75 per acre for Huntington Canyon "grazing land," which he would secure from the federal government for an average $15 an acre even though it was actually valued at up to $300 an acre because of the presence of coal. This transaction had to be completed March 1, 1906.[40]

Despite this damning document, the government could not prove fraud against any other members of the consortium. It lost the case. The Freeds and their associates, including developer Don Robbins and lawyer E. W. Senior, passionately wished to protect their reputations. They funded the publication of the entire transcript of testimony, running to several volumes, which had resulted in their vindication. Undaunted, Maynard requested permission to appeal to the commissioner of the General Land Office, writing to Attorney General Wickersham: "In my opinion . . . the Freed case involves interests [the Union Pacific] substantially as large and valuable as the [Alaskan] Cunningham case, and I believe that the proof contained in the record is stronger than was offered in the latter case." Maynard promised "a hard fight on my part."[41]

This reference to the Cunningham cases may have been unfortunate. Wickersham was mired in "the work of the [Justice] Department, which is very exacting, and the intrusions of the various investigating committees,"[42] as he had complained to Theodore Roosevelt in August 1911. Repeatedly called to testify before Congress on the Alaskan coal claims, Wickersham could not give Maynard his full attention.

Maynard persisted in seeking departmental support, contacting Marsden C. Burch, his former superior in the original Utah coal land suits. Dwelling on the Peabody-Palmer litigation in his letter to Burch, Maynard revisited the ticklish doctrine of relationship. Maynard rejected the claims of the Peabody consortium that they had financed earlier development by the Rio Grande Western Construction Company and the Pleasant Valley Coal Company, which would accord them protection under the doctrine of relationship. Instead, citing his old foes, "Bird, the land attorney, and Bob Forrester, its geologist," Maynard envisioned a paper empire, not actual development. If he was right, the government had a case; if not, he would have to withdraw the suit. Despite his bravado when writing to the attorney general, Maynard acknowledged to Burch that this would be a difficult case. He added: "I have no pride of opinion in this matter. . . . If . . . you think the suit should be discontinued I will cheerfully concur." He also bolstered his case by referring to "the numerous investigating committees of the Democratic House of Representatives," who might "take great pleasure in adding this case to their list," presumably of Republican failures.[43]

The trust-busting impulse had certainly caused far-reaching ripples. The Cunningham claims scandal had helped the Democrats to gain a majority in the House, where they intensely investigated the predominantly Republican executive branch. Attorney General Wickersham, dodging congressional fire, had less time to devote to ongoing coal-land fraud cases, even those involving the still-mighty Union Pacific. As the premium on government success grew, the Justice Department simply could not afford to pursue a case it could not win.

CHAPTER 13

New Developments

By the beginning of 1912, Attorney General Wickersham had decided to support Maynard's suit against the Palmer-
Peabody group to get restitution for coal illegally mined in Utah before
the Gould takeover. However, perhaps leery of Maynard's messianic
zeal and his recent lack of supervision, the Justice Department offered
Marsden C. Burch the job of chief prosecutor. In considering this
assignment, Burch delved more deeply into the history of Utah Fuel's
land acquisitions at Sunnyside. Special agent Isaac Lamoreaux, of
Interior, back in the field, had just unearthed Robert Kirker's Sunnyside placer mining claim and Holladay's corporate involvement with
the Tidwells. Lamoreaux also reported to Burch that the Tidwells
had actually worked under the direction of Robert Forrester as agents
for the Pleasant Valley Coal Company. When they had obtained
official title, they immediately deeded their Sunnyside lands to Royal
C. Peabody, of New York, a dummy Rio Grande executive. For the
first time, the Justice Department fully comprehended the intricacies
of the Rio Grande's elaborate corporate structure and its Utah land-
grab scheme.[1]

Burch was already familiar with most of the case due to his labors
on the original 1906 bills in equity against the PVCC and the Utah
Fuel Company. He tried to refresh his memory as to whether Palmer
and associates had been involved in those. As Burch recalled, Maynard
had later amended the first 1912 complaint to state that:

> all the while the coal was being taken it was the intention of the
> defendants, of course, by fraudulent processes, to obtain these lands
> and this coal and the title thereto. If this latter complaint be true,
> there is no possibility that it was not embraced in the suits already dis-
> missed.[2]

Still, Burch vacillated. He wrote to the attorney general in considering this new assignment, recapitulating differences that had arisen
between himself and Maynard in the original litigation. He reminded

the attorney general that Maynard had not wanted to proceed against Royal Peabody in New York, but had agreed only when Burch had insisted he do so, "pointing out to him that we should be no respecter of persons." When Ernest Knaebel (who, as noted in the preceding chapter, had overlooked Maynard among his charges) had assumed leadership in the Division of Land Fraud, Burch said:

> I practically gave notice everywhere that I would not be responsible for anything Mr. Maynard would do, for reasons not herein necessary to be mentioned, and heard no more of this case until you brought it to my attention and asked me to take charge of it.[3]

One of the unpublicized reasons for Burch's withdrawal may have been Maynard's tacit understanding with the Utah State Land Board. When the Justice Department had spread its dragnet beyond the railroad trusts in 1907, Maynard had verbally assured the State of Utah that it would not be made party to the suit against the Milner-Gilson syndicate, probably in an attempt to soothe long-standing federal-state animosity.[4]

While Burch mulled over his falling-out with Maynard, he tried to obtain a copy of the amended complaint to see if the doctrine of relationship applied. If, as Peabody insisted in his demurrer, this doctrine applied, the government would have no case. Regrettably, for Burch, the amended complaint had not been included in the paperwork he received. However, relying on Maynard's verbal assurances of its content, Burch reported:

> I then stated, and believed, that the suit should be tried at least, rather than dropped, lest the somewhat awkward attempts at settlement and adjustment which I learned that Mr. Maynard had made might cause the Department [of Justice] to be suspected (in this case that would have meant you [the attorney general]) of having attempted to begin a suit to obtain a settlement and, finding it could not do so, dismissed the same.[5]

When Burch actually received the amended complaint, he was appalled at its terms.

> in the amended complaint Mr. Maynard not only admitted, but alleged the whole case to have been planned from the start by the defendants with the purpose and intent of procuring title to the land; that the coal had been mined in the process of obtaining such title, and that the circumstance of taking the coal had come way down into the time when the bills were pending that were subsequently settled by us.[6]

Burch faced a terrible predicament. As he lamented to the attorney general: "I see no other way now than to dismiss the case, humiliating as it seems to be." He was also embarrassed to write to Maynard, having already verbally assured him that he would prosecute. Burch ended with a plea to the attorney general to write to "Mr. Maynard, so that he may not think I have acted unfairly toward him. Perhaps," he added, "the whole of the letter should not be quoted." Although Burch had made his final decision, Attorney General Wickersham, for the time being, did nothing.[7]

Part of the federal confusion resulted from the way in which the original compromise had been reached. Although the Interior and Justice Departments had cooperated reasonably well to prosecute the case, the Treasury Department had belatedly injected itself into the settlement process, due to the importance of the bonds sales by the defendant corporations based on allegedly clear title to the coal lands involved. Force of circumstances had pressured Burch and Maynard into letting the Treasury dictate the wording of the receipts.[8]

Correspondence issuing from the railroad's legal offices early in 1912 emphasized the importance of these bonds. On January 9, while Burch was still debating the possibility of a new federal case, the railroad's attorney in Denver wrote to Mark Braffet in Salt Lake City requesting descriptions of patented lands in Utah and Colorado under the two Utah coal subsidiaries and the proceeds of bonds on properties under mortgage. He also requested information on lands in Utah and Colorado, still unpatented or held by others "in trust" for either Utah Fuel or Pleasant Valley Coal.[9]

Braffet's very exhaustive reply described surface rights valuable for timber in the Pleasant Valley district, and another surface parcel claimed at Castle Gate. In the Sunnyside district, the company had achieved title to most of its claims through the first federal settlement.[10] Three other nearby tracts, held in trust, were soon to pass to the Fuel company. A later Braffet letter computed the holdings of PVCC throughout Utah at 17,424.87 acres, and that of Utah Fuel at 22,096.41 acres.[11]

A 1920 report commissioned by the State of Utah also emphasized the importance of protecting bondholders in the 1909 compromise of the cases against the Rio Grande system. It stated:

> For some strange and unaccountable reason the testimony bearing upon fraudulent entries was cut short and legal obstacles built up relative to jurisdiction in the matter of the Morton Trust Company, being made a party to the action. . . . One is at a loss to determine

how it occurs that a title to property acquired by fraud and conspiracy becomes valid when mortgaged to a trust company which refuses to surrender the security. ... The compromise reads: "Hence as to any property to which the lein of the mortgage has attached, it is impossible to release the same since there is no power in the Morton Trust Company to do so."[12]

Although, for the time being, the coal-land mortgages offered some protection, precisely these same bonds would later threaten the railroad's economic survival.

Early in 1912, at the same time Burch was feeling his way through the proposed coal-fraud prosecution, the Rio Grande came under the control of Rockefeller interests and underwent an administrative shuffle. Benjamin F. Bush emerged as D&RG president, and E. T. Jeffery became president of the Western Pacific and chairman of the Rio Grande board of directors, the latter appointment easing out George Gould. Under Bush's leadership, Rio Grande policy emphasized system maintenance and a more conciliatory approach to economic rivals, two radical departures from the Gould style. These qualities might serve the railroad well, as Bush also inherited the controversy with Fred Sweet.[13]

In January 1912, Sweet had rejoined his battle for fair freight rates, still before the Interstate Commerce Commission. On January third, he wrote to the ICC complaining of a four-month car shortage that had allegedly resulted from inequitable car distribution by the Rio Grande. While Sweet and other independents had received half as many cars as the railroad mines, the Rio Grande had refused to reallocate cars until the ICC decided the pending case. In the meantime, the Sweets' Consolidated Fuel Company could not deliver the amounts promised its clients, and a "fuel famine" gripped the region.[14]

The ICC commissioner not only replied to Sweet but also forwarded his grievance to the D&RG. The newly installed president, Benjamin Bush, on a tour of inspection in Salt Lake City, promptly conferred with Sweet and others in an attempt to speed the movement of coal. During this conference, Bush suggested a distribution plan that, he hoped, would be acceptable to all the independents. He reached an impasse with Sweet, however, over the exact number of cars to be distributed. Bush proposed new calculations based on current production; Sweet wanted to use older figures, to give him a significant edge over all other competitors.[15]

Although the Rio Grande did not know it, Sweet had been pushing for major growth along the Black Hawk vein—a development that

Workers and officials of the Denver and Rio Grande Western pose at Helper with Engine 843, designed to pull heavy loads up the steep Prince Canyon grade. Behind it is the coal car, loaded with the fuel that prompted the land and transportation monopoly battles described in this book. Courtesy of the Western Mining and Railroad Museum, Helper, Utah.

would require additional cars. The first hint of change had come earlier in January when two of Mohrland's original incorporators, A. J. Orem and James G. Berryhill, transferred their interests in the Castle Valley Coal and Railroad Companies to associate James H. Mays. Two months later, the local newspaper, which had been speculating on the probable results of this transaction, trumpeted news of a sale. The lead story, in a full front page of mining reports, announced the purchase of the Castle Valley–owned Black Hawk Mine by the United States Smelting, Refining and Mining Company (USSR&M), headed by William G. Sharp, formerly superintendent of PVCC and then general manager of Utah Fuel. Sharp had led his New York–based firm back into the Book Cliffs field, where it took an option on the Sweets' Consolidated Fuel. The USSR&M officials consummating this deal were accompanied by David Eccles, of Ogden, Utah's first million-aire, whose interest in the transaction probably stemmed not only from his own holdings in the area, but from his son LeRoy's little-known federal coal claim to the disputed Sweet section. Adding further discomfort to the Rio Grande, Eccles branded as "largely exaggerated" the report that the new owners would build a railroad south into Emery County, or north, paralleling the D&RG.[16] But the possibility festered.

The extent of USSR&M investment was made public as the *Carbon County News* carried an advertisement declaring "Top Price Paid for Consolidated Fuel Co. Stock," in tandem with an article announcing major stock purchases by the smelting giant. USSR&M had allegedly bought $750,000 of Castle Valley Coal stock, all of Black Hawk's stock valued at $600,000, and an option on Consolidated Fuel stock for $1,200,000. In addition, USSR&M had assumed the outstanding bonds of the Castle Valley Coal Company and Consolidated Fuel at a cost of $1,200,000 and $800,000, respectively. The price of the Southern Utah Railroad, which connected the Black Hawk district to Price, was also being considered in the deal, at an estimated $5 million.[17]

Coal-land prices skyrocketed in eastern Utah. By April, the ecstatic local paper screamed: "Carbon Coal Land Tops The Market." The U.S. land office in Salt Lake City had just accepted $5,800 for forty acres of coal land two miles northwest of Helper. A follow-up article on the deal swung by USSR&M, as finally concluded in June 1912, put $1 million into the pockets of the Sweets. USSR&M received controlling stock in the Consolidated Fuel Company and five thousand acres of bituminous coal land, Hiawatha township, and a one-half interest in the Southern Utah Railroad. For the time being, Fred Sweet remained as president of the company and shepherded the transfer of its litigious legacy. In purchasing Hiawatha, USSR&M had also acquired the Sweets' disputed state title to section 32, still awaiting a decision in the Eighth Circuit Court of Appeals. It had also acquired the railroad-rate suit against the D&RG and twenty-five other carriers, pending before the ICC.[18]

Fred Sweet had continued to pursue the rate problem during the transfer of Consolidated Fuel to USSR&M. In March, he wrote again to the ICC commissioner, stating that the D&RG had begun to provide a satisfactory numbers of cars, "principally [due] to the fact that you exercised your good offices in our behalf." However, he complained that the rate structure of all the western railroad defendants had not yet been adjusted, and asked for the probable date of an ICC hearing. He got the relief he sought that summer. A June ICC decision, followed by a July hearing, caused the D&RG representatives to sit down with the companies mining the Black Hawk vein. Together, they resolved the issues discussed at Denver, and informed the ICC that all further complaints in which those parties were involved should be dismissed.[19]

Spurred by both business interests and this new Rio Grande policy of conciliation, the USSR&M approached the D&RG about direct railroad service to its recently purchased Black Hawk properties. This inquiry led railroad officials to reassess the entire coal district south and west of the Black Hawk developments, site of a proposed new railroad route that avoided transshipping at Price. Rio Grande officials agreed that the USSR&M's new holding could indeed provide valuable freight. Further southwest, the Freed holdings in Huntington Canyon offered 4,640 acres of good coal but no real commercial prospects, for reasons that included allegations of land fraud and the cancellation of receiver's receipt by order of the General Land Office.[20] Other nearby coal land still in the public domain offered coal-mine development opportunities, however. According to C. H. Gibbs, Robert Forrester's replacement, "unless the coal land law is changed it will be exceedingly difficult for individuals or companies to acquire sufficient area for mine operations. ... The prices put upon these lands are practically prohibitive to individuals at least."[21] Under the circumstances, the D&RG chose not to build.

Prosecutions earlier begun under the same defective coal-land law began to mature. Despite complications and continuations in the Utah coal-land cases, the Justice Department finally had some success in Colorado. In April 1912, the General Land Office awarded the government 8,465 acres of Colorado coal land, worth an estimated $1,755,750. These lands were relinquished by Utah Fuel and the Calumet Fuel Company, another D&RG subsidiary. Fortunately for the Justice Department, all but 640 acres were unpatented, facilitating federal triumph.[22]

The unpopular compromise in the first, flashy, Utah coal-land fraud case remained stuck in the public memory, however. On June 1, a New York journalist forwarded to Attorney General Wickersham an allegation from a Minneapolis lawyer, "for your information." The lawyer was quoted as saying:

"When Garfield was in Roosevelt's cabinet, he settled with the Union Pacific Railroad for millions of dollars worth of coal lands which it held under the name of the Utah Fuel Company, for a mere song. He also stopped one suit against the Union Pacific for the recovery of millions of dollars worth of coal lands after the special U.S. attorneys had spent months working on them."[23]

Wickersham quickly wrote to Ernest Knaebel: "Is not this a mistake, and doesn't he refer to the settlement with the Utah Fuel Company which we made in 1909?" Knaebel assured Wickersham that, yes, indeed, the Minneapolis attorney was in error; that the Union Pacific case had been in Wyoming and involved flagrant fraud in the use of soldiers' scrip. The government had won a measured victory there, obtaining return of the lands and a forfeiture of the payment price. On the other hand, Utah Fuel and the PVCC had been successful in winning a compromise awarding them Utah coal land worth millions of dollars, while returning a minimal acreage and paying a paltry fine. The attorney general then responded to the journalist's letter, saying that Wickersham himself had settled the Utah Fuel cases, "where a large amount of money was paid and a large amount of coal lands restored to the Government. I don't know of any other Utah Fuel Company matter having been settled [then]."[24] Meanwhile, Wickersham still neglected to act on Burch's recommendations that the latest suit against Palmer, Peabody, et al. be dismissed. The problems of litigating Utah coal-land-fraud lingered on.

Burch's request had been made in January and he was increasingly concerned that nothing as yet had been done. On June 25, he sent an official, seven-page, "Memorandum for the Attorney General," again outlining all the circumstances and the reasoning behind his views of the pending cases, especially the doctrine of relationship. He referred to his role in the original Utah litigation and ended with a renewed plea for dismissal, "unless Mr. Maynard can, in some manner, convince you to the contrary."[25]

The next day Wickersham dashed off a one-page letter to the secretary of the interior that revealed his confusion. He referred by number to the Palmer-Peabody cases "for coal alleged to have been unlawfully taken from the public lands in Colorado [sic: he meant Utah]" and recommended their dismissal. After further misdated references by Wickersham to "the Colorado case" and "the New York case," the second series of suits against Rio Grande coal fraud in Utah ignominiously ended.[26]

Although the Justice Department had left the fray, internal legal assaults against the Rio Grande's fraudulently acquired lands were brewing. An increasingly vicious power struggle between Utah Fuel attorney Mark Braffet and D&RG vice president Alexander H. Cowie would help force congressional attention to the still-unreformed national coal-land law, in the way that the federal legal assault never could. At the moment, however, all seemed calm. The D&RG, now totally free of the threat of federal litigation over Utah coal, began surveying a new grade over the mountains that linked the eastern Utah coal fields to Salt Lake City. Officials also planned a change from steam to electric power, and the stringing of telephone lines along the new route. This project was billed as "the biggest piece of single railroad construction undertaken in the West in a long time," with full credit going to its president, Benjamin Bush.[27]

In December 1912, another event occurred that strengthened the relative position of the Rio Grande among western railroads. Although the D&RG had successfully repulsed federal litigation, the Union Pacific had not. A federal court dissolved the UP-SP line that combined routes from New Orleans to San Francisco and Portland. This case, begun under Roosevelt in 1908 and continued through the Taft administration, was hailed as "the biggest decision since the Northern Securities merger was declared illegal" in 1904. In January 1913, the lower court's verdict was upheld by the U.S. Supreme Court, which additionally ruled that, in order to "dissolve" the monopoly, Union Pacific stockholders could not buy Southern Pacific stock held by the Union Pacific Railroad Corporation. The case then returned to the Utah district court where it originated for complete resolution.[28]

This increased economic strength had political repercussions. As the political crosscurrents of 1912 swept eastern Utah, both the railroad and the independents used party affiliations to enhance their power. Utah Fuel attorney Braffet had long acted as puppeteer to both the local Democratic Party and the Republican Party, insuring friendly elected officials in the Utah coal district. In reaction, independent coal-mine developers had organized in 1910 as the Progressive Party, allying at the national level with former President Theodore Roosevelt. In 1912, the Democrats nominated Woodrow Wilson, opposing Republican Taft and causing a three-way race. Roosevelt and Taft split the Republican vote, ushering Democrat Wilson into the presidency.

Events in eastern Utah were almost as dramatic. For the first time, the Rio Grande kingmaker, Braffet, lost control of the Carbon County Commission—the top local government body. Two progressives filled the open commission seats, presaging a long slide for Braffet in company power and prestige.[29] As a result, he sought to refurbish his position, partly through contests for coal land.

The D&RG was also losing ground economically, first to USSR&M on the Black Hawk vein and then to Mormon businessman "Uncle" Jesse Knight, whose fortune came through ownership of the Provo Mills, a beet sugar refinery, hard-rock mines, and an ore smelter in

Hauling rail ties to build the 4.5-mile Spring Canyon Railroad, west of Helper. This line was used to tap a new canyon commercially developed first by "Uncle" Jesse Knight in 1912–1913. Courtesy of the Western Mining and Railroad Museum, Helper, Utah.

Utah's Tintic Mining District. In 1912, his Knight Investment Company bought lands in Spring Canyon, opening up an area about two miles west of Helper for commercial development. Knight next put up $250,000 for a railroad to serve the lands of his Spring Canyon Coal Company, which was completed in May 1913. He promptly toured his new investment in a Pullman car loaded with distinguished visitors, showing his guests an estimated $500,000 worth of improvements. These had been erected despite a dispute over the land on which they stood.[30]

Knight's legal problems stemmed from forty acres acquired from the state in 1912, originally part of Utah's grant under its enabling act. As such, the land had to be nonmineral, but a small coal outcrop lay exposed in one corner. A subsequent claimant, William F. Olson, of Price, filed on the property with the federal government under the coal-land laws and Knight made his expensive improvements. Olson claimed that the forty acres was indeed coal land, therefore it could neither pass to the state nor could it belong to Knight. Olson intended to take the whole spread—improvements and all. Resolution of this case had to await a decision on the similarly disputed Sweet section, still pending in the courts. Taking a sizeable financial risk, Knight plowed ahead with development.[31]

The recent shift from a Republican to a Democratic regime prolonged matters: Wilson was putting together his Cabinet. Initially, litigation instigated by Republican administrations continued under its own steam. In March 1913, just as Wilson entered the White House, the ICC ruled on the freight rate case instigated by Fred Sweet and others, involving all western carriers. Western Classification 51, the basis for all railroad rates between the Mississippi River and the Pacific Coast, was overturned by the ICC as discriminatory. A revised rate schedule was demanded by March 31. The railroads immediately appealed the decision. Three months later, attorneys for both parties in this suit petitioned the ICC to allow a uniform freight rate for coal from the mines on the Black Hawk vein with those of the D&RG. Utah's independent developers had finally put a brake on the Rio Grande.[32]

Bush's conciliatory D&RG administration moved to comply. On June 20, 1913, three days after the decision on the uniform freight rate, the Utah Railway and the Rio Grande signed an agreement granting the D&RG the right to operate all of the trackage out of the Black Hawk vein in return for the cancellation of independent plans for a parallel railroad north from Price. The Rio Grande also reduced its price twenty-five cents a ton for its competitors. In June 1914, the U.S. Supreme Court upheld the ICC rate decision in two cases heard on appeal, thus resolving one portion of the coal-and-railroads controversy in eastern Utah.[33]

Concurrently, the D&RG faced internal financial problems, stemming from Contract B, which pledged the assets of the Rio Grande to support the Western Pacific. Payments due on WP first mortgage bonds led to the threat of receivership for both lines and caused a corporate shakeup in midsummer 1913. Personnel shifted in both lines, although Bush retained the D&RG presidency, allowing a continuation of his policy of accommodation.[34]

None of these railroad issues directly affected coal-fraud issues; however, controlling this valuable land assumed renewed importance. Trying to maintain federal momentum, in July 1913, Maynard wrote to the attorney general requesting leave to visit Washington to represent the government in the secretary of the interior's hearing on the Freed suit, involving more than four thousand acres of coal land in Emery County. Dubbing this case, "one of the most important that

I have had in my charge since I have been connected with the Government," Maynard recapitulated his unsuccessful progress through the courts and his subsequent loss before the register and receiver of the Salt Lake land office. Although the government had won on appeal before the commissioner of the General Land Office, the Freed-Filer appeal to the secretary of the interior would result in a binding, unappealable decision. Maynard viewed this case as "quite as important as the celebrated Cunningham coal lands" and perhaps had some professional pride riding on the outcome. Yet he still had to wait almost three more years for a hearing.[35]

The change to a Democratic administration was part cause of this delay. It also excited fears of new litigation in eastern Utah. Suddenly, Utah Fuel scrupulously observed the law in claiming an additional three hundred acres at Sunnyside in April 1913. The company explicitly reserved "to the United States all coal in the lands conveyed ... [as required by] an Act of Congress approved March 3, 1909 [the Mondell Act]."[36] Shortly thereafter, an apprehensive Utah Fuel official wrote to the company vice president:

> Last night ... [I talked] with the head of the Government Secret Service in this district. He informed me that ... the Department of Justice is very suspicious of the [Utah coal lands cases] settlement made, and further thinks that undue influence or even bribery was resorted to. ... Naturally the democrats would be quite willing to show that the methods used in the [Republican] settlement of land suits in the west were not of the best, and further, that the department had been unduly lenient with various coal companies.[37]

The writer also mentioned that, in the government's opinion, none of the operating eastern Utah companies could withstand much investigation into their land titles, including the Castle Valley Coal Company, Consolidated Fuel Company, Independent Coal Company, and the new Spring Canyon Coal Company formed by Mormon Jesse Knight. Yet the federal agent had remarked that "all corporations looked alike to him, ... and if his superiors wished to favor certain corporations and prosecute others it was all right with him." The Utah Fuel official concluded: "There is undoubtedly a serious effort being made to make further trouble for the Utah Fuel Company and its subsidiaries."[38]

CHAPTER 14

Sweet Solution

Fears of new litigation seemed increasingly unrealistic as the pending western coal-land cases remained stalled in the courts. As early as July 1911, Judge Marshall, of Utah's federal district court, had warned government prosecutor Maynard to expect significant delays in the Sweet and Milner cases. At the time, Marshall was preoccupied with opinions he would have to write for the circuit court of appeals, and told Maynard: "It would be far better to wait until he was ready to give his attention to the cases and dispose of them before an argument was had."[1]

In the next few years, coal-mine development boomed, despite numerous defective land titles. Swept up in this economic riptide, the Sweet brothers and their associates returned to Utah's coal fields, bringing fresh capital from the sale of their Consolidated Fuel properties (including the disputed Sweet section) to USSR&M. They invested their profits in the Spring Canyon district, uphill from Knight's disputed property. In June 1913, the Sweet group incorporated the Standard Coal Company, supposed to "set the standard" for a model coal operation and company town. Fred Sweet became president, and Leon F. Rains joined the company in 1914 as manager. His business acumen and personal ambition would later make trouble for his employers, but, in the beginning, he ran a model operation.[2]

In Washington, D.C., Congress remained unmoved by the ongoing boom. Senator Reed Smoot tried to draw his colleagues into the task of regularizing western coal-land titles. First in 1912, and again in 1913, he proposed a statute of limitations on the legal vulnerability of school sections granted to the state—the issue involved in the Sweet section litigation, then already pending for a half dozen years. After weathering his second defeat, he predicted in 1914: "I do not believe that the United States Supreme court will ever decide that the enabling act granted to Utah known coal or known mineral lands."[3]

That same year, Maynard finally got to argue precisely this point in the Sweet case before John Marshall's federal district court. Maynard presented voluminous testimony taken in 1910, including that of federal surveyor Joseph A. Taff, who had testified regarding the high commercial value of the coal deposits in the disputed section 32. Appearing for the Sweets, a mining engineer and mine operator had traced the coal outcroppings on the Sweets' land across miles of country from its known occurrence at Castle Gate, concluding that "the coal exposures on Section 32 would have no value whatever as a workable coal mine." A second Sweet witness had also compared the Miller Creek coal horizon with that of Castle Gate, and found the former decidedly inferior. But Judge Marshall favored the prosecution, returning the Sweet section to the public domain in February 1914. USSR&M, purchaser of the property, immediately appealed.[4]

This consistent comparison between the Sweet section and Castle Gate initially involved only the values of their respective coals. Soon, however, Castle Gate would win its own attention in litigation. It was the first area where coal fraud had been pinpointed, by a government agent in 1905. Shortly thereafter, the agent had left the investigation, so his observations had never been cause for action. The Castle Gate coal field, widely recognized as one of the richest in eastern Utah, had never been the subject of a suit. That omission, and a number of shifting corporate and legal circumstances, would one day threaten to embroil this area in its own controversy. For the time being, however, Castle Gate was simply recognized the a standard for an excellent coal seam.[5]

A few months later, Judge Marshall also handed down a decision on the Milner-Gilson property. This case involved 5,564 acres of land claimed by the estate of the late Stanley B. Milner, which had been claimed by Milner from the State of Utah as in lieu sections under Utah's enabling act. Unlike the Sweet section, the land had not yet proceeded to patent—thus title remained with the state. The federal government was contesting the Milner claim on the basis of fraud perpetrated by the Milner group when they claimed coal land as grazing land from the state. By agreement between Maynard and the Utah land board, the state was considered an innocent party to the fraud. In June 1914, Judge Marshall decided that the title to the Milner lands also rested in the national government. The state, hopeful that its rights might be resorted in the circuit court, waited for the result of the Milners' appeal. Once again, land titles remained uncertain pending further deliberation.[6]

Litigious considerations quickly paled beside world events. The American public watched in horror as the "civilized" nations of Europe stumbled into a bloody world war. By the end of the summer of 1914, foreign belligerency had even affected Utah coal. Salt Lake Valley copper mines and smelters reduced their forces by one-half, further diminishing the demand for local coal and coke. Needing fewer trains, the railroads cut their coal orders by 100,000 tons. Utah's coal fields suffered acute economic distress.[7]

Further political setbacks also plagued the Utah Fuel Company in late 1914. Although Braffet's cronies had recaptured local municipal offices in 1913, they had, at best, a tenuous electoral hold. Incensed at the return of the Utah Fuel "machine," the Progressives even mobilized their women. Organizing a Women's Betterment League, the wives and sisters of independent developers campaigned for an end to saloons, gambling, and prostitution, and for a clean local government, increasingly focusing their sights on Utah Fuel.[8] A bit of political doggerel published by a "Mrs. Grundy" in the *Carbon County News* lampooned "the company, fierce as a shark, / Whose principal tool's a fellow named Mark, / Who works to let Graft have its sway."[9] These attacks further blackened the standing of the Rio Grande system in the eyes of the community.

This proindependent political drive had severe economic repercussions for the railroad when, in the fall of 1914, Progressive candidates swept all offices except that of the county clerk. The now fully-Progressive Carbon County Commission immediately revised the tax rates, basing them on the 1914 commercial assessed value rather than on original purchase price. The Rio Grande system had acquired most of its properties as grazing land (and title based on this fraudulent evaluation had been confirmed by the government compromise). As a result, railroad affiliates had been paying bargain-basement taxes for years. Now, under the Progressives, levies on Utah Fuel and Pleasant Valley coal acreage soared to an estimated $10,000 annually. Nonpayment meant foreclosure, and Braffet rushed to the local district court to sue for unlawful taxation. At Braffet's request, the court issued a restraining order, barring sale of the lands while it deliberated the merits of the case. For the first time, it appeared that the D&RG might actually lose its valuable coal properties, or have to pay on their actual worth. Like other issues, however, this question hung for years on the court's deliberations and possible state legislative action.[10]

With the immediate political fight over, the Rio Grande system returned to consideration of pending internal concerns. In the fall of 1914, a well-known engineer, hired to report on the physical condition of the railroad, issued a scathing report. Rails had not been maintained;

high freight rates had eliminated possible shippers along the route; rolling stock was antiquated and inadequate; in short, the railroad was falling apart. Furthermore, Rio Grande assets, now so clearly required for physical improvements, were pledged to support its sister line, the WP. The Western Pacific had been heavily indebted since its creation in 1903 to challenge the Union Pacific's route to the West Coast. It had been capitalized by three contracts—A, B, and C—supported by Rio Grande revenues. Contract B was especially notorious, later dubbed a "signed, blank check [to the WP] to be honored by the Rio Grande companies," which included its related coal concerns. The WP's long-standing tendency to lose money was exemplified by its 1914 performance: it lost $138,398.94 during the first half of that year alone. A WP bond payment was due the following September 1, and the railroad lacked the funds to cover it. The D&RG had to cover the debt.[11]

This clearly unequal relationship dominated discussion of the Rio Grande board of directors until the spring of 1915, when the courts were asked to decide if the D&RG system could really be made liable for the debts of the WP. Meanwhile, a reorganization committee was formed under the leadership of an official of the Equitable Trust Company (successor to the Bowling Green Turst Company), which now held the railroad's mortgages. No matter what the corporate outcome, the glory days of railroad/coal expansion were over.[12]

The Sweets faced their own financial setback during 1915. That summer, while Fred Sweet, the Standard Coal Company president, was in California, his manager, Rains, made his move. Using Standard's time and money, Rains appropriated Standard's water surveys, filed for water rights in his own name, and began preliminary mine development work on an adjacent area. Rains then brought in prospective investors, including P. J. Quealy, of the Union Pacific's Wyoming mines, and L. R. Wattis, president of the Utah Construction Company and business associate of the Eccles family. On August 15, 1915, Rains resigned from his position with Standard Coal. A month later, he set up his own corporation, the Carbon Fuel Company. Wattis and W. W. Armstrong, among others, joined Rains on the board of directors. Infuriated, Sweet challenged Rains's land title and his water shares in court. Sweet lost for all but a small amount of the water. Now Rains, too, was in the coal business.[13]

Simultaneously, however, Sweet received a modicum of comfort from the federal courts. On September 27, 1915, the Eighth Circuit Court of Appeals finally ruled on the Sweet section, upholding the ownership claims of Sweet and of his successor, USSR&M. In reaching its decision, the court specifically explored the terms of Utah's enabling act, national legislative intent, public-land policy, and the distinction between a sale and a grant. Overturning the decision of Utah's profederal Judge Marshall, the circuit court judges declared that Congress had possessed the right to exempt mineral lands from the Utah land grant, but it had not done so. Simply because such lands were reserved from *sale* did not mean they could not be *granted* to a state. Furthermore, eighteen years had passed since Utah had assumed it had been granted this property, and many transactions rested on valid state ownership. The appellate court reasoned that severe injustice would result if the state were forced to relinquish its chosen school sections. Therefore, the court vested the title of Section 32, Township 15 South, Range 8 East, Salt Lake Base and Meridian in the State of Utah, and, through sale, in Frederick A. Sweet and USSR&M. Even more importantly, throughout the West, coal-bearing school sections became state property. Appalled at this decision, the Justice Department decided to appeal the case to the Supreme Court.[14]

The Sweet decision had an immediate impact on much of Utah's coal-land ownership. Dozens of patient claimants found their titles temporarily secure. Among these, Jesse Knight breathed more easily as W. F. Olson's claim to the Spring Canyon Coal Company townsite was invalidated, pending the upcoming appeal. The Sweet appeals decision did not cover all Utah's contested coal lands, however. It did not resolve the issue of in lieu mineral lands, those chosen when the numbered sections in place had proven unsuitable for sale because of aridity, topography, previous preemption, or some other reason. Therefore, the Sweet decision had no bearing on the lands claimed by the Milner consortium, which were coal-bearing in lieu sections.

Recognizing this fact, the circuit court heard *Milner v. United States* immediately after the Sweet case. Here, judicial reasoning favored the federal government. In the Milner case, the judges held that, although Utah was entitled to school sections regardless of their content, this right did not extend to in lieu sections. Furthermore, the new definition of coal land—invalidating the old requirement that coal must be exposed on every forty-acre parcel—worked against the Milner group. The judges stated: "Gilson and Milner were both men of mature years and had great experience in the business of mining," so their "grazing land" fiction was a clear attempt to defraud. The eighth circuit thus confirmed Marshall's earlier decree, depriving the Milner group of the land.[15]

The Milner-Gilson hard-luck story did not stop there. That same month, the commissioner of the General Land Office also upheld the fraudulent nature of their claims, and declined to let them gain title through his office. As a result, the tracts in question were restored to the public domain.[16] Yet no other developer stepped forward to claim this land under federal law. The absence of any new claimant unintentionally helped to extend the life of Utah's coal-land controversies.

The new definition of coal land, so damaging to the Milner group, had just been established that April in *Diamond Coal and Coke v. United States.* At trial, the history of the company emerged, revealing the huge dimensions of the frauds that had originally been attacked in Utah. In brief, Diamond Coal and Coke had been incorporated in Salt Lake City in 1894. Its agents promptly began mining veins, discovered by Robert Forrester, that lay exposed just over the state line, in the southwest corner of Wyoming. Yet this first attempt at development was aborted due to accusations of coal-land fraud based on the old forty-acre definition. Then, thirty-four other claims, representing 2,840 acres of land, were acquired in the same area, beginning in 1899, and passed to patent in 1901. On these, the coal lay below the surface. In a variation on the Utah scheme, two dummies had utilized homestead laws and soldiers' scrip to acquire the land, filing the usual affidavit that the land did not contain coal. The local land office accepted their assertions as "proof."[17]

This situation might have remained unaltered had federal attorneys not tried a different approach in this case: a challenge of the method for defining coal land. As all geologists and coal developers knew, coal formed in huge sheets, which spread for many, many miles through a given geological area. (For example, on the basis of this knowledge, Forrester had made claims ranging from Wyoming, through Utah, Colorado, and New Mexico.) Therefore, the old federal requirement of coal exposure on every forty-acre parcel not only ignored reality, it hamstrung prosecution. By attacking the definition of coal land itself, the Justice Department had hit on one of the very weakest points in an admittedly faulty body of law.

In the case against Diamond Coal and Coke, prosecutors relied on federal surveys made in 1874 that showed lands adjacent to those in question as coal bearing. The Justice Department then moved to set aside the patents on the basis that the area was known coal land, and that the claimants were, in fact, dummy entrants. The local court awarded the land to the coal company, but the decision was reversed on appeal. Diamond Coal and Coke then brought the case before the Supreme Court, where the government won. Most importantly, the decision declared: "There is no fixed rule that lands become valuable for coal only through its actual discovery within its boundaries. On the contrary, they may, and often do, become so through adjacent disclosures and other surrounding external conditions."[18] This judicially defined doctrine of inference, as it was known, eased the way for many a federal coal-land prosecution.

This new judicial definition may have been a factor in the beginning of litigation over a previously untouched Utah area: Castle Gate. The problems there had begun when an original entryman, Stephen R. Marks, essentially sold his land twice to two different buyers, first as a claim and then with title. The situation became more complicated when one of the "owners" passed the land on to others. By 1914, the two claimants of the Marks entry were coming into open conflict, enlivening the fracas over Utah coal.

To be more specific, Marks had first entered on 160 acres in 1888 under federal coal-land law. In 1891, he received his patent on the basis that he was obtaining the land for himself and no other. In the interim, however, Marks had sold his claim to intermediaries, who passed it to the Pleasant Valley Coal Company. Under these circumstances, Marks's affidavit that he wanted the tract for his own use was questionable, at best. Under judicial scrutiny, the PVCC could stand accused of obtaining a fraudulently acquired bit of land. To make matters worse, PVCC had erected much of its company town and its coal-sorting tipple on the Marks entry property, and had been paying taxes on the land and improvements for years.[19]

The Marks entry later attracted a second buyer, a fact uncovered only after a long saga of western growth. Early in 1913, Truman Ketchum had gone to the Castle Gate area intent on opening a mine. His knowledge of eastern Utah probably stemmed from the days when he had been a special agent for the D&RG. In 1898, he had gone to Price to testify for the railroad in an unspecified legal case, probably *Holladay v. Kirker,* over coal land at Sunnyside. In the strike of 1903–1904, he had worked in company with Gunplay Maxwell as a guard for the PVCC. Ketchum's law enforcement experiences had honed his investigative skills. A business colleague described him as "an exceedingly dangerous man to have on one's track ... if there was anything K[etchum] could seize hold of." By 1913, he resided in Oregon, but renewed his interest in Utah coal through the Salt Lake incorporation of the Ketchum Coal Company, through which he obtained eighty acres of land adjoining the Marks entry on the northeast.[20]

By 1914, Ketchum had made great progress in developing his eighty acres of coal land. First, he had solved the ubiquitous problem of getting capital by selling all but 15 percent of the Ketchum Coal Company stock to LeRoy Eccles, of Ogden. Eccles had long been looking for the main chance in eastern Utah coal. In 1908, he had quietly filed on the Sweet section under federal law, but his success there still hinged on the pending Supreme Court case. His chances had recently been damaged by the appeals court decision; perhaps a different vein in the same coal field might offer more promise. Consequently, Eccles employed the assets inherited as one of the sons of Utah's first millionaire, David Eccles, and bought a majority ownership in the Ketchum Coal Company. However, although Eccles owned all the bonds, he allowed Ketchum to retain title to the land in trust for the company, perhaps to minimize public awareness of his family's sizeable financial holdings. (His father had done much the same thing in backing the Wattis-owned Utah Construction Company.)[21]

Once the Ketchum Coal Company was sufficiently financed, its owners had to begin actual development work. This included obtaining land for a tramway necessitated by the location of the coal vein, seventy-three feet up on the canyon wall. The tramway would extend from the mine portal on the side of the cliff to a tipple, a huge building used for sorting coal by size, located astride the tracks of the D&RG along the Price Canyon floor. The coal could be dumped directly from the tipple into boxcars destined for points West. The land needed for the tramway and tipple did not belong to Ketchum, but it could be condemned under a Utah statute (earlier upheld in the U.S. Supreme Court) that authorized a private mine operator to condemn land needed for his own development. (Such eminent domain statutes, aiding miners and irrigators alike, were a common outgrowth of the turn-of-the-century desire to develop the West.) The proposed tramway-tipple strip led directly across the Marks entry claimed by the PVCC. As the Ketchum group began a land-title search on which to base their condemnation suit, they discovered that two parties, not one, claimed the land.[22]

Enter Charles Nelson Sweet (or C. N.), brother and corporate associate of the late Arthur A. Sweet and Fred Sweet. C. N. Sweet had long been leasing mines in the Castle Gate area, and had no doubt followed all local coal-land litigation, given his family's involvement in much of it. In 1913, he discovered the weakness in the PVCC title to the Marks entry based on recent court decisions invalidating ownership on the basis of fraud.[23] Sweet approached Marks to purchase the land anew, and Marks, having sold his claim to PVCC intermediaries around 1890, sold the title to the same 160 acres a second time, to Sweet. Recognizing this conflict he had thus created, Marks added a stipulation: that if Sweet achieved title to the property he would pay Marks an additional amount. The distinction in the two sales was this: in 1888, Marks had simply sold his claim to the land, not the actual title, which he obtained three years later, allegedly for his own use (an untrue assertion, since he had already sold it to another). Therefore, since Marks had perpetrated fraud in not obtaining the title for himself alone, the first sale, which had led to PVCC "ownership," was invalid. Marks allegedly still owned the land, so he could sell it again to Sweet. Litigation was needed to establish this story in a court of law. Consequently, Sweet began a suit in April 1914 in the Utah district court for Carbon County to quiet title to his newly purchased property by challenging PVCC ownership.[24]

Given the Sweets' relish for litigation, the next step came as a surprise. On June 28, two or three days before the case was to come to trial, Sweet dropped the suit. Even Sweet's attorney did not know why, although he confessed he had found "some nice and doubtful questions involved and ... was at a loss to predict what might be their outcome" (see below).[25]

Meanwhile, the Ketchum Coal Company began condemnation proceedings in state court against both Sweet and the PVCC, as conflicting claimants of the Marks entry, to get its tramway strip. Shortly thereafter, LeRoy Eccles sought to simplify the tangled land claims by buying Sweet's interest in the Marks entry for an undisclosed amount. Sweet agreed, and Eccles's purchase may have accounted for the surprising end to Sweet's suit, although documentation of the timing is unclear.[26]

Despite some fuzziness over cause and effect, the next step was clear. After Sweet's exist from the Castle Gate controversies, the Ketchum Company fell on the PVCC with a vengeance. Soon the railroad-coal company found itself the subject of suits over essentially the same parcel of land, in cases involving the same litigants, but in two courts and under two very different bodies of law. The Ketchum Coal Company was first tying to condemn a strip of land in local district court for its development needs. Second, Ketchum Coal attorneys filed a suit in federal court to quiet title to a 160-acre tract that contained many PVCC improvements, worth perhaps $250,000. Fortunately for the Rio Grande system, this suit was dismissed a few months later, although larger troubles were just beginning.[27]

These twin Ketchum suits came at a particularly inopportune time for the Rio Grande, given the aftereffects of the financial struggles between the WP and D&RG. Economic competition from a new, independent mine worried the railroad fully as much as renewed litigation. The Ketchum Coal Company, if it started operation, could offer the same high grade of Castle Gate coal, so well-known through-out the West, that had previously been available only through the Rio Grande system. Furthermore, the railroad could not hope to strangle the Ketchum operation with exorbitant freight rates, as it had done in the past, due to the recent strengthening of the ICC. Other tech-niques were required. Leading the assault, Vice President Cowie personally saw to it that material to construct the Ketchum tipple and tramway stayed on the train at Castle Gate. The Ketchum Coal Company obtained a court injunction to stop the delay, but their construction lagged.[28]

The Ketchum group, under majority stockholder LeRoy Eccles, vigorously pursued their claim to the Castle Gate lands. In 1915, the president of the D&RG, Benjamin Bush, succinctly outlined the problems that Eccles and associates had created. Writing to Rio Grande chairman E. T. Jeffery, Bush pointed out that Eccles, with interests in Wyoming coal and numerous manufacturing enterprises, was keen on using superior Utah coal for locomotive fuel. Although he refused to buy coal from the D&RG subsidiaries, he would use the railroad to ship his own output if allowed to open Ketchum's mine. Therefore, allowing the Ketchum company to develop their mine need not be totally bad for business. The first step was to allow them to build the disputed tramway. President Bush urged such a settlement, even authorizing preliminary discussions with Eccles. His proposed plan estimated $12,000 as the amount the Rio Grande would have to spend on trackage and yards to ship the Ketchum Coal Company output, a probable thirty thousand tons annually. This compromise proposal lay on the desk of Utah Fuel's vice president, A. H. Cowie, when Bush was peremptorily fired in a board of directors dispute a month later. Bush's conciliatory attitude toward Eccles and Ketchum evapo-rated under new railroad management, exemplified by Cowie.[29]

Prior to his departure, Bush clarified the issue of the dual Marks entries and the ownership of Castle Gate for his superior in a way that also hinted at the animosity between Cowie and the Sweets. As Bush wrote:

> When the property of the Ketchum Coal Company was acquired, the same parties [the Eccleses] took over the disputed title to the property at Castle Gate, a portion of which is occupied by the Town, tipple and coke ovens. ... In an effort to obtain other concessions from Mr. Cowie Mr. Eccles offered to buy from Mr. Sweet and turn over to Mr. Cowie, all the adverse claims upon which Mr. Sweet's suit depended. However, Mr. Cowie is of the opinion that he can successfully defend title to all of the property, and he considers the pending suit merely a scheme to blackmail the Utah Fuel Company, and he possibly has the erroneous impression that Mr. Eccles is a party to such enterprise.[30]

LeRoy Eccles had also voiced the opinion that even this generous offer would not mollify Vice President Cowie, who seemed determined to enhance his own power and that of the Rio Grande at virtually any cost. After all, the old Gould system had rebuffed the Justice Department with just such an approach. But times had changed, the financial climate had altered, and internal dissention was rapidly weakening the Rio Grande system. For example, Mark Braffet, who had ambitions of his own, dismissed Cowie's machinations as the result of "a morbid fear that something might happen to the company in those suits which only the utmost of vigilance on his part can avert."[31] Braffet himself would shortly become yet another contestant for Utah lands obtained through coal-land fraud.

As each side in the Ketchum controversy became more intractible, Truman Ketchum unilaterally decided to attack the despised Cowie on a personal level: his investigative talents had unearthed one of Cowie's buried skeletons. Ketchum wanted to file an indictment against Cowie under the White Slave Act (or Mann Act) for transporting a woman across state lines for immoral purposes. He had obtained complete information, including the woman's name, but Eccles refused to condone this sleazy litigation. Since the two men were so closely associated in a business way, Eccles felt his own name would be blackened by this seamy personal attack. Ketchum grudgingly backed off.[32] The Eccles family had been understandably publicity-shy, particularly since suffering through unwanted, prurient attention upon the death of paterfamilias David Eccles in December 1912. The settlement of his considerable estate had led to published reports of the existence of Eccles's two polygamous families, not generally well known during his lifetime. Furthermore, a third woman had stepped forward, claiming marriage to Eccles, and successfully litigated for a chunk of his sizeable fortune for herself and her son.

However, although Cowie received a lucky break in regard to the white-slave accusation, nothing had been resolved regarding the Castle Gate coal lands.[33] To complicate matters, other Castle Gate lands near the Marks entry had attracted a new claimant: Cyrus W. "Doc" Shores, another former D&RG employee. Taking his side, Braffet insisted that the Shores filing under federal law (based on defining the area in question as coal land, under the new doctrine of inference) was "friendly" to the railroad's interest. As Braffet explained to the company attorney, Henry McAllister:

> Mr. Shores as an honest man and never at any time designed to do anything but good for the Utah Fuel Company. He filed at Castle Gate because I informed him that under the law as it was then laid down by Judge Marshall [in the Sweet case], the land was open to entry and I knew of various persons who were unfriendly and who had designs upon it; Cowie was one of them.[34]

Obviously, Braffet was using the dispute over Castle Gate to escalate his feud with Cowie.

In this tangled web of industrial rivalry, many of the combatants were personally as well as professionally acquainted. For example, Shores had been partners with Ketchum in an oil well at Sunnyside. The two had also worked together as special agents for the D&RG during the bitter coal miners' strike of 1903–1904. Shores had also served in several law enforcement posts, including being sheriff of Gunnison County, Colorado, where, around 1890, he had befriended cowboy detective Charlie Siringo, who had investigated the polygamy charges against Senator Smoot. In this instance, Shores appeared to be aligned with Braffet, who claimed unswerving allegiance to the Rio Grande system. Braffet alleged that the Shores claim was simply a protection for a decision favoring the federal government in the Sweet case, which could also affect every other coal-land claim made through the state. Under the eighth circuit decision, the PVCC was protected, but no one knew what the Supreme Court would do. The D&RG general counsel predicted: "It will probably not be heard until 1917."[35] In fact, his estimate was a year early.

Meanwhile, infighting with the railroad bureaucracy increasingly decimated the ranks of those considered "friends." The rift between Braffet and Cowie soon widened into a chasm. In December 1915, Cowie informed Braffet that he would supervise Braffet's department, approve his correspondence, and endeavor to keep separate all affairs related to the railroad from those of Braffet's employer, Utah Fuel. The men parted amicably, but, as Braffet later sniffed: "I have not taken his instruction seriously."[36] Cowie, already tangling with Ketchum and Eccles, and suspecting Shores, was about to make a dangerous new enemy.

CHAPTER 15

Double Trouble

While Rio Grande system officials bickered, the Freeds celebrated. The Freed consortium finally won clear title to 4160 acres of disputed property in March 1916, by the unappealable decision of Wilson's interior secretary, Franklin K. Lane. The alleged coal-land fraud, in litigation since 1907, had been the cause for federal criminal indictments that were dismissed in 1909 when federal prosecutor Maynard could locate only witnesses hostile to the government. Seeking success through a civil procedure, beginning in 1910, Maynard had lost his case before the register and receiver of the Salt Lake land office in 1911—more than a year after the death of the leading defendant, Charles M. Freed. The commissioner of the General Land Office had overturned this decision in 1912, but, on appeal, the Freeds had finally won their case and their land in the civil court of last resort.[1]

In reporting this decision, the Price newspaper, the *News-Advocate,* noted that the Freed lands, originally bought at $40,800, were now valued at $296,240, and had an estimated market value of up to $4 million. Of more importance to the Freeds, however, was the clearing of the family name. The devious Walter Filer, who had entered into a secret agreement with the manager of the Union Pacific Coal Company, D. O. Clark, had since been divorced from the family. Despite the Clark deposition, in which Clark admitted to this complicity, the government could not prove conspiracy to commit fraud in contravention to the Coal Land Act of 1873. The defect in this document—and in Maynard's case—was that it could not be proved that this agreement was signed before the Freed-Filer consortium took up the land. Claude Freed, a son of the late Charles Freed, explained that several of the entrymen and entrywomen indeed borrowed money from Walter Filer (who may or may not have an agreement with anybody). When they sold their lands, months later, to Charles Freed, they did so in good faith, not as UP dummies. Yet the upbeat local paper, in reporting this vindication, failed to note a fact found in the county's land records. In July 1916, four months after Lane's decision, Walter Filer transferred forty acres by quitclaim deed to the federal government, allegedly "eliminated from the grantor's [Filer's] coal claim as non-coal land."[2] After almost ten years of litigation, the federal government reclaimed forty acres of land of dubious value, and relinquished more than four thousand acres of known coal land. Obviously, the government did not trumpet this "success." Furthermore, the longed-for success in establishing federal claims to the coal-bearing public domain remained chimerical.

While matters smoothed out for the Freeds, the Rio Grande system tightened its complex knot. The Ketchum-Eccles-Shores scrapping over Castle Gate lands forced the Pleasant Valley Coal Company to countersue to clear its own title, the first time a Rio Grande affiliate had brought litigation over disputed coal land. No doubt done in trepidation, in March 1916, company attorneys filed a suit against Ketchum in federal district court over the Marks entry. PVCC officials were especially concerned with protecting improvements, including "boarding houses, bunk houses and wash houses ... 42 dwellings ... coke ovens ... a store and office building" and other construction worth a grand total of almost $300,000. Protecting these assets had outweighed the risk of bringing cloudy coal land titles to the attention of the law.[3]

Rio Grande officials, trying to present a united front in the Ketchum suits, sat atop a steaming volcano of company controversy. The Cowie-Braffet conflict was about to blow up. Cowie railed at Braffet's insubordination and in April 1916 turned to the D&RG's chairman of the board, E. T. Jeffery. He requested Braffet's "immediate retirement from ... [Utah Fuel] affairs as his continued presence in our family circle is dangerous and demoralizing." Jeffery agreed that Braffet should be discharged. However, Cowie hesitated, pending a meeting with railroad general counsel McAllister, Braffet's immediate superior.[4]

At exactly the same time, Braffet fired off a long letter to McAllister about Cowie's behavior. Braffet said that while he had no objection to the new legal firm engaged by Cowie for the Ketchum case, he objected to their amended complaint. It appeared to assert that the Marks entry might indeed be fraudulent, based on perjury, and it "might challenge action on the part of the Department of Justice. ... A parallel can be imagined where a plaintiff [claims] ... that he came by the property involved by stealing it from some person not a party to the suit." The whole idea of theft of the public lands was certainly nothing new in Utah, but the use of fraud had a new importance since the Milner decision.[5]

Abandoning the corporate perspective, Braffet began a personal attack on Cowie. He cited a fatality at the Clear Creek mine that had prompted the widow to file suit for damages. Feeling he should have handled the matter, Braffet referred to his own experience "of more than 250 settlements of death claims ... at an average cost of around $600 per claim, including 161 of the [Winter Quarters] mine explosion cases." But Cowie had chosen C. H. Gibbs, the company geologist, to meet with the Clear Creek widow. Gibbs, in Braffet's opinion, was so inept that "no worse bungler could be found for such a task." By inference, Cowie was no better.[6]

Braffet went on with other grievances. He complained of Cowie's "systematic undermining" of his political power, a particularly sore point for Braffet, following his loss of the Helper city council in the 1915 election. He further complained of Cowie's ineptness in dealing with the new Utah branch of the American Mining Congress. This body had organized to fight off a new tax amendment that was being considered by the state legislature, whereby all mines in Utah would be assessed at current value, not purchase price. Braffet explained: "Our taxes would probably be increased at least $100,000 per year; Utah Copper ... taxes would be raised from about a quarter million to approximately five millions." A fund-raising drive geared to defeat the proposition had elicited Cowie's " 'moral' support," but no money. According to Braffet, this refusal had lost Utah Fuel many friends in the mining community, just as the company was likely to need it.[7]

Finally, Braffet picked the scabs off old wounds involving litigation. First, he alleged that Cowie's demand of noncompliance with Ketchum on the matter of his tramway had resulted in a finding that Utah Fuel was acting in contempt of a standing court injunction, pending a further hearing. Meanwhile, Cowie had libeled Ketchum in the Price newspaper, the *Sun,* read by virtually every eligible juror. That libel, claimed Braffet, would likely emerge in the trial, to the detriment of Utah Fuel. Under these circumstances, Braffet assumed that Cowie lied when he claimed jurisdiction over Braffet's department. Braffet then offered his resignation, if he was in error. "I can be of little service to the company if required to take direction from Mr. Cowie. Besides, I would not consider working for him."[8]

Three days later, Braffet repented of his final offer. He typed another caustic letter to McAllister, alleging Cowie's personal graft, including a $3,000 kickback on the building of Castle Gate company houses. Additionally, Braffet alleged, Cowie and his sidekick, geologist Gibbs, had conspired against Utah Fuel in Spring Canyon. Braffet wrote:

> Finally Jesse Knight opened a mine there [Spring Canyon] when it developed that the State Selection lands which everybody thought were held in trust for the company, were declared to be owned by Cowie and Gibbs, and they promptly sold the same . . . for $26,800.00 as I remember. The profit was about $26,000.[9]

Braffet alleged that Cowie had boasted: "I am here to feather my nest by God, that is how old Jay Gould got his." He then raised the specter of further abuses, alarmed that, since recent reorganization, Cowie's "sole signature unlocks the treasure of this company."[10] The conclusion was obvious. Braffet should stay. Cowie should go.

The Cowie-Braffet controversy had exploded under pressures rending the entire Rio Grande system. First, in August 1915, the ICC had upheld the right of the Union Pacific to close the Ogden Gateway, foisting a potentially damaging revenue loss on the Rio Grande. Second, that fall, Rio Grande infighting resulted in the installation of an executive committee of George Gould's family members to head the system. Third, and most seriously, a group of anti-Gould businessmen, some affiliated with New York's Equitable Trust Company, maneuvered a foreclosure sale of the Western Pacific on July 1, 1916. They then held the Rio Grande system liable for an approximately $38 million difference between the value of the old WP bonds and the price of the road, based on the onerous Contract B. To recover this amount, the Equitable Trust Company brought suit in the courts of New York.[11]

Throughout 1916 and 1917, the D&RG general counsel, Henry McAllister, alternated between attempted settlements of the Castle Gate litigation (involving Ketchum, Eccles, Shores, Braffet, and Cowie) and the Equitable suit. In this context, he was forcibly reminded of the threat of the Braffet-Cowie feud by an alarmed E. T. Jeffery, who wired:

> [it is] a very inopportune time for such an unwarrantable controversy to become public property . . . which . . . may have effects on pending litigation in Ketchum case and furthermore may have bearing on what we have in mind for next fall.[12]

Jeffery also suggested:

a truce ... between Cowie and Braffet ... even though it be only
to end this calendar year. Any public controversy ... during next
six or eight months will be most unfortunate and carry in its train
consequences which you and I are compelled to regard most seriously.[13]

The basis for Jeffery's concern with the next six to eight months,
and the reference to "what we have in mind," was never made explicit.
However, the attack on the whole Gould system and the concurrent
corporate reorganization offers a plausible explanation.

Other concerns may have bothered Jeffery. The 1916 presidential
election threatened local repercussions: Utah Progressives were still
demanding a new assessed valuation on mining properties, with subsequent increased tax revisions. The Marks entry at Castle Gate had to
be litigated, and could set a precedent affecting coal lands throughout
eastern Utah and Colorado. Finally, the Cowie-Braffet conflict, clearly
irreconcilable, would ultimately have to be resolved by firing one or
the other, and who knew what would happen then?

In consequence, Jeffery had given McAllister a most difficult task:
maintaining company peace. The cause of the conflict was clearly
perceived to be Utah coal-land litigation. As McAllister wrote: "I had
realized that this particular crisis [the Braffet-Cowie war] had arisen
out of the so-called Ketchum litigation—both the condemnation suit
and the suit to quiet title." Jeffery then suggested moving Braffet from
Utah Fuel and Cowie's domain to the offices of the D&RG itself.
However, a temporary truce was arranged, simply by removing Braffet
from defending the Ketchum suits that so preoccupied Cowie. In
addition, Braffet would continue to report to McAllister, as he had
previously, rather than to Cowie. McAllister himself had to hammer
out these particulars over more than two hours of separate conferences
with Braffet and Cowie, feeling that bringing them together would
"develop into sores which would be hard to heal." After an agreement
was almost concluded, "while I was talking with Braffet, a summons
was served by Ketchum personally upon Cowie in a personal injury
suit [brought by the widow in the Clear Creek fatality]." Cowie
immediately exploded and blamed Braffet, saying he was in collusion
with the Ketchum Coal Company. It took all of McAllister's conciliatory powers to heal the breach.[14]

Privately, to Jeffery, McAllister discounted Cowie's allegation, but
did agree that "the Ketchum people (including Eccles in this reference)
have become very bitter and intend to attack the Company and Cowie

wherever possible." For example, they were investigating charges of
Cowie's corruption, including some of those made by Braffet. In
addition, they were "thinking about laying the matter before the
Interstate Commerce Commission to secure a severance of the Utah
Fuel Company from the Denver and Rio Grande"—which would be
the very first time the alleged monopoly might be attacked by an
antitrust suit.[15]

For the time being, the Ketchum land suits proved far more
worrisome. McAllister felt that Cowie's handling of the matter was
not particularly astute, and that Braffet, though shrewd, resourceful,
and not disloyal, was "not a very able attorney." In an era of varied
threats to the Rio Grande system, its supposed legal assets had become liabilities.[16]

To circumvent the Braffet-Cowie fracas and eliminate its "cause,"
McAllister invited William D. Riter, one of Eccles's new attorneys
involved in the Ketchum case, to visit Denver to discuss face-to-face
the possibility of an out-of-court settlement of the Ketchum suits. The
two attorneys made these arrangements without telling either Cowie
or Braffet; only the chairman, Jeffery, was kept informed. Cowie had
botched an earlier attempt at compromise, as Jeffery now recalled.
Apparently, Ketchum, Eccles, and Cowie had met in November 1915
and the D&RG representatives had offered to buy the eighty acres
held by the Ketchum Coal Company in return for dropping the quiet
title suit on the Marks entry. Eccles, the major Ketchum company
stockholder, had left the meeting saying he would consider the offer.
He had never responded further. Now McAllister had to follow up
this lead.[17]

Riter agreed to travel to Ogden, Eccles's home, to reopen negotiations, although, as McAllister reported, "Eccles has the reputation of
being arbitrary and rather difficult to influence and he [Riter] knows
of no one who has close relations with him who might act as an
intermediary." (Riter eventually suggested another attorney, who had
assisted the family at the time of the death of its head, David Eccles,
in December 1912, when an alleged illegitimate son had made a
successful claim on the family fortune. Anyone competent in such
delicate circumstances could certainly be useful here).[18] However, with
the possibility of an intermediary still unresolved, Riter met with
McAllister, after receiving firm assurances that Cowie had been excluded from the negotiation process. Riter then went to Eccles and
reported the response:

E[ccles] had his fighting clothes on; ... he felt very bitter in the
matter, more particularly against Cowie; that he had put his money
into this [Ketchum] mine because of assurances from the railroad
officials that they would take care of him, & now there was a concerted
scheme to put him out of business; that he had given instructions
to spare no expense, & that if it were possible to "bump" the coal
co. or the railroad co.—I use the exact word—in any legitimate way,
to do so.[19]

The negotiations continued in secret. On May 18, Riter reported
that Eccles was sincerely willing to negotiate, even for an alternate
tramway site. They had also discussed the possibility of the Rio Grande
buying the eighty-acre Marks entry held by the Ketchum Coal Company. But the asking price was high; Eccles estimated his probable
net yearly profits at $70,000 to $75,000, or 10 percent of $750,000, a
sum the Rio Grande system might find hard to reach.[20]

To complicate legal matters further, Ketchum injected the issue
of the Marks entry ownership into his condemnation suit, in which
the two opposing parties were still dickering over the cost of the land's
purchase. Initially, when the Ketchum Coal Company needed a strip
of land for its tramway across the disputed Marks entry, Ketchum
had slapped a condemnation suit on the Rio Grande system (assuming
railroad ownership). Subsequently, Ketchum had also deeded the
Marks entry to the Ketchum Coal Company (assuming *he* owned it).
As a result, any litigation over the tramway right-of-way had to address
the matter of who owned the land sought through the condemnation
proceeding: the Rio Grande, that had first bought Marks's claim, or
Sweet and his successor, Ketchum, who had bought the title.[21]

Meanwhile, Cowie, pursuing his instincts, attempted to approach
Eccles about the pending suits. On May 22, Riter worriedly wired
McAllister that Cowie, unaware of ongoing negotiations, wanted to
force Eccles to prepare a court deposition. Cowie's insistence could
easily lead to charges of Rio Grande duplicity, destroying any rapport
the intermediaries had so far achieved. Riter begged McAllister to
dissuade Cowie from this action. But by then negotiations were thoroughly stalled.[22]

This delay was partly intentional. McAllister confided his fears
and reasons in a long letter to his superior, E. T. Jeffery. As McAllister
pointed out, part of the land involved in the disputed Marks entry
lay in a school section. Although the circuit court had recently ruled
in the Sweet case that Utah could legally claim mineral lands under
its enabling act—hence the state would owe the school section—the

Justice Department had appealed this decision to the Supreme Court. No one could predict the decision there on *U.S. v. Sweet.* Furthermore, the Milner case, also still on appeal to the Supreme Court, had been lost by the state in the same circuit court (the eighth) because it involved in lieu sections. Under the doctrine of inference, the Milner consortium had been found to have committed fraud, and fraud also tainted the Marks claim acquired by the Rio Grande system. (At the time Stephen Marks sold his claim to intermediaries for the D&RG, he had not yet received title. He did so only through swearing that the land was for his own use—an obvious lie.) Clearly, the pending court cases—*U.S. v. Sweet* on the right of Utah to claim mineral school sections and *Milner v. U.S.* bearing on the importance of fraud—could impact D&RG ownership at Castle Gate. McAllister was particularly concerned about the allegation of Marks's fraud, which could lead to

> the disqualification of the Pleasant Valley Company as an entryman, which we supposed were settled several years ago when the government compromise was effected [in the original Utah coal land suits]. This same issue is being injected into the condemnation suit, because much, if not all, of the right of way is over this Marks' land.[23]

As McAllister well understood, the Marks entry case potentially involved thousands of acres of coal-bearing land in Utah and elsewhere, much of it obtained under the same sort of cloudy titles. An adverse decision at Castle Gate could put immense tracts at risk, if someone were willing and persistent enough to ferret out all the landholding details. Just such a determined enemy was in the making as the Braffet-Cowie feud reached its conclusion.

In the meantime, McAllister concentrated on the two Ketchum suits. First, he reported his concerns about where the cases would be heard. McAllister thought the federal court, where the quiet-title countersuit had been filed, would be more sympathetic to company interests; therefore, a decision in the state court on the tramway condemnation had to be delayed, to prevent a possible bar to the federal suit. Second, an out-of-court settlement with Eccles still held out the best overall hope for the railroad, but an agreement had to be forged quickly to preserve secrecy. Although Cowie remained unaware that his superiors were negotiating behind his back, in his fight with Braffet word might leak out any day. Third, the Rio Grande stood to lose crucial revenue if Eccles actually opened his mine, but, as McAllister reported, "blocking competition will bring us into trouble, and ... it is much better to suffer some inconvenience and

loss through competition than to incur disfavor on larger questions."
Finally, McAllister was haunted by the possibility of an adverse decision
in the Supreme Court on *U.S. v. Sweet* that would throw out all titles
on school sections known to contain coal at statehood, which included
the Marks entry.[24]

In an attempt to resolve the Marks entry ownership, W. D. Riter
continued his negotiations with Eccles, and reported at length to
McAllister. Just as McAllister had bypassed Cowie in the Rio Grande
organization, Eccles negotiated without the knowledge of Ketchum,
who held in trust the deed to the Marks entry. In mid-May, Eccles
revealed to Riter the details of the actual Marks entry ownership.
When Sweet bought the Marks entry, he allowed Marks to retain a
one-half interest in the property. Sweet then sold a one-quarter interest
to the Ketchum Coal Company, for an unreported sum, and Eccles,
on his own, bought out Marks's one-half interest for $2,500. Effectively,
then, Eccles, who owned 85 percent of the stock in Ketchum Coal,
controlled a three-quarter interest in the Marks entry. Later, Sweet
sold his remaining one-quarter interest directly to Ketchum for $3,500,
before Eccles was aware that it was on the market. After hearing this
explanation, Riter tried to negotiate with Eccles to settle his interest
in the Marks entry by compromise, raising what Eccles called a "nice
legal question," especially in regard to the effect that such a move
might have on the one-fourth portion owned by the Ketchum Coal
Company. The two men consequently discussed how "reasonable"
Ketchum might be in disposing of his portion of the Marks entry
(meaning the size of the price tag). Their dealings were further complicated by the fact that Ketchum held the deed to the entire property
in trust—whether with or without a written declaration, Riter was
unable to discover.[25]

Later in the conversation, Eccles himself brought up the larger
issue of fraudulently obtained titles. As reported verbatim by Riter,
Eccles began:

> "Let me make this prediction: a year from now you will be glad to
> pay a million to hold your Willow Creek mine." I replied: "The
> Willow Creek mine is not on this property." . . .
>   "I know that but the title was obtained fraudulently, & Walton's
> boy & others have already filed on it, so if you are going to clean
> this whole thing up you will have to pay them, and they are not
> going to get off the property for nothing."[26]

Hitting another nerve, Eccles continued:

The railroad-built company town of Castle Gate, Utah, at the turn of the century. A coal mining town, Castle Gate exemplifies the union of rails and coal. The disputed Willow Creek Mine is up the canyon at the rear, left. Courtesy of the Western Mining and Railroad Museum, Helper, Utah.

"A year ago you could have gotten the whole thing [the Marks entry] for a mere song if it hadn't been for the obstinacy of that man Cowie, and for the life of me I can't see how the stockholders of the U[tah] F[uel] Co. would ever permit such a man to be in control of their affairs."[27]

Eccles concluded his discussion with Riter with the sincere belief that his lawyers would win the title suit. Rio Grande hopes for an out-of-court settlement faded.

As PVCC attorneys grudgingly continued regular court procedures, Ketchum made his move. On June 14, 1916, he filed the first antimonopoly case ever brought against the railroad system. The case was brought to federal court under the commodities clause of the Interstate Commerce Act, as amended, which said that no railroad could carry its own coal or coke. Ketchum supported his allegation with an exhaustive description of the interlocking directorates of the Denver & Rio Grande Railroad, the Pleasant Valley Coal Company, and the Utah Fuel Company, to underscore their common ownership. Based on the fact that he owned ten shares of Rio Grande stock,

Ketchum alleged that the company's actions would jeopardize his investment.[28]

Almost immediately, Ketchum revised his complaint by accusing the Rio Grande of being a combination in restraint of trade in violation of the amended version of the Sherman Anti-Trust Act of 1890. He claimed that, while the D&RG handled the trade of its subsidiaries with alacrity, it denied him simple access. The railroad had, "continuously since April 5, 1916, maintained a large number of wires charged with electric current of a voltage of 4,400 volts" across the right-of-way Ketchum had been granted, and he asked the federal courts for relief.[29]

These antitrust allegations created major difficulties for the attorneys trying to litigate the other Ketchum suits. Suddenly, the railroad and its coal subsidiaries had to behave as completely separate organizations. Henry McAllister, of the D&RG, regretfully wired Riter that neither of them should represent the coal companies in the upcoming litigation. He also recommended that the pugnacious Mark Braffet be brought back into the fray, despite his rift with Cowie, to beef up the Utah Fuel legal task force.[30]

While railroad officials were still adjusting to these new exigencies, Utah's seventh district court (Carbon County) dismissed Ketchum's condemnation suit against the PVCC, as initial owners of the Marks entry, although the Rio Grande remained a defendant. The court made this ruling because Ketchum had deeded the tram right-of-way to the Ketchum Coal Company, supposedly to convert the condemnation suit into a means for quieting title, a use the court found unacceptable. McAllister characterized Ketchum's move as the result of "stupidity which might be expected of parties in collusion." Although the condemnation suit remained against the railroad for that portion of the tramway strip that crossed the original Rio Grande right-of-way, the Marks entry case was over. The enforced separation of the railroad from its coal-mining subsidiaries had brought one minor victory to the Rio Grande system.[31]

According to McAllister, Cowie responded jubilantly to this decision, revealing "what he says is a long cherished idea of clearing the [PVCC] land sought to be taken by the Ketchum Coal Company for its tipple and tracks, of the old and abandoned coke ovens now thereon, and of laying additional trackage." Since the PVCC (and its owner, Utah Fuel), and the D&RG now had to behave as separate entities, a few legalistic steps were in order. First, Cowie's track extensions would probably impinge on the Rio Grande right-of-way. No one could be certain, however, because its exact location had been lost, along with the old narrow-gauge maps and plats. Second, Cowie might have to demonstrate in court that this new track was necessary for PVCC business, not simply an additional attempt to block the Ketchum Coal Company. Cowie proposed to spend about $25,000 on these improvements, which might be seized if the Ketchum Coal Company won its continuing litigation. With characteristic bravado, Cowie brushed aside this risk, announcing he would "brook no interference in the carrying out of his plans."[32]

At the same time that McAllister reported these new plans of Cowie's to E. T. Jeffery, he forwarded his views regarding the Ketchum antitrust suit still pending against the D&RG:

> Now that the thing has been opened up I believe it would be just as well, from our standpoint, for the Attorney General to investigate the situation, and to determine whether or not we are violating the law. ... I think that if the government should take any action it would be a suit (such as it brought in the Pennsylvania anthracite cases) to enjoin further violations. Notwithstanding all of the litigation between the government and the Pennsylvania roads, it has never yet sought to impose any criminal penalties.[33]

McAllister's cautious acceptance of this new possibility failed to consider the magnitude of recent shifts in public policy and the diminishing importance of the domestic scene. Not only did the Wilson administration lack Roosevelt's muckraking spirit and Taft's passion for legalism; major international threats were fast encroaching on national consciousness. Wilson was running for a second term on the slogan, "He kept us out of war." His tenacity against Germany, the belligerent in a growing European conflict, had extracted the Sussex Pledge the previous May. This agreement freed the United States from attacks by German submarines—and the increasing possibility of going to war—at least until the following January. Wilson had also moderated his earlier stance on Mexico, saying: "Some of the leaders of the revolution may often have been mistaken and violent and selfish, but the revolution itself was inevitable and is right." Even more importantly, the president felt satisfied with government regulation of the railroads to date. In December 1915, he had concluded his third message to Congress with the words: "The regulation of the railways of the country by federal commission has had admirable results and has fully justified the hopes and expectations of those by whom the policy of regulation was originally proposed." Given these preoccupations and pronouncements from the chief of state, a vigorous antitrust prosecution hardly seemed likely.[34]

A shift at the federal level did not save the Rio Grande from other combatants, however. By mid-July, attacks on the Castle Gate lands under various guises had become so complicated that General Counsel McAllister felt compelled to explain each of them in its entirety. In a fifty-page document, accompanied by a jumbo-sized map, he reported to Jeffery on all the pending litigation on Castle Gate, involving the Marks entry, the shores filing, Ketchum's condemnation suit, the uncertain D&RG right-of-way, and, last, Ketchum's latest allegations of railroad antitrust transgressions. The combined result of this litigation was summarized by McAllister:

> There must be no collusion between the companies. In other words, regardless of intercorporate relations, we must endeavor to get at, and to stand upon, the true facts, regardless of the effect upon the companies. We cannot afford to admit, without justification in law, an abandonment of the right of way, or carelessly fix the original location of the first trackage, simply because the Pleasant Valley Company may benefit in litigation or otherwise. I have instructed the Railroad's attorney that the case must be treated as though we had no interest in the Pleasant Valley Company.[35]

In fact, if not in law, the railroad and its coal affiliates had finally been sundered, the desired effect of the original federal bills in equity of 1906. But this event had come at a time when fewer and fewer federal officials cared. Furthermore, the ownership of much western coal land remained in doubt, at least as long as the Supreme Court pondered the Sweet and Milner cases. Lastly, the underlying problem of finding a workable national coal-land law was a long, long way from a solution.

CHAPTER 16

Wartime

Competition for the Marks entry remained the liveli-
est of the ongoing coal land suits. In August 1916, two new developments enlarged the scope of this litigation. First, the Utah Supreme
Court reinstated the PVCC as a party to the Marks entry suit, in a
move indicating to Henry McAllister that the court "had become more
or less partisan on this question" of resolving title, probably to the
detriment of the rail system. Second, this decision prompted McAllister
to call for a speedy trial in the supposedly less partisan federal court
of the case to quiet title to the Marks entry. Otherwise, an adverse
ruling in the state court might influence a federal court decision,
although it would not be binding. McAllister admitted that the issue
of ownership of the Marks entry could not now be kept out of the
condemnation suit, as he had earlier hoped. Even the litigation over
the small strip of land for a tipple and tramway might jeopardize the
whole 160 acres patented by Marks, and, by extension, thousands of
acres of coal land claimed in the heyday of freewheeling acquisitions.[1]

McAllister's concerns with sober legal precedents contrasted with
Mark Braffet's down-home personal pettiness. Ever contentious,
Braffet gleefully forwarded to McAllister a newspaper account of a
new fraud case against A. H. Cowie involving his Wasatch mine, one
of the businesses he ran elsewhere with company geologist Gibbs.
Although, Braffet alleged, Cowie had suppressed the article in the Salt
Lake newspapers through his control of D&RG advertising revenues,
Braffet had himself secured its publication in Ogden, the Eccles's
stronghold. Lost in the thick of his own battles, Braffet had apparently
not considered any detrimental impact such publicity might have on
the corporation as a whole. Furthermore, McAllister had heard from
Cyrus "Doc" Shores, who had accosted him on two separate occasions
to complain of his loss of the Salt Lake police chief job and his bitterness
toward the Rio Grande. Writing to Jeffery, McAllister dismissed the
tirades with: "I do not believe his 'bite' will be so dangerous. ... In
fact, I do not believe he will hold any Utah position which he may

secure, for any length of time." McAllister's lighthearted dismissal of Shores's threat belied other worries. The Cowie-Braffet conflict escalated when Cowie's hired detective reported Braffet's drunken carousing with Riter, the Eccles go-between, in a night on the town in Salt Lake City. McAllister, still in Denver, told his chairman, Jeffery, that he thought the whole thing was a lie and the informant unreliable, but this persistent bickering must have been hard to take as legal matters rose to a head.[2]

By September 15, McAllister reported to Jeffery: "The [Ketchum] litigation is every day becoming more troublesome." He had "received some intimations that at one time at least Cowie was favoring the separation of the Coal Companies from the Railroad Company, think-ing his own interests might be served thereby." McAllister was still trying to expedite the hearing of the Marks entry case in federal court. At the same time, Cowie continued to push McAllister for Braffet's removal, asking—as McAllister told Jeffery—"You let me know promptly when we can throw him out on his head." Dodging Cowie, McAllister wrote to Jeffery: "I am entirely willing that the onus for retaining Braffet at present be thrown on me. I think it would be disastrous in a number of ways to discharge him at this juncture." Obviously, the Rio Grande and its now virtually severed coal compa-nies had far too much at stake to create further animosity with Braffet.[3]

Part of the pressure on the railroad was relieved at the beginning of October 1916, when the federal district court for Utah sustained McAllister's motion to dismiss Ketchum's antitrust suit. Ketchum vowed an appeal, but, even at that, the case would not be heard until September 1917. Railroad attorneys had some breathing room on a least one lawsuit. The respite also gave McAllister the chance to concentrate on other matters. The suit of the Equitable Trust Company immediately claimed his energies.[4]

Conflict over the financial relationship of the D&RG and its sister line, the Western Pacific, had led to litigation in 1915. By the time the court case ensued, the Equitable Trust Company of New York held most of the notes on the WP. Under the onerous Contract B, Equitable tried to attach all the assets of the Rio Grande to make good on its investment. Specifically, it wanted the shares of Utah Fuel. In October 1916, the beleagured McAllister informed Jeffery of the bank's contentions:

> The principal defense is that the Utah Fuel Company is a mere
> agency of the Denver and Rio Grande Company, that the Denver

and Rio Grande was by contract to make good in any deficiencies in Western Pacific operating accounts, and that supplying the coal in question was merely a method of performing the contract, the same as though the coal had been paid for and the Denver Company called upon to make good the cost.[5]

Ironically, the same sort of interlocking corporate relationship that had protected Rio Grande coal land from further federal suits now threatened destruction for the D&RG. Regardless of the outcome of Ketchum's antitrust suit against the railroad, its ownership of the Utah Fuel and the PVCC might ultimately vanish.

However, the Rio Grande's luck seemed to be changing. The Ketchum logjam was breaking up. The day after McAllister typed the above letter, he again wrote Jeffery about the Utah litigation, marking the letter *Personal*. He cited "overtures ... from the other side for a settlement of the Castle Gate condemnation suit, which, of course, should carry with it all of the other collateral litigation [of the Marks entry]." These overtures had included a discussion of the tramway issue and "an indication on the part of the Eccles' interests to sell their Castle Gate holdings." On October 12, McAllister wrote to the attorneys handling the condemnation suit for the PVCC and Utah Fuel. He reminded them to be sure to leave a strong record of ownership of the Marks entry, since the state court (though not the federal court) had said that the two issues could be settled in the same litigation. The next day, a cipher telegram announced Utah Fuel's monetary offer for the eighty-acre tract held by the Ketchum Coal Company and Eccles's interest in the Ketchum Marks entry case. Unfortunately, the amount cannot now be deciphered. McAllister continued: "However believe Eccles and Ketchum more or less inharmonious and ... it is probably best to settle condemnation case by itself and remove[?] Eccles from situation."[6]

Perhaps Eccles had simply tired of the long litigation and wanted to write off a bad investment. On the other hand, the December date for the Eighth Circuit Court of Appeals decision on the Rio Grande–Utah Fuel–PVCC interlocking directorates was fast approaching, and the subject must have made Eccles uncomfortable. Eccles himself was on the board of the Wyoming Coal Company. His brother Royal and his half brother Marriner served as officers in Lion Coal, which owned the Wattis mine just north of Hiawatha. M. S. Browning, from Lion Coal, also had helped incorporate Black Hawk Coal, which operated at Hiawatha, along with David Eccles, another brother, and Daniel and John Heiner, whose relative, Moroni, had been one of the founders of Castle Valley Coal just to the south. All of these mines were served by the Utah Southern Railway, further strengthening the corporate unity. Although similar relationships linked almost all of the "independent" mines of eastern Utah, Ketchum, who sat on only one board, may not have been aware of the possible impact of attracting attention through his antitrust suit.[7]

In addition, the 1916 elections were coming up, and major changes were expected in this presidential year. In Utah, events on both the local and state level promised major repurcussions. In Carbon County, Mark Braffet's political power had been gutted by Cowie's insistence on running elections through his own man. This Utah Fuel infighting had effectively enfranchised miners whose votes had previously been cast at company direction. Consequently, in November 1916, fired by independent rhetoric, the voters threw out the corporate machine. For the first time since Braffet had received his madate to run the county in 1909, the railroad's coal fields were totally free of his political control. Outcomes at the state level mirrored the upheaval that ushered Democrat Woodrow Wilson into the White House for a second term. Utah elected a predominantly Democratic legislature, and, for the first time since statehood in 1896, a Democrat sat in the Utah governor's mansion. The threat of higher taxes on mining properties, still in limbo, became an evermore concrete possibility.[8]

In another interesting twist to the Democratic sweep, Utah's Senator George Sutherland (Republican) was defeated in his bid for reelection. His first Senate win, in 1906, had been clouded by insinuations of his involvement in Utah coal-lands fraud due to his service as counsel for Utah Fuel. His espousal of the railroad cause and Utah's states rights had led President Roosevelt into increasing rapproachment with Utah's other Republican senator, Reed Smoot, a more Progressive man. This political union had helped squelch persistent allegations of continuing polygamy in Utah as the state achieved a final measure of "respectability" with Roosevelt's public defense of Smoot in the *Collier's* article of 1911.

Sutherland's career was far from over, however. Upon leaving the Senate, he became president of the American Bar Association and remained active in the Republican Party. His stalwart party affiliation and his former senatorial friendship with Republican Warren Harding (Ohio) enhanced his stature in the Republican Party. The crowning achievement of his career—a Supreme Court appointment—was still far in the future, however.[9]

The successful contender for Sutherland's seat, William H. King, had first come to state prominence as the attorney who defended union organizers in the 1903–1904 strike of coal miners. During the trial of King's client, harrassment by Braffet (on behalf of Utah Fuel) and the court's obvious bias in favor of the company had led to statewide ridicule of the entire Carbon County judiciary. Derision had gradually given way to political action, as the power of the independent-backed Progressives grew apace, leading to King's election in 1916, just as Braffet tried to justify the political loss of Carbon County to Utah Fuel.

Perhaps sensing this sea change, Braffet's ally, Truman Ketchum, busied himself with his mine. In November and December 1916, work expanded on the Castle Gate property claimed by the Ketchum Coal Company. Doc Shores, another Braffet affiliate, appeared at Castle Gate, ostensibly visiting an old friend, but pumping for information about demolishing the old PVCC coke ovens. The friend reported immediately to PVCC officials. He said the two of them (he and Shores) had gotten "a little irritated" over the Cowie-Braffet controversy, in which Shores unequivocally supported Braffet. The informant continued: "I told Mr. Shores Mr. Cowie had never skinned me on any mining deals. But I believed M. Braffet had good and plenty." Recognizing that Shores was "working for a strong Corporation—and I am working for another one," he ended with protestations of company loyalty. Shores's visit probably prompted increased surveillance of the Ketchum development work. In mid-December the Castle Gate superintendent cabled that "three strangers at Castle Gate ... [are] taking measurements on ground between track four and County road" and also sent the numbers of the railroad cars the Ketchum Coal Company had loaded. From the perspective of the Rio Grande system, Ketchum production at Castle Gate seemed to be moving along disturbingly well.[10]

At the end of 1916, the railroad system and the coal companies (now legally separate) seemed to get a break from all this bad news. On December 29, the battery of specially hired, self-consciously non-railroad lawyers wired Cowie:

> Ketchum case decided in our favor. Court confirms title of Marks entry in Pleasant Valley Coal Company on three grounds, namely, paper title, adverse possession and by estoppel. Also holds coke oven site has been put to public use and cannot be condemned. Further holds track nine had also been put to public use and such use must not be interfered with by Ketchum Coal Company.

Court does not allow them to condemn sixty foot strip to within
five feet of north rail of track nine. Regard this as being absolutely
useless to them.

Complaint dismissed as to railroad company.[11]

With this decision, the time had come for final resolution of the
Utah Fuel infighting. The need for a "united front" had disappeared.
On January 10, 1917, McAllister, ever the go-between, wrote to Braffet
quoting a recent resolution from Utah Fuel's board of directors:

> RESOLVED, That the Vice-President [Cowie], . . . and the General
> Counsel [McAllister], . . . are hearby directed to arrange forthwith for
> the retirement of Mr. M. P. Braffet from the service of the Company.

Braffet was callously instructed to surrender all his files directly to
Cowie.[12] He left Utah Fuel forever, carrying with him a strong grudge
against his former employers. He soon found ways to make them rue
his release.

As the fight between Braffet and Cowie ended, overseas, World
War I went on. Like many other corners of America, Utah's coal
district writhed under wartime pressures. The conflict in Europe
and President Wilson's Underwood Tariff had disrupted the flow of
foreign coal into the Pacific Northwest. American suppliers, including
Utah mines, rushed to fill the fuel vacuum. Locally, the coal shortage
worsened and the Carbon County newspaper dramatized this plight:
"Utah Mines Far Behind Orders," it screamed in March 1917, reporting
a backlog of half a million tons. Witnesses testifying before a special
investigating committee of the Utah legislature blamed the D&RG
for the shortage. The president of the Independent Coal and Coke
Company testified: "I should say in the first place, the shortage is
undoubtedly due, in very large part, to the service rendered by the
Denver & Rio Grande road." Fred Sweet, now of the Standard Coal
Company, echoed his complaint. He said the D&RG "has not got the
number of cars today that it had in 1913. It has not got the same
number of locomotives today that it had in 1913." The numbers
he produced, from Rio Grande reports to the ICC and to its own
stockholders, indicated more than two thousand fewer cars and thirty-
five fewer locomotives. A summary of public attitudes emerged in
the testimony of John Critchlow, who was asked about the delay in
coal shipments: "I think a good railroad would have had a bad time,
and I don't think the Denver & Rio Grande is a good railroad."[13]

These views reflected the painful reality of Rio Grande finances.

The Equitable Trust Company of New York was still trying to garnish the earnings of the Utah Fuel Company to pay Western Pacific debts. However, the court had yet to hear testimony on this complex intertwining of railroad/mine fiscal responsibilities. As attorneys prepared their briefs in 1917, war had intervened.

World War I—the Great War, as it was at first known—had an immediate impact on the financial fate of the Rio Grande. Almost paralleling events in Europe as America entered the fray, the railroad strove to defend its assets on several fronts at once. First, in March 1917, the D&RG fought in federal district court in Colorado over the Utah Fuel bonds demanded as payment by the Equitable Trust Company. Then "Doc" Shores, whose alleged title to some of the Castle Gate lands had not yet been adjudicated, intervened in the Equitable's suit, claiming his own right to some of the Utah Fuel assets. The issue was complicated by a dispute over the ownership of the Utah Fuel bonds. D&RG attorney McAllister maintained that the bonds were committed to the receiver when the railroad went into receivership in 1917. However, the receiver had not taken actual physical possession of the bonds before wartime railroad reorganization began. In explaining the matter to his superiors, McAllister wrote:

> On December 27, 1917, immediately prior to government control, and also prior to the appointment of receivers of the Denver and Rio Grande Company (on January 26, 1918), The Equitable Trust Company . . . instituted a suit . . . to recover the judgment previously entered in the Federal court, and . . . levied [an attachment] upon the equity of the Denver Company in the Utah Fuel stock.[14]

The Equitable company was advertising these shares for sale in June. McAllister hastily applied for an injunction to prevent this sale, as violating the court appointment of a receiver, and the sale was postponed for a few weeks as the court deliberated.[15]

Meanwhile, the federal government exercised sweeping control of the nation's economy after the United States entered the war on April 6, 1917. For example, after a brief interval of reliance on industrial "cooperation," the federal government organized a formal structure for the regulation of coal, then the fuel of choice for America's industrial machine. On August 21, 1917, President Wilson created a Fuel Administration, with sweeping regulatory powers. The Fuel Administration immediately set new national prices for coal, and set up a system of state fuel administrators to enforce them.[16]

The Utah fuel administrator met with his colleagues from Oregon,

Washington, California, Nevada, and Idaho that October. To help
alleviate the fuel shortage plaguing the West, they decided to create
a "car and motive power bureau" to manage railroad transportation
of coal, with the approval of the ICC. Montana and Wyoming later
joined this network. This system fell nicely into a larger federal
framework when Congress organized the Railroad Administration
the following December 26. Through this process, using sweeping
emergency powers, the government seized temporary control of the
coal mines and railroads that it had so laboriously been trying to
litigate into submission to the national will.[17]

Wartime government control of railroads and mines seriously
retarded the prosecution of the Utah coal-land frauds suits. The suit
of the Equitable Trust Company (for $38 million of the Rio Grande
assets), for example, was forestalled, pending the resumption of railroad
private ownership at war's end. Until then, all the assets of the D&RG
and its related companies (including Utah Fuel and the PVCC) pledged
to the national war effort. Similar arrangements affected other produc-
ing Utah coal mines. Even more importantly, World War I sounded
the death knell for the long federal antimonopoly crusade, dating
back to Roosevelt's first term. Even before the entry of the United
States into the war, President Wilson confided in a friend:

> Every reform we have won will be lost if we go into this war.
> We have been making a fight on special privilege. ... War means
> autocracy. The people we have unhorsed will inevitably come into
> control of the country for we shall be dependent upon the steel, ore
> and financial magnates. They will run the nation.[18]

A recent historian, Gabriel Kolko, offered an even more compel-
ling argument: "A synthesis of business and politics on the federal
level was created during the war, ... that continued throughout the
following decade. ... It was during the war that effective, working
oligopoly and price and market agreements became operative in the
dominant sectors of the American economy."[19]

Certainly these views played out nicely in the resolution of some
of the Utah coal-land litigation. For example, the Denver and Rio
Grande received more sympathetic treatment in federal court than it
had a decade earlier. On May 10, 1917, the U.S. district court for
Utah, ruling on *Pleasant Valley Coal Company v. Ketchum,* awarded title
to the Marks entry to the PVCC. This settled most of the ownership
questions, although the suit to condemn a strip of land for a tramway
and tipple, in which the Marks entry ownership had been injected,

was still on appeal to the state supreme court. In September, the state also ruled in favor of the PVCC regarding the Marks entry ownership, although the Ketchum Coal Company was awarded the right to condemn tramway land across it. Even the conservative McAllister found this decision "highly gratifying."[20]

In the pause between federal and state court hearings on the Marks entry, McAllister had prepared his arguments for the Eighth Circuit Court of Appeals on Ketchum's antitrust suit, *Ketchum v. D&RG Railroad Company*. In December 1917, as the national government took over the administration of America's railroads, the appeals court rendered a decision on the Denver and Rio Grande and its interlocking directorates with Utah Fuel and Pleasant Valley Coal. The court ruled that Ketchum could show no harm to himself by the admitted interlocking of the three companies. Not only was Ketchum's ten-stock share too small to sustain damage, but the Rio Grande's ability to transport its own coal and coke "is very beneficial to the company, and therefore to its stockholders." Furthermore, Ketchum's complaint about the Rio Grande monopolizing the coal trade came about seven years after the practice began. The court recognized that "the real trouble which has given rise to the present suit is the quarrel between the Ketchum Coal Company and the railroad company in regard to the shipment of coal," which had already been adjudicated in another court. Thus this case had become a grudge suit. The appeals court sustained the lower court's decision that threw out Ketchum's complaint.[21] Besides, it was wartime. Consolidation, not antitrust, had become the norm.

As Bernard Baruch explained in his final report on the War Industries Board, winning World War I had depended on more than the nation's military strength. He described his view of ultimate preparedness: "There must be a mobilization of her [the United States] full economic resources—industrial, agricultural and financial. These must be organized, coordinated, and directed with the same strategy that governs the operations of the purely military arms of service."[22] For the duration of the war, industry and America were one.

One result of this war-winning strategy bloomed in the 1920s, as described by historian William Leuchtenburg:

> The 1920's represent not the high tide of laissez faire but of Hamilton-ianism, of a hierarchical concept of society with a deliberate pursuit by the government of policies most favorable to large business inter-ests. No political party, no national administration, could conceivably have been more co-operative with business interests.[23]

In this context, America's railroads had become part of the war effort. Their strength was that of the nation. Former legal adversaries had become allies.

Yet in the complex legal tangle that included coal land, some railroads fared better than others. When in January 1918 the D&RG was declared liable for the debts of the Western Pacific, the Equitable Trust Company gained the right to the shares and bonds of Utah Fuel. As the deal was finally hammered out by June 1918, Utah Fuel securities were sold for "$4,000,000 to parties acting in the interest of the Western Pacific Railroad Corporation, which is the large beneficiary in the judgment which the Equitable Company is enforcing."[24] The Equitable Trust Company itself recovered $4 million as part of the damages awarded by the court, and the Western, whose insolvency had forced the Rio Grande into receivership in the first place, acquired one of its most valuable properties. Utah Fuel, long a creature of the Rio Grande, now belonged to its sister line. Despite this change in ownership, however, the old railroad/coal combination remained un-

The town of West Hiawatha, part of the Hiawatha complex, in 1916, four years after its purchase by the United States Smelting, Refining and Mining Company. This view illustrates the steep canyon terrain, where ownership of a single section of land, such as the long-litigated Sweet section, could lock up much of the valuable coal vein behind it. Courtesy of the Western Mining and Railroad Museum, Helper, Utah.

broken. The original antitrust goal of the first Progressive prosecution had still not been met.

Another event of 1918 drastically changed the parameters of Utah coal-land litigation. When the Rio Grande system bowed out as the touchstone for national coal-land policy, the Sweet section stepped in. In January 1918, the U.S. Supreme Court reached its decision on the Sweet case. The Sweets and their successors, who had been awarded the long-disputed section by the Eighth Circuit Court of Appeals, lost before the court of last resort. This land, now part of the Hiawatha development acquired in 1912 by United States Smelting, Refining and Mining, had to be returned to the public domain. Of even greater importance, the Supreme Court used the Sweet case to rule on whether or not states could acquire known mineral lands to support public schools under their enabling acts when the legislative language was ambiguous. In deciding for the government, the justices ruled that Congress had not intended to transfer mineral-bearing public land to the states in school sections granted in place. They made no distinction between *sale* of such land and *grants* to the states, a matter emphasized by the lower court.[25] As a result, the Sweets, their grantees, USSR&M, and the State of Utah, all lost their claims to the land.

Throughout the West, known coal-bearing school sections sold as grazing land suddenly had cloudy titles. The means by which land was "known" to contain coal—the recently established "doctrine of geological inference"—gained enhanced importance. And a new burden loomed for the courts, as entrepreneurs leaped at the chance to claim under federal law the myriad sections, earlier granted to states, that became suddenly available.

Two newspaper articles reporting on the Sweet case explained the local ramifications of the decision. All similar coal lands, except those already compromised in other suits (notably Sunnyside), reverted to the federal government. The state had to repay the purchasers the "grazing" price paid. Claimants then had to rebuy the property— at coal-land prices—from the federal government. The state could eventually select in lieu sections to make up for the coal-bearing tracts it lost. In concluding one article, the author briefly referred to a similar case, *U.S. v. Truth A. Milner,* involving 5,500 acres of Carbon County coal (although these were in lieu lands, not sections granted in place). The Milner case had already reached the U.S. Supreme Court but had been remanded back to the U.S. district court for further hearings. Because of the slightly different circumstances, in this suit (as in several others), the Sweet decision did not offer a final solution.[26]

A second contemporary article erroneously reported the sale of the Sweet section to moneyed interests from Salt Lake City for almost $130,000. This report was in error, because, although the men mentioned had indeed filed under federal law, the Sweet section had already been claimed in a similar manner by LeRoy Eccles and associates. Despite the Supreme Court decision, the title to the property could not yet be quieted.[27]

The Supreme Court's decision on the Sweet case was only one indication of a changing legal mentality. America needed her coal reserves and money from the sale of recently reclaimed public land sales to fight the war. Federal control of the nation's industry was exemplified by the very recent nationalization of mines and railroads that marked an abrupt shift from protecting private property to promoting the public good. But this shift, while powerful in the short run, was widely recognized as being highly temporary. As U.S. economic and political policy endured a dramatic flip-flop during roughly three short years from 1917 to 1920, the legal system, whipped by action and reaction, tried ponderously to keep up. Policymakers readjusted their attitudes, and an impact on Utah coal-land litigation, while difficult to trace, was felt as significantly as in other, better-studied areas of American jurisprudence.[28]

Another coal-land case, concluded in Colorado in May 1918, illustrated this shift toward endorsing federal power rather than protecting private property. There, 3,400 acres of coal-bearing land, illegally claimed as in lieu land when the national forests were created, were reclaimed by the nation. This tract, worth an estimated $1 million, was relinquished by John D. Rockefeller's Colorado Fuel and Iron Company in return for the right to another 5,800 acres. Rockefeller, the creator of the "trust" and quintessential "robber baron," had previously obtained title to the reclaimed land through the decisions of the General Land Office and the secretary of the interior. His assertions that these decisions were final could only be overruled because the government introduced new evidence of fraud when it brought the case in federal court—another indication of new-found federal strength.[29]

This wartime shift had a far-reaching impact on ongoing coal-land fraud litigation, and, by extension, the eventual disposition of the remaining public domain—including determinations of to whom and by whom it must be transferred. Many of the details of this impact had yet to be settled in the courts and appropriate administrative agencies. The Progressive Era coal-land fraud suits—a virtual extension of the era's trust-busting, antirailroad crusade—became converted to other uses that were emerging only in the heat of the wartime fray. In this crucible, perhaps the old cry for a federal coal-leasing statute, articulated by President Roosevelt in 1906, might yet be heard. But even a change in the law would not resolve cases already in the courts. The end of a long, hard legal battle was not yet in view.

To a large extent, the Supreme Court's decision in the Sweet case in January 1918 changed the rules of the game. Since the federal government could now claim all the school sections known to contain coal at statehood, purchasers who had acquired these lands from the State of Utah—independents and railroad affiliates alike—stood to lose vast tracts of coal. So, the first question to be addressed was: Who actually owned the land? Or, put more practically: Whose claim took precedence? In the tangled web of Utah coal-land controversy, each case had to be adjudicated individually through the courts or the Department of the Interior, at least as long as Congress remained silent.

Almost unnoticed in the local brouhaha over the Sweet case, the suit over Knight's Spring Canyon tipple and townsite tract wrestled with the definition of *known* coal land. In hearing this case in the spring of 1918, the General Land Office in Washington, D.C. considered the Supreme Court's 1914 findings in *Diamond Coal and Coke v. United States,* by which the company's patents had been cancelled on the basis of fraud perpetrated through knowledge that the lands were coal-bearing prior to their acquisition. This knowledge had been gained through "the doctrine of geological inference;" that is, if coal existed in lands contiguous to the disputed parcel, coal was "known" to be present in the disputed land. This doctrine relied on coal geology: the expert knowledge that coal typically lay in huge sheets over thousands of square miles. In the Knight case, the commissioners pondered: Did the existence of a coal outcrop near this property provide sufficient proof that the land was "coal-bearing"? William Olson's coal claim— filed with the federal government—rested on the principle that it did. Furthermore, he asserted that the mineral nature of Knight's property was known at statehood, so, according to the Sweet decision, the land had been illegally procured by the state, and Knight's title was null and void. Jesse Knight countered that the land was neither coal-bearing at statehood nor in the present, because one small outcrop did not constitute proof of its minerality. Not surprisingly, the State of Utah backed Knight's case.[30]

By August 1918, the GLO made its decision. It awarded the land containing surface improvements—including almost the entire company town and the tipple—to Knight's Spring Canyon Coal Company. But it granted the remainder of the unimproved land and all the mineral rights underlying the tract to Olson. Almost unnoticed in the fuss over Knight's improvements, the wording that separated the surface from the underlying mineral rights was a harbinger of future legal solutions. Unimpressed by this aspect of the decision, however, Olson greedily appealed to the secretary of the interior, demanding the entire property, including the surface land that housed Knight's developments.[31]

In March 1919 came the next ruling on the Knight case. The local paper optimistically announced: "The final chapter to the years of litigation over title to Utah school lands found to be mineral bearing, especially coal bearing, appears to have been written." The paper's statement was made about a dozen years too soon, but other information in the article was accurate. It correctly described "the tangled condition of affairs" plaguing Utah's coal-land titles, often claimed under conflicting state and federal law. The Sweet case had prompted much of this confusion, as federal, state, and federal claims had been consecutively unheld. Jesse Knight, caught in the crossfire, had expended more than $200,000 on improvements on land he thought he had bought from Utah in the halcyon days when the federal appeals court had awarded the Sweet section to the claimants from the state. Recently, the U.S. Supreme Court, in *U.S. v. Sweet,* had given final title to the federal government. A strict interpretation of the Sweet decision in the Knight case, however, would give the property back to the federal government, with which Olson had filed.[32]

The secretary of the interior had ruled otherwise. As reported in the *Sun,* he declared that "the [Spring Canyon Coal] company's improvements should be respected. Neither the ground on which they stand nor essential control over them should be handed to a third party." This decision was made on the basis of equity—on the grounds that Knight had done his development in good faith. It did not refer to the doctrine of geological inference, nor any other determinant of the mineral nature of disputed land on which the improvements rested. Olson had lost his case for the meantime, but an appeal to the federal courts followed.[33]

While these precedent-setting decisions were being formulated, the war continued. As the federal government assiduously ran mines and railroads in keeping with wartime policy throughout the summer and fall of 1918, its bureaucracy became more complex and its regulations tighter. The system was working at full tilt when peace came unexpectedly on November 11. Suddenly, stockpiled coal became a glut, not a military necessity. Private enterprise reasserted its claims over the nation's railroads, although Congress hesitated to act. Even more importantly, the nation sat back, loosened its belt, and invited normalcy—whatever that was—to come on in. The days for great national crusades were over.

PART III

The Results of Reform

CHAPTER 17

"Herald of a New Era"

Although Utah Fuel now belonged to the Western Pacific, not the D&RG, this decision did little to alter the basic relationships between railroad corporations and Utah coal. Furthermore, the war had left an ironic corporate legacy. As one cynical writer observed just before the end of hostilities:

> To begin with, the trusts that were busted into many parts do not seem to have suffered at all, for each part has grown almost as big as the original trust. Stranger yet, numbers of previously small independents have grown so enormously that they now almost resemble the original trusts.[1]

These issues of size and other hallmarks of a "trust" colored the ongoing controversy over the Sweet section. Although the Supreme Court had returned it to the public domain in 1918, this transfer was only to allow its sale by the proper—that is, the federal—authorities. Next, the issue became: To whom should it be sold? Two major claimants faced the government with outstretched palms. First, the Sweets and their successors, the United States Fuel Company of the USSR&M (United State Smelting, Refining and Mining Company) claimed a "good faith" purchase dating back to 1912. Seeking to establish its rights, the USSR&M appealed to the House of Representatives, bringing a private bill (addressing its own particular, individual needs) in 1919. In opposition came LeRoy Eccles and associates, who had held a federal claim on the same land since 1908.[2]

Acrimonious debate blazed in the House Subcommittee on Public Lands. Capturing the moral high ground seemed to be the key to success given the recent Jesse Knight decision. Consequently, the opposing claimants began simultaneously asserting their own purity and besmearing the reputations of their adversaries.

The published results of these lengthy hearings reviewed almost the entire scope of the Utah coal-land cases, as well as mentioning similar conditions in other land-grant states. Remarks made in the debate excoriated both sides: "speculators" (presumably Eccles) were said to have bought up conflicting claims just to harrass others; claims of "innocence" (made for Sweet and USSR&M) were derided.[3] An Eccles associate in the Lion and Wyoming Coal Companies, who had been the Wyoming distributor for the Fuel Administration during the war, D. H. Pape, represented the Eccles group at the hearing. In countering the "speculator" argument, he claimed that in fact the Sweets had stolen the mantle of justice from its rightful owners, the Eccles consortium. In reviewing years of Utah coal-lands development, Pape indignantly thundered:

> There is a certain class of men down there in Utah who have preyed on the coal lands of the State. Mr. Sweet and his crowd is [sic] one of this class. It is common knowledge that they grabbed the land comprising the holdings of the Independent Coal & Coke Co., from private information taken over the telegraph wires while one of them was in the employment of the Denver & Rio Grande Railroad Co. They unloaded that onto other people immediately and then they secured other lands which they transferred to the Consolidated Fuel Co., which was organized by them.[4]

In essence, Pape accused the Sweets of being aspiring monopolists. His underlying assumption replicated that of the original Progressive anticoal land fraud cases: monopoly was to be punished by federal intervention.

Pape described the purported evils this alleged concentration had wrought:

> They have demoralized the coal situation in the West for years by their cut-throat competitive methods, which enabled them to build up the market and then they unloaded the Consolidated Fuel Co. upon the United States Fuel Co. Then they got into the Standard Fuel Co., another property which they want to sell. . . . [A]nd that is the kind of men that come here and plead "innocent purchasers" and charge LeRoy Eccles et al. with being "speculators."[5]

The vision of capitalistic good and evil was obviously intended to sway the congressmen. Accordingly, after this blast, one of Sweet's associates, Robert R. Barnes, asked if the Sweets had not provided the first economic competition to what was then the monopolistic Denver and Rio Grande Western's Utah Fuel Company. Pape heatedly replied that the Union Pacific and its affiliates had tried to compete with the Western's mines, but finally admitted that Sweet was indeed the first of what had now become at least six or seven nonrailroad competitors in coal. Yet he reiterated that United States Fuel could hardly be called an innocent purchaser, since it was "not in the habit of buying land without looking into the title." Barnes painted a different picture: the low price Sweet offered, reflecting what he had paid the state, had induced the smelting giant to take a chance on the disputed section—and reflected Sweet's capitalistic "innocence."[6]

Fighting for the moral high ground, Pape responded that Eccles, far from being a speculator, was simply an honest citizen who wanted to buy the land from the national government and was willing to pay full purchase price. He then accused the United States Fuel Company of wanting to acquire section 32 to block out others from the government-owned lands behind it, assuring them competition-free development without having to pay the rising state taxes on additional lands under their control.[7]

Barnes countered that LeRoy Eccles's father, millionaire David Eccles, had been one of the biggest businessmen in the West. His

This huge block of coal from the Black Hawk Mine, sent to the Panama-Pacific Exposition in 1915, illustrates the tremendous value of Black Hawk's wide seams. Coal was more usually mined in smaller pieces, as evident in an illustration on page 120. Courtesy Utah State Historical Society, Salt Lake City.

involvement in the Black Hawk Coal Company, Ketchum Coal Company, Lion Coal Company, and many other enterprises fully balanced the clout of United States Fuel. Was this, then, a struggling independent? Further mudslinging smeared the names of E. W. Senior and the Freeds of Huntington Canyon, and Mark Braffet for his interest in Castle Gate. After other testimony, the subcommittee adjourned.[8]

This sulphurous interchange indicated the perceived importance of corporate "morality" even after the nation's era of idealism—the Progressive Era—was supposed to have ended. Perhaps Congress had grown jaded or indifferent; or perhaps this highly personal exchange simply confused those present. In any event, the bill to resolve the ownership of the Sweet section died right there in committee. Since it was never reported out, the only avenue not yet exhausted lay in the executive branch. To the Department of the Interior the combatants would eventually turn.

In the meantime, other Utah coal-land claimants were pursuing their own routes toward money, power, or control. Barnes's reference to Mark Braffet's latest claims marked the most dangerous challenge so far to the sliding fortunes of Utah Fuel. In 1918, shortly after the Supreme Court's Sweet decision, Braffet had filed a federal application for the Willow Creek section of Castle Gate, obtained from the state by the Pleasant Valley Coal Company (later a wholly-owned subsidiary of Utah Fuel). Its fragile title was common knowledge, noted by Eccles in his conversations with Riter as an area where "if you are going to clean this whole thing up you will have to pay."[9] Additionally, Braffet had claimed another school section number 32 that adjoined the Willow Creek number 2 mine at Castle Gate. Like Olson in Spring Canyon and Eccles on the Black Hawk vein, Braffet turned to federal law, as administered through the agencies of the Interior Department, to challenge long-established ownership based on transfer from the state.

Braffet's school section contest first went to the Salt Lake branch of the General Land Office for a hearing. There, according to a *Sun* report, he trotted out the doctrine of geological inference established in *Diamond Coal and Coke* to support his claim to "known" coal land:

> Coal bearing sedimentary rocks ... are obvious throughout that district, and were at all times known to dip into said Sec. 32, carrying with them large seams of coal naturally exposed in adjacent canyons in many of which operating mines were opened prior to the passage of the enabling act.[10]

Therefore, the state knew the land to be coal-bearing at statehood. Utah's title, he insisted, could not hold.

In considering Braffet's arguments for determining the known presence of coal, the Utah federal land office for the first time had to consider this judicial definition of known coal land, which materially strengthened Braffet's case. (The "good faith" argument, successfully utilized by Jesse Knight, was not brought here.) Based on his insider's knowledge, Braffet additionally pinpointed other Gould system coal-land frauds. In testimony entered in the Castle Gate contest he accurately described the dummy system perpetrated at Sunnyside and elsewhere. He claimed that the State of Utah had sold his former employer more than 20,000 acres of coal land as state selections from the public domain. As he well knew, some of this property had never been litigated, and Braffet carefully targeted the tracts still legally vulnerable.[11] The whole proceeding had the tinny ring of a grudge suit.

Not surprisingly, Braffet was also willing to help others to relieve his former employers of disputed tracts. In his lawyer's guise, he assisted the Milners, whose Carbon County Land Company had been denied claims to over 5,500 acres of coal land by the Eighth Circuit Court of Appeals. Braffet's new law partner, Samuel A. King, may have helped cement this union. After all, Sam King's older brother, one of the U.S. senators for Utah, William H. King (George Sutherland's nemesis), now sat on the board of the Carbon County Land Company, exemplifying a new link between state politics and coal. Consequently, in October 1919, Braffet and Sam King appeared before the Utah State Land Board to discuss the Milner interests northeast of Price. Braffet and King asserted that the title to these lands "undoubtedly" rested with the state, based on statements allegedly made by federal prosecutor Fred Maynard in 1907. As reported by the newspaper, "Maynard expressed to the State board . . . that it was not the intention of the government to contest the state's rights to these lands, but rather to protect the state against improper disposition of the same." The attorneys further argued that, since these were in lieu lands, not regular school sections, the Sweet decision did not pertain to them. They noted that the federal government had so far taken no action to reassign title to the Sweet section, and by now the statute of limitations had run in favor of the state's claim. Braffet and King asked permission to use the state's name in requesting clarification of ownership from the federal government. They then proposed to complete the payment of grazing-land prices for the property, tendered by the Milner group to Utah. When the state balked at this last item, the attorneys began negotiating to purchase 2,560 acres, the largest acreage allowable in Utah, from the state.[12] Oddly enough, Braffet's attempt to aid competitors of the Rio Grande system would ultimately help clarify the application of federal coal-land law to Utah in a way that federal litigation against the railroad consortium itself was never able to do.

Regarding the immediate issue at hand, Utah and the Milners soon reached a compromise. The state contended that the initial price of $1.50 an acre would do little to support public schools; besides, the land contained coal. But the state was willing to offer generous payment terms to the group that had helped it assert its rights to these in lieu lands, as against those of the federal government. The land board therefore offered the Milner consortium a contract for purchase of the original 5,564 acres for $556,428, under mortgage to the state, repayable in installments beginning in 1925 and ending in 1950. The Milners, delighted at a second chance to acquire a very valuable property, accepted.[13]

It is unclear whether or not the federal government was informed of these arrangements, or even contacted regarding the ambiguous status of the title to the Milner land. However, it is very clear that Congress finally took the long-recommended steps to reform the unrealistic national coal-land law. Congress was finally willing to listen to complaints about the Coal Land Act of 1873, similar to those voiced by the secretary of the interior in 1907. In that first flush of Progressive reform, the Justice Department had been pressing its prosecution against the Rio Grande system based on exactly that statute, and had just begun its cases against Arthur A. Sweet and the Milners. Faced with its obvious defects, the interior secretary had complained:

> The futility of this law [of 1873] is shown in the fact that since its enactment less than 500,000 acres of coal lands have been patented under it, while millions of acres of coal lands have been taken under other forms of entry . . . in order to avoid the terms of the coal-land act, coal lands being the highest-priced lands offered by the Government. . . .
>
> These lands have almost uniformly passed into the hands of speculators or large combinations controlling the output or the transportation, so that the consumer is at the mercy of both in the greater portion of the West. The inducements for much of the crime and fraud committed under the present system can be prevented by separating the right to mine from the title to the soil.[14]

A later historian interpreted the slight acreage acquired under the Coal Land Act of 1873 as indicative of the slight importance of coal land in the larger picture of the public domain. In 1951, Louise Peffer wrote: "Coal lands as such had never been a large item of land-office business because of the [restrictive] terms of the mining laws ... [and the later-set price] so high that none could afford to buy the lands."[15] This more recent interpretation of the insignificant volume of coal-land transfers in reality illuminated the astounding extent to which fraud had been the preferred mode of coal-land acquisition. That reality, well recognized in the Progressive Era, may have been one of the casualties of the industrial, as well as perceptional, shifts caused by World War I.

By the end of that war, the nation had become fascinated with the battles for oil lands, rather than coal. This new source of power had more promise and glamor than the dirty, black mineral that had powered nineteenth-century industrial growth.[16] In a move characterized by one historian as President Taft's "most audacious act," the president had engineered the passage of the Pickett Act through Congress in 1910. This statute allowed for the withdrawal of all potentially oil-bearing lands from the public domain, which, after classification, could be disposed of under the applicable laws. Even Wyoming Representative Frank Mondell, chairman of the Public Lands Committee, had supported this bill, a major reversal of the attitude with which he had greeted President Roosevelt's coal-land withdrawals. Mondell cited recognition of "large public sentiment" for these presidential policies as the reason for his changing views.[17]

Although Mondell's claim may have been disingenious, public reliance on oil—and a growing Congressional interest in disposition of oil lands—grew between 1910 and 1920. This decade marked the shift from the navy's reliance on coal to oil, and the subsequent congressional creation of naval oil reserves, beginning in 1912. The first of these reserves, in Elk Hills and Buena Vista Hills, California, were followed in 1914 by the creation of the Teapot Dome reserve in Wyoming (later to attain notoriety). In a tangential public-land matter with later importance for Utah coal, the 1914 Congress put Alaskan coal lands on a leasing basis. In 1915, the Supreme Court ruled the Pickett Act constitutional in *United States v. Midwest Oil Company,* legitimizing a series of roughly 250 earlier executive orders regarding the public domain, and placing greater pressure on Congress to legislate if it wanted to regain control of the public lands. Then, in 1916, Congress expanded its oil-land policy by setting aside three oil-shale reserves, two in Colorado and one in Utah.[18] With this last action, the interest of Utah's Senator Reed Smoot, now chairman of the Senate Public Lands Committee, became actively engaged in oil as well as coal, setting the stage for his committee's hearing on a new land-leasing act.

In 1918, Congress began the debate that led up to the passage of the Mineral Leasing Act of 1920. In general, westerners wanted to open up the public domain to enhance their own development, but disagreed on the method. The argument in favor of leasing was presented by Rep. John Kendrick (Wyoming) in 1918, as he noted that the new leasing proposal "marks the passing of an old system, the tendency of which was to produce great wealth and extreme poverty side by side." In a surge of optimism about the new proposal, he continued: "It is the herald of a new era: it reveals a new vision of national responsibility which, while providing for the welfare of the present, protects and safeguards the interests of future genera- tions."[19] By his reckoning, the dilemma of western lands—including Utah's coal lands—was about to be solved.

Not everyone agreed with this assessment. Mirroring the days of the first federal litigation of Utah coal-land fraud, the state's two senators were again divided over public-land policy. As the leasing debate continued into 1919, Senator William King (a director of the Carbon County Land Company, which was purchasing more than 5,500 acres of coal-bearing land from the State of Utah), thundered: "I am absolutely opposed to the leasing system, the paternalism, the bureaucracy, the autocracy, the un-American system that leasing entails."[20]

Utah's other senator, Smoot, as chairman of the committee on public lands, followed his own agenda. After a hiatus of six years in the coal-land fight, he pressed forward in 1919 with a bill that would confirm to the states ownership of all school sections regardless of mineral content. When the secretary of the interior received a copy of this bill, he respectfully reminded Utah's senior senator of the recent 1918 Sweet decision that had specifically reserved mineral lands to the federal government. Smoot's bill quietly died in committee. Next, Smoot largely drafted the bill (later heavily amended by the House) that put a mineral-leasing system in place. The leading historical treatment of congressional debate on public land law focuses on provi- sions regarding oil and oil shale, but other minerals (gas, phosphate, and coal) were included under the new Mineral Leasing Act.[21]

In regard to coal, the most significant land-policy change was the separation of surface and mineral rights. Buyers could purchase only the former. The minerals below the surface belonged to the United States in perpetuity and could be worked only under lease. Additional provisions included raising the legal acreage limit to 2,560 coal-bearing acres, offering a two-year prospecting lease as well as a development lease of indeterminate length, and setting the low royalty of 5¢ a ton on coal mined and a maximum of $1 per acre rental per year. Remaining mindful of the earlier power of railroad–coal monopolies, Congress added other sections, limiting railroad holdings to those necessary for corporate use. No company could hold more than one lease per state, and railroads could hold only one lease per two hundred miles of track in any state. Other provisions addressed the need to mine for domestic use only and outlined special rules for municipalities.[22]

While generally heralded as a reform, the Mineral Leasing Act added complexities to land titles already under adjudication. Although most of the best coal lands in the West had already passed into private ownership, the title of many tracts was uncertain. Questions included: Were disputed titles acquired through the state as school sections (or as in lieu lands) automatically voided? What was the effect of proven fraud? Could adjudicated coal lands still be purchased under state law, as the Milners had contracted to do, or did all such lands now have to be leased from the federal government? Could states offer a lease? Precisely which tracts fit the new definition, *coal-bearing by geological inference?* Had this knowledge of the land's mineral content existed at statehood? How did that knowledge affect the status of the land?

For three years, the State of Utah had been wrestling with similar questions, and had come up with some findings just as Congress passed the Mineral Leasing Act. An auditor's report, in preparation since 1917, was issued in 1920. It identified thousands of acres sold by the state that had subsequently been found to contain coal. Listing each parcel by specific geographical description, the report noted where title had been conferred by the out-of-court-settlement of the government's first ("landmark") coal-land case against the Rio Grande system, dubbing the compromise "one of the most flagrant miscarriages of justice and farci[c]al terminations of an important case at bar in the history of the State of Utah."[23] More than a decade later, the original federal Utah coal-land cases were still seen as an ignominious failure.

This thoroughgoing report also dealt at length with all independently owned coal-land tracts, and outlined those few instances in which coal had been reserved to the state, listing properties still under litigation. In boldface, referring to Utah's own mineral leasing statute, it stated: "The State Board of Land Commissioners have never been authorized by law to sell lands containing deposits of coal," damning the practice as negligent in protecting the interests of the state. The report also castigated the state board of equalization, which continued to tax these illegally acquired coal lands on the basis of their purchase price as grazing lands, rather than at their commercial value, despite earlier attempts at a state constitutional amendment to raise taxes on mineral lands. A 3 percent proceeds tax to benefit public schools was still being fought in the courts. Another boldface statement in the auditor's report warned: "No proceedings have ever been instituted by the state for the recovery of such lands." The report forcefully recommended that this oversight be immediately corrected.[24] Even as Congress finally reformed the defective Coal Land Act of 1873 that had necessitated so much land fraud, the results of the earlier defective law still rankled in Utah.

The state call for retribution overlooked widespread changes wrought by World War I. One such change fulfilled the prophetic warning of President Wilson: international belligerency had ended the public urge to bust the trusts. According to historian Gabriel Kolko: "The war period represents the triumph of business in the most emphatic manner possible . . . big business gained total support from the various regulatory agencies and the Executive."[25] The brand of public opinion that had so spurred Burch, Maynard, and other members of the original prosecution team had long since faded. A pro-business spirit now pervaded the press. For example, in 1920 the *New West Magazine* devoted an entire month's issue to Utah's Book Cliffs coal field. An article by John B. Forrester, Utah Fuel employee and younger brother of Robert, praised the thirteen operating coal companies in the area, where previously agents of the Rio Grande system had worked alone. The Western's coal companies emerged in print as the "Father of Coal Mining in Utah," and former Western employees were reportedly "in responsible positions in about every other company in the district." This image of the railroad as benevolent sire of a bevy of cooperative corporations was a long, long way from Roosevelt's view of combinations as a multi-tentacled trust.[26]

The old Rio Grande bogeyman, now humbled, had also undergone a transformation. More than a year after the 1918 armistice, Congress passed the Esch-Cummings Bill, which returned all railroads to private ownership, as of March 1, 1920. As the Rio Grande's receivership ended, the railroad emerged as two new corporations: the Denver and Rio Grande Western Railroad Company (D&RGW) and the Western Pacific Railroad Corporation, a holding company for the new D&RGW and for the old Western Pacific, now the owner of Utah Fuel. Although initially united under the leadership of the president of the Equitable Trust Company, these companies proved so economically unstable that renewed receivership, bankruptcy, and trusteeships colored their existence until 1947.[27]

As the Rio Grande system emerged from the fold of receivership, a wolf was waiting. Mark Braffet, still after valuable Utah coal lands, challenged his former employers for previously unlitigated Castle Gate properties. In 1922, he won a contest in the General Land Office for 160 acres of disputed land there that the PVCC had obtained from the state. The PVCC appealed the decision, and turned to face another weapon in the Braffet arsenal, the Beehive Coal Corporation, newly charted in the state of Delaware. Braffet tendered Beehive's bid for the mineral-leasing rights on 1,560 acres of lands adjacent to those already in litigation. In response, the PVCC paid the federal government a new leasing record of $50,100, in compliance with the provisions of the new Mineral Leasing Act. The new federal lease provisions also obligated the company to spend $200,000 on development during the next two years or risk losing the property. Beehive Coal touched the PVCC for further expenditures in 1922, when its officials offered to sell another school section near Castle Gate. Based on insider knowledge of fraudulent state-based land titles, Beehive employees had purchased this tract from the federal government just four months before the passage of the Mineral Leasing Act. To protect its Castle Gate operation, Utah Fuel, the owner of the PVCC, had to buy. The two companies signed an agreement whereby "thru Mark P. Braffet, the said Utah Fuel Company offers to purchase the above described property for the sum of Fifty Thousand Dollars ($50,000.00) cash."[28] Braffet got his share of the take, and his former employers undoubtedly rued his release.

Not all of the early coal-land claimants suffered as severely as the Rio Grande system. Jesse Knight's tenacity in holding his Spring Canyon coal land had finally paid off in January 1921, when the District of Columbia Court of Appeals ruled to protect his property. The decision turned on the ability of the secretary of the interior to ignore the Sweet decision in making a ruling. The appeals court ruled that the secretary was indeed within his rights in acting to protect Knight as an innocent purchaser. The Spring Canyon townsite tract was at last safe from Olson's grasp.[29]

In 1913, some miners still lived in tents (foreground) in the coal company town of Spring Canyon. Unfortunately for owner Jesse Knight, all the land on which he had erected the town was claimed by a rival interest that alleged he had obtained the land by fraud. Courtesy of the Western Mining and Railroad Museum, Helper, Utah.

Just two months later, the old question of the ultimate ownership of the Sweet section was resolved. Although the Supreme Court had used the litigation of this school section to rule that states could not claim known mineral lands at statehood based on their enabling acts, the only immediate effect of the decision had been to return the Sweet section to the public domain. Neither of the competing claimants— USSR&M with a state claim and LeRoy Eccles and associates with a federal claim—had been successful in getting a resolution in Congress, which had further expressed its will in regard to coal lands with the passage of the Mineral Leasing Act of 1920. Although this law forbade any private ownership of coal-bearing lands, it did not specifically apply to lands already in dispute. As a result, the secretary of the interior, the appropriate official in the executive branch, could render a final decision on who owned the Sweet section, since all other avenues of adjudication had already been exhausted.

Traditionally, and for practical reasons, the secretary of the interior published only a small fraction of all the cases brought to him for adjudication. The Sweet case was not among them. According to a newspaper report, however, he awarded the Sweet section, then worth an estimated $500,000, to Eccles in February 1921. On March 3, 1921, the very last day of his presidency, the stricken Woodrow Wilson signed a federal patent conveying this strategic, coal-rich section to Eccles and associates. Less than two months later, the Eccles group sold the land to the USSR&M for an undisclosed amount.[30]

The following year, Congress belatedly regularized this decision-making process with a new law. It empowered the commissioner of the General Land Office, in accordance with regulations approved by the secretary of the interior, to decide on suspended cases involving public lands (most of which had been pending since the Sweet case was appealed to the Supreme Court in 1917). The secretary had to approve these decisions, and could act only to divest the United States of land titles. He was also required to issue new patents when outstanding patents under dispute were surrendered. Yet even this establishment of legal authority promised no speedy resolution to ongoing coal-land disputes. As the secretary himself remarked in 1921: "Entirely too much red tape has been used and too many technicalities imposed in the matter of granting final patents. ... I discovered recently that there are now pending approximately 19,000 cases before the General Land Office"—all of which he might now have to decide.[31]

As the federal machinery for clearing coal-land titles grew increasingly efficient, Utah raced to establish its own claims. In the fall of 1921, the state took a new interest in the Castle Gate operations of Utah Fuel and Pleasant Valley Coal. Belatedly following its auditors' advice, Utah claimed possession of a 160-acre school section, part of the huge Castle Gate parcel that had just been leased by the federal government to the PVCC. If successful, the state could benefit from the lease revenues from the property. In addition, Utah became an intervenor in the ongoing Ketchum suit for ownership of the same property.[32]

Meanwhile, the coal market slumped. Increasingly, private developers had less reason to pursue expensive, time-consuming litigation. Although the local paper disingenuously announced the inaccessibility of the Book Cliffs coal as the reason for the dip, other causes abounded. First, several economic sectors nationwide had suffered a downturn with the end of wartime demands. During the war, Book Cliffs coal, like other industries, had overexpanded. Second, companies had faced labor problems with a nationwide coal strike in 1922. Third, specific mines had experienced a strain on the resources at their command;

notably those associated with the Rio Grande system, which had previously offered a tempting litigation target.[33]

In this bleak atmosphere, coal-land decisions left a spotty legacy. First, in July 1922, the secretary of the interior ruled that the General Land Office, headed by a former Utah governor, William Spry, had erred when it had supported the Utah land office in awarding Mark Braffet his claim to 160 acres at Castle Gate. The secretary based his finding on the fact that the PVCC and the State of Utah (which had allegedly sold the land to the company) had not been allowed to give evidence in the case; therefore, it was remanded to the Utah land office for further hearings. A year later, the secretary ruled that, while the PVCC might not be able to claim title to this disputed property (in presumed future litigation), Braffet's allegation of PVCC wrongdoing did not give him preference rights to ownership of the area. If this decision over preference rights were to become binding, much of the acquisitive motive behind pending litigation would disappear. What would be the advantage in pursuing expensive litigation to void a title when immediate rights to the subsurface coal were not gained? Meanwhile, Utah withdrew its ownership claims to the tract that Braffet wanted and leased the land to the PVCC. Braffet appealed, but his case was dismissed in January 1924. However, he was not yet finished with his old employers.[34]

In his assaults on the ownership of the Castle Gate lands, Braffet continually relied on the doctrine of geological inference as the proper way to determine the presence of coal on the sections of land he desired. This doctrine (which, as noted earlier, based the definition of coal-bearing on nearby geological indications, rather than a visible outcrop) also propped up the case of Braffet's friend, "Doc" Shores. Shores had filed with the federal government on the same Castle Gate parcel claimed by Truman Ketchum and the PVCC from the state. By a coincidence, Shores had filed his federal ownership claim in 1915, when William Spry, now commissioner of the General Land Office, had been governor of Utah. In his new federal position, Spry now had the power to vindicate, or at least clarify, the decisions of his former administration.[35]

In 1923, Spry and his land office colleagues had decided that the Shores claim was known to be coal-bearing at statehood based on geological inference. In other words, an administrative decision finally mirrored reality: when Utah became a state, geologists had known where coal existed based on evidence on adjoining lands. Because of this knowledge, the state could neither legally claim this land nor sell it to others. This portion of the decision effectively invalidated the claims of the PVCC and Ketchum. Spry's administration had further ruled, however, that the passage of the Mineral Leasing Act three years earlier meant that Shores could not now buy the land from the federal government (unlike Eccles, who had achieved private ownership of the Sweet section in an unreported decision i.e., one that set no precedent). Undaunted, Shores appealed to the secretary of the interior, perhaps hoping for the same kind of treatment that Eccles had received, as revealed by the local newspaper. As a former Rio Grande special agent and police officer, Shores was familiar with dogged pursuit, but courts needed more time than criminals. A huge backlog of cases gave him years to wait for an answer.[36]

Meanwhile, in separate actions, the secretary of the interior was asked to rule on whether or not the State of Utah held title to the lands it sold to Ketchum and the PVCC. The decision was reserved pending other litigation. Spry, as commissioner of the General Land Office, denied the PVCC ownership to another disputed Castle Gate section, originally purchased by Spotter Owen (now a State of Utah land assessor), then conveyed to the Rio Grande system in 1903. Once again, this case continued on appeal as the executive branch sought to sort out the tangle of Utah coal-land titles.[37] The new Mineral Leasing Act might settle such disputes in the future, but the heavy legacy of Progressive coal-fraud litigation remained unresolved.

CHAPTER 18

No Longer Necessary

In the 1920s, the practical issue of Utah coal-land ownership slouched toward resolution. Although future acquisitions bowed to the legal parameters set by Congress with the Mineral Leasing Act of 1920, the law could not be made retroactive. Old warhorses seasoned in earlier coal-land battles remained on the field. The tortuous process of land litigation wound to its conclusion through a maze of now outdated statutes and decisions.

This lengthy legal endeavor took place in an age worn out by the recent, ghastly war. The old reform fire was gone. Tired Progressive Frederic Howe spoke for a generation when he wrote:

> At fifty I saw myself as I saw the political state. I had lost the illusions I had spent a lifetime in hoarding. I had lost the illusions of myself. Much of my intellectual capital had flown. Drafts on my mind came back endorsed: "No funds."[1]

The political and legal climate had also changed pace. Herbert Hoover, now secretary of commerce, had developed an activist, associative vision of the federal role that would soon come to sanction corporate cooperation as a pillar of the U.S. economy. Likewise, the federal courts no longer judged monopolies by their composition, but by their results. Under the "rule of reason," the legality of restraint was judged on whether or not it promoted or restricted competition. Even at the state level, policies and legislation tended to liberalize corporate law (often modeled on New Jersey's statutes), simultaneously strengthening antitrust measures, presumably to stimulate beneficial mergers while weeding out uncompetitive ones.[2]

Numerous historians have sought the reasons for this change. In 1959, Arthur Link reviewed a number of early theories when he asked: "What Happened to Progressivism in the 1920s?" He acknowledged the intellectual exhaustion of middle-class reformers like Howe, but struck a more optimistic note than most. In Link's view, certain progressive impulses survived into the 1920s—but even Link could

find them only among farmers and planners for public power development.[3] A dozen years later, Otis Graham claimed that the glacial pace
of change had proved wearisome to progressives; the masses had
remained ignorant; would-be reformers had split over urban-rural
differences and cultural antagonisms, and the state had continued to
favor conformity. As a result, large economic interests could continue
to plunder the public domain (among other nefarious activities). In
this situation, Graham surmised: "Economic reform would have to
wait until the more important matters of morals and behavior and
ideas were dealt with."[4] More recently, historians Ellis Hawley, Morton
Keller, and Herbert Hovencamp have explained the same changes as
a trend toward the rationalization of business based on new economic
theories, themselves an outgrowth of a dynamic, industrializing
nation.[5]

Certainly the mood of the 1920s was light years away from the
paced, rational approach of the prewar era. During the hedonistic
Roaring Twenties, youth rebelled in an orgy of the Charleston and
bathtub gin, while their elders speculated wildly on the stock market.
The passage of the Eighteenth Amendment and the Volstead Act led
to widespread disregard for the law and a growing contempt for its
enforcement. Meanwhile, President Calvin Coolidge, equating the
national purpose with business itself, stated his opinion: "Brains are
wealth and wealth is the chief end of man."[6] In this climate, amassing
riches through corporate measures achieved a new respectability.

By the 1920s, controlling Big Business through litigation had become impractical and anachronistic. If the Progressive Movement had
once lived, it was now gone—and according to historian Peter Filene
it had never existed. Writing in 1970, Filene claimed that the Progressive Era itself was "characterized by shifting coalitions around different
issues, with the specific nature of these coalitions varying on the federal,
state, and local levels."[7] Certainly, the growing antirailroad consensus
that had united suspicious Mormons with zealous federal attorneys
in a mutual trust-busting effort had evaporated over time.

In the new entrepreneurial climate, even those who might otherwise have sought to regulate Utah coal-land acquisitions leaped into
mining development. Utah's junior U.S. Senator, William H. King,
for one, had joined the board of the Carbon County Land Company
(CCLC), the corporation chartered by Sam Gilson and Stanley Milner.
King had first risen to prominence in Utah as the attorney who
defended union organizers in the face of Utah Fuel intimidation
during the strike of 1903–1904. By the 1920s, he was as eager to be

involved in the coal industry as many of his contemporaries, and he fought his Senate colleague, Reed Smoot, over public-land policies.[8]

The CCLC (with King as a member) had, prior to the passage of the Mineral Leasing Act, contracted to buy five thousand acres of coal land from the State of Utah. In a speculative move typical of the 1920s, King was now involved in selling off part of this property, even before his corporation had achieved clear title. Independent Coal and Coke Company (IC&C), charted by the Sweets in 1906 as the first nonrailroad affiliate to enter the Book Cliffs field, bought the bulk of it. Another smaller parcel was lost to Carbon County in a tax sale. In actuality, all of these new owners could receive only a claim, since payment to the state had not yet been made in full and, therefore, title had not been perfected. King and his legal partner, the ubiquitous Mark Braffet (King's legal opponent in the 1903 organizer's trial), promised to clear up any possible title disputes through negotiations with the federal government.[9]

Building on this uncertain venture, King's associates, along with Californian capitalists, had recently formed the Pacific Steel Corporation, a giant steel consortium run on Utah coal. The ability to assure the corporate fuel supply through private ownership of valuable coal land had become a marketing magnet, especially since competitors would presumably be able to obtain a federal coal-land lease only under the Mineral Leasing Act of 1920.[10]

The local press avidly reported these coal/steel transactions throughout the fall of 1922. Reporters detailed a visit of "Eastern and Pacific Coast steel interests" to the old Milner-Gilson holdings. The CCLC and IC&C, trying to consummate deals in private, refused to make a statement for the papers, but the press persisted. The California business meetings of Senator King got coverage. So did the activities of Leon F. Rains, who had earlier misappropriated the Sweets' water shares above Standardville, when he joined the Utah-California steel and coal combination during a hush-hush meeting in San Francisco. Piquing public interest, the aggregate worth of the consortium was reported at an estimated $60 million, indicating the continuing importance of investment in Utah coal.[11]

These figures may have attracted federal attention; or Braffet and King may have duly made contact regarding the possible conflict in coal-land claims; either way, the Justice Department reacted. In 1924, the government publicly reasserted its rights to the old Milner property, as established by the Eighth Circuit Court of Appeals in 1914. The United States brought suit against the new constellation of owners—

the Independent Coal and Coke Company, the Carbon County Land
Company, and Carbon County—in the U.S. district court in Salt Lake
City, where the original federal Utah coal-land fraud cases had begun
in 1906.[12]

Once again, coal developers had to wait for the wheels of justice
to grind out a decision. Meanwhile, Utah's governor tried to stimulate
congressional interest in finalizing the ownership of unlitigated school
lands to avoid the very real possibility of continuing, protracted federal
suits. In 1923, Governor Charles Mabey called on his fellow governors
to influence their senators "to secure the passage of a law by congress
. . . fixing a time beyond which the government cannot defeat school
grants to the states on the grounds that they are mineral in character."[13]
Under such prodding, Senator Andrieus Jones (New Mexico) followed
closely by Utah's Senator Smoot, introduced twin bills on school
sections into the 1923 Senate Committee on Public Lands. Yet for
two years, these and similar proposals did not reach the floor of
the Senate.[14]

In the meantime, the U.S. district court for Utah was ready to
hear the new case on the old Milner-Gilson claims. The doctrine of
geological inference, now the judicially established definition of known
coal land, had strengthened the government's claim to this acreage.
As of the Sweet decision in 1918, known coal land could not pass to
a state as a numbered school section in place under its enabling act.
On the other hand, although the Sweet section was just such a numbered parcel, the old Milner lands were in lieu sections that the
federal government had specifically granted to the state of Utah when
requested to do so. As the defense reasoned, the state had the superior
claim under this different set of circumstances. Additionally, the defendants relied on statements allegedly made in 1907 by Justice Department attorney Fred Maynard as he pursued the Progressive target of
the railroad-coal "trust." Defense attorneys asserted that, according to
Maynard, the federal government had then simply sought to protect
the state from fraud in litigating the original Milner-Gilson transaction,
not to reacquire the land in question. Certainly Utah had never been
a party to the suit, indicating that the federal government had no
direct quarrel with the state. The major issue here must therefore be
fraud—and now that the state had agreed to sell this tract as known
coal land at an appropriate price, no fraud was being perpetrated.
The state, not the nation, should be able to dispose of this land.[15]

At trial, it became clear that the U.S. district court had abandoned
its earlier, strongly profederal stance with the departure of Judge

Marshall. In January 1925, the court dismissed the United States' complaint, holding that the State of Utah had a valid claim to the land that had now come under the protection of the six-year statute of limitations. The state could therefore dispose of the property as it wished, and the IC&C, CCLC, and Carbon County held valid titles. The judge determined that the Sweet case had no bearing here, since these were in lieu lands, not school sections. The Justice Department appealed, resulting in September 1925 in an appellate court reversal of the lower court's decision. In so doing, however, the Eighth Circuit Court of Appeals remanded the case to district court in order to strike Carbon County from the list of defendants, on the basis that it could hardly be accused of fraudulent entry for gain after acquiring the land in a tax sale. The developers in the IC&C and CCLC, given hope for possession by the conflicting court decisions, appealed the case to the U.S. Supreme Court, which agreed to hear the case. The State of Utah, still frustrated in its attempt to get congressional action on the subject, filed a brief of amicus curiae, indicating its strong interest in the outcome.[16]

In preparing for a hearing before the Supreme Court, William Riter, formerly an attorney for the victorious Eccles consortium in the Sweet case, developed a new argument for IC&C and the CCLC. Riter centered his brief on the significance of fraud. Asserting that, since the State of Utah had not been a party to the first Milner case, concluded in 1914, it had never been deprived of the property and therefore had been within its rights to dispose of the disputed land in any appropriate manner. The only result of the first Milner case, he reasoned, was that the Milners and associates had been forced to acknowledge their perpetration of fraud and relinquish fraudulently obtained coal land *to the state*. Because they and other coal developers had since repented of the error of their ways and contracted to rebuy the property legally *from* the state, they should be awarded clear title. Whether or not the Supreme Court would agree with this line of reasoning had to wait until May 1927 for a decision.[17]

In the meantime, Mark Braffet was awaiting his own decision on his federal filing on Castle Gate coal lands from the court of the District of Columbia, the next resort in a series of appeals brought through the Department of the Interior. (This route was unavailable for cases that had *already* gone through the courts; in those instances, the secretary of the interior had the final say.) Braffet had appealed his case over the Willow Creek Number 2 Mine, one of the earliest school section acquisitions of the PVCC, now the property of his enemy, Utah Fuel. Braffet's tenacity was rewarded when he won the case in April 1926. Six other plaintiffs holding federal filings, including Cyrus "Doc" Shores, directly benefited from this decision. The local *Sun* newspaper speculated whether Utah Fuel/PVCC would try to effect a compromise over the Number 2 Mine, which they had been working on lease from the federal government since 1918. When reporters asked Braffet whether he would seek compensation from Utah Fuel for coal previously extracted, he claimed "he was unprepared to say at this time."[18] Braffet had apparently won his revenge against the company that had sided with A. H. Cowie.

At the same time that Braffet received satisfaction from the District of Columbia court, Congress busied itself with mopping up details of coal-land ownership. The first result was the Coal Trespass Law of 1926, which outlawed practices such as had occurred at Sunnyside, the basis of the second series of federal suits against the old Rio Grande system. This law made it "unlawful to mine or remove coal of any character ... from beds or deposits in lands of the United States," marking the end of a long-standing abuse.[19] Another statute passed the same year abolished the limitation of one coal lease per person per state.[20]

Next, Congress tackled the tangled web of state selections, mineral and otherwise, through the Jones Act, passed on January 25, 1927. Named after Senator Jones of New Mexico, it was entitled "An Act Confirming in States and Territories title to lands granted by the United States in aid of common or public schools." The Jones Act contained specific language reflecting the national separation of surface and mineral rights and stated unequivocally that the school sections granted in place, whether mineral or not, belonged to the states, at the same time explicitly excluding in lieu lands from its provisions. The Jones Act also indicated who would get the revenue from the nation's newly disposed coal lands. In the designated school sections, the mineral rights could only be leased from the states, not sold into private ownership. The revenues from the state leases covered by this law had to go to the support of public schools, along with profits from the sale of the surface. The act continued: "Any lands or minerals disposed of contrary to the provisions of this Act shall be forfeited to the United States by appropriate proceedings instituted by the Attorney General." A final provision of the bill specifically exempted "any pending suit or proceedings in the courts of the United States" from its provisions. Thus the ownership of much Castle Gate land, as well as the in lieu Milner claims, remained an open question.[21]

Further stumbling blocks on the road toward Utah coal-lands ownership resulted from contradictions between recent judicial decisions and new federal legislation. For example, the secretary of the interior balked at issuing Braffet a patent to the Willow Creek lands, recently awarded by the court of the District of Columbia, because such an action contradicted the Mineral Leasing Act of 1920. The secretary therefore brought a suit to the Supreme Court.[22]

Before a decision could be reached, Mark Braffet died. On January 3, 1927, the leading Utah paper reported:

> Mark P. Braffet, 56, for more than a quarter of a century prominent in legal circles of the state and city, . . . died Sunday in his home in Price. . . .
>
> The deceased came into prominence during the hearing here 20 years ago of the so-called coal land fraud cases, when several prominent coal operators and railroad men were indicted by the federal grand jury here. Mr. Braffet secured settlement favorable to his company. For several years he was counsel for the Utah Fuel company. . . .
>
> He was recognized as a political power in Carbon county and a shrewd business man. It is doubtful if the extent of his holdings is actually known.[23]

Not only was the extent of his holdings not known, it had yet to be decided. The Willow Creek litigation ultimately went to the U.S. Supreme Court, where a decision was rendered in April 1928. Posthumously, Braffet lost this final contest. Citing the welter of recently passed coal-land laws, especially the Mineral Leasing Act of 1920, the court ruled that Braffet, by his earlier victory, had simply voided PVCC ownership, not transferred it to himself. As of 1920, in the absence of a valid patent, coal land must be leased. The federal government and the states now had to come to an equitable agreement as to the recipient of the lease money. In this instance, due to the year-old Jones Act, Utah retained the ownership it had claimed under its enabling act, despite the known character of the land as bearing coal. Utah could confirm surface rights to the PVCC and the Ketchum Coal company; the coal it could only lease.[24]

With the decision against the late Mark Braffet, a series of Utah coal land cases came to a close. Among them was the Shores case. Shores had filed a federal claim on some Castle Gate school land illegally acquired by the PVCC from the state. The same property had been claimed by Ketchum. Shores, now the only adverse claimant, was continuing the case on appeal to commissioner Spry's General Land Office. In October 1928, he received the verdict: the board had reviewed the evidence presented, with attention to indications that the land might have been known as coal bearing at statehood, based on the doctrine of geological inference. Echoing the original 1881 report of Rio Grande geologist Ellis Clark, the decision noted:

> A massive bed of sandstone, 80 to 120 feet thick ... is exposed on both sides of Price Valley ... and for many miles to the east along a prominent escarpment ... known as the Book Cliffs. ... [Near] the tract in question a mine, known as the Castlegate No. 1, was opened on this seam in 1888 or 1889, and many millions of tons of coal were taken from it during its operation.[25]

Further testimony indicated that in 1896, when Utah achieved statehood, the only value of the land derived from the likely presence of coal. Therefore, the state could not claim the land as school sections under its enabling act. On the other hand, Utah had subsequently achieved ownership through the 1927 Jones Act. Shores, who had filed with the federal government, had lost. So had the other claimants who had relied on federal law. Yet the state, too, had to change its ways. As the newspaper reporting the case warned: "Notice has been served on the state that it must cancel the sale of the land ... and ... reserve the mineral deposits to the state" for lease.[26]

These decisions yielded multiple results. First, individuals were now thoroughly discouraged from pursuing litigation of ambiguous coal-land titles. Second, the question of state versus federal claims to coal-bearing school sections in place had been decided in favor of the states. Third, all subsurface coal land must now be leased and the recipients of the lease money had been clearly defined. Yet the original Progressive goal—to restore fraudulently obtained Utah coal lands to the public domain—remained unfulfilled. In addition, the ownership of coal-bearing in lieu sections had yet to be resolved. This last issue could become the means of fulfilling the Progressive dream.

The ultimate vehicle for deciding this matter became the Milner case, now up in a new form as a contest between the United States and the land's new owners, the IC&CC and the Carbon County Land Company (Milner's and Gilson's original corporation). Although a question existed over whether the state or the federal government could convey this property, the State of Utah was not a party to the suit. Not surprisingly, therefore, the Supreme Court's initial decision, rendered on May 31, 1927, was inconclusive. Although the justices held (in a six-three decision) that the CCLC had acted improperly in rebuying the land from the State of Utah, they referred the case back to the Utah district court for further review. The problems with the case as presented were twofold: first, title to the lands in question had already been granted to the United States, not the state, in the first federal litigation completed in 1914 against Truth A. Milner, et al. Hence, the nation needed to protect its title rather than pursue corporate claimants who had received title from the state. (In that matter, the statute of limitations would not be a bar to litigation.) Second, in order for a decision to be binding, the State of Utah needed to be made party to the suit.[27]

In rendering this opinion, one of the dissenting votes was cast by Utah's George Sutherland, former U.S. senator and member of the Supreme Court since 1922. Although Justice Sutherland offered no written argument explaining his dissent, his past certainly offered some reasons for his stance. For one, Sutherland had had a previous affinity with the developers of Carbon County coal. Specifically, almost twenty-five years before he had recommended Hiram Booth for the CCLC's board of directors. Second, his early legal career had included a stint as legal counsel for Utah Fuel and Pleasant Valley Coal. Third, he had voiced the general Utah distrust of the federal government occasioned by the repressive federal tactics of his youth, as indicated by some of the few of his legal papers he preserved for posterity.[28]

Among Sutherland's slim collection remain two undated briefs from his early legal career, classified only as 1888–1901, but probably dating from 1896, the year of Utah statehood. The first involved Utah's consistent political nemesis, polygamy. Sutherland had represented accused polygamist Peter M. Baum in John Marshall's federal district court. Before statehood, Baum had been convicted of adultery, a common charge leveled against polygamists. Baum was awaiting sentencing when Utah became a state, which prompted Sutherland to bring an action to dismiss the case. Sutherland argued that, since Utah had just achieved statehood and marriage was regulated by the state, the power to punish adultery under the federal Edmunds-Tucker Act had ceased. Therefore, the case against Baum should be dismissed. Judge Marshall disagreed. He reasoned that if "the law under which this indictment was found has been repealed by implication with respect to Utah, still the power to punish past offenses under it is saved," even more so if the law was not thus repealed. Baum was duly sentenced.[29]

In the second instance, Sutherland had again relied on the constitutional separation of powers of the nation and the state in his attempt to defend a near-monopoly among coal retailers in Salt Lake City. In this case, he argued that, because the action was brought in Utah Territory under the federal Sherman Anti-Trust Act, Utah's statehood had voided federal power to regulate what was essentially a state matter (i.e., internal sales, and not restraint of interstate trade). Again, Sutherland lost.[30]

From a more theoretical standpoint, Sutherland's biographer later noted that the justice was a consistent supporter of three "constitutional ultimates[,] . . . the separation of powers, . . . limited government and dual federalism."[31] Sutherland's ultimate fame, as the intellectual leader of the Four Horsemen who opposed so much New Deal legislation on constitutional grounds, rang consistent with his dissent on the Milner-Gilson coal lands case.

The local newspaper carefully reported this 1927 Supreme Court decision. Abandoning its earlier smear tactics (which had implied Sutherland's complicity in the first federal coal-lands suits), the *Sun* philosophically discussed the question of state or federal ownership of disputed tracts of coal land. In reviewing the Supreme Court's IC&CC-CCLC decision, the paper announced: "The question now arises as to whether or not the land in question comes under the Jones bill passed by the last session of congress. . . . [Perhaps] the land involved in the case . . . would revert to the state of Utah as soon as the litigation is ended."[32] But the Jones Act applied only to numbered school sections in place. Would the Supreme Court recognize a similar application to in lieu lands?

Eagerly awaited by many, the Milner-Gilson coal lands contest made its second trip to the Supreme Court in 1932, after a seven-year hiatus. It was now entitled *Utah et al. v. United States,* with the state finally a party as directed. Utah had continued to claim that the United States was estopped from prosecution based on statements made by Fred Maynard "in a conversation between him and members of the Board of Land Commissioners in 1907, when he delivered to them a copy of the bill of complaint in the first suit." In its final decision, the Supreme Court felt compelled explicitly to deny this repeated argument. The majority found that Maynard "was obviously without authority to dispose of the rights of the United States in its mineral lands and could not estop it from asserting rights which he could not surrender." The court upheld the decision of the circuit court of appeals. Once again, Justice Sutherland dissented, leaving no record of his reasons why.[33] The United States had finally reclaimed part of the coal-bearing public domain fraudulently acquired in Utah.

Thus, in 1932, the last of Utah's Progressive Era coal-land suits ended. As a result of the case between the United States and Utah, more than five thousand coal-bearing acres were restored to the public domain. In 1933, a small (but front-page) article (notable for its lack of capitalization) appeared in the current eastern Utah newspaper, the *Sun-Advocate*. It announced that lands "lost to the Carbon County Land company through a decision of the United States supreme court will be restored to public entry by the general land office on July 26."[34] In the depths of the Great Depression, this notice elicited little excitement.

Even though the long-pending coal-land cases had ended, not all Utah tracts enjoyed clear title. Several "owners" clung tenaciously to unlitigated school sections of known coal land obtained by fraud. Barring further adjudication, their disposition had to await actions of the Congress and of the Interior Department.

In 1934, two years after the Supreme Court finally decided on the Milner lands, Congress passed yet another law to settle the ongoing problems of these state selections. It authorized the secretary of the interior to grant titles to the states of all numbered school sections in place in accordance with the Jones Act. The law continued: "In all inquiries as to the character of the land for which patent is sought the fact shall be determined as of the date when the state's title attached."[35] Land "known" to be coal-bearing at statehood could still be litigated. However, in the depressed 1930s, no one cared to inquire about this "knowledge." Such probing might all too easily lead to conflicting claims and expensive litigation. The result was a decade of legal inactivity.

Subsequently, the western coal industry as a whole jumped from bust to boom and back again to bust. After the Depression, the demands of World War II pushed coal production beyond any previous limit. Although coal land became a good investment for the first time in two decades, the general prosperity gave no cause for litigation. In the 1950s, a bust again plagued western coal districts. As production levels plunged, interest in ownership of coal land and leases waned. The same dismal economic trend—and resultant disinterest—continued into the 1960s.[36] In a nation more and more dependent on oil, coal, the mineral that had once powered national progress, had lost much of its significance.

Concurrently, the national coal-land law was subject to congressional revision. In 1948, the earlier 2,560-acre lease maximum limit was doubled. Separate statutes governing Alaskan coal were consolidated with the Mineral Leasing Act in 1959. In 1964, the Mineral Leasing Act of 1920 was amended to allow a huge 10,240 acres per lease, with a total of 46,000 acres allowed per company per state.[37] At last, a parcel of reasonable commercial size had become legally obtainable.

In the 1960s, the fate of Utah's remaining unlitigated coal lands was decided when the Department of the Interior made its ultimate determination on some remaining Utah school sections containing coal. For example, one of these, near Castle Gate, had been claimed by a PVCC dummy in 1902, contested almost twenty years later by Mark Braffet, and worked under a state coal lease since the 1920s. But the actual title had never officially been cleared. In a general mopping-up operation, in September 1964, the United States formally deeded this Castle Gate land to the State of Utah in accordance with the Jones Act and the statute of 1934. More than a dozen other school sections in eastern Utah and hundreds throughout the rest of the West had their ownership formally confirmed to the states at this time.[38]

As a result, more than half a century of friction over Utah coal ownership finally ceased. Although the process took several decades, Congress had hammered out workable coal-land law. Unrealistically small coal-land allowances had been changed to generous tracts.[39] Developers could now legally obtain workable, commercial acreage, although, after 1920, only under lease. A spate of legal contests for coal and coal-land ownership among individuals, the state, and the federal government had all been resolved. The era of necessary fraud was over.

Conclusion

What were the outcomes of this series of Utah coal-land cases? First, each of them had an immediate effect: securing title to a disputed parcel of land, stymieing an attempt at monopoly, or establishing a new legal precedent. The major cases discussed in this book are here summarized, listed by date initiated:

1898: *Holladay v. Kirker et al.*, brought in Utah's seventh judicial court (Carbon County), which helped solidify Rio Grande system control of Sunnyside when Holladay lost the following year.

1902: *Arthur A. Sweet v. Charles Mostyn Owen,* resulting in a partial victory in the local district court for Sweet, involving Sunnyside lands he subsequently sold to an agent of the Pleasant Valley Coal Company.

1903: Nine different cases were brought by the United States in the federal Land Office in Salt Lake City, the most important of which was *United States v. Utah.* Weak government preparation was cited as the reason for government failure to win a conviction at Salt Lake and on appeal in Washington, D.C.

1906: *Albert L. Simmons v. Owen L. Davies* in the General Land Office, which, when Simmons won, stymied a dummying attempt by the Rio Grande system.

1906: Bills in Equity, the beginning of the federal antirailroad litigation between the United States and the Pleasant Valley Coal Company (two bills) and the Utah Fuel Company (two bills), which were resolved in 1909 in an out-of-court settlement. The only lands reclaimed by the federal government were undeveloped properties in Salina Canyon, far from Utah's richest coal district. The Rio Grande system achieved clear title to the other disputed parcels, including Utah's best coking coal, at Sunnyside.

1907: *U.S. v. Freed, Filer, Robbins, and Senior* over lands in Huntington Canyon, brought first in federal court, where the case was dismissed in 1909. In 1910, federal prosecutors then tried litigation through the General Land Office, taking the case all the way to the secretary of the interior, where in 1916 the Freeds were vindicated.

1907: *U.S. v. Arthur A. Sweet* (and, after his death, v. Frederick Sweet), in federal court, which resulted in a Supreme Court decision in 1918 awarding the land to the federal government. This case set the precedent for federal ownership of lands known at statehood to contain coal (or other minerals).

1907: *United States v. Milner et al.*, brought in federal court to resolve ownership of in lieu lands known at statehood to contain coal. This was the last case to be resolved, making two trips to the U.S. Supreme Court. The final decision came in 1932 in *Utah et al. v. United States,* involving essentially the same land and the exact same issues. The federal government won.

1912: *U.S. v. Palmer, Peabody, et al.*, a second federal attempt on Sunnyside, which was quickly dismissed at federal request due to problems arising from the doctrine of relation.

1914: William Frances Olson sued Jesse Knight in the federal land office at Salt Lake City over lands claimed by Knight that included his entire company town in Spring Canyon. Eventually, the State of Utah, which had granted Knight his patent, took on Olson. A series of appeals resulted in a 1921 decision in favor of Utah and Knight.

1917: *Ketchum v. Denver and Rio Grande Railroad* and, in 1919, *Ketchum v. Pleasant Valley Coal Company* in state and federal courts were both unsuccessful attempts by Truman Ketchum to break the railroad's grip on an important part of its Castle Gate holdings. In this effort he was aided by Cyrus W. "Doc" Shores, who began his own land office litigation in 1918. These suits prompted countersuits by the railroad and coal companies, the first time they had willingly entrusted their affairs to the courts. These suits also forced the two linked concerns to behave in a totally independent fashion. Ultimately, the railroad and its coal-mine company won, assuring ownership of lands they had developed for more than forty years.

1919: Mark Braffet, formerly a lawyer for the Utah Fuel Company, brought a case in the Salt Lake branch of the General Land Office against his former employer and the Pleasant Valley Coal Company over Castle Gate lands. It continued on appeal, in various forms, to the Court of Appeals in the District of Columbia. There, the 1928 decision stipulated that, although the coal companies had illegally gained the lands and now had to work them under lease, Braffet had no prior rights of entry.

As the foregoing list indicates, litigation begun during the Progressive Era had a very long life and far-reaching consequences. These results were felt on the local, state, and national levels, and each perspective deserves separate comment.

Locally, during the era of the Utah coal-land fraud cases, the Saints' isolated "last Utah frontier" was forever bound to regional and national networks. Economically, for example, the old barter economy was replaced by cash, leading such hard-scrabble Mormon farmers as Heber J. Stowell to try to hook his cart to the rising economic star of the Sweets. They, in turn, pursued development work with a group of Italian immigrant miners, laid off by the railroad mines and more than happy to work for a competitor of their former employers. Increasingly, all employment in the area stemmed from the mines, the railroads which served them, or the service centers which sprang up nearby. This pattern still predominates.

In politics, too, coal-mine competition shaped events. For example, Mark Braffet, Utah Fuel king-maker, saw his power exploded not only by an internal corporate rivalry but by the efforts of Progressive-minded women (not coincidentally aligned with independent mine developers), who demanded multiple political and societal reforms. Mine ownership also made a difference, and one result of the Progressive Era coal-land litigation was a shift in the local balance of power.

The Utah coal-land cases also proved to be a vehicle for clarifying issues of state-federal relationships. To a large extent, creating and maintaining the dynamics necessary to prosecute suits over a quarter of a century altered Utah's relationship with the national government. Ramifications touched the organization and power of the LDS Church, particularly during and after the Smoot hearings. While Utahns became more reliant on the federal government to right certain coal-land frauds within their state, they became correspondingly less dependent on the might of the LDS Church to answer all of their needs. Although, before the antipolygamy raids of the 1880s, the Mormon "State of Deseret" (the original Mormon name for what became Utah) enjoyed relative social and economic independence, federal investigations of the church as a result of the Roberts and Smoot hearings closed the doors on any return to those old ways. Historian Jan Shipps explained this shift most succinctly: "External pressure (especially political pressure from the United States government) played ... an enormous role in forcing Mormons to change. ... Virtually universal agreement exists, too, that buried within that antipolygamy campaign were issues as much economic and political as social and moral."[1] The progress of the Utah coal-land fraud cases illuminate specifics of this transformation.

Technically, the government "saved" few of the Utah lands that had already been fraudulently claimed, excepting those in Salina Canyon. Most of the other tracts remained in private ownership, although the Utah coal-land cases did foster a certain amount of redistribution of lands, notably from railroad control into the hands of other capitalists. This result spread some of Utah's coal-land wealth. Not all of those involved lived long enough to experience the outcome, however; for example, Arthur A. Sweet, Robert Forrester, Stanley Milner, Samuel Gilson, Charles M. Freed, and Mark Braffet. Nonetheless, the broadening of coal-land ownership fostered mine development and enhanced economic ties with regional and national market systems.[2] Recent historians saw in this result "the triumph of eastern capitalism . . . [in which] the economic fortunes of Utah came to depend upon decisions and centers of control that lay far outside the confines of the state."[3]

In fact, the power to affect Utah and its coal district increasingly shifted to Washington, D.C., at least during the Progressive Era. In the course of litigating these cases, and as a direct result of some of them, a new body of coal-land law was established. Much of this success was due to the continuing efforts of the prosecution team of Marsden C. Burch and Fred A. Maynard, who had begun Utah litigation with measured apprehension, resulting from the *Detroit Timber* and *Clark* cases.[4] They subsequently secured a judicial definition of coal land, which replaced the requirement that coal be exposed on every forty-acre parcel, a detriment to earlier government prosecutions. Furthermore, some legal precedents set by the Progressive Era Supreme Court still stand, notably from the *Sweet* case, decided in 1918.[5]

The Utah coal-land litigation also demanded change from the other branches of government, especially Congress and the Department of the Interior (including the General Land Office), specifically in regard to defects of the Coal Land Act of 1873. Congress responded in 1920, passing the Mineral Leasing Act, which required that subsurface coal land be leased from the federal government, forever preventing the kind of abuse discussed here.[6] Administrative decisions of the General Land Office and the secretary of the interior implemented and clarified these changes. Although the 1920 act has undergone modification, today it still remains the law of the land.

Business, too, at all levels, responded to this coal-land litigation. Eventually, the "visible hand" of the capitalist was stayed by an "invisible hand"—not of market pressures of supply and demand, but of increasingly effective government regulation.[7] This is not to say that deals are not still consummated in private, or that personal understandings no longer color economic decisions; however, since the instigation of these cases, the force of law has restrained the human acquisitive impulse, in contrast to an earlier era, when flouting an unrealistic, restrictive statute seemed the only route to industrial development.

All of these events took place in a larger context that was then shaping responses to the American West. The predominant perception that the frontier had "closed" led to reassessment of who deserved this diminishing patrimony. The optimism of the Progressive philosophy, coupled with new perceptions about conservation, of Big Business as so-called trusts, and of the necessity of governmental control, melded together to address this problem.[8] Land fraud was admittedly widespread, hence the conscious government effort to bring corrective litigation—against timber-land fraud in Oregon, copper-land fraud in Montana, and coal-land fraud in Utah. The complications involved in litigating the latter were almost impossible to foresee.

Nonetheless, one could argue for the ultimate achievement of a Progressive victory in the Utah coal-land fraud litigation. The results of these suits approached the era's goal as defined by Robert Wiebe, with emphasis on "certain broad social, political, and economic issues," including a desire "to regulate the economy in the public interest."[9] One should also consider the immediate objectives of Justice Department prosecutor Burch, when he debated approaching even "the President himself, and see if something cannot be done to check, and finally prevent the wholesale misappropriation—I might say theft—of lands that is going on." In 1906, Burch knew the solution: "compel [C]ongress to repeal the Coal Land Act altogether, and thus save these lands," which were then subject to "the wasteful and,—if it had been intentional,"—wicked disposition of the ... lands of the government."[10] From his perspective, success was complete. Congress did indeed repeal the act, although it took some fourteen years to do so. And, as a result of suits lasting into the 1930s, land "theft" ultimately ceased, thanks in large part to the litigation that Burch and others so doggedly pursued.

Notes

INTRODUCTION

Each work cited here is representative of a much larger body of literature listed in the bibliography.

1. Nash, *American West*, esp. pp. 31–33, 70, 100–101, and discussion of Henry Kaiser's empire, pp. 205–09, in that Kaiser later acquired Sunnyside; Rickard, *History of American Mining*; Smith, *Rocky Mountain Mining Camps*, and Smith, *Mining America*.

2. Spence, *Mining Engineers*; Spence, *British Investments*; Young, *Mining Men*; Miller, *Stake Your Claim*, esp. pp. 182–83 as specific to material discussed here; Paul Wallace Gates, *History of Public Land Law Development*, (Washington, D.C.: Government Printing Office, 1968). The chapter in Gates by Robert W. Swenson is of particular use.

3. Peffer, *Closing of the Public Domain*; Wyant, *Westward*; Mayer and Riley, *Public Domain*.

4. Nelson, *Making of Federal Coal Policy*.

5. Marcosson, *Anaconda*; Fahey, *Hecla*; Scamehorn, *Pioneer Steelmaker*; Arrington with Hansen, "*Richest Hole on Earth.*"

6. Malone, *Battle for Butte*; Sonnichsen, *Colonel Greene*.

7. Ringholtz, *Uranium Frenzy*.

8. Powell, *The Next Time We Strike*; Whiteside, *Regulating Danger*; Papanikolas, *Buried Unsung*; McGovern and Guttridge, *Coalfield War*.

9. Bowen, *Three Dollar Dreams*; Gardner and Flores, *Forgotten Frontier*. Bowen makes reference to problems with a railroad coal-land grant on pp. 217–18 and pp. 360–63; Gardner and Flores discuss coal-land litigation on pp. 119–24.

10. This particular contradiction is explicitly addressed in Leuchtenburg, *Perils*, pp. 124–27. A complete discussion of the pertinent literature on Progressivism is found in chapter 1.

CHAPTER 1

1. Arthur Sweet, Coal Certificate #172, GLO #1947, Book 6, Carbon County Recorder's Records; *Arthur A. Sweet v. Charles Mostyn Owen*, Civil

253

272, Utah 7th Judicial District, Carbon County Clerk's Records, *Abstract of Mining Locations*, T. 14 S. R. 14 E., Carbon County Recorder's Records, all in Carbon County Courthouse, Price, Utah.

2. Coal Land Act, 17 Stat. 607 (1873).

3. Memorandum, "Sunnyside Selections Made for Utah Fuel Company," MS 154, Utah Fuel Collection, Box 9, Folder 3, Lee Library, Brigham Young University, Provo, Utah.

4. "Coal Lands Inquiry," (Price) *Eastern Utah Advocate* (hereafter EUA), 6 Dec. 1906.

5. Theodore Roosevelt's true "Progressivism" has been a subject of historical debate. Roosevelt's reluctance publicly to leave the Republicans and join the Progressive Party is discussed in Gable, *Bull Moose*. Mowry, in *Era of Roosevelt*, views Roosevelt as a man in tune with his era, though not necessarily a leader in espousing progressive impulses. He makes this point explicitly in *Roosevelt and the Progressive Movement*, p. 11, in which he states, "Theodore Roosevelt did not beget the progressive movement." Mowry instead assigns the movement's beginnings to Populism. The entire notion of Roosevelt as a reformer is brought into question by Kolko, in *Triumph*. Roosevelt himself, in *Autobiography*, especially chapter 12, makes much of his New Freedom and the numerous reforms of his administrations, but he sees radical progressives as returning to a nineteenth-century individualism and finds business combinations to be indispensable in the modern era, despite their opposition to much of his reform package.

6. Civil 272; "Coal Lands Inquiry."

7. "Coal Lands Inquiry."

8. Ibid.

9. "Verbatim Report of Testimony and Proceedings . . . to investigate the question of coal shortage . . . beginning on the 29th day of January, A.D. 1917," MS 479, Manuscripts Division, Special Collections Department, University of Utah Libraries, Salt Lake City, Utah, pp. 216–17.

10. 41 Cong. Rec. 450 (1906) (House), 41 Cong. Rec. 2077 (1907) (Senate), quoted in Paul W. Gates, *History of Public Land Law Development* (Washington, D.C.: Government Printing Office, 1968), p. 727.

11. Peffer, *Closing of the Public Domain*, pp. 69–71; Maynard [and] Booth to attorney general, 7 Dec. 1906, Record Group 60, U.S. Department of Justice Straight Numerical Files, Box 654, Case 48590, National Archives, Washington, D.C.

12. G. F. Pollock to secretary of the interior, 22 Dec. 1906, Papers of Theodore Roosevelt [microfilm], Series 1, Reel 70.

13. Historians' views of the Progressive Era vary widely. Thought by some to be an artificial historical construct (see Filene, "Obituary"), it is defined by most historians on the basis of some common denominator. Josephson, in *Robber Barons*, defined a progressive as one who opposes Big Business. Nye, in *Midwestern Progressive Politics*, p. 197, stressed that "the rule of the majority

should be expressed in a stronger government, one with a broader social and economic program and one more responsive to popular control." To some extent, Nye's book illustrates those tendencies. Another broad definition comes from Barck and Blake, *Since 1900*, p. 33, in which progressives were "liberals in all parties who were seeking to advance social justice through political action." This altruism is not a part of the story of Utah coal. Others saw progressives primarily in terms of class orientation. Mowry, in *California Progressives*, pp. 86–104 and Hofstadter, in *Age of Reform*, pp. 131–72, viewed progressives as urban, middle-class Americans who felt their status challenged by Big Business, Big Labor, and political machines. A strong working-class identification is evident in Huthmacher's "Urban Liberalism," where he claims that the poor, who suffered most from the established order, spearheaded reform. All of these views of Progressivism as a reform movement contrast sharply with the work of Kolko, especially *Triumph*, which claims that many in big business wanted government regulation to stabilize the marketplace and reduce competition. Perhaps the actions of Frederick Sweet described here illustrate that tendency, but he was hardly successful in his attempt. An even more extreme statement of an upper-class basis for Progressivism comes from Weinstein, in *Corporate Ideal*, (p. ix), which claims: "The ideal of a liberal corporate social order was formulated and developed under the aegis and supervision of those who then, as now, enjoyed ideological and political hegemony in the United States: the more sophisticated leaders of America's largest corporations and financial institutions." Finally, the most useful definition of progressivism for this work comes from Wiebe, in *Businessmen and Reform* (p. 211), who wrote that "the progressive movement did center about certain broad social, political, and economic issues: to provide the underprivileged with a larger share of the nation's benefits; to make governments more responsive to the wishes of the voters, and to regulate the economy in the public interest." While this work relies on the definition provided by Wiebe, it can only be with the caveat that the pursuit of his three specific goals sometimes led to certain friction.

14. Cutright, *Theodore Roosevelt*, pp. 213–37.

15. "Coal Titles Should Remain in the Government, says President," EUA, 6 Dec. 1906; Peffer, p. 70.

16. 17 Stat. 607.

17. Theodore Roosevelt's presumed devotion to trust-busting remains a subject of historical debate. See Kolko, *Triumph*, and, by the same author, *Railroads and Regulation*; also Baldwin, *Antitrust*, pp. 36–37. Recognition of Roosevelt's efforts in regulating railroads and public lands, however, have been highlighted in more recent works, such as Sklar, *Corporate Reconstruction*, pp. 182–285, and Mayer and Riley, *Public Domain, Private Dominion*, pp. 114–33.

18. And hence the filing of bills in equity, rather than indictments or complaints.

19. A good, brief description can be found in Hechler, *Insurgency*, pp. 16–44.

20. A good description of the development of Mormonism can be found in Allen and Leonard, *Story*, especially pp. 1–288. An exclusively economic treatment is in Arrington, *Great Basin Kingdom*. Three different views of the centrality of polygamy to the statehood issue can be found in Lamar, *Far Southwest* (pp. 362–409, where polygamy is seen as one factor among many), Larson, *"Americanization" of Utah* (who argues that it was used as a pretext to mobilize the anti-Utah statehood drive), and Lyman, *Political Deliverance* (who argues that polygamy was the central issue in retarding Utah statehood). The most thorough work on Mormon polygamy, with specific details of the political control referred to in the text, is Hardy, *Solemn Covenant*.

21. Furniss, *Mormon Conflict*, pp. 186–87, 199–203; Lamar, *Far Southwest*, pp. 338–51.

22. No title, (Salt Lake City) *Deseret News*, 17 Aug. 1859.

23. No title, (Camp Floyd, Utah) *Valley Tan*, 17 Aug. 1859. See also Furniss, p. 224.

24. Larson, "Government, Politics and Conflict," in Poll et al., *Utah's History*, pp. 243–74.

25. Jensen, ed. *History of Railroads*, p. 111; Henry McAllister Jr., "Colorado Land and Improvement Companies, Colorado Springs, 1884," courtesy of the Bancroft Library, University of California, Berkeley; Allen and Leonard, pp. 95, 323, 524.

26. "An act granting to railroads the right of way through the public lands of the United States," 18 Stat. 482 (1875).

27. Jensen, p. 111.

28. Quoted in Athearn, *Rebel*, p. 41.

29. 18 Stat. 482.

30. Arthur Ridgway, "History of Transportation in Colorado: 'Royal Gorge War,' " MS 513, Denver and Rio Grande papers, Box 22, Folder 5315, Colorado Historical Society, Denver, Colorado.

31. Ibid; Athearn, *Rebel*, pp. 64–69, 85–87; Arthur Ridgway, "Denver & Rio Grande, Development of Physical Property in Chronological Narrative," 1 Jan. 1921, MS 513, Box 45, filed after the 1921 divider; Ridgway, "Chart of the Denver & Rio Grande Railroad Co." (hereafter Chart), MS 513, Box 19, Folder 5212; Riegel, *Story of Western Railroads* (1926; reprint ed.; Lincoln: University of Nebraska Press), pp. 185, 188; LeMassena, *Colorado's Mountain Railroads*, vol. 2, pp. 27, 28.

32. Athearn, *Rebel*, p. 98; "Denver & Rio Grande Western Railway Company Annual Report of Chief Engineer for year ending December 31st, 1881," (hereafter Chief Engineer's Report), MS 513, Box 42, Folder "Annual Report of Chief Engineer, 1881," p. 1.

33. Hannah M. Mendenhall, "The Calico Road," in Reynolds, *Centennial Echoes*, pp. 150–51.

34. Chief Engineer's Report.

35. "A Little Mixed," *Salt Lake Herald*, 14 May 1881.

36. Ellis Clark Jr. to General William J. Palmer, 11 Oct. 1881, MS 513, Box 51, Folder 865.

37. Holbrook, *American Railroads*, pp. 190–92.

38. "Samuel H. Gilson, Widely Known in West, Is Dead," (Salt Lake City) *Deseret Evening News*, 3 Dec. 1913; Newell C. Remington, "A History of the Gilsonite Industry" (Master's thesis, University of Utah, 1959), p. 37; Kretchman, *Gilsonite*, p. 28; Brooks, *Mountain Meadows*; Gilson's reward poster is reproduced following p. 184 in Larson, *"Americanization."*

39. Remington, p. 45; "State Land Board Minutes for December 1, 1896," State Land Board Records, Administrative Division, Series: Minutes, Box 1, pp. 42–46, Utah State Archives, Salt Lake City, Utah.

40. Chief Engineer's Report, p. 24.

41. William Jackson Palmer to A. G. Renshaw, 27 Oct. 1881, quoted in Athearn, *Rebel*, p. 107.

42. Fred A. Maynard to Ernest Knaebel, 8 Dec. 1909, RG 60, Box 654, Case 48590.

43. Athearn, *Rebel*, pp. 115–16; Ridgway, "Chart."

44. Bancroft, *History of Utah* pp. 736–37.

45. Klein, *Union Pacific*, pp. 53–55, 148–50, 154–56, 175–76; Arrington, *Great Basin Kingdom*, pp. 258–65, 275–76; Athearn, "Coming," 128–42.

46. "First Annual Report of the Board of Directors of the Denver & Rio Grande Western Railway Company. December 31st, 1883," MS 513, Box 42, Folder 3927.

47. Ibid., pp. 4–11; Athearn, *Rebel*, pp. 144, 149–53.

48. A. C. Watts, "Opening of First Commercial Coal Mine Described," in Reynolds, pp. 37–38; Union Pacific, *History*, p. 124.

49. Arrington, "Abundance From the Earth: The Beginnings of Commercial Mining in Utah," pp. 211–18 and Elroy Nelson, "The Mineral Industry: A Foundation of Utah's Economy," both in *Utah Historical Quarterly* 31 (summer 1963).

50. Watts, "Opening," in Reynolds pp. 37–38.

51. "Record—Sevier Railway Company," courtesy of the Bancroft Library, University of California, Berkeley, pp. 1–2; Record Book 1, p. 203; Record Book 2, pp. 17, 19, 31, 39, 45, 61; Record Book 3, pp. 61, 65, 67, 69, 71, 73–75, 84, 87, 132–33; Record Book 1, p. 197; Record Book 3, pp. 119, 104, all in Carbon County Recorder's Records, Carbon County Courthouse, Price, Utah.

52. "Report by Professor Gardiner, on the Coal Situation along the Rio Grande Western Railway, made for the Railway Company," MS 513, Box 8, Folder 1618.

53. Whitney, *History of Utah*, vol 3 City: 1892–1902), quoted in Stewart Lofgren Grow, "A Study of the Utah Commission," (Ph.D. dissertation, University of Utah, 1954), pp. 273–74.

54. Lyman, *Political*, p. 71.

55. Lamar, *Far Southwest*, pp. 305–78; Lamar, "Statehood," pp. 307–27; Seifrit, "Diary," pp. 358–81; Wilford Woodruff *Journal*, 8 Aug. 1894, quoted in Seifrit, p. 381; Lyman, p. 74.

56. Lyman, pp. 81, 103, 107; James S. Clarkson to Woodruff, 11 July 1894, copy, A. T. Volwiler Papers, Lilly Library, Indiana University, Bloomington, Indiana, p. 10; *Montana 37*.

57. Clarkson to Woodruff, 11 July 1894, pp. 4,5. Lyman pp. 132–37; Larson, *"Americanization"*; D. Michael Quinn, "LDS"; Hardy, *Solemn*, pp. 127–66.

58. Charles H. Madsen, ed., 'Carbon County; A History," mimeographed history prepared for Utah State Centennial, 1947, p. 19; "Castle Gate Coal Lands," MS 154, Utah Fuel Collection, Box 9, Folder 3, Lee Library, Brigham Young University, Provo, Utah; Athearn, *Rebel*, pp. 175–80.

59. Clarkson to Woodruff, p. 9; Roberts, *Comprehensive History*, vol. 6, pp. 288–90; Utah Enabling Act, 28 U.S. 107 (1894).

60. Rawlins, *Unfavored*, p. 187.

61. Ibid.

CHAPTER 2

1. Athearn, *Rebel*, p. 183.

2. *Official Report of the Proceedings and Debates of the Convention Assembled at Salt Lake City on the Fourth Day of March, 1895, to Adopt a Constitution for the State of Utah*, (hereafter Proceedings] vol. 2 (Salt Lake City: Star Printing Company, 1898), pp. 1469–72.

3. Ibid., pp. 1873–74.

4. Ibid., p. 1607.

5. Ibid., pp. 1609–11, 1879.

6. Poll, "A State Is Born," pp. 9, 29–30; Larson and Poll, "The Forty-Fifth State," in Poll, ed., *Utah's History*, pp. 387–404.

7. Poll et al., *Utah's History*, pp. 704–06.

8. Roberts, *Comprehensive History*, vol. 6, p. 334.

9. R. Bitton, "The B. H. Roberts Case," pp. 28–29; Lyman, *Political*, note 1, p. 6; G. Durham, "Administrative Organization."

10. Poll, "A State Is Born," pp. 28–29.

11. Joseph F. Smith, *Another Plain Talk: Reasons Why the People of Utah Should Be Republicans*, courtesy of the Huntington Library, San Marino, California.

12. Ibid., pp. 6–9. A very good description of the "pen" community can be found in Larson, *"Americanization"*, pp. 183–206.

13. Smith, pp. 12–13, 15.

14. "Memoranda made by Clio [Hiram B. Clawson] of things he has learned at various times from personal observation or from being told by others, the past four years," (hereafter Clio Memo) attached to James S. Clarkson to Wilford Woodruff, 11 July 1894, copy, A. T. Volwiler Papers, Lilly Library, Indiana University, Bloomington, Indiana.

15. Ibid; Lyman, *Political*, pp. 78–79.

16. Various letters, U.S. Land Board Correspondence, 1910–1913, Administrative Division, Correspondence Series, State Land Board Records, Box B115H3, Utah State Archives, Salt Lake City, Utah. Despite the title of the folder, correspondence from the 1890s is also contained in it.

17. S. W. Lamoreaux to Register and Receiver, 29 December 1896, in "Minutes Sept. 25, 1896 to June 7, 1898," Box 1, Department: Land Board, Series: Minutes, Utah State Archives, pp. 72–75.

18. Ibid.

19. Utah Enabling Act, 28 Stat. 107 (1894).

20. "Minutes of June 3, 1897," Division: Administration, Series: Minutes Sept. 25, 1896 to Jun. 7, 1898, Box 1, Utah State Archives, p. 173.

21. Minutes of the State Land Board, July 30, 1897 and Sept. 9, 1897, Box 1, pp. 218, 261; "Local News," EUA, 28 Oct. 1897.

22. Utah 7th Judicial District, Civil Case 227, Remittitur, p. 8, Carbon County Courthouse, Price, Utah; "Bob Kirker Has Another Story," EUA, 27 Dec 1906. Some local histories claim that the area was originally known as Verdi. According to Arthur Gibson, "Sunnyside," in Reynolds, *Centennial Echoes*, "There was a station on the main line of the Denver & Rio Grande Western Railroad, 20 miles east of Price by that name [Sunnyside] and it was thought by the officials of the railroad and the Utah Fuel Company that his would be an appropriate name for the new coal mine, therefore a change was made, the new mine being called Sunnyside and the former Sunnyside being called Verdi," p. 203. According to an unpublished mimeograph (listed as Teachers, pupils and patrons of the Carbon School District, "A Brief History, 1933, p. 22) the original source for much of *Centennial Echoes*, this change took place after 1898. EUA refers to the area as Whitmore Canyon until 1899.

23. Charles H. Madsen, ed., "Carbon County: A History," 1947, mimeo, pp. 23–25.

24. "Pioneer Citizen Called By Death," (Price) *Carbon County News*, (hereafter CCN), 27 Nov 1913; "Wellington," in Reynolds, pp. 156–68; Mildred E. Brown, "History: Justus Wellington Seeley II," typescript, Castle Dale, 1970, copy in possession of the author. The family surname is spelled variously as Seely and Seeley. The spelling used here follows that in Lever, *History*, pp. 618–20, entries contributed by the Seelys themselves.

25. Lever, ibid.

26. *Index to Mining Locations*, Book 8, pp. 1–5, Carbon County Recorder's Records, Carbon County Courthouse, Price, Utah.

27. "Bob Kirker Has Another Story."

28. *Index to Mining Locations*, Book 8, pp. 151, 156, 185; Coal Land Act, 17 Stat. 607 (1873).

29. "Articles of Incorporation, Holladay Coal Company," College of Eastern Utah Special Collections, Price, Utah.

30. *Report of the Coal Mine Inspector for the State of Utah for the years of 1897 and 1898* (Salt Lake City: Deseret Publishing Company, 1899), p. 29.

31. Ibid.

32. "Coal Lands Inquiry," EUA, 6 Dec. 1906.

33. "Means Much for Price," EUA, 28 Oct. 1897.

34. *U.S. v. George Foster Peabody*, Answer to Complaint, and *U.S. v. Utah Fuel Company*, Bill of Complaint No. 867, both in Record Group 60, U.S. Department of Justice Straight Numerical Files, Box 654, Case 48590, National Archives, Washington, D.C.; *Abstract of Mining Locations*, T 14 S R 14 E and T 15 S R 14 E, Carbon County Recorder's Office, Carbon County Courthouse, Price, Utah.

35. "Happenings Ten Years Ago This Week," EUA, 24 Oct. 1907.

36. *Holladay v. Kirker, et al.*, 20 Utah 192 (1899) at 197, 198.

37. "Coal Lands Inquiry."

38. Ibid.

39. "Another Tale of Sunnyside Mine," (Salt Lake City) *Deseret News*, 15 Dec. 1906.

40. Ibid.

41. Ibid.

42. M. C. Burch to the attorney general, 17 Jan. 1912, RG 60, Box 654, Case 48590.

43. "Coal Lands Inquiry."

44. "Again Come Together," EUA, 15 Dec. 1898; "The Holladay Case," EUA, 29 Dec. 1898; no title, EUA, 9 Feb. 1899.

45. "More Tilts Come in Coal Hearing," *Deseret Evening News*, 8 April 1908; "Old Timer Takes Witness Stand," *Deseret Evening News*, 7 Apr. 1908.

46. *Holladay v. Kirker, et al*, 7th Judicial District Court Records, Carbon County Clerk's Office, Carbon County Courthouse, Price, Utah. An index preserved there shows the documents generated by the case, although only the order transferring it to the state supreme court is preserved in the records. A telephone call to the state supreme court revealed that there are no *Holladay v. Kirker, et al.* records there, although the research librarian, who refused to give his name, said that a state supreme court justice allegedly took several court records home with him years ago. Other information (notably and especially the name of this justice) was refused.

47. "Personal Mention," EUA, 20 Oct. 1898.

48. "Lands Thrown Open," EUA 27 Oct. 1898.

49. "Under Lease and Bond," EUA, 8 Dec. 1898; "Personal Mention," EUA, 22 Dec. 1898; B. R. McDonald to C. H. Gibbs, 12 May 1911, MS 154, Utah Fuel Company Papers, Box 16, Fd. 7, Lee Library, Brigham Young University, Provo, Utah; "Two Hired Hands are Fired from Their Jobs," EUA, 10 Sept. 1908.

50. EUA, 15 Dec. 1898.

CHAPTER 3

1. "District Court Proceedings," EUA, 16 Feb 1899; "Coal Lands Inquiry," EUA, 6 Dec. 1906; "At Work on Coal," EUA, 15 June 1899.

2. "At Work on Coal." Italics added.

3. Arrington with Hansen, *"Richest Hole,"* pp. 16–18.

4. Ibid., pp. 18–48; Gary B. Hansen, "Industry of Destiny: Copper in Utah" *Utah Historical Quarterly* 31 (summer 1963): 267–72.

5. "At Work On Coal."

6. *Report of the Coal Mine Inspector for the State of Utah, for the years 1899 and 1900* (Salt Lake City: Deseret News, 1901), pp. 21, 5, 8, 16.

7. Fred A. Maynard to Ernest Knaebel, 8 Dec. 1909, Record Group 60, U.S Justice Department Straight Numerical Files, Box 654, File 48590, National Archives, Washington, D.C.; *Annual Report of the Rio Grande Western Railway Company to the Stockholders for the Year Ending June 30, 1892* (New York: William H. Clark, 1892), p. 1. MS 513, Denver & Rio Grande Collection, Box 43, Folder 3937, Colorado Historical Society, Denver, Colorado.

8. Maynard to Knaebel, 8 Dec. 1909.

9. "Coal Lands Inquiry"; *Third Annual Report of the State Board of Land Commissioners of the State of Utah for the year ending December 31, 1898* (Salt Lake City: Deseret News Print., 1899), p. 2.

10. "Delinquent Tax List: Wellington," EUA, 15 Dec. 1898; W. H. Lever, *History*, pp. 618–19.

11. Don Carlos Grundvig, "The Evolution of the Mind of Man," p. 284, mimeo, copy in possession of the author. Italics added.

12. As a very cordial letter put it: "The question you ask is an easy answer, although it is not the reply I would like to give to you. The correspondence of the First Presidency for that period of time is not available." Ronald G. Watt to Nancy J. Taniguchi, 27 Aug. 1987.

13. Wilford Woodruff, George Q. Cannon and George M. Smith to Morris M. Estee, 18 Dec. 1894, Woodruff Papers, LDS Church Historical Society, quoted in Lyman, *Political*, p. 245; Woodruff Journal, 30 Dec. 1896, cited in Lyman, p. 254, note 73. The originals are currently unavailable to researchers.

14. Harold H. Dunham, "Some Crucial Years of the General Land Office," in Carstensen, *Public Lands*, pp. 181–201.

15. Roberts, *Comprehensive History*, vol. 6, p. 362.

16. "Rolapp to be Beaten," *Salt Lake Tribune*, 4 Sept. 1898; Roberts, *Comprehensive History*, p. 363.

17. Quoted in Bitton, "The B. H. Roberts Case," p. 35.

18. Ibid., Roberts, *Comprehensive History*, pp. 363–64.

19. "Personalities," EUA, 23 Feb. 1899; " 'Spotter' Owen in Richfield," (Salt Lake City) DEN, 25 Sept. 1899; "Prest. Snow Is Accused By Owen," DEN, 9 Oct. 1899; "C. Mostyn Owen After Roberts," DEN, 16 Oct. 1899.

20. Roberts, *Comprehensive History*, p. 364. Roberts had been well aware of the explosiveness of the polygamy issue as far back as the state constitutional convention, when he argued *against* women's suffrage, in contrast to the prevailing views of other Mormon leaders. As he explained, he did so in order that the state constitution might be acceptable in Washington, D.C., realizing that Utah women, originally enfranchised, had been disfranchised by federal statute when they failed to support antipolygamy legislation. See *Official Report of the Convention* pp. 421–29 and discussion in Bakken, *Rocky Mountain*, pp. 94–98.

21. Quoted in Roberts, p. 370.

22. "Owen 'Turned Down,' " DEN, 10 Oct. 1899; "President Snow's Case Is Dismissed," DEN, 14 Oct. 1899; "Owen Consults Streeper Today," DEN, 11 Nov. 1899; quoted in Edmund T. Olson, *Coal Lands Report in Charge of Joseph Ririe, State Auditor* (Kaysville, Utah: Inland Printing Company, 1920), pp. 12, 13.

23. Malone, *Battle for Butte*, pp. 112–30, 148–56; "Clark, William Andrews," *Who Was Who*, p. 225; Mangam, *The Clarks*, pp. 73–74; Wyant, *Westward in Eden*, pp. 35–36.

24. Malone, *Battle for Butte*, pp. 195–97; Hulse, "W.A. Clark," pp. 48–55.

25. *Report of the Coal Mine Inspector for the State of Utah, for the years 1899 and 1900* (hereafter Mine Report), (Salt Lake City: Deseret News, 1901), p. 33.

26. 20 Utah 192 (1899).

27. "Robert Forrester Dead," (Price) *Carbon County News* (hereafter CCN), 23 Dec. 1910.

28. "Peabody Tells His Story," EUA 26 Dec. 1907; "Happenings Ten Years Ago This Week," EUA, 24 Oct. 1907; "Coal Lands Inquiry."

29. "First Annual Report of the State Board of Land Commissioners of the State of Utah for year ending December 31, 1896," State Land Board Records, General Administration Division, Series: Annual Reports, 1896–1904, Utah State Archives, Salt Lake City, Utah, p. 4.

30. "The New Railroad," EUA, 15 June 1899.

31. Mine Report, pp. 21, 22.

32. "Sunnyside Line Being Inspected," DEN, 9 Nov. 1899; "Short Stories," EUA, 29 June 1899.

33. For this reason, the U.S.G.S. *Mineral Reports of the United States* (Washington, D.C.: Government Printing Office, various years) resorted to

combining the total coke production of Colorado and Utah to avoid revealing a corporate secret. See 1900, pp. 461, 467; 1901, pp. 452, 479; 1902, 357, 432. As of 1903, the U.S.G.S got around this difficulty by listing all coal production (including both coal and coke) for each state—valued as a whole—listing only separate tonnage as "made into coke." See pp. 360–62.

34. Mine Report, p. 4.

35. Mine Report, pp. 16, 22–30.

36. Maynard to Knaebel, 8 Dec. 1909.

37. MS 513, Denver and Rio Grande Papers, Box 11, Fd. 4521, Colorado Historical Society, Denver, Colorado; "The New Railroad," EUA, 15 June 1899; quoted in Maynard to Knaebel, 8 Dec. 1909.

38. No title, EUA, 28 Dec. 1899; Maynard to Knaebel, 8 Dec. 1909.

39. Maynard to Knaebel, 8 Dec. 1909; Athearn, *Rebel*, pp. 192–96.

40. Athearn, pp. 192–96.

41. 31 Stat. 1133 (1901).

CHAPTER 4

1. Quoted in McCullough, *Mornings on Horseback*, pp. 349–50.

2. McGeary, *Gifford Pinchot*, pp. 19–44.

3. Ibid., pp. 45–61.

4. Andrews, *Theodore Roosevelt*, p. 214.

5. Pinchot, *Breaking New Ground*, pp. 245–46.

6. "The Control of Corporations," Address at Providence, Rhode Island, 23 Aug. 1902, in Roosevelt, *American Problems*, vol. 18, pp. 77–81.

7. Ibid.

8. Union Pacific, *History*, pp. 41, 43, 59, 165; M. C. Burch to solicitor general, 26 Mar. 1909, Record Group 60, U.S Justice Department Straight Numerical Files, Box 654, Case 48590, National Archives, Washington, D.C.

9. 24 Stat. 379 (1887); 32 Stat. 847 (1903).

10. *Congressional Record*, 58th Congress, 2d Session (1903–04), xxxviii, 4029.

11. *Milner et al. v. United States*, 228 Fed. 431 (1915) at 432–36.

12. *Report of the Coal Mine Inspector for the State of Utah for the Years 1901 and 1902* (Salt Lake City: Star Printing Company, 1903), pp. 34, 94; "Coal Land Deals Worrying Them," EUA, 26 July 1906.

13. *Milner, et al. v. United States*, at 435, 436; "Coal Land Deals Worrying Them."

14. "John B. Millburn Shot Down," EUA 12 Oct. 1905; "Millburn and Gilson Contest Coal Lands," EUA, 3 Sept. 1903.

15. "Millburn Wins His Coal Lands Case" EUA, 29 October 1903.

16. "Millburn and Gilson Contest Coal Lands."

17. "Sam H. Gilson Canes President Roosevelt," EUA, 28 May 1903.

18. "Millburn and Gilson Contest Coal Lands."

19. John B. Millburn, Coal Certificate #186, GLO #2168, Book 6, Carbon County Recorder's Records, Carbon County Courthouse, Price, Utah; "John B. Millburn Shot Down."

20. R. Forrester to A. H. Cowie, 3 Aug. 1905, MS 154, Utah Fuel Company Papers, Box 17, Folder 2, Lee Library, Brigham Young University, Provo, Utah.

21. Merrill, *Reed Smoot*, pp. 21–27.

22. Salt Lake *Truth*, 30 July 1904, quoted in Merrill, *Reed Smoot*, p. 28.

23. Quoted in Merrill, *Reed Smoot*, p. 28.

24. Van Wagoner, *Mormon Polygamy*, pp. 164–66.

25. Quoted in Merrill, *Reed Smoot*, p. 28.

26. Merrill, *Reed Smoot* pp. 29–30.

27. Van Wagoner, *Mormon Polygamy*, pp. 152, 164–66; *Journal History* 16 Aug. 1900, quoted in Van Wagoner, p. 154. A tentative list of 220 post-Manifesto marriages is in Hardy, *Solemn*, pp. 394–425.

28. Merrill, *Reed Smoot*, pp. 39–47; Bills in Equity, Nos. 869, 870, RG 60, Box 654, Case 48590.

29. Hardy, *Solemn*, pp. 252–53; Van Wagoner, *Mormon Polygamy* p. 169; Merrill, *Reed Smoot*, pp. 50–51.

30. Merrill, *Reed Smoot* pp. 52–53; Van Wagoner, pp. 173–75, 183.

31. Van Wagoner, pp. 173–74; quote from Hardy, *Solemn*, pp. 260–61.

32. Ibid., pp. 174–94; Merrill, *Reed Smoot*, pp. 50–51.

33. Siringo, *Cowboy Detective*, pp. 387, 394.

34. Ibid., pp. 392–93; Shipps, "Utah Comes of Age,"; Merrill, *Reed Smoot*, pp. 63–65; Hardy, *Solemn*, p. 252.

35. Pinchot, *Breaking New Ground*, pp. 244, 248.

36. Ibid., pp. 245, 246.

37. Ibid., pp. 246–48; "Report of the 1903 Land Commission," Gifford Pinchot Manuscript Collection, Library of Congress, Box 680, quoted in Mayer and Riley, *Public Domain*, p. 10.

38. Mayer and Riley, p. 10; Pinchot, *Breaking New Ground*, pp. 246–48.

39. Jerry A. O'Callaghan, "The Disposition of the Public Domain in Oregon," (Ph.D. dissertation, Stanford University, 1951), published as *Memorandum of the Chairman to the Committee on Interior and Insular Affairs, United States Senate* (Washington, D.C.: Government Printing Office, 1960); Peffer, *Closing of the Public Domain*, pp. 42–45; William K. Wyant, *Westward in Eden*, p. 133; Pinchot, *Breaking New Ground*, p. 244.

40. "Memorandum" accompanying M. C. Burch to attorney general, 26 Mar. 1909, RG 60, Box 654, Case 48590.

CHAPTER 5

1. "Our Uncle Sam Sits On Grazing Land," (Price) EUA, 8 Oct. 1903; Peffer, *Closing of the Public Domain*, pp. 32–45. Peffer also highlights the

magnitude of western land fraud, organizing this discussion in relation to the various acts abused. See, for example, the problems with the Desert Land Act (p. 18), the Homestead Act (p. 42), the Reclamation Act (p. 43), the railroads and scrip (p. 54), and problems created by the administration of a body of admittedly bad land law in general (p. 149). Sometimes land fraud began at the first step of federal control, with inept surveys themselves. See Paul W. Gates, *History of Public Land Law Development* (Washington. D.C.: Government Printing Office, 1968), pp. 420–22. In other words, land fraud was varied, widespread, and initially limited only by the imagination and chutzpah of the claimant.

2. "Government Agent is Looking After Titles"; "Our Uncle Sam Sits On Grazing Land"; "Why the Salina Cutoff Has Suspended Work," all in EUA, 8 Oct. 1903; Utah Enabling Act, 28 U.S. 107 (1894).

3. "Why the Salina Cutoff Has Suspended Work"; "Government Agent is Looking After Titles."

4. William H. Bird to Robert Forrester, 9 Feb. 1905; R. Forrester to Major Wm. H. Bird, 11 Feb. 1905; William H. Bird to Robert Forrester, 14 Feb. 1905, all in MS 154, Utah Fuel Company Papers, Box 8, Fd. 5, Lee Library, Brigham Young University, Provo, Utah.

5. Hardy, *Solemn*, preceding p. 341, shows a close-up of Owens's face from these photographs, as the only known photographic image of him. But Hardy eschews reproducing the entire photograph, based on its tasteless representation of Mormon temple garments.

6. H. G. Williams to W. G. Sharp, 24 Dec. 1901, MS 154, Box 8, Fd.5; Book 5, pp. 101, 154, Carbon County Recorder's Records, Carbon County Courthouse, Price, Utah.

7. H. G. Williams to G. W. Kramer, 14 March 1902, MS 154, Box 7, Fd. 10.

8. 19 L.D. 23; Williams to Kramer, 14 March 1902.

9. H. G. Williams to G. W. Kramer, 17 March 1902, MS 154, Box 8, Fd. 5.

10. Athearn, *Rebel*, pp. 202–04; R. A. LeMassena, "1902," *Colorado's Mountain Railroads, Vol. II* (Golden, Colorado: Smoking Stack Press, 1965), n.p.

11. Arrington, *David Eccles*, pp. 251, 252.

12. LeMassena, "1902," n.p.; Arrington, *David Eccles*, pp. 251–53.

13. Athearn, pp. 207, 208.

14. "Complaint," *United States v. Palmer, Peabody, et al.*, RG 60, United States Department of Justice Straight Numerical Files, Box 654, Case 48590, National Archives, Washington, D.C.

15. Arthur A. Sweet, Coal Certificate 172, GLO #1947, Book 6, Records of Carbon County, Recorder's Office, Carbon County Courthouse, Price Utah; Warrum, *Utah Since Statehood*, vol. 3, p. 232.

16. *Arthur A. Sweet v. Charles Mostyn Owen*, Civil 272, Utah 7th Judicial

District, Carbon County Clerk's Records, Price, Utah; "Coal Lands Inquiry," EUA, 6 Dec. 1906.

17. Civil 272; Memorandum, "Sunnyside Selections Made for Utah Fuel Company," MS 154, Box 9, Fd. 3; "Coal Lands Inquiry," EUA, 6 Dec. 1906; "Verbatim Report of Testimony and Proceedings . . . to investigate the question of coal shortage . . . beginning on the 29th day of January, A.D. 1917," MS 479, Manuscripts Division, Special Collections Department, University of Utah Libraries, Salt Lake City, Utah, pp. 216, 217.

18. Powell, *Next Time*, pp. 51–80.

19. "Bitter Legal Fight Occurs in Court At Scofield," *Salt Lake Tribune*, 11 Dec. 1903; Taniguchi, "No Proper Job," pp. 145–64.

20. "Bitter Legal Fight."

21. "Still Another of Lovey's Jokelets," reprint, EUA, 17 Dec. 1903.

22. "Department Is with Salt Lake," 7 October 1909; "Utah Fuel Company Charged With Fraud in Affidavit Filed In the Land Office," EUA, 12 Mar. 1905.

23. "After The Fuel Co.," EUA, 31 Mar. 1904.

24. Ibid.

25. *Albert L. Simmons v. Owen L. Davies*, contest in the United States Land Office, MS 154, Box 10, Folder 18.

26. Mine Report, 1899 and 1900, pp. 26, 106; Ibid., 1901–1902, pp. 33–34, 94.

27. Heber Stowell Patent, RG 49, Desert Land Entries, F.C. File 920, National Archives, Washington, D.C.

28. Civil 493, *W. H. Lawley v. A. A. Sweet and Henry Wade*, Utah 7th Judicial District, Carbon County Clerk's Records, Carbon County Court-house, Price, Utah.

29. S. K. Smith to D. Crow, 7 Dec. 1904; S. Kedzie Smith to H. G. Williams, 9 Dec. 1904; both in MS 154, Utah Fuel Company Papers, Box 8, Fd. 5, Lee Library, Brigham Young University, Provo, Utah.

30. H. G. Williams to S. Kedzie Smith, 12 Dec. 1904, MS 154, Box 8, Fd. 5.

31. "Clark, William Andrews," *Who Was Who*, p. 225; "Utah State News," EUA, 10 March 1904; Riegel, *Story of Western Railroads*, pp. 315, 316; Malone, *Battle for Butte*; Hulse, "W. A. Clark," pp. 48–55.

32. Civil 493, Utah 7th Judicial District.

33. M. P. Braffet to H. G. Williams, 14 Dec. 1904; S. Kedzie Smith to D. Crow, 14 Dec. 1904; J. H. Cory to D. Crow, 15 Dec. 1904, all in MS 154, Box 8, Fd. 5.

34. J. H. Cory to D. Crow, 15 Dec. 1904, MS 154, Box 8, Fd. 5.

35. "Declaration of Intention to Purchase Coal Land"; Forrester to Schlacks, 8 Mar. 1905, both in MS 154, Box 8, Fd. 5.

36. *United States v. Robert Forrester*, MS 154, Box 9. Fd. 6.

37. William H. Bird to R. B. [*sic*—B. R.] McDonald, 5 Jan. 1905, MS 154, Box 8, Fd. 5.

38. *Simmons v. Davies*.

CHAPTER 6

1. Hardy, *Solemn*, pp. 251, 260–61; Merrill, *Reed Smoot*, pp. 47–48.

2. Merrill, *Reed Smoot*, pp. 50, 90; Roberts, *Comprehensive History*, vol. 6, pp. 395–97; 409–10. The American Party was, in its focus on anti-Mormonism, a revivication of the old Liberal Party begun during the antebellum era and strongly resurgent during the antipolygamy crusades of the 1880s. It was initially opposed by the Mormon People's Party, which divided into Republicans and Democrats in anticipation of Utah statehood, forcing the Liberals to take similar sides. A full discussion of this process is found in Lyman, *Political*. See also Alexander, "Political Patterns of Early Statehood, 1896–1919," in Poll et al., eds., *Utah's History*, p. 417. Shipps, "Utah Comes of Age," has much valuable information, although it has been partly replaced by Hardy, *Solemn*.

3. George W. Moyer to W. H. Moody, 3 Jun. 1905, Record Group 60, U.S. Justice Department Straight Numerical Files, Box 654, Case 48590, National Archives, Washington, D.C. In the context of national and state politics and the Smoot hearings, the timing of Moyer's letter is suggestive of a possible cause-and-effect relationship, although much further research is necessary to substantiate this speculation.

4. Merrill, *Reed Smoot*, p. 63.

5. Roberts, p. 396; Hardy, p. 258.

6. "Light Cast on Methods Used to Grab Coal Lands," *Salt Lake Herald*, 12 March 1905.

7. Ibid. Another way of looking at the dummy system, certainly more prevalent during the nineteenth century, is the concept of "release of energy" used to increase productivity, as discussed in Hurst, *Law*, pp. 8–32. In this sense, the dummy system fostered development because of relatively lower risk of venture capital resulting from reduced investments as compared with the legal method.

8. Ibid.

9. "Grand Jury May Probe Coal Grab," *Salt Lake Herald*, 13 March 1905.

10. "Mothers' Congress and Mormonism," *Salt Lake Herald*, 12 March 1905.

11. Merrill, *Reed Smoot*, p. 57. The importance of public consensus to the Mormon Church is hard to overemphasize. It resolves the conflict pinpointed in O'Dea, *The Mormons*, p. 243: "These two tendencies [of "free agency of man" and a highly organized church hierarchy established by divine revelation] demanded some kind of accomodation to each other if serious conflict was to be avoided. In terms of church government, there

has resulted a democracy of participation within the context of hierarchical organization and authoritarian operation." Reed Smoot's refusal to sustain his brother apostles indeed constituted "serious conflict." Mormon historians Arrington and Bitton also emphasize the importance of consensus in *The Mormon Experience*. Quoting from another author, they stress "how much more elaborated and theologically central was the Mormon concern for authoritative religion" than the contemporaneous Campbellites and Shakers (p. 39). The power of authority in relation to intellectual inquiry, discussed on p. 260, refers to "the authority of the apostles [of the Quorum of the Twelve] and prophets as sole adjudicators of church doctrine" and to the penalty of excommunication accorded to "an unbeliever who speaks out publically against the church." Obviously, Smoot strongly desired to *support* his church, but his public display of dissent, while not approaching the level necessary for excommunication, nonetheless played havoc with the idea of a divinely ordained hierarchy, for how could God send the leaders of his church more than one message?

12. R. Forrester to C. H. Schlacks, 8 Mar. 1905, with enclosures, MS 154, Utah Fuel Collection, Box 8, Folder 5, Lee Library, Brigham Young University, Provo, Utah.

13. "George A. Whitmore Dies; Long A Prominent Figure," (Price) *News-Advocate*, 6 Nov. 1917; "James M. Whitmore," *Utah Since Statehood* (Chicago-Salt Lake City: S. J. Clarke, 1919), pp. 500–03.

14. Civil 227, Seventh Judicial District, Carbon County Clerk's Records, Price, Utah.

15. Ibid.

16. R. Forrester to H. G. Williams, 22 May 1905, MS 154, Box 8. folder 8, with map of Range Creek watershed.

17. R. Forrester to H. G. Williams, 23 May 1905, MS 154, Box 8, Folder 8.

18. H. G. Williams to C. H. Schlacks, 23 May 1905, MS 154, Box 8, Folder 8.

19. "Justice Sutherland Dies In East," (Salt Lake) *Deseret News*, 18 Jul. 1942.

20. Williams to Schlacks, 23 May 1905.

21. William H. Bird to Robert Forrester, 12 May 1905, MS 154, Box 8, Folder 5.

22. Moyer to Moody, 3 June 1905.

23. C. S. [Charles Schlacks?] to A. E. Welby, 15 Jul. 1905; A. E. W[elby] to F. E. B., 17 July 1905; both MS 154, Box 17, Fd. 2.

24. F. E. B. to Mr. Welby, 18 Jul. 1905; A. E. W[elby] to A. C. Ridgway, n.d.; A. C. Ridgway to Mr. Cowie, 25 Jul. 1905, all MS 154, Box 17, Folder 2.

25. A. H. C[owie] to Bob [Robert Forrester], 29 Jul. 1905, idem.

26. E. T. Jeffery to W. G. Sharp, 3 Oct. 1901; [W.G. Sharp] general manager to E. T. Jeffery, 8 Oct. 1901, both in Ms 154, Box 10, Fd. 19.

27. R. Forrester to H. G. Williams, 30 Jun. 1905, MS 154, Box 17, Folder 2.

28. B. R. McDonald to R. Forrester, 3 Jul. 1905, MS 154, Box 17, Fd. 2.

29. "Field Man for Utah Coal Companies Dies," (Salt Lake City) *Deseret News*, 8 Jan. 1923; Mine Report, 1901 and 1902, pp. 95, 36.

30. R. Forrester to H. G. Williams, 5 Jul. 1905, MS 154, Box 17, Fd. 2.

31. Ibid.

32. Ibid.

33. C. H. Schlacks to R. Forrester, 12 July 1905, MS 154, Box 17, Folder 2; "Western Takes San Pete Valley," EUA, 3 Oct. 1907; "San Pete Valley Railway Co. Minutes, 1893–1910," Minutes of 3 Oct. 1907, attached to p. 45, courtesy Bancroft Library, University of California, Berkeley.

34. W. J. T[idwell] to R. Forrester, 11 Jul. 1905, MS 154, Box 17, Folder 2.

35. W. J. T. to R. Forrester, 17 Jul. 1905, idem.

36. Ibid.

37. Ibid., 25 Jul. 1905.

38. Ibid.

39. H. G. Williams to C. H. Schlacks, 18 Jul. 1905, MS 154, Box 17, Fd. 2.

40. W. J. Tidwell to H. G. Williams, 20 Jul. 1905, idem.

41. R. Forrester to Mr. Cowie, 3 Aug. 1905, MS 154, Box 17, Fd. 2, Lee Library, Brigham Young University, Provo, Utah; "New Railroad Planned in Northeastern Utah," attached; "New Railroad To Carry Coal," attached; H. G. Williams to Mr. Schlacks, 18 Aug. 1905, MS 154, Fd. 17, Box 2; "Road From Coal Fields," attached; R. Forrester to H. G. Williams, 13 Oct. 1905, ibid.; "Colonel Milner Files Maps of his Proposed Road into this County," attached; "Milner to Build Railroad," attached.

42. Complaint, *Henry Wade v. Arthur A. Sweet*, Civil Case 9420, Utah Third Judicial District, Salt Lake County Clerk's Office, Salt Lake City, Utah; "Wade Sues His Son-in-law," EUA, 1 Aug. 1907.

CHAPTER 7

1. W. J. T[idwell] to H. G. Williams, 19 Aug. 1905, MS 154, Utah Fuel Collection, Box 17, Folder 2, Lee Library, Brigham Young University, Provo, Utah.

2. Joseph A. Taff, "U.S. Geological Survey Mine Notes," MS 210, U.S.G.S. Coal Lands Survey (1905–1908), Box 1, Fd. 1, Manuscripts Division, Special Collections Department, University of Utah Libraries, Salt Lake City, Utah.

3. Ibid.

4. Joseph A Taff to the director of the Geological Survey, 5 September 1905, quoted in *Joint Hearings before the Committee on Public Lands. February 11 and 12, 1926* (Washington, D.C.: Government Printing Office, 1926), p. 151.

5. Ibid.

6. J. Harwood Graves to attorney general, 30 Aug. 1905, RG 60, Box 654, Case 48590.

7. Sudbury affadavit, attached to Graves to attorney general.

8. Graves to attorney general.

9. Ibid.

10. Ibid.

11. Ibid.

12. Ibid.

13. J. D. Dixon to Gomer Thomas, Sept. 15, 1905, Correspondence of the State Coal Mine Inspector, Special Collections Department, University of Utah Libraries; Clifton Lowe to J. D. Dixon, 1 Nov. 1905, State Land Board Administrative Correspondence (Abstracts), Utah State Archives, Salt Lake City, Utah.

14. Carstensen, *Public Lands*, p. 508; W. A. Richards to Register and Receiver, 30 December 1905, State Land Board Administrative Correspondence (Abstracts); *Reports of the Department of the Interior. 1907*, Vol. I (Washington, D.C.: Government Printing Office, 1907), p. 14; Frank D. Hobbs to State Board Land Commissioners, 2 Feb. 1906; and Frank D. Hobbs to Messrs. Higgins & Senior, Att'y for Gideon Snyder, 2 Feb. 1906, both in State Land Board Administrative Correspondence (Abstracts).

15. A. H. Cowie to [?], 25 Nov. 1905, MS 154, Box 10, Folder 18.

16. R. Forrester to A. H. Cowie, 25 Nov. 1905, MS 154, Box 10 Folder 18.

17. D. O. Clark deposition, attached to Ernest Knaebel to attorney general, 28 Jul. 1911, RG 60, Box 655, Case 48590.

18. Ibid.

19. *"United States v. C. M. Freed, et al.*, Involving Title to Certain Coal Lands Situate in Emery County, Utah, Vol. I," Records of the State Land Board, Utah State Archives, Salt Lake City, Utah.

20. N. E. D. to A. H. Cowie, 30 Dec. 1905, MS 154, Box 10, Folder 18.

21. Ibid.

22. N. E. D. to A. H. Cowie, 29 Dec. 1905, MS 154, Box 10, Folder 18.

23. Will [Foster] to Marsena [Foster], 12 Jan. 1906, MS 154, Box 10, Folder 18.

24. Shipps, "Utah Comes of Age," pp. 98, 99; Reed Smoot to Joseph F. Smith, 24 Nov. 1905, quoted in Merrill, *Reed Smoot*, p. 91.

25. Merrill, pp. 91–92, 72.

26. "Confidential" to [F.A.] Maynard, 10 Apr. 1906; George W. Moyer to W. H. Moody, 7 Mar. 1906; ibid., 13 Mar. 1906, all in RG 60, Box 654, Case 48590.

27. George Albert Smith to Reed Smoot, 2 Feb. 1906, MS 1187, Reed Smoot Papers, Box 25, Folder 2, Lee Library, Brigham Young University, Provo, Utah.

28. Ibid.

29. Ibid.

30. Smith to Smoot, 20 Feb. 1906, MS 1187, Box 25, Folder 9; *Simmons v. Davies*, MS 154, Box 10 Folder 18; *McDonald V. Davies*, MS 154, Box 8, Folder 4.

31. [Decision] *Albert L. Simmons v. Owen L. Davies*, 26 Feb. 1906, MS 154, Box 10, Fd. 18. On the battle for public lands, see Alexander, "Smoot and Land Policy," pp. 245–64, which discusses the dispute from a conservation standpoint. I believe that the ownership of coal lands was a significant factor in determining antagonists. See particularly p. 247, including footnote 4, which includes among the "states' righters" coal company friends and affiliates Clarence Don Clark of Wyoming, and Utah's George Sutherland and William H. King, whose story is told later in this work.

32. Tillman-Gillespie Resolution, 34 Stat. 823 (1906).

33. W. A. Richards to secretary of interior, 18 Apr. 1906; E. A. Hitchcock to attorney general, 22 May 1906; W. A Richards to secretary of interior, 10 May 1906, all in RG 60, Box 654, Case 48590.

34. "Hot Air Story on Coal Lands," EUA, 22 Mar. 1906.

35. "W. G. Sharp Expected in Utah at Any Time," EUA, 5 Apr. 1906.

36. Joseph A. Taff, "U.S. Geological Survey. Township Plats. Department [of] Justice, 1906," (hereafter Taff, 1906), MS 210, Box 1, Folder 2; acting attorney general to secretary of the interior, 2 Mar. 1906, RG 60, Box 654, Case 48590; *Reports of the Department of the Interior 1907*, Vol. I, (hereafter Interior Reports) (Washington, D.C.: Government Printing Office, 1907), pp. 363, 12.

37. "Pangs of Thirst" EUA, 18 Oct. 1906.

38. Taff, 1906, pp. 1–8.

39. G[eorge] E. Hair to commissioner of the General Land Office, 24 October 1905, RG 60, Box 654, Case 48590.

40. "Is On Big Coal Land Deal," EUA, 1 Feb. 1906; "Utah Fuel Company Buys," EUA, 8 Feb. 1906; "Is Going Over To Durango," EUA, 12 April 1906; "Of A More of Less Personal Nature," EUA, 10 May 1906; Mine Report, 1905 and 1906, pp. 45–46.

41. "Lucius Curtis Cash Entry #4732," RG 49, Homestead Papers, National Archives, Washington, D.C.

42. Burch to attorney general, 3 Jul. 1906, RG 60, Box 654, Case 48590.

43. "Federal Action Started at Zion Against Leading Coal Company," EUA, 12 Jul. 1906.

44. Burch to attorney general, 13 Jul. 1906, RG 60, Box 654, Case 48590; "Booth Removes Coal Land Lid," EUA, 19 Jul. 1906.

45. M. C. Burch to solicitor general, 30 Jul. 1906, RG 60, Box 654, Case 48590.

46. Ibid.

CHAPTER 8

1. "Coal Land Deals Worrying Them," (Price) EUA, 26 Jul. 1906.

2. Bill of Complaint No. 876, *U.S.v. Utah Fuel Company*; Bill of Complaint No. 868, *U.S. v. Pleasant Valley Coal Company*, both in Record Group

60, U.S. Justice Department Straight Numerical Files, Box 654, Case 48590, National Archives, Washington, D.C.

3. Ibid.; Bill of Complaint No. 869, *U.S. v. Utah Fuel Company;* Bill of Complaint No. 870, *U.S. v. Pleasant Valley Coal Company*, RG 60, Box 654, Case 48590.

4. M. C. Burch to solicitor general, 30 Jul. 1906, RG 60, Box 654, Case 48590.

5. Ibid.

6. Ibid.

7. Ibid.

8. Link and McCormick, *Progressivism*, pp. 36–39.

9. Ibid.

10. Ibid. See also Gardner and Flores, *Forgotten Frontier,* pp. 119–24.

11. Merrill. *Reed Smoot*, pp. 70–76.

12. Burch to solicitor general, 30 Jul. 1906.

13. Shipps, "Utah Comes of Age"; Hardy, *Solemn*, pp, 259–68.

14. Burch to solicitor general, 30 Jul. 1906. The cases mentioned by Burch, *United States v. Detroit Timber and Lumber Company*, 200 U.S. 321 (1906) and *United States v. Clark*, 200 U.S. 601 (1906) involved using the law as then interpreted by the courts to disguise the true nature of a fraudulent transaction. Burch and Fred Maynard, who were teamed in the Utah coal-land cases, had also prosecuted these. In the *Detroit Timber* case, the government failed to recover timber land that had been transferred from a previous owner, the Martin-Alexander Lumber Company, to Detroit Timber and for which patent had issued resulting in conveyance. For the tracts not yet cónveyed, patents were cancelled, resulting in seventeen tracts returning to the public domain while twenty-seven remained with the company. The reasoning was that, although the original grantee may have committed fraud, Detroit Timber purchased the lands in good faith. The Clark case, decided immediately afterward, reiterated the idea that a presumably innocent purchaser (this time of eighty patents for timber lands) could not be punished for the acts of a guilty entryman and that the guilt of the purchaser had to be clearly established in order to return the land to the public domain. Although the first case pertained to companies and the second to individuals, the message was the same: sale to a second party offered protection from conviction for fraudulent entry and deprived the government of the land unless clear proof of fraud on the part of successive owners could be obtained.

15. Ibid.

16. "Would Confiscate Sunnyside," EUA, 2 Aug. 1906.

17. "Fisher Harris Is Now Explaining," EUA, 9 Aug. 1906.

18. Ibid.

19. "United States Senator May Be Drawn Into Net," EUA, 19 Jul. 1906; George Sutherland Papers, "General Miscellaney—Scrapbooks 1902–1917," Box 9, Scrapbook 1, 1902–13, containing article "Sutherland Comes Back

at Justice M'Carty," *Salt Lake Herald*, 14 Aug. 1906, Library of Congress, Washington, D.C.; "Sutherland Gets Out of the Old Law Firm," EUA, 2 Aug. 1906; [Editorial], EUA, 30 Aug. 1906. The editorial identifies the firm: Sutherland, Van Cott and Allison. Waldemar Van Cott assisted Washington, D.C. attorney A. S. Worthington in defending Smoot. See Hardy, p. 252.

20. Frank L. Campbell to H. M. Hoyt, 7 Aug. 1906, RG 60, Box 654, Case 48590.

21. H. W. Hoyt to H. C. Lewis, 10 Aug. 1906, RG 60, Box 654, Case 48590.

22. M. C. Burch to solicitor general, 5 Sept. 1906, RG 60, Box 654, Case 48590.

23. M. C. Burch and Fred Maynard to attorney general, 28 August 1906; M. C. Burch to solicitor general, 7 Sept. 1906; acting attorney general to John S. Vreeland, 7 Sept. 1906, all in RG 60, Box 654, Case 48590.

24. "Complaint Is Sworn Out for President J. F. Smith," (Salt Lake) *Evening Telegram*, 12 Sept. 1906; Anthon H. Lund to Heber J. Grant, 12 Sept. 1906, MS 1233, Heber J. Grant Papers, Box 52, Fd. 22, LDS Church Archives, Salt Lake City, Hardy, p. 261; diary of Joseph Fielding Smith, pp. 111, 116–17, MS 4250, Joseph Fielding Smith Papers, Box 5, Historical Department, LDS Church, Salt Lake City. The Smith diary is currently unavailable for research. These pages were photocopied earlier and bear the citation then current.

25. Alexander, "Reed Smoot and Land Policy," pp. 245–64, especially p. 247.

26. "The Utah Fuel Company Enters Demurrers in Coal Land Cases," EUA, 11 Oct. 1906; "Certain to Help Carbon County," EUA, 20 Sept. 1906.

27. "Sensational Charges Against Coal Company," EUA, 4 Oct. 1906; "Stole Coal Land Right and Left," EUA, 11 Oct. 1906; "Rio Grande and Coal Companies to be Looked into by Commission," EUA, 22 Nov. 1906.

28. Burch quoted in "Utah Coal Lands May Be Released," EUA, 25 Oct. 1906.

29. "Utah Fuel Case Heard," EUA, 15 Nov. 1906.

30. "Federal Grand Jury Is Likely to Get Busy," EUA, 15 Nov. 1906; "Grand Jury Now Resting," EUA, 29 Nov. 1906.

31. "Federal Grand Jury Is Likely to Get Busy."

32. "Grafting Government Official Kicked Out of the Land Office," EUA, 15 Nov. 1906.

33. "Coal Lands Inquiry," EUA, 6 Dec. 1906.

34. Maynard [and] Booth to attorney general, 7 Dec. 1906, RG 60, Box 654, Case 48590; "Federal Grand Jury Gets Busy," EUA, 13 Dec. 1906.

35. "Forrester As A Mormon Elder," EUA, 13 Dec. 1906.

36. EUA, 13 Dec. 1906.

37. "General Manager Williams and Others Indicted Furnish Bonds," EUA, 13 Dec. 1906.

38. "Land Board Will Make No Contest," EUA, 13 Dec. 1906.

39. "Land Board Called Down," EUA, 6 Dec. 1906; "Coal Land Titles Should Remain In The Government, Says the President," EUA, 6 Dec. 1906.

40. Peffer, *Closing of the Public Domain*, pp. 52–58; 69–71.

41. "Memorandum Relative to the Secretary of the Interior's Explanatory Letter to the President Dated December 17, 1906," attached to G. W. Woodruff to Theodore Roosevelt, n.d., Theodore Roosevelt Papers, Series 1, Reel 70, pp. 6,7.

42. Ibid.

CHAPTER 9

1. "Bonaparte, Charles Joseph," in Sobel, *Biographical Directory* pp. 30, 31; Ethan Allen Hitchcock to President Theodore Roosevelt, 19 January 1907, Theodore Roosevelt Papers, Series 1, Reel 71.

2. Remarks of Senator Boies Penrose, reported in a reminisence by Frances T. Plimpton at Amherst College in *Reader's Digest* 72 (1 Jun. 1958), p. 142; Milton R. Merrill, "Reed Smoot," *Utah Historical Quarterly* p. 348; Merrill, *Reed Smoot*, pp. 76–80; Van Wagoner, *Mormon Polygamy*, p. 180; Meyer and Riley, *Public Domain, Private Dominion*, pp. 126–30.

3. Miller, *Stake Your Claim!* pp. 182–83.

4. Reisner, *Cadillac Desert*, pp. 85, 86; E. A. Hitchcock to T. Roosevelt, 1 Mar. 1907, Theodore Roosevelt Papers, Series 1, Reel 72, p. 172.

5. Theodore Roosevelt to the secretary of the interior, 12 Mar. 1907, Theodore Roosevelt Papers, Series 6, Reel 428, Vol. 1, p. 414; ibid., p. 415.

6. Pinchot, *Breaking New Ground*, p. 395.

7. "Knocks Out Coal Land Titles," EUA, 24 Jan. 1907.

8. "Four More Are Nailed To Cross," EUA, 24 Jan. 1907; "Before the Secretary of the Interior: *United States of America v. Rilla Snyder et al.*," RG 60, United States Department of Justice Straight Numerical Files, Box 40, Case 48590, pp. 7,8.

9. M. C. Burch to attorney general, 9 Apr. 1907.

10. Ibid.

11. Ibid.

12. Ibid.; Huitt to attorney general, 22 Apr. 1907; attorney general to M. C. Burch, 24 April 1907, all in RG 60, Box 654, Case 48590.

13. "Promoter and Lawyer Sweet in Trouble Over Coal Lands," EUA, 24 Jan. 1907.

14. "Articles of Incorporation of the Independent Coal and Coke Company," Special Collections, College of Eastern Utah, Price, Utah; "It Means Much to Both Towns," EUA, 3 Jan. 1907; "Curtis Tells What His Company Is Now Doing," EUA, 7 Mar. 1907; "Independent Coal People Are Employing About Hundred Men," EUA, 21 March 1907; "Improvements Being Made By the Independent Coal and Coke Co.," EUA, 2 May 1907; "New Cable

Now Going In," EUA, 15 Aug. 1907; "Anxious To Get Out A Hundred Tons Daily," EUA, 14 Nov. 1907.

15. "Land Board Will Make No Contest," EUA, 13 Dec. 1906; Civil 272; "Coal Lands Inquiry"; *Hearings Before the Subcommittee of the Committee on the Public Lands, House of Representatives, Sixty-Fifth Congress, Third Session, on H.J. Res. 282* (Washington, D.C.: Government Printing Office, 1919), p. 67.

16. "The Land Board to Make Fight," EUA, 4 Apr. 1907; "Twelfth Annual Report of State Board of Land Commissioners for fiscal year ending Nov. 30, 1907," Department: State Land Board, Division: General Administration, Series: Annual Reports, Utah State Archives, Salt Lake City, Utah, p. 5.

17. Twelfth Annual Report, 1907, p. 5; "Coal Land Purchased," (Price) *Sun*, 1 Mar. 1918.

18. "Millburn Wins His Coal Lands Case," EUA, 29 Oct. 1903; "Milner Coal Holdings Get In Federal Court," EUA, 22 Apr. 1909; "Sidney D. [*sic*] Milner Dies Suddenly At Salt Lake," EUA, 10 May 1907; "Coal Lands Deals Worrying Them," EUA, 26 Jul. 1906; "Milner Coal Holdings Get Into Federal Court;" EUA, 22 Apr. 1909; "Title to Coal Lands Goes to Government," EUA, 28 May 1914.

19. "Status of the Milner Coal Holdings Is Sought," *Sun*, 17 Oct. 1919; G. Hair to William Spry, 27 Dec. 1909, State Land Board Correspondence 1896–1900, Utah State Archives, Salt Lake City, Utah.

20. "Coal Land Deals Worrying Them."

21. "Robert Forrester Again Indicted in Colorado," EUA, 27 Jun. 1907; "May End Coal Land Disputes," EUA, 18 Jul. 1907.

22. James Rudolph Garfield to attorney general, 16 Apr. 1907, RG 60, Box 654, Case 48590.

23. "Order of the Secretary of the Interior Garfield," 35 L.D. 655; "Commissioners Choosing Lands," EUA, 17 Oct. 1907.

24. "Union Pacific Has Cold Feet," EUA, 11 Apr. 1907; "Coal Company Restores Lands to Uncle Sam," EUA, 23 May 1907.

25. *Reports of the Department of the Interior for the fiscal year ending June 30, 1907*, Vol 1 (Washington, D.C.: Government Printing Office, 1907), pp. 12–15.

26. John C. Cutler to State Board of Land Commissioners, 29 Jul. 1907, Division: State Land Board, Series: Correspondence, Box: "Report to the Board of Title Investigations and Individual Pieces of Land," Utah State Archives.

27. "Memorandum by the Attorney General," 6 Nov. 1907, Theodore Roosevelt Papers, Series 1, Reel 78.

28. Maynard and Booth to attorney general, 2 Sept. 1907; attorney general to James R. Garfield, 4 Oct. 1907, both in RG 60, Box 654, Case 48590.

29. Fred A. Maynard to attorney general, 16 Sept. 1907, RG 60, Box 654, Case 48590; "The Utah Fuel Company Cases Up Again At Zion," EUA, 7 Nov. 1907.

30. "J. M. Whitmore and J. W. Warf," EUA, 14 Nov. 1907; Joseph A. Taff, "U.S. Geological Survey Mine Notes, 1907," MS 210, U.S.G.S. Coal Mine Survey Notes (1905–1908), Box 1, Fd. 3, Manuscripts Division, Special Collections Department, University of Utah Libraries, Salt Lake City, Utah; "Prof. Taff Returns To Zion From Sunnyside," EUA, 21 Nov. 1907; M. C. Burch to Joseph A. Taff, 27 Apr. 1907, RG 60, Box 654, Case 48590.

31. "Judge Lewis in Limelight Now," EUA, 26 Dec. 1907; "Judge John A. Marshall Rules Opposite Colorado Jurist," EUA, 26 Dec. 1907; "Not in Violation of the Statutes," EUA, 2 Jan. 1908; "And, It Is to Be Hoped, the Same Will Apply in the Utah Cases," EUA, 2 Jan. 1908; 34 Stat. 1246 (1907).

CHAPTER 10

1. Hiram E. Booth to attorney general, 31 Dec. 1907, Record Group 60, U.S. Department of Justice Straight Numerical Files, Box 654, Case 48590, National Archives, Washington, D.C.

2. "Utah Fuel Has More Trouble," EUA, 7 Jan. 1908; J. F. Vaile to M. C. Burch, 4 Jan. 1908, with enclosure J. F. Vaile to Charles J. Bonaparte, 4 Jan. 1908; Burch to attorney general, 5 Jan. 1908, both in RG 60, Box 654, Case 48590.

3. M. C. Burch to attorney general, 6 Jan. 1908, RG 60, Box 654, Case 48590.

4. M. C. Burch to attorney general, 14 Jan. 1908, RG 60, Box 654, Case 48590; "Sudden Close In The Land Frauds," EUA, 16 Jan. 1908; "Royal C. Peabody Goes On Record," EUA, 16 Jan. 1908.

5. M. C. Burch to attorney general, 17 Feb. 1908, RG 60, Box 654, Case 48590.

6. Fred A. Maynard and Hiram E. Booth to attorney general, 18 Feb. 1908; ibid., 19 Feb. 1908; M. C. Burch to attorney general, 20 Feb. 1908; all in RG 60, Box 654, Case 48590.

7. Attorney general to M. C. Burch, 4 Mar. 1908; attorney general to Hiram E. Booth, 10 March 1908, both in RG 60, Box 654, Case 48590.

8. M. C. Burch to attorney general, 20 Feb. 1908.

9. "Outlook Is Bad for Coal and Coke Industry," 30 Jan. 1908; "Putting on More Miners," 4 June 1908; "Price of Coal is Reduced," 9 Jan. 1908; "Utah Fuel Company is Curtailing its Output," 16 Jan. 1908; all in EUA; Athearn, *Rebel* reprint, p. 214.

10. Attorney general to Fred A. Maynard, 8 Oct. 1907; Maynard to attorney general, 22 Jan. 1908; attorney general to William Spry, 16 Apr. 1908; Maynard to attorney general, 8 Apr. 1908; M. C. Burch to attorney general, 25 Apr. 1908, all in RG 60, Box 654, Case 48590.

11. Maynard and Hiram E. Booth to Burch, 7 May 1908, RG 60, Box 654, Case 48590.

12. Charles J. Bonaparte to the president, 12 Mar. 1908, Theodore Roosevelt Papers, Series 1, Reel 81.

13. Ibid.

14. Andrews, *Theodore Roosevelt* pp. 233–36; Bishop, *Roosevelt and His Time*, vol. 2, pp. 56–59.

15. "Coal Lands Cases Resumed," EUA, 5 Mar. 1908; "Smooth Graft Is Worked At Zion," ibid.; "Truth and Gossip, EUA, 2 Apr. 1908; "Coal Cases Are On Again," ibid.; "Old Timer Takes Witness Stand," EUA, 7 Apr. 1908.

16. Quoted in "Old Timer."

17. "More Tilts Come In Coal Hearings," (Salt Lake) *Deseret Evening News* (hereafter DEN), 8 Apr. 1908; "Joseph Seeley Tells Just Why," DEN, 9 Apr. 1908; "Wellingtonite As Witness," EUA, 9 Apr. 1908; "Demon Rum In The Coal Cases," DEN, 10 Apr. 1908.

18. Maynard and Booth to attorney general, 27 May 1908; Bonaparte to Maynard, 2 Jun. 1908; Maynard to attorney general, 7 Aug. 1908; all in RG 60, Box 654, Case 48590.

19. "Government About Done," EUA, 18 June 1908.

20. "Mrs. Robert Forrester Testifies In Coal Cases," EUA, 12 Nov. 1908.

21. Athearn, *Rebel*, p. 195; "San Pete Valley Railway Company Minutes, 1893–1910," pp. 45–50, courtesy of the Bancroft Library, University of California, Berkeley; "Record-Sevier Railway Company," pp. 89–110, also courtesy of the Bancroft Library; LeMassena, *Mountain Railroads*, vol. 2, "Part IV, The Denver & Rio Grande Railroad Company (Consolidated) 1908"; "Great Things for Future," EUA, 28 May 1908; "Gould Is to Inspect Mines," EUA, 6 Aug. 1908.

22. "Ogden Gateway Opened to Carbon County Coal" and "Tariff Rates on Coal to North Announced," both in EUA, 1 Oct. 1908; "Babcock Confidential With the Public Now," EUA, 4 Feb. 1909.

23. "Robert Forrester Dead," (Price) *Carbon County News*, 23 Dec. 1910; "Lewis To Preside In Coal Land Transfer," EUA, 8 Oct. 1908; "Government Amends Its Complaint In Coal Suit," EUA, 15 Oct. 1908.

24. Frank Hall to attorney general, 1 Oct. 1908, RG 60, Box 654, Case 48590; ibid., attorney general to secretary of interior, 5 Oct. 1908, ibid., Thomas Ward Jr. to attorney general, 15 Feb. 1909; ibid. attorney general to Hall, 19 Feb. 1909.

25. Pinchot, *Breaking New Ground*, p. 377.

26. Ibid., pp. 379–80.

27. *United States v. Keitel*, 211 U.S. 370 (1908).

28. "J. H. Eccles Dead," EUA, 12 Nov. 1914; "Figuring on Local Mines," EUA, 21 Mar. 1907; "In Re. House Joint Resolution 282," MS 154, Utah Fuel Collection, Box 7, Fd. 10, Lee Library, Brigham Young University, Provo, Utah.

29. Fred Dennett to register and receiver, 24 Dec. 1908; E. D. R. Thompson and M. M. Kaighn to E. W. Senior, 2 Jan. 1909, both in Utah

State Land Board Records, "Report to the Board of Title Investigations on Individual Pieces of Land" folder, Utah State Archives; Burch to Ernest Knaebel, 5 Nov. 1909, RG 60, Box 654, Case 48590.

30. "Coal Lands Cases Up In News Form," EUA, 17 Dec. 1908; "Defense Rests In Case Of Utah Fuel Company," EUA, 31 Dec. 1908.

31. "Morton Trust Is in the Limelight," EUA, 21 Jan. 1909; "Was the Fuel Company or Uncle Sam the Winner?" EUA, 8 Apr. 1909.

32. Bonaparte to the president, 14 Jan. 1909, T. R. Papers, Series 1, Reel 87.

33. State Board of Land Commissioners to the governor, 18 February 1909, "Report to the Board of Title Investigations on Individual Pieces of Land," State Land Board Records, correspondence, Utah State Archives. Mondell Act, 35 Stat. 844 (1909).

34. 35 Stat. 844; "Quite Vast Broadening of Coal Lands Policy," EUA, 10 Jun. 1909.

35. "Quite Vast Broadening."

36. C. W. Hayes, quoted in Mayer and Riley, *Public Domain, Private Dominion*, p. 155.

37. "Wickersham, George," in Sobel, *Biographical Directory*, p. 356; attorney general to secretary of interior, 11 Mar. 1909; RG 60, Box 654, Case 48590; Maynard to attorney general, 11 Mar. 1909, RG 60, Box 654, Case 48590.

38. M. C. Burch to attorney general, 26 Mar. 1909, RG 60, Box 654, Case 48590.

39. Burch to attorney general, 6 Jan. 1908, RG 60, Box 654, Case 48590; Burch to attorney general, 26 March 1909.

40. Maynard and Booth to attorney general, 30 Mar. 1909; John B. Vreeland to attorney general, 31 Mar. 1909, both in RG 60, Box 654, Case 48590.

CHAPTER 11

1. "Some Figures of Coal Case Fines," EUA, 22 Apr. 1909; "Some Facts About Coal Lands Frauds," *Salt Lake Tribune,* 16 Apr. 1909.

2. "Some Facts About Coal Lands Frauds."

3. "Victory for Local Men," newspaper clipping from unidentified paper attached to JRH to Mr. Mikkelson, n.d., RG 60, U.S. Dept. of Justice Straight Numerical Files, Box 654, Case 48590, National Archives, Washington, D.C.

4. Ibid.

5. Burch to attorney general, 26 March 1909; Maynard to Burch, 10 Apr. 1909; both in RG 60, Box 654, Case 48590.

6. Burch to attorney general, 14 April 1909; attorney general to Maynard, 15 Apr. 1909, both in RG 60, Box 654, Case 48590.

7. E. N. Clark to C. H. Schlacks, 10 April 1909, MS 513, Denver and Rio Grande Papers, Box 13, Fd. 4586, Colorado Historical Society, Denver.

8. Taniguchi, "No Proper Job," pp. 145–64.

9. Maynard to attorney general, 13 May 1909, Burch to attorney general, 15 Jun. 1909, both in RG 60, Box 654, Case 48590.

10. Maynard to attorney general, 13 May 1909.

11. Burch to Attorney General, 15 Jun. 1909.

12. Mark P. Braffet and John M. Zane to Burch, 23 Jun. 1909, and ibid., 28 Jun. 1909; attorney general to Maynard, 30 Jun. 1909, all in RG 60, Box 654, Case 48590; "Forrester Gets it In Colorado," EUA, 10 Jun. 1909.

13. Maynard to attorney general, 29 Jun. 1909, RG 60, Box 654, Case 48590.

14. Attorney general to Maynard, 30 Jun. 1909.

15. "Utah Fuel Gives Up More Money," EUA, 29 Jul. 1909.

16. "Coal Lands Are Now Reconveyed," EUA, 7 Oct. 1909.

17. "Wyoming Coal Lands Restored," EUA, 29 Jul. 1909.

18. "After Milner Coal Lands," EUA, 22 Jul. 1909; "Status of Milner Coal Holding is Sought," (Price) Sun, 17 Oct. 1919.

19. "Why Should The Delay Be Here?" EUA, 22 Apr. 1909; "Department Is with Salt Lake," EUA, 7 Oct. 1909; "Some Facts About Coal Land Frauds," (Salt Lake) Tribune, 16 Apr. 1909.

20. [Fred A. Maynard] to Burch, 8 Oct. 1909, RG 60, Box 654, Case 48590.

21. Ibid.

22. Ibid.

23. Burch, "Memorandum for Mr. Knaebel," 5 Nov. 1909, RG 60, Box 654, Case 48590.

24. "Don C. Robbins Gives His Side of the Story," EUA, 18 Nov. 1909; special assistant [Fred A. Maynard] to attorney general, 22 Jul. 1913, RG 60, Box 654, Case 48590.

25. R. A. Ballinger to attorney general, 29 Nov. 1909, RG 60, Box 654, Case 48590.

26. W. G. Candland to George E. Hair, 29 Dec. 1909, U.S. Land Board correspondence 1896–1900, State Land Board, Utah State Archives.

27. Maynard to Ernest Knaebel, 8 Dec. 1909, RG 60, Box 654, Case 48590.

28. Ibid.

29. Ibid.; ibid., 27 Dec. 1909; RG 60, Box 654, Case 48590.

30. Letter to Maynard, (unsigned), 26 Jan. 1910, RG 60, Box 654, Case 48590. It is initialed "EK-GM" in the upper right hand corner, supposed by Maynard to represent "Ernest Knaebel-Miss Grace Murphy" (his secretary). See Maynard to Knaebel, 10 Mar. 1910.

31. Maynard to Knaebel, 7 Feb. 1910, RG 60, Box 655, Case 48590; Maynard to Knaebel, 10 Mar. 1910, RG 60, Box 654, Case 48590.

32. Maynard to Knaebel, 10 Mar. 1910.

CHAPTER 12

1. *Hearings before Committee of Investigation of Interior Department and Bureau of Forestry,* 61st Congress, 3rd Session, Sen. Doc. 719, Vol. 8, p. 4507;

Pringle, *Life and Times,* p. 491; Mason, *Brandeis,* p. 256; Mason, *Bureaucracy;* Hechler, *Insurgency,* pp. 154–55; Pennick, *Progressive Politics,* pp. 105–36; Coletta, *William Howard Taft,* pp. 84–100. The significance of the Ballinger-Pinchot affair reached far beyond the effects discussed here. To give an example: the controversy is briefly described by Grauman in "Kennecott: Alaskan Origins of a Copper Empire" (pp. 202–203), wherein she succinctly explains the "handmaiden" role of coal in the copper industry (copper obviously being her major topic). Despite the exposure of the Cunningham frauds, Alaskans were generally far more sympathetic to the Guggenheims as builders of the territory than were the citizens of the lower forty-eight states, as discussed by Slotnick in "The Ballinger-Pinchot Affair in Alaska."

2. Maynard to Knaebel, 8 Dec. 1909; Knaebel to Maynard, 3 Jan. 1910; G. W. Wickersham to Maynard, 22 Jan. 1910; Maynard to Knaebel, 10 Mar. 1910; Wickersham to Maynard, 26 Jan. 1910, all in RG 60, U.S. Justice Department Straight Numerical Files, Box 654, Case 48590, National Archives, Washington, D.C.

3. Maynard to Knaebel, 8 Dec. 1909, RG 60, Box 654, Case 48590.

4. Unsigned carbon copy to Maynard, 15 Mar. 1910, RG 60, Box 654, Case 48590.

5. George A. Williams to Charles Nagel, 23 Jun. 1910 and Maynard to Knaebel, 19 Jul. 1910, both in RG 60, Box 654, Case 48590; *Official Register, 1909* Vol. I (Washington, D.C.: Government Printing Office, 1909), p. 52.

6. Secretary of interior to attorney general, 9 Aug. 1910 and acting attorney general to secretary of interior, 13 Aug. 1910, both in RG 60, Box 654, Case 48590.

7. Hechler, pp. 28–82; Mason, p. 257, 258; Paschal, *Sutherland,* pp. 61–62, 105–14.

8. Quoted in Pinchot, *Breaking New Ground,* pp. 430–31.

9. Elbert F. Baldwin to William Howard Taft, 13 Jan. 1909, quoted in Hechler, *Insurgency,* p. 154.

10. Pinchot, pp. 395–98; Andrews, *Theodore Roosevelt,* pp. 209, 210.

11. Peffer, *Closing of the Public Domain,* p. 240.

12. Ibid., pp. 241–42.

13. Chief clerk to Mr. Cole, 5 March 1910, RG 60, Box 654, Case 48590; Mason, *Brandeis,* pp. 258–76.

14. 36 Stat. 539 (1910).

15. 36 Stat. 583 (1910); "Coal Lands Re-appraised," (Price) *Carbon County News* (hereafter CCN), 3 June 1910; Editorial, CCN, 23 Dec. 1910.

16. Quoted in "Message from the President of the United States," Document No. 644, Senate Documents Vol. 61, 61st Congress, 2nd Session, (Washington, D.C.: Government Printing Office, 1910), p. 2.

17. Ibid.

18. "Robert Forrester Dead," CCN, 23 Dec. 1910; "Funeral of Robert

Forrester," CCN, 30 Dec. 1910; "Prominent in the West's Development," CCN, 14 Jan. 1911.

19. "Arthur A. Sweet Dead," DEN, 21 July 1910; Warrum, *Utah,* pp. 232–33.

20. "Hiawatha," EUA, 2 Sept. 1910.

21. United States, *Statutes at Large,* Dec. 1905 to Mar. 1907, Chapter 3591, Section 1; Record Group 134, "Records of the Interstate Commerce Commission," Formal Docket 7933; Ibid., Formal Docket 3811, both in the National Archives, Washington, D.C.

22. "Petition," filed 31 Jan. 1911, Record Group 134, "Records of the Interstate Commerce Commission," Formal Docket 7933; ibid., Docket 3811, both in National Archives; "Claim Unfair Discrimination," EUA, 9 Feb. 1911.

23. GMS to Mr. Holmstead, n.d., attached to docket 3811, RG 134.

24. Will C. Higgins, "Success of the Consolidated Fuel Company," *Salt Lake Mining Review* (hereafter SLMR) 13 (15 Apr. 1911): 20; idem, "Business Men Examine Hiawatha Mines," SLMR 13 No. 4 (30 May 1911), pp. 15–17; "Coal Company Entertains Party," EUA, 18 May 1911.

25. "Castle Valley Coal Property," EUA, 23 Mar. 1911; "Coal Company Making Strides," EUA, 30 Mar. 1911; "Pettit Writes of the Castle Valley's Veins," EUA, 20 Apr. 1911; "Utah Coal Is to Supply Coast," EUA, 27 Apr. 1911; "First Car Party Enjoy their Trip," EUA, 8 Jun. 1911; Will C. Higgins, "The Castle Valley Coal Company," SLMR 13 No. 6 (30 Jun. 1911): 15–18; Secretary of Utah Territory, Territorial Executive Papers, Series 241, Reel 13, Box 5, Folder 23], "Annual Report, Robert Forrester, U.S. Mine Inspector, 1892," p. 13490.

26. "The Castle Valley Coal Company."

27. "Fisher Defends Coal Land Policy," EUA, 5 Oct. 1911.

28. J. B. to attorney general, 9 Aug. 1910, RG 60, Box 654, Case 48590.

29. Pinchot, p. 461; Mason, *Brandeis,* p. 258.

30. Mason, *Brandeis,* pp. 281–82; Pinchot, pp. 460, 495–96.

31. "Mr. Roosevelt to the Mormons," *Collier's,* 15 Apr. 1911; *Deseret News Almanac,* p. 291.

32. Maynard to Knaebel, 25 Apr. 1911, RG 60, Box 654, Case 48590.

33. Maynard to attorney general, 27 Apr. 1911, RG 60, Box 655, Case 48590.

34. Maynard to Knaebel, 25 Apr. 1911; Maynard to attorney general, 27 Apr. 1911.

35. Ibid.

36. Knaebel to Maynard, 17 May 1911; Knaebel to attorney general, 18 May 1911, both in RG 60, Box 655, Case 48590.

37. Maynard to attorney general, 21 May 1911, RG 60, Box 655, Case 48590.

38. [unsigned—probably Maynard] to Burch, 8 Oct. 1909, RG 60, Box 654, Case 48590.

39. Maynard to attorney general, 27 Apr. 1911 and 21 May 1911; "Freeds Win Out in Bitter Fight," (Price) *Sun,* 17 Mar. 1916.

40. Clark deposition, attached to Knaebel to attorney general, 28 July 1911, RG 60, Box 655, Case 48590; "Union Pacific Was After Freed Coal," EUA, 20 Jul. 1911.

41. Maynard to attorney general, 10 Jul. 1911, RG 60, Box 655, Case 48590.

42. Wickersham to Roosevelt, 1 Aug. 1911, Theodore Roosevelt Papers, Series I, Reel 111.

43. Maynard to Burch, 27 Nov. 1911, RG 60, Box 655, Case 48590.

CHAPTER 13

1. Burch, "Memorandum for the Attorney General," 18 Jan. 1912, RG 60, U.S. Justice Department Straight Numerical Files, Box 654, Case 48590, National Archives.

2. Ibid.

3. Burch to attorney general, 24 Jan. 1912, RG 60, Box 654, Case 48590.

4. 284 U.S. 534 at 545 (1932).

5. Burch to attorney general, 24 Jan. 1912, RG 60, Box 654, Case 48590.

6. Ibid.

7. Ibid.

8. Maynard to attorney general, 21 May 1911, RG 60, Box 655, Case 48590.

9. J[oel] F. Vaile to M. P. Braffet, 9 Jan. 1912, MS 154, Utah Fuel Collection, Box 9, Fd. 10, Lee Library, Brigham Young University, Provo.

10. Braffet to Vaile, 19 Jan. 1912, ibid.

11. Ibid.; idem, 4 Feb. 1912.

12. Edmund T. Olson, *Coal Lands Report in Charge of Joseph Ririe, State Auditor* (Kaysville, Utah: Inland Printing Company, 1920), pp. 13–14.

13. Athearn, *Rebel,* pp. 218, 219.

14. Fred Sweet to Interstate Commerce Commission, 3 Jan. 1912; RG 134, Commission Records, Docket 3811, National Archives.

15. E. N. Clark to James S. Harlan, 3 Feb. 1912, RG 134, Docket 3811.

16. "Castle Valley Coal Property Is Sold," CCN, 12 Jan. 1912; "Millions Going Into Eastern Utah Coal Mines and Railroads," EUA, 7 Mar. 1912; Arrington, *David Eccles.*

17. "Top Price Paid," CCN, 8 Mar. 1912; ibid., "Salt Lake Version of Big Coal Deal."

18. "Carbon Coal Land Tops the Market," CCN, 5 Apr. 1912; "Big Coal Deal Closed Saturday," CCN, 6 Jun. 1912.

19. Fred Sweet to James M. Harlan, 22 Mar. 1912, RG 134, Docket 3811; ibid., "Stipulation."

20. C. H. Gibbs to A. H. Cowie, 21 Jun. 1912, MS 154, Box 9, Fd. 1.

21. Ibid.

22. "Uncle Sam Recovers Valuable Coal Lands," CCN, 26 Apr. 1912; Athearn, *Rebel*, pp. 218, 219.

23. William Barnes Jr. to George W. Wickersham, 1 Jun. 1912, RG 60, Box 655, Case 48590.

24. Wickersham, "Memorandum for Mr. Knaebel," with note signed "E. K.," 3 Jun. 1912, RG 60, Box 655, Case 48590.

25. Burch, "Memorandum for the Attorney General," 25 Jun. 1912; RG 60, Box 655, Case 48590.

26. Attorney general to secretary of interior, 26 Jul. 1912, RG 60, Box 655, Case 48590.

27. "Soldier Summit to Be Electrified," EUA, 21 Nov. 1912; "Spending Millions In Improvements," EUA, 12 Dec. 1912.

28. 226 U.S. 470 (1913); "Harriman Combine Will Be Dissolved," CCN, 5 Dec. 1912; "Loses Contest in Highest Court," CCN, 9 Jan. 1913.

29. "Letter From Scofield," CCN, 7 Oct. 1910. "Sunnyside Closed to Progressives," CCN, 31 Oct. 1912; "The Official Returns," EUA, 7 Nov. 1912; Taniguchi, "No Proper Job." In some respects, this rural movement conformed to urban efforts recently studied by modern historians. However, fine points of correlation (or lack thereof) need further study. See, for example, McCarthy, "Urban Optimism" and DiGaetano, "Urban Political Reform."

30. "Jesse Knight Looking Up Coal Proposition," EUA, 8 Aug. 1907; Arrington and Alexander, *Dependent Commonwealth* p. 29; "Utah State News," CCN, 30 May 1912; "City and County," CCN, 13 Feb. 1913; "County Business Transacted," CCN, 17 Apr. 1913.

31. "Townsite Title Cleared," *Sun,* 8 Mar. 1918; "Many Titles Rest on Olson Case," *Sun,* 26 Apr. 1918.

32. "Notable Victory for the People," CCN, 20 Mar. 1913; "Stipulation," 17 Jun. 1913, RG 134, Interstate Commerce Commission, Docket 3811, *Consolidated Fuel Co. et al. v. Atchison, Topeka & Santa Fe Railroad, et al.,* National Archives, Washington, D.C.

33. "Denver and Rio Grande Takes Over Two Roads," EUA, 26 Jun. 1913; "Coal Road to End at Castle Gate," CCN, 6 Nov. 1913; "New Railroad Soon To Build," EUA, 20 Jul. 1911; "Western Railroads Hit Hard By Supreme Court," EUA, 25 Jun. 1914; "Los Angeles Switching Case," 234 U.S. 294 (1914); 234 U.S. 276 (1914).

34. Athearn, *Rebel*, pp. 220–24.

35. [Fred A. Maynard] to attorney general, 19 Jul. 1913, RG 60, Box 655, Case 48590.

36. Entry 11905, Utah Fuel Company, Book 2A, p. 114, Carbon County Recorder's Records, Carbon County Courthouse, Price, Utah; 35 Stat. 844 (1909).

37. Unsigned carbon copy to A. H. Cowie, 30 Jul. 1913, MS 154, Box 14, Fd.12.

38. Ibid.

CHAPTER 14

1. Maynard to attorney general, 10 Jul. 1911, RG 60, U.S. Justice Department Straight Numerical Files, Box 655, Case 48590, National Archives.

2. "Sweets Back in the Coal Game," EUA, 3 Jul. 1913; "Helper News Notes," CCN, 20 Nov. 1913; "Standard Company Has Splendid Record," EUA, 14 June 1914; "Price and Vicinity," EUA, 6 Aug. 1914.

3. *Joint Hearings Before the Committee on Public Lands and Surveys, United States Senate and the Committee on the Public Lands, House of Representatives, 69th Congress, First Session, on S. 3078 and H.R. 9182. February 11 and 12, 1926* (Washington, D.C.: Government Printing Office, 1926), p. 107; *Hearings Before the Subcommittee of the Committee on Public Lands, House of Representatives, Sixty-Fifth Congress, Third Session, on H.J. Res. 282.* (Washington, D.C.: Government Printing Office, 1919), (hereafter Land Hearings), p. 35.

4. "Transcript of Record, Supreme Court of the United States, October Term 1914, No. 99, *United States v. Frederick A. Sweet, Administrator of the Estate of Arthur A. Sweet, deceased,* RG 267, Supreme Court Appellate Files, File 25120, pp. 12, 13, National Archives, Washington, D.C.; "Sweet Loses Contest," CCN, 26 Feb. 1914.

5. J. Harwood Graves to attorney general, 30 Aug. 1905, RG 60, Box 654, Case 48590.

6. "Transcript of Record, *Independent Coal and Coke v. United States,* 8th Circuit Court of Appeals, 21 Nov. 1925," RG 267, File 31707; G. E. Hair to William Spry, 27 Dec. 1909 and [W. D. Candland] to Hair, 29 Dec. 1909, both in State Land Board Records, correspondence, Utah State Archives; "Title to Coal Land Goes to Government," EUA, 21 May 1914.

7. Mine Report, 1913–1914, p. 101; "Effect of War on Utah," *Salt Lake Mining Review* 16 (15 Aug. 1914): 26.

8. "Women Organize Betterment League," CCN, 26 Feb. 1914; "Hundreds of Women Petition the Council," CCN, 5 Mar. 1914; "The Betterment League," CCN, 19 Mar. 1914.

9. "The Carbon County Vampire," CCN, 26 March 1914.

10. "Progressive Party Sweets the County," EUA, 5 Nov. 1914; *Pleasant Valley Coal Company v. Alpha Ballinger as County Treasurer,* Civil 856 (1914) and *Utah Fuel Co. v. Alpha Ballinger as County Treasurer,* Civil 857 (1914), both in Utah's Seventh Judicial District, Carbon County Clerk's Records, Carbon County Courthouse, Price, Utah; "The Utah Fuel Company Restrains Sale of Lands," EUA, 24 Dec. 1914.

11. Athearn, *Rebel* reprint, pp. 220–25.

12. Ibid., pp. 225–28.

13. Mine Report, 1915–1916, p. 281; "City and County," (Price) *News-Advocate* (hereafter NA), 3 Sept. 1915; "Carbon Fuel Incorporates," NA, 17

Sept. 1915; *Carbon Fuel Coal Company v. Standard Coal Company and C. W. Bemis,* Civil 941 (1915), Utah Seventh Judicial District.

14. 28 U.S. 107 (1894); 228 Federal 421 (1915).

15. *Milner et al. v. United States,* 228 Fed. 431 (1915) at 439.

16. "Milner Entry Is Cancelled," *Salt Lake Herald-Republican,* 15 Sept. 1915; "Milner Coal Entry Has Been Cancelled," NA 17 Sept. 1915.

17. *Diamond Coal and Coke Company v. United States,* 233 U.S. 236 (1914); "Robert Forrester Dead," CCN, 23 Dec. 1910; Incorporation Papers, Diamond Coal and Coke Company, Division of Corporations and Commercial Codes, Department of Commerce, State of Utah, Salt Lake City, Utah; 233 U.S. 236 at 233–49.

18. 233 U.S. 236 at 237.

19. "Report of Henry McAllister, Jr. to E. T. Jeffery, Chairman," 10 Jul. 1916, MS 513, Denver and Rio Grande Collection, Box 15, Fd. 3315, Colorado Historical Society, Denver, Colorado. The PVCC was thus able to use the private law of property to set up an alternative legal theory in order to substantiate its land claim by operating its business openly and notoriously and by paying taxes on it. This alternative ground was later among those approved in court.

20. "Personal Mention," EUA, 13 Oct. 1898; "Castle Gate Interested In Big Suit," NA, 3 Mar. 1916; [no title], EUA, 16 Jan. 1913; "Ketchum Coal Company Strikes New Coal Vein," EUA, 21 May 1914; W. D. Riter to Henry McAllister Jr., 19 May 1916, MS 513, Box 15, Fd. 3304.

21. "Judge Christensen Holds Special Session to Hear Coal Land Case," *Sun,* 28 Apr. 1916; B. F. Bush to Jeffery, 23 Sept. 1915, MS 513, Box 15, Fd. 3251; Riter to McAllister, 20 May 1916, MS 513, Box 15, Fd. 3305–7.

22. "Exhibit E, Amended Bill of Complaint," *Pleasant Valley Coal Company v. Truman A. Ketchum,* MS 513, Box 15, Fd. 3315, pp. 20–22. The case applicable here, *Highland Boy Gold Mining Company v. Strickley* (1904), 28 Utah 215, is cited by Bakken in *Development of Law* in support of his discussion on the flexible nature of the power of eminent domain with reference to irrigators, part of the legal framework for development of the West. See p. 75 and note 17 on pp. 169–70.

23. 233 U.S. 236 (1914); 228 Fed. 431 (1915).

24. Riter to McAllister, 19 May 1916, MS 513, Box 15, Fd. 3304.

25. Ibid.

26. Ibid.

27. "Exhibit E, Amended Bill of Complaint," *Pleasant Valley Coal Company v. Truman A. Ketchum,* MS 513, Box 15, Fd. 3315, pp. 20–22.

28. "Judge Christensen Holds Special Session to Hear Coal Land Case," *Sun,* 28 April 1916; Bush to Jeffery, 23 Sept. 1915, MS 513, Box 15, Fd. 3251; Riter to McAllister, 20 May 1916, MS 513, Box 15, Fd. 3305-7; McAllister, to Jeffery, 5 Jul. 1916, MS 513, Box 29, Letterbook 12.

29. Bush to Jeffery, 23 Sept. 1915, MS 513, Box 15, Fd. 3251; Jeffery to A. H. Cowie, 27 Sept. 1915, MS 513, Box 16, Fd. 3504; Athearn, *Rebel*, p. 231; Riter to McAllister, 20 May 1916, MS 513, Box 15, Fd. 3305–7.

30. Bush to Jeffery, 23 Sept. 1915, MS 513, Box 15, Fd. 3251.

31. Ibid; M. P. Braffet to McAllister, 18 Apr. 1916, MS 513, Box 15, Fd. 3271, p. 2.

32. Riter to McAllister, 19 May 1916, MS 513, Box 15, Fd. 3304.

33. Hardy, *Solemn,* pp. 184–85; Arrington, *David Eccles,* pp. 140–58, 170–86.

34. Braffet to McAllister, 18 Apr. 1916, MS 513, Box 15, Fd. 3271.

35. "Personal Mention," EUA, 13 Oct. 1898; "Ketchum & Shores to Resume Work at their Sunnyside Well," EUA, 7 May 1903; Siringo, *Cowboy Detective,* pp. 66–69, 192, 306; "Report of McAllister to Jeffery, Chairman," 10 July 1916, MS 513, Box 15, Fd. 3315, pp. 3–5.

36. Braffet to McAllister, 18 Apr. 1916, MS 513, Box 15, Fd. 3271, pp. 1–2.

CHAPTER 15

1. "Freeds Win Out in Bitter Fight," *Sun,* 17 Mar. 1916.

2. "Big Coal Land Scrap Settled," NA, 17 March 1916; "No Fraud In Freed Entries Is Decision," attached to Knaebel, "Memorandum for the Attorney General," 28 Jul. 1911, RG 60, U.S. Justice Department Straight Numerical Files, Box 655, Case 48590, National Archives, Washington, D.C.; Book A-1, Quit-Claim Deeds, p. 214, Carbon County Recorder's Records.

3. "Exhibit E, Amended Bill of Complaint," *Pleasant Valley Coal Company v. Truman A. Ketchum.* MS 513, Rio Grande Papers, Box 15, Fd. 3315, Colorado Historical Society, Denver, pp. 30–33, 20–22.

4. Braffet to McAllister, 18 Apr. 1916, MS 513, Box 15, Fd. 3271, pp. 1–2; E. T. Jeffery to McAllister, 18 Apr. 1916, MS 513, Box 15, Fd. 3272-3; McAllister, to Jeffery, MS 513, Box 15, Fd. 3274-81.

5. Braffet to McAllister, 18 Apr. 1916, MS 513, Box 15, Fd. 3271, pp. 1–2.

6. Ibid.

7. Braffet to McAllister, 18 Apr. 1916.

8. Braffet to McAllister, 18 Apr. 1916.

9. Braffet to McAllister, 21 Apr. 1916, MS 513, Box 15, Fd. 3274-81.

10. Ibid., allegedly quoting Cowie; ibid.

11. Athearn, *Rebel* reprint, pp. 226–34.

12. Jeffery to McAllister, 25 Apr. 1916, MS 513, Box 15, Fd. 3274-81. See also Letterbooks 12 and 13, MS 513, Box 29.

13. Jeffery to McAllister, 25 Apr. 1916.

14. McAllister, to Jeffery, 28 Apr. 1916, MS 513, Box 15, Fd. 3274-81.

15. Ibid.

16. Ibid., 1 May 1916, MS 513, Box 15, Fd. 3274-81.

17. Jeffery to McAllister, 4 May 1916, MS 513, Box 15, Fd. 3291-5; [Henry

McAllister, Jr.] to Jeffery, 5 May 1916, MS 513, Box 15, Fd. 3296-3302; "Ketchum Wins At Castle Gate," *Sun,* 7 May 1916; McAllister, to Riter, 9 May 1916, MS 513, Box 15, Fd. 3291-5; McAllister to Jeffery, 9 May 1916; ibid.; Jeffery to McAllister, 10 May 1916, ibid.

18. McAllister, to Jeffery, 14 May 1916, MS 513, Box 29, Letterbook 12.

19. Riter to McAllister, 15 May 1916, MS 513, Box 15, Fd. 3296-3302.

20. Riter to McAllister, 18 May 1916; Jeffery to McAllister, 19 May 1916, both in MS 513, Box 15, Fd. 3296-3302.

21. McAllister to Riter, 19 May 1916, MS 513, Box 15, Fd. 3303.

22. Van Cott, Allison, and Riter to McAllister, 22 May 1916, MS 513, Box 15, Fd. 3305-7.

23. [Henry McAllister, Jr.] to Jeffery, 19 May 1916, MS 513, Box 15, Fd. 3303.

24. Ibid.

25. Riter to McAllister, 19 May 1916, MS 513, Box 15, Fd. 3304.

26. Riter to McAllister, 20 May 1916, MS 513, Box 15, Fd. 3305-7.

27. Ibid.

28. *Ketchum v. D&RG,* 248 Fed. 106 (1917).

29. McAllister, to Jeffery, 30 Aug. 1916, MS 513, Box 29, Letterbook 12; ibid., 3 July 1916; 248 Fed. 106.

30. McAllister, to Van Cott, Allison, & Riter, 3 July 1916, 513, Box 29, Letterbook 12; ibid., 5 Jul. 1916.

31. "Ketchum Wins A Round In Court," NA, 7 July 1916; "Report of General Counsel Henry McAllister, Jr., to E. T. Jeffery, Chairman," 16 Jun. 1916, MS 513, Box 15, Fd. 3315.

32. McAllister to Jeffery, 8 Jul. 1916, MS 513, Box 29, Letterbook 12.

33. McAllister, to Jeffery, 8 Jul. 1916, MS 513, Box 29, Letterbook 12.

34. Daniels, *Woodrow Wilson,* pp. 258–61; Eaton and Read, *Woodrow Wilson,* p. 262; Link, *Woodrow Wilson,* pp. 70–80.

35. "Report of Henry McAllister, Jr., General Counsel, to E. T. Jeffery, Chairman."

CHAPTER 16

1. McAllister to A. C. Ellis, 25 Aug. 1916, MS 513, Denver and Rio Grande Papers, Box 29, Letterbook 12, Colorado Historical Society, Denver.

2. McAllister, to Jeffery, 15 Aug. 1916 and idem, 31 Aug. 1916, both in MS 513, Box 29, Letterbook 12.

3. McAllister, to Jeffery, 12 Sept. 1916 and idem, 15 Sept. 1916, both in MS 513, Box 29, Letterbook 12.

4. "Ketchum Case is Thrown Out," *Sun,* 13 Oct. 1916; McAllister to Jeffery, 9 Oct. 1916, MS 513, Box 29, Letterbook 12.

5. McAllister to Jeffery, 8 Oct. 1916, MS 513, Box 29, Letterbook 12.

6. Transmitted in cipher as: "However believe Seraph and Ketchum

more or less inharmonious and … it is probably best to monarch breaded bliss by itself and martagon Seraph from multure" in McAllister to Jeffery, 9 Oct. 1916; idem, 13 Oct. 1916, both in MS 513, Box 29, Letterbook 12.

7. Arrington, *David Eccles,* pp. 150, 157; Don Strack, "A History of the Development of Coal Mining and Railroads in Carbon County, Utah," 7 Jun. 1983, copy in possession of the author.

8. "Republicans Get but Three Places on County Ticket," NA 9 Nov. 1916.

9. "Justice Sutherland Dies in East," (Salt Lake City) *Deseret News,* 18 July 1942.

10. J. F. Cory to Mr. [William] Littlejohn, 13 Nov. 1916; J. S. T[hompson] to Cowie, 18 Nov. 1916; Thompson to Cowie, 19 Dec. 1916, all in MS 154, Utah Fuel Collection, Box 2, Fd. 17, Lee Library, Brigham Young University, Provo, Utah.

11. Riter, Ellis, Lucas, and Gibbs to Cowie, 29 Dec. 1916, MS 154, Box 2, Fd. 7.

12. McAllister, to Braffet, 10 Jan. 1917, MS 513, Box 29, Letterbook 12.

13. "New Field Open to Local Mines," NA, 29 Mar. 1917; Isaac F. Marcosson, *Metal Magic,* pp. 218, 231; Arrington and Alexander, *Dependent Commonwealth,* pp. 70–71; "Utah Mines Far Behind Orders," NA, 29 Mar. 1917; "Verbatim Report of Testimony and Proceedings … 29th day of January A.D. 1917," (hereafter Legislative Hearings) ACC 479, Manuscripts Division, Special Collections Department, University of Utah Libraries, Salt Lake City, pp. 64, 181–89, 217–18, 307–15.

14. McAllister, to Charles B. Eddy, 24 Jun. 1918, MS 513, Box 30, Letterbook 13.

15. McAllister to Jeffery, 13 Mar. 1918; McAllister, to A. J. Shores, 18 Mar. 1918; McAllister to Walter H. Sanborn, 4 Jun. 1918; McAllister to A. R. Baldwin, 4 June 1918, all in MS 513, Box 30, Letterbook 13.

16. "Strevell Helping," NA, 31 May 1917; Charles R. Van Hise, *Conservation and Regulation in the United States During the World War* (Washington: Government Printing Office, 1917) in facsimile reprint as *The United States in World War I* (n.p.: Jerome S. Ozer, 1974), pp. 139–41.

17. Record Group 67, "Records of the Fuel Administration, Bureau of State Organizations, Utah," Box 841, Folder 1, W. W. Armstrong to Herbert Hoover, 31 Jul. 1917; ibid., C. E. Groesbeck to Armstrong, 7 Jul. 1917; ibid., Armstrong to Mr. Snead, 24 Oct. 1917; Van Hise, p. 218; RG 67, Box 841, Fd. 2, Armstrong to Dr. Harry A. Garfield, 24 Oct. 1917; ibid., Whitcomb, Holmes, Schwabacher, Walker, Gooding, and Armstrong to Garfield, 20 Oct. 1917, all in National Archives, Washington, D.C.

18. Woodrow Wilson to Josephus Daniels, in Baker, *Woodrow Wilson,* vol. 1, p. 506.

19. Kolko, *Triumph,* pp. 286–87. Similar views are expressed by Hawley, *Search for a Modern Order,* pp. 23–25 and by Keller, *Regulating,* pp. 33–35.

Hovencamp, in *Enterprise,* comes to similar conclusions without explicitly mentioning World War I. See particularly his discussion of economic hypotheses on pp. 175–82, including: "This book argues that American judges had an economic point of view. . . . Their political economy convinced them that questions about economic regulation should be treated as nothing more than questions about economic efficiency," questions that obviously had implications for national security during wartime (p. 176).

20. McAllister, to Jeffery, 17 May 1917 and idem., 26 Sept. 1917, both in MS 513, Box 29, Letterbook 12.

21. 248 Fed. 106, at 111 (1917).

22. Baruch, *American Industry,* p. 4.

23. Leuchtenburg, *Perils,* p. 103.

24. McAllister to Eddy, 24 Jun. 1918; Athearn, *Rebel* reprint, pp. 234–37.

25. 245 U.S. 563, at 573 (1918).

26. "State Loses Title to Valuable Lands," *Sun,* 1 Feb. 1918.

27. "Coal Land Purchased," *Sun,* 1 Mar. 1918.

28. The shift in legal culture from Progressive idealism to the legal realism of the 1930s has been explored primarily through a look at rights of workers and civil liberties. Very little has been done in regard to federal regulatory agencies or public land policies. A number of works, however, speak of the shift as one from reliance on legal traditions to reliance on "public policy"; hence, the discussion of public land policy has some bearing here. See, for example, Friedman, *History,* pp. 591–92; and Johnson, *American Legal Culture,* pp. 130–39. Also of interest are Hall, *Magic Mirror,* pp. 226–66, which shows the shift while omitting the issues at hand here, and Hall, Wiecek, and Finkelman, *American Legal History,* pp. 365–92, which speaks eloquently of the contradictions haunting the federal regulatory state in the early twentieth century. An approach focusing on "Scholarly Thought" can be found in White, *Patterns,* pp. 99–135.

29. "Coal Lands Are Given Up To The Government," *EUA,* 8 May 1918.

30. "Many Titles Rest on The Olson Case," *Sun,* 26 Apr. 1918; *Diamond Coal and Coke v. U.S.* (1914), 233 U.S. 236.

31. "W. F. Olson and Jesse Knight Are Given Decision," *Sun,* 23 Aug. 1918; "Ketchum Loses In Castle Gate Case," *Sun,* 28 Sept. 1917.

32. "W. F. Olson is Jarred from Townsite at Storrs," *Sun,* 21 Mar. 1919.

33. Ibid.

CHAPTER 17

1. Albert W. Atwood, "Mergeritis," *Saturday Evening Post,* 13 July 1918, pp. 16 ff, reprinted in Trask, *World War I,* p. 104.

2. Land Hearings.

3. Ibid., pp. 14–15, 61–67.

4. Ibid., p. 66.

5. Ibid.

6. Ibid., pp. 67–72.

7. Ibid., pp. 67–75.

8. Ibid., pp. 77–85.

9. Reported in Riter to McAllister, 20 May 1916, MS 513, Denver and Rio Grande Papers, Box 15, Fd. 3305-7, Colorado Historical Society, Denver.

10. "Utah Fuel, the State and M. P. Braffet Battle," *Sun,* 24 Oct. 1919.

11. Ibid.

12. "Status of the Milner Coal Holdings is Sought," *Sun,* 17 Oct. 1919; 228 Fed. 431 (1915).

13. "Compromise Reached in the Big Land Dispute," *Sun,* 19 Dec. 1919; Edmund T. Olson, *Coal Lands Report in Charge of Joseph Ririe, State Auditor* (Kaysville, Utah: Inland Printing Co., 1920).

14. 17 Stat. 607 (1873); R. A. Ballinger, "Recommendations Regarding Legislation," *Report to the Secretary of the Interior* (Washington, D.C.: Government Printing Office, 1907), p. 14.

15. Peffer, *Closing of the Public Domain,* p. 119.

16. Mayer and Riley, *Public Domain, Private Dominion,* pp. 155–208.

17. Robert W. Swenson, "Legal Aspects of Mineral Resources Exploitation," in Paul W. Gates, *History of Public Land Law Development* (Washington, D.C.: Government Printing Office, 1968), pp. 734–35; 45 Cong. Rec. 4644 (1910).

18. Wyant, *Westward in Eden,* pp. 84, 85; Swenson, 741.

19. Cong. Rec. 65th Congress, 2nd session, p. 391.

20. Cong. Rec. 66th Congress, 1st Session, p. 4111.

21. *Joint Hearings Before the Committee on Public Lands and Surveys, United States Senate, and the Committee on the Public Lands, House of Representatives, 69th Congress, First Session. February 11 and 12, 1926* (hereafter Joint Hearings) (Washington, D.C.: Government Printing Office, 1926), p. 113; Swenson, pp. 741–45.

22. 41 Stat. 437 at 438–440 (1920).

23. Olson, pp. 13–15.

24. Ibid., p. 26.

25. Kolko, *Triumph,* p. 287.

26. J. B. Forrester, "Carbon County Coal Properties," *New West Magazine,* vol. 11, no. 2 (Feb. 1920): 28–30.

27. "D&RG Under New Control," [Los Angeles?] *Times,* 1 Aug. 1921, MS 513, Box 19, Fd. 3548; "Brief Comments on History of The Denver and Rio Grande Western Railroad Company and Predecessors," MS 513, Box 56, Fd. "History;" Athearn, *Rebel,* pp. 240–327.

28. 49 LD 212 (1922); "Commissioner Would Give Coal Land To Braffet," *Sun,* 4 Mar. 1921; "Higher Price for Valuable Coal Lease," *Sun,* 8 July 1921; "Resolution," Book 3H, pp. 224, 225, Carbon County Recorder's Records, Carbon County Courthouse, Price, Utah.

29. 47 L.D. 58 (1919); "Coal Lands Decision of Much Interest Locally," *Sun,* 28 Jan. 1921.

30. "United States Fuel Is Loser In Big Land Case," *Sun,* 18 Feb. 1921. *Decisions of the Secretary of the Interior In Cases Relating to the Public Lands,* Vol. 47, January 1, 1919–January 31, 1921 (Washington, D.C.: Government Printing Office, 1921) and idem., Vol. 48, Feb. 1, 1921–Apr. 30, 1922 (Washington, D.C.: Government Printing Office, 1922) do not mention LeRoy Eccles nor any of his associates, nor the Sweet section itself, but the title transfer is recorded in Patent Book 6, pp. 250, 251 and Book 5H, pp. 207, 208, both in Carbon County Recorder's Office.

31. 42 Stat. 857 (1922); *Annual Report of the Secretary of the Interior for the fiscal year ended June 30, 1921* (Washington, D.C.: Government Printing Office, 1921), p. 12.

32. "State to Defend Title to Land at Castle Gate," *Sun,* 16 Sept. 1921; "Carbon's Immense Coal Field Described by Uncle Sam's Geologists," *Sun,* 10 Feb. 1922.

33. "No Route to Book Cliffs Coal," *Sun,* 14 Apr. 1920; Chandler, *Visible Hand,* pp. 456, 457; "State to Defend Title to Land at Castle Gate," *Sun,* 16 Sept. 1921.

34. 49 L.D. 212 (1922); "Involves Local Land," *Sun,* 26 May 1922; "Mark P. Braffet Loses His First Round With the Utah Fuel," *Sun,* 11 Aug. 1922; "Title to Lands in Castle Gate District Now Up in Washington, D.C.," *Sun,* 20 July 1923; "Land Title Denied," *Sun,* 7 Sept. 1923; 276 U.S. 560 (1928), 563.

35. 52 L.D. 503 (1928), 504; "Castle Gate Coal Land Case Goes Against Cyrus Shores," *Sun,* 10 Feb. 1922; Carstensen, *Public Lands,* p. 509.

36. "Cyrus W. Shores Loses Out in Castle Gate Coal Land Litigation," *Sun,* 9 Mar. 1923; 52 L.D. 503 (1928).

37. "State to Defend Title to Land at Castle Gate," *Sun,* 16 Sept. 1921; "State's Title To Valuable Tract of Coal Land in Carbon Upheld," *Sun,* 23 Feb. 1923; "Title to Lands in Castle Gate District Now Up in Washington, D.C.," *Sun,* 20 July 1923; "Land Title Denied," *Sun,* 7 Sept. 1923.

CHAPTER 18

1. Howe, *Confessions,* p. 325.

2. Hawley, *Search for a Modern Order,* pp. 100–03; Keller, *Regulating,* pp. 34–40; Hovencamp, *Enterprise,* pp. 266–67, 304–05.

3. Link, "What Happened?" pp. 833–51.

4. Graham, *Great Campaigns,* pp. 117–26; quote p. 123.

5. Hawley, pp. 45–49, 66–71, 100–04; Keller, pp. 34–42; Hovencamp, pp. 241–307.

6. Quoted in Leuchtenburg, *Perils,* p. 188.

7. Filene, "Obituary," p. 33.

8. "Milner Property to be Developed," NA, 7 Sept. 1922; Alexander, "Smoot and Land Policy," pp. 245–64.

9. Ibid; "Experts Go Over the Milner Lands at Price," *Sun,* 21 Oct. 1922.

10. "Big Deal in Carbon County Coal Lands Now Being Made on the Coast," *Sun,* 24 Nov. 1922.

11. "Experts Go Over," *Sun,* 23 May 1923 and "Big Deal."

12. "Milner Lands Title Again in Court Action," *Sun,* 23 May 1923.

13. "Utah's Governor Gets Busy on Land Titles While on His Trip Back East," *Sun,* 26 Oct. 1923.

14. Joint Hearings, p. 108.

15. "Milner Lands Title Again in Court Action."

16. "(Opinion): United States Court of Appeals, Eighth Circuit," RG 267, Supreme Court Appellate Cases, Case 984, File 31707, National Archives, Washington, D.C.

17. "Petition for Writ of Certiorari;" "Motion of State of Utah for leave to appear as *amicus curiae*"; Charles Elmore Cropley to Wilson & Barnes, Esqs., 6 Aug. 1927; all in RG 267, Case 984, File 31707.

18. "No Overtures as Yet for Compromise," *Sun,* 16 Apr. 1926.

19. 44 Stat. 891 (1926).

20. Mineral Leasing Act of 1920, as amended 30 U.S.C. 181.

21. 44 Stat. 1026 (1927), at 1027.

22. *Work, Secretary of the Interior, v. Braffet,* 275 U.S. 514 (1926).

23. "Mark P. Braffet Funeral Tuesday," *Deseret News,* 3 Jan. 1927.

24. 276 U.S. 560 (1928); "State Wins Fight Over Coal Lands After Long Dispute," *Sun,* 15 Nov. 1928.

25. 52 L.D. 503 (1928), at 506.

26. 52 L.D. 503; "State Wins Fight."

27. 274 U.S. 640 (1927).

28. "Sutherland Gets Out of the Old Law Firm," EUA, 2 Aug. 1906.

29. *U.S. v. Peter M. Baum,* in AC 11,908, George Sutherland Papers, Box 10, "Legal Briefs, 1888–1901," Library of Congress, Washington, D.C.

30. *U.S. v. Carpenter and others,"* idem.

31. Paschal, *Sutherland,* p. 149.

32. 274 U.S. 640; "Carbon County Land Company Loses Out in Supreme Court," *Sun,* 3 Jun. 1927.

33. 284 U.S. 534 (1932), at 545; "Carbon County Coal Lands Restored For Entry," [Price] *Sun-Advocate,* 29 Jun. 1933.

34. "Carbon Coal Lands Restored for Entry."

35. 48 Stat. 1185 (1934).

36. Taniguchi, "Perceptions and Realities," pp. 184–90.

37. Mayer and Riley, *Public Domain, Private Dominion,* p. 142.

38. 71 L.D. 392 (1964); Book 93, p. 206, Carbon County Recorder's Office.

39. Under these expanded provisions, Congress later determined that too much coal land had been leased under terms unfavorable to the federal

government, which resulted in the passage of the Federal Coal Leasing Amendments Act in 1976. See discussion in Mayer and Riley, pp. 140–45.

CONCLUSION

1. Jan Shipps, "In the Presence of the Past: Continuity and Change in Twentieth-Century Mormonism," in Alexander and Embry, *After 150 Years,* p. 9.

2. Arrington and Alexander, *Dependent Commonwealth,* p. 7.

3. Arrington, *From Wilderness,* p. 17.

4. *United States v. Detroit Timber & Lumber Co.,* 200 U.S. 321 (1906); *United States v. Clark,* 200 U.S. 601 (1906).

5. See, for example, *Kadish v. State Land Department,* 747 Pac. 2nd 1183 (1988).

6. Mineral Leasing Act, 41 Stat. 437 (1920).

7. This language is borrowed from Chandler, *Visible Hand.*

8. Many versions of this idea exist in the literature. See, for example, Nash, *Creating the West,* pp. 11–14.

9. Wiebe, *Businessmen and Reform,* p. 211.

10. Burch to solicitor general, 30 July 1906, Record Group 60, Justice Department Straight Numerical Files, Box 654, Case 48590, National Archives, Washington, D.C.

Selected Bibliography

SECONDARY SOURCES

Abraham, Henry J. *Justices and Presidents: A Political History of Appointments to the Supreme Court.* 2nd ed. New York: Oxford University Press, 1985.

Alexander, Thomas. "Senator Reed Smoot and Western Land Policy, 1905–1920," *Arizona and the West* (fall 1971):245–64.

———, ed. *"Soul-Butter and Hog Wash," and Other Essays on the American West.* Provo, Utah: Brigham Young University Press, 1978.

——— and Jessie L. Embry, eds. *After 150 Years: The Latter-day Saints in Sesquicentennial Perspective.* Provo, Utah: Brigham Young University Press, 1983.

Allen, James B. *The Company Town in the American West.* Norman: University of Oklahoma Press, 1966.

——— and Glen M. Leonard. *The Story of the Latter-day Saints.* Salt Lake City: Deseret Book, 1976.

Anderson, Nels. *Desert Saints: The Mormon Frontier in Utah.* Chicago: University of Chicago Press, 1942.

Andrews, Wayne, ed. *The Autobiography of Theodore Roosevelt.* New York: Charles Scribner's, 1958.

Arrington, Leonard J. *The Changing Economic Structure of the Mountain West, 1850–1950.* Logan, Utah: Utah State University Press, 1963.

———. *David Eccles: Pioneer Western Industrialist.* Logan: Utah State University Press, 1975.

———. *From Wilderness to Empire: The Role of Utah in Western Economic History.* Salt Lake City: University of Utah Institute of American Studies, 1961.

———. *Great Basin Kingdom: An Economic History of the Latter-day Saints, 1830–1900.* Cambridge: Harvard University Press, 1958. Reprint, Lincoln: University of Nebraska Press, Bison Books, 1966.

——— and Thomas Alexander. *A Dependent Commonwealth: Utah's Economy from Statehood to the Great Depression.* Provo, Utah: Brigham Young University Press, 1974.

——— and Davis Bitton. *The Mormon Experience: A History of the Latter-day Saints.* New York: Alfred A. Knopf, 1979.

295

———— with Gary P. Hansen. *"The Richest Hole on Earth": A History of the Bingham Copper Mine.* Logan: Utah State University Press, 1963.

Athearn, Robert G. *Rebel of the Rockies: A History of the Denver and Rio Grande Western Railroad.* New Haven: Yale University Press, 1962. Reprint, Lincoln: University of Nebraska Press, 1977, under the title *The Denver and Rio Grande Western Railroad: Rebel of the Rockies.*

————. "The Independence of the Denver & Rio Grande." *Utah Historical Quarterly* 26 (1958):2–21.

————. *Union Pacific Country.* Chicago: Rand McNally, 1971.

————. "Utah and the Coming of the Denver and Rio Grande Railroad." *Utah Historical Quarterly* 27 (1959):127–42.

Baker, Ray S. *Woodrow Wilson: Life and Letters.* 8 vols. New York: Greenwood, 1927–1939.

Bakken, Gordon Morris. *The Development of Law on the Rocky Mountain Frontier: Civil Law and Society, 1850–1912.* Westport, Conn.: Greenwood, 1983.

————. *Rocky Mountain Constitution Making, 1850–1912.* New York: Greenwood, 1987.

Baldwin, William Lee. *Antitrust and the Changing Corporation.* Durham, N.C.: Duke University Press, 1961.

Bancroft, Hubert Howe. *History of Utah.* San Francisco: Bancroft, 1889.

Barck, Oscar Theodore Jr. and Nelson Manfred Blake. *Since 1900: A History of the United States in Our Times.* 4th ed. New York: Macmillan, 1965.

Baruch, Bernard M. *American Industry in the War.* New York: Prentice-Hall, 1949.

Beebe, Lucius, and Charles Clegg. *Rio Grande: Mainline of the Rockies.* Berkeley: Howell-North, 1962.

Bickel, Alexander M. and Benno C. Schmidt, Jr. *The Judiciary and Responsible Government, 1910–21.* vol. 9 in *History of the Supreme Court of the United States.* New York: Macmillan, 1984.

Bindler, Norman. *The Conservative Court, 1910–1930.* Associated Faculty, 1986.

Bishop, Joseph Bucklin. *Theodore Roosevelt and His Times.* 2 vols. New York: Charles Scribner's, 1920.

Bitton, R. Davis. "The B. H. Roberts Case of 1898–1900." *Utah Historical Quarterly* 25 (January 1957):27–46.

Black, Henry Campbell. *Black's Law Dictionary.* 3rd ed. St. Paul: West Publishing, 1933.

Blum, John Morton. *The Progressive Presidents: Roosevelt, Wilson, Roosevelt, Johnson.* New York: W. W. Norton, 1980.

Bowen, Lynne. *Boss Whistle: The Coal Miners of Vancouver Island Remember.* Lantzville, British Columbia: Oolichan Books, 1982.

————. *Three Dollar Dreams.* Lantzville, British Columbia: Oolichan Books, 1987.

Brooks, Juanita. *The Mountain Meadows Massacre.* Palo Alto, Ca.: Stanford University Press, 1950.

Brown, Ronald C. *Hard Rock Miners: The Intermountain West, 1860–1920.* College Station: Texas A&M University Press, 1962.

Bryant, Keith L. Jr. *History of the Atchison, Topeka and Santa Fe Railway.* Lincoln: University of Nebraska Press, 1974.

Carstensen, Vernon, ed. *The Public Lands: Studies in the History of the Public Domain.* Madison: University of Wisconsin Press, 1968.

Chandler, Alfred D. *Strategy and Structure.* Cambridge, Mass.: MIT Press, 1962.

————. *The Visible Hand: The Managerial Revolution in American Business.* Cambridge: Harvard University Press, 1977.

Coletta, Paolo E. *The Presidency of William Howard Taft.* Lawrence: University Press of Kansas, 1973.

Cutright, Paul Russell. *Theodore Roosevelt: The Making of a Conservationist.* (Urbana: University of Illinois Press, 1985).

Daniels, Josephus. *The Life of Woodrow Wilson, 1856–1924.* N.p.: Will H. Johnson, 1924.

Davis, John Hagy. *The Guggenheims: An American Epic.* New York: William Morrow, 1978.

Deseret News. *1991–1992 (LDS) Church Almanac.* Salt Lake City: Deseret News Press, 1990 [*sic*].

DiGaetano, Alan. "Urban Political Reform: Did It Kill the Machine?" *Journal of Urban History,* vol. 18, no. 1 (November 1991):37–67.

Dilley, James W. *History of the Scofield Mine Disaster.* Provo, Utah: Skelton, 1900.

Doelling, Helmut Hans. *Central Utah Coal Fields.* Salt Lake City: University of Utah Press, 1972.

Downey, Mathew T., et al., eds. *The Progressive Era and the First World War (1900–1918).* New York: Macmillan, 1992.

Durham, G. Homer. "Administrative Organization of the Mormon Church." *Political Science Quarterly* 57 (March 1942):51–71.

Eaton, William Dunsneath and Harry C. Reed. *Woodrow Wilson: His Life and Work.* N.p.: C. E. Thomas, 1919.

Fahey, John. *Hecla: A Century of Western Mining.* Seattle: University of Washington Press, 1990.

Fausold, Martin L. *Gifford Pinchot: Bull Moose Progressive.* Syracuse, N.Y.: Syracuse University Press, 1961.

Fell, James E. Jr. *Ores to Metals: The Rocky Mountain Smelting Industry.* Lincoln: University of Nebraska Press, 1979.

Filene, Peter J. "An Obituary for 'The Progressive Movement.'" *American Quarterly* 9 (1970):20–34.

Fisher, John Sterling. *A Builder of the West: The Life of General William Jackson Palmer.* Caldwell, Idaho: Caxton Printers, 1939.

Friedman, Lawrence, *A History of American Law*. New York: Simon and Schuster, 1973.

———. *Total Justice*. New York: Russell Sage Foundation, 1985.

Friedman, Leon and Fred L. Israel. *The Justices of the United States Supreme Court, 1789–1969: Their Lives and Major Opinions,* Vol. III. New York: Chelsea House, 1969.

Furniss, Norman F. *The Mormon Conflict, 1850–1859.* New Haven: Yale University Press, 1960.

Gable, John Allen. *The Bull Moose Years: Theodore Roosevelt and the Progressive Party.* Port Washington, N.Y.: Kennikat, 1978.

Gale, Hoyt Stoddard. *Coal Fields of Northwestern Colorado and Northeastern Utah.* Washington: Government Printing Office, 1910.

Gardner, A. Dudley and Verla R. Flores. *Forgotten Frontier: A History of Wyoming Coal Mining.* Boulder, Colo.: Westview, 1989.

Garraty, John A. *The New Commonwealth, 1877–1890.* New York: Harper and Row, 1968.

Goldman, Eric F. *Rendezvous With Destiny.* New York: Alfred A. Knopf, 1952.

Graham, Otis L. Jr. *The Great Campaigns: Reform and War in America, 1900–1928.* Englewood Cliffs, N.J.: Prentice-Hall, 1971.

Grauman, Melody Webb. "Kennecott: Alaskan Origins of a Copper Empire," *Western Historical Quarterly* 9 (April 1978):197–211.

Hall, Kermit. *The Magic Mirror: Law in American History.* New York: Oxford University Press, 1989.

———, William M. Wiecek, and Paul Finkelman. *American Legal History: Cases and Materials.* New York: Oxford University Press, 1991.

Hammond, Otis G., ed. *The Utah Expedition, 1857–1858.* Concord, N.H.: New Hampshire Historical Society, 1928.

Hansen, Klaus J. *Quest for Empire: The Political Kingdom of God and the Council of Fifty in Mormon History.* Lincoln: University of Nebraska Press, 1967.

Hardy, B. Carmon. *Solemn Covenant: The Mormon Polygamous Passage.* Urbana: University of Illinois Press, 1992.

Hawley, Ellis W. *The Great War and the Search for a Modern Order, A History of the American People and Their Institutions, 1917–1933.* New York: St. Martin's, 1979.

Hays, Samuel P. *Conservation and the Gospel of Efficiency: The Progressive Conservation Movement, 1890–1920.* (Cambridge: Harvard University Press, 1959.

——— "The Politics of Reform in Municipal Government in the Progressive Era." *Pacific Northwest Quarterly* 55 (1964):157–69.

———. *The Response to Industrialism, 1885–1914.* Chicago: University of Chicago Press, 1957.

Hechler, Kenneth W. *Insurgency: Personalities and Politics of the Taft Era.* New York: Russell & Russell, 1964.

Higgins, Will C. "Business Men Examine Hiawatha Mines." *Salt Lake Mining Review* 13 (30 May 1911):15–17.

————. "The Castle Valley Coal Company." *Salt Lake Mining Review* 13 (30 June 1911):15–17.

————. "Success of the Consolidated Fuel Company." *Salt Lake Mining Review* 13 (15 April 1911):20–21.

Hill, Marvin S. and James B. Allen, eds. *Mormonism and American Culture.* New York: Harper and Row, 1972.

Himmelberg, Robert F., ed. *The Monopoly Issue and Antitrust, 1900–1917.* New York: Garland, 1994.

Hines, Walker D. *War History of American Railroads.* New Haven: Yale University Press, 1928.

Hofstadter, Richard. *The Age of Reform: From Bryan to F.D.R.* New York: Alfred A. Knopf, 1955.

Holbrook, Stewart H. *The Story of American Railroads.* New York: Crown, 1947.

Hoogenboom, Ari Arthur and Olive Hoogenboom. *A History of the ICC: From Panacea to Palliative.* New York: W. W. Norton, 1976.

Hovencamp, Herbert. *Enterprise and American Law, 1836–1937.* Cambridge: Harvard University Press, 1991.

Howe, Frederic H. *The Confessions of a Reformer.* 1925. Reprint. New York: Quadrangle, 1967.

Hulse, James W. "W. A. Clark and the Las Vegas Connection: The 'Midas of the West' and the Development of Southern Nevada." *Montana* 37 (winter 1987):48–55.

Hurst, James Willard. *Law and the Conditions of Freedom in the Nineteenth-Century United States.* Madison: University of Wisconsin Press, 1956.

Huthmacher, Joseph. "Urban Liberalism in the Age of Reform." *Mississippi Valley Historical Review* 49 (September 1962): 231–41.

Jenks, J. W. *Great Fortunes: The Winning: The Using.* New York: McClure Phillips, 1906.

Jensen, Oliver, ed. *The American Heritage History of Railroads in America.* New York: American Heritage, 1981.

Johnson, John W. *American Legal Culture, 1908–1940.* Westport, Conn.: Greenwood, 1981.

Josephson, Matthew. *The Robber Barons: The Great American Capitalists, 1861–1901.* Published 1934. Reprint, New York: Harcourt, Brace, Jovanovich, 1962.

Journal of the West 8 (July 1974).

Keller, Morton. *Regulating a New Economy: Public Policy and Economic Change in America, 1900–1933.* Cambridge: Harvard University Press, 1990.

Kennedy, David M., ed. *Progressivism: The Critical Issues.* Boston: Little, Brown, 1971.

Klein, Maury. *The Life and Legend of Jay Gould.* Baltimore: Johns Hopkins Press, 1986.

———. *Union Pacific: Birth of a Railroad, 1862–1893.* Garden City, New York: Doubleday, 1987.

Kirkland, Edward Chase. *Industry Comes of Age: Business, Labor and Public Policy.* New York: Holt, Rinehart, and Winston, 1961.

Knight, Jesse William. *The Jesse Knight Family.* Salt Lake City: Deseret News Press, 1940.

Kolko, Gabriel. *Railroads and Regulation, 1877–1916.* Princeton: Princeton University Press, 1965.

———. *The Triumph of Conservatism: A Reinterpretation of American History, 1900–1916.* New York: Free Press of Macmillan Co., 1963.

Kretchman, Herbert F. *The Story of Gilsonite.* Salt Lake City: American Gilsonite Company, 1957.

Lamar, Howard R. *The Far Southwest, 1846–1912: A Territorial History.* New Haven: Yale University Press, 1966.

———. "Statehood for Utah: A Different Path." *Utah Historical Quarterly* 39 (fall 1971):307–27.

Lambert, Neal. "Saints, Sinners and Scribes: A Look At the Mormon in Fiction." *Utah Historical Quarterly* 36 (winter 1968):63–76.

Lamborn, John E. and Charles S. Peterson. "The Substance of the Land: Agriculture v. Industry in the Smelter Cases of 1904 and 1906." *Utah Historical Quarterly* 53 (fall 1985): 308–25.

Larson, Gustive O. *The "Americanization" of Utah for Statehood.* San Marino, Calif.: Huntington Library, 1971.

LeMassena, R. A. with Jackson Thode. *Colorado's Mountain Railroads.* 5 vols. Golden, Colorado: Smoking Stack, 1965.

Leonard, William Norris. *Railroad Consolidation Under the Transportation Act of 1920.* New York: Columbia University Press, 1946.

Leuchtenburg, William E. *The Perils of Prosperity, 1914–32.* Chicago: University of Chicago Press, 1958.

Lever, W. H. *History of Sanpete and Emery Counties, Utah.* Salt Lake City: Tribune, 1898.

Link, Arthur S. *Woodrow Wilson and the Progressive Era, 1910–1917.* New York: Harper & Row, 1954.

———. "What Happened to the Progressive Movement in the 1920s?" *American Historical Review* 64 (July 1959):833–51.

——— and Richard L. McCormick. *Progressivism.* Arlington Heights Ill.: Harlan Davidson, 1983.

Lyman, Edward Leo. *Political Deliverance: The Mormon Quest for Utah Statehood.* Urbana: University of Illinois Press, 1986.

McCarthy, Michael P. "Urban Optimism and Reform Thought in the Progressive Era," *The Historian* 51 (February 1989):239–62.

McCullough, David. *Mornings on Horseback*. New York: Simon and Schuster, 1981.

McGeary, M. Nelson. *Gifford Pinchot: Forester-Politician*. Princeton, N.J.: Princeton University Press, 1960.

McGovern, George Stanley and Leonard F. Guttridge. *The Great Coalfield War*. Boston: Houghton Mifflin, 1972.

Malone, Michael P. *The Battle for Butte: Mining and Politics on the Northern Frontier, 1864–1906*. Seattle: University of Washington Press, 1981.

Mangum, William D. *The Clarks: An American Phenomenon*. New York: Silver Bow, 1941.

Marcosson, Isaac F. *Anaconda*. New York: Dodd, Mead, 1957.

————— *Metal Magic: The Story of the American Smelting and Refining Company*. New York: Farrar, Straus, 1949.

Mason, Alpheus Thomas. *Brandeis: A Free Man's Life*. New York: Viking, 1946.

—————. *Bureaucracy Convicts Itself: The Ballinger-Pinchot Controversy of 1910*. New York: Viking, 1941.

—————. *The Supreme Court from Taft to Burger*. Baton Rouge: Louisiana State University Press, 1979.

Mayer, Carl J. and George A. Riley. *Public Domain, Private Dominion: A History of Public Mineral Policy in America*. San Francisco: Sierra Club Books, 1985.

Merrill, Milton R. *Reed Smoot: Apostle in Politics*. Logan: Utah State University Press, 1990.

—————. "Reed Smoot, Apostle-Senator." *Utah Historical Quarterly* 28 (October 1960):342–49.

Miller, Charles Wallace Jr. *Stake Your Claim! The Tale of America's Enduring Mining Laws*. Tucson: Westernlore, 1991. *Montana* 37 (autumn 1987).

Mowry, George E. *The California Progressives*. Berkeley: University of California Press, 1951.

—————. *The Era of Theodore Roosevelt and the Birth of Modern America, 1900–1912*. New York: Harper & Row, 1958.

—————. *Theodore Roosevelt and the Progressive Movement*. Madison: University of Wisconsin Press, 1947.

"Mr. Roosevelt to the Mormons." *Collier's,* 15 Apr. 1911: 28.

Mumey, Nolie. *John Williams Gunnison (1812–1853), The Last of the Western Explorers: A History of the Survey Through Colorado and Utah with a Biography and Details of his Massacre*. Denver, Colo.: Artcraft, 1955.

Murphy, Miriam. "The Great 'Smoke Nuisance.'" *Beehive History* 9 (1983):18–22.

Nash, Gerald D. *The American West in the Twentieth Century: A Short History of an Urban Oasis*. Englewood Cliffs, N.J.: Prentice-Hall, 1973.

—————. *Creating the West: Historical Interpretations, 1890–1990*. Albuquerque: University of New Mexico Press, 1991.

Nelson, Robert H. *The Making of Federal Coal Policy.* Durham, N.C.: Duke University Press, 1983.

New West Magazine 11 (1920).

Notarianni, Philip F., ed. *Carbon County: Eatern Utah's Industrialized Island.* Salt Lake City: Utah State Historical Society, 1981.

———. "Utah's Ellis Island: The Difficult 'Americanization' of Carbon County." *Utah Historical Quarterly* 47 (1979):178–93.

Nye, Russell B. *Midwestern Progressive Politics: A Historical Study of Its Origin and Development, 1870–1950.* East Lansing: Michigan State University Press, 1951.

O'Dea, Thomas F. *The Mormons.* Chicago: University of Chicago Press, 1957.

Official Report of the Proceedings and Debates of the Convention Assembled at Salt Lake City on the Fourth Day of March, 1895, to Adopt a Constitution for the State of Utah. 2 vols. Salt Lake City: Star Printing, 1898.

Papanikolas, Helen Zeese, ed. *The Peoples of Utah.* Salt Lake City: Utah State Historical Society, 1976.

———. "Utah's Coal Lands: A Vital Example of How America Became A Great Nation." *Utah Historical Quarterly* 43 (1975):104–24.

Papanikolas, Zeese. *Buried Unsung: Louis Tikas and the Ludlow Massacre.* Salt Lake City: University of Utah Press, 1982.

Paschal, Joel Francis. *Mr. Justice Sutherland: A Man Against the State.* Princeton, N.J.: Princeton University Press, 1951.

Paul, Rodman Wilson. *Mining Frontiers of the Far West, 1848–1880.* New York: Holt, Rinehart, and Winston, 1963.

Peffer, E. Louise. *The Closing of the Public Domain: Disposal and Reservation Policies, 1900–1950.* Stanford: Stanford University Press, 1951.

Pennick, James Jr. *Progressive Politics and Conservation: The Ballinger-Pinchot Affair.* Chicago: University of Chicago Press, 1968.

Peterson, Richard H. *The Bonanza Kings: The Social Origins and Business Behavior of Western Mining Entrepreneurs, 1870–1900.* Lincoln: University of Nebraska Press, 1971.

———. "Jesse Knight, Utah's Mormon Mining Mogul." *Utah Historical Quarterly* 57 (1989):240–53.

Pinchot, Gifford. *Breaking New Ground.* New York: Harcourt, Brace, 1947.

Plimpton, Frances T. [Reminiscence.] *Reader's Digest,* 1 June 1958:142.

Poll, Richard D. "A State Is Born." *Utah Historical Quarterly* 32 (winter 1964):9–31.

———, Thomas G. Alexander, Eugene E. Campbell, and David E. Miller. eds., *Utah's History.* Provo, Utah: Brigham Young University Press, 1978.

Powell, Allan Kent. *The Next Time We Strike: The Utah Coal Fields During the Non-Union Era.* Logan: Utah State University Press, 1985.

———. "Tragedy at Scofield." *Utah Historical Quarterly* 41 (spring 1973).

Pringle, Henry F. *The Life and Times of William Howard Taft.* New York: Farrar & Rinehart, 1939.

Quinn, D. Michael. "LDS Church Authority and New Plural Marriages, 1890–1904." *Dialogue* 18 (spring 1985):8–23.

The Railroad Red Book: An Exponent of Irrigated Farming, a Magazine of Rocky Mountain Travel 34 (January 1917).

Rawlins, Joseph L. (Alta Rawlins Jensen, ed.). *The Unfavored Few: An Auto-Biography of Joseph L. Rawlins.* Salt Lake City: privately printed, 1954.

Reisner, Marc. *Cadillac Desert: The American West and Its Disappearing Water.* New York: Viking, 1986.

Resek, Carl, ed. *The Progressives.* New York: Bobbs-Merrill, 1967.

Reynolds, Thursey Jessen, comp. *Centennial Echoes From Carbon County.* Salt Lake City: Daughters of Utah Pioneers, 1948.

Rickard, Thomas A. *A History of American Mining.* New York: McGraw-Hill, 1932.

———. "The Utah Copper Enterprise." *The Mining and Scientific Press* (1918):41, 47.

Riegel, Robert Edgar. *The Story of the Western Railroads.* New York: Macmillan, 1926.

Ringholz, Raye C. *Uranium Frenzy: Boom and Bust on the Colorado Plateau.* New York: W. W. Norton, 1989.

Robbins, George W. "Land Policies of the United States Applied to Utah to 1910." *Utah Historical Quarterly* 20 (July 1952):239–51.

Robbins, Roy M. *Our Landed Heritage: The Public Domain, 1776–1936.* Glouster, Mass.: Peter Smith, 1960.

Roberts, B. H. *A Comprehensive History of the Church of Jesus Christ of Latter-day Saints, Century I, in Six Volumes.* Reprint. Provo, Utah: Brigham Young University Press, 1965.

Roosevelt, Theodore. *American Problems: Works of Theodore Roosevelt.* New York: Charles Scribner's, 1925.

———. *Autobiography.* New York: Charles Scribner's, 1913.

Rumble, Wilfrid E. *American Legal Realism.* Ithaca: Cornell University Press, 1968.

Scamehorn, H. Lee. *Pioneer Steelmaker in the West: The Colorado Fuel and Iron Company, 1872–1903.* Boulder, Colo.: Pruett, 1976.

Schlesinger, Arthur M. Jr. *The Age of Roosevelt: The Crisis of the Old Order, 1919–1933.* Boston: Houghton Mifflin, 1957.

Seifrit, William C. "To Get U(tah) in U(nion)': Diary of a Failed Mission." *Utah Historical Quarterly* 51 (fall 1983):358–81.

Seltzer, Curtis. *Fire in the Hole: Miners and Managers in the American Coal Industry.* Lexington: University Press of Kentucky, 1985.

Semonche, John E. *Charting the Future: The Supreme Court Responds to a Changing Society, 1890–1920.* Westport, Conn.: Greenwood, 1978.

Shipps, Jan. "Utah Comes of Age Politically: A Study of the State's Politics in the Early Years of the Twentieth Century." *Utah Historical Quarterly* 35 (spring 1967):91–111.

Siringo, Charles A. *A Cowboy Detective: A True Story of Twenty-Two Years With a World-Famous Detective Agency.* 1912. Reprint. Lincoln: University of Nebraska Press, 1988.

Sklar, Martin J. *The Corporate Reconstruction of American Capitalism, 1890–1916: The Market, the Law, and Politics.* Cambridge: Cambridge University Press, 1988.

Slotnick, Herman. "The Ballinger-Pinchot Affair in Alaska." *Journal of the West* 10 (April 1971):337–47.

Smith, Duane A. *Mining America: The Industry and the Environment, 1800–1980.* Lawrence: University Press of Kansas, 1987.

————. *Rocky Mountain Mining Camps: The Urban Frontier.* Bloomington: Indiana University Press, 1967.

Sobel, Robert, ed. *Biographical Directory of the United States Executive Branch, 1774–1977.* Westport, Conn.: Greenwood, 1977.

Sonnichsen, C. L. *Colonel Greene and the Copper Skyrocket.* Tucson: University of Arizona Press, 1983.

Spence, Clark C. *British Investment and the American Mining Frontier, 1860–1901.* Ithaca, N.Y.: Cornell University Press, 1958.

————. *Mining Engineers and the American West: The Lace-Boot Brigade, 1849–1933.* New Haven: Yale University Press, 1970.

Standard Coal Company. *Standard Coal: The Story of the Mining of Standard Coal.* Salt Lake City, c. 1947.

Strevell, Charles N. *As I Recall Them.* Salt Lake City: Stevens & Wallis, n.d.
———— "Coal Situation for 1917." *Salt Lake Mining Review* 16 (30 April 1917):30.

Summers, Harrison Boyd and Robert E. Summers. *The Railroad Problem.* New York: H. W. Wilson, 1939.

Taniguchi, Nancy J. "No Proper Job For A Stranger: The Political Reign of Mark Braffet." *Utah Historical Quarterly* 58 (spring 1990):145–64.

————. "Rebels and Relatives: The Mormon Foundation of Spring Glen, 1878–90." *Utah Historical Quarterly* 48 (1980):366–78.

Thelen, David P. "Social Tensions and the Origins of Progressivism." *Journal of American History* 56 (Sept. 1969):323–41.

Trask, David F., ed. *World War I At Home: Readings in American Life, 1914–1920.* New York: John Wiley, 1970.

Turner, Frederick Jackson. "The Significance of the Frontier in American History." *Proceedings of the Forty-First Annual Meeting of the State Historical Society of Wisconsin.* (Madison, Wisconsin, 1894):79–112.

Union Pacific Coal Company. *History of the Union Pacific Coal Mines, 1868 to 1940.* Omaha, Nebraska: Colonial, [1940].

Utah Historical Quarterly 31 (summer 1963).

Van Hise, Charles R. *Conservation and Regulation in the United States During the World War.* 1918. In facsimile reprint as *The United States in World War I.* N.p.: Jerome S. Ozer, 1974.

Van Wagoner, Richard S. *Mormon Polygamy: A History.* Salt Lake City: Signature, 1986.

Warrum, Noble, ed. *Utah Since Statehood.* 3 vols. Salt Lake City: S. J. Clarke, 1919.

Weinstein, James. *The Corporate Ideal in the Liberal State, 1900–1918.* Boston: Beacon, 1968.

White, G. Edward. *Patterns of American Legal Thought.* New York: Bobbs-Merrill, 1978.

White, Leonard D. *The Republican Era: 1869–1901.* New York: Macmillan, 1958.

Whiteside, James. *Regulating Danger: The Struggle for Mine Safety in the Rocky Mountain Coal Industry.* Lincoln: University of Nebraska Press, 1990.

Whitnah, Donald R., ed. *Government Agencies.* Westport, Conn.: Greenwood, 1983.

Whitney, Orson F. *History of Utah.* 4 vols. (Salt Lake City: George Q. Cannon, 1892–1904.

Who Was Who in America, Vol. I, 1897–1942. Chicago: A. N. Marquis, 1943.

Wiebe, Robert H. *Businessmen and Reform: A Study of the Progressive Movement.* Chicago: Quadrangle Paperback, 1968.

———. *The Search for Order, 1877–1920.* New York: Hill and Wang, 1967.

"With Coal Producers." *Salt Lake Mining Review* 22 (1920):35.

W.P.A. *Utah, A Guide to the State.* New York: Hastings House, 1941.

Wunderlin, Clarence E. Jr. *Visions of a New Industrial Order: Social Science and Labor Theory in America's Progressive Era.* New York: Columbia University Press, 1992.

Wyant, William K. *Westward in Eden: The Public Lands and the Conservation Movement.* Berkeley: University of California Press, 1982.

Wyman, Mark. *Hard-Rock Epic: Western Miners and the Industrial Revolution, 1860–1910.* Berkeley: University of California Press, 1979.

Young, Otis E. Jr. *Black Powder and Hand Steel: Miners and Machines on the Old Western Frontier.* Norman: University of Oklahoma Press, 1976.

———. *The Mining Men.* Kansas City, Mo.: Lowell, 1974.

PUBLIC DOCUMENTS

Carbon County. Civil Cases, 1896–1924. Criminal Cases, 1896–1924. Commissioners' Minutes, 1906–1918. Recorder's Records. All in Carbon County Courthouse, Price, Utah.

Price, Utah. Bureau of Land Management Lease Record Cards.

Salt Lake County. Third Judicial District Records. Salt Lake County Clerk's Office, Salt Lake City, Utah.

United States. Coal Commission. *Report of the United States Coal Commission, Dec. 10, 1923.* Washington, D.C.: Government Printing Office, 1925.

————. *Congressional Record* 45 Cong.; 58 Cong. 2d Sess.; 65 Cong. 2d Session; 66 Cong. 1st Sess.

————. House Reports. *Hearings Before the Subcommittee of the Committee on the Public Lands, House of Representatives, Sixty-Fifth Congress, Third Session, on H.J. Res. 282.* Washington, D.C.: Government Printing Office, 1919.

————. Interior Department. Bureau of Mines. *Mineral Yearbook.* Appropriate years.

————. Interior Department. *Decisions of the Secretary of the Interior In Cases Relating to the Public Lands, Vol. 47, Jan. 1, 1919–Jan. 31, 1921* (Washington, D.C.: Government Printing Office, 1921) and *Vol. 48, Feb. 1, 1921–April 30, 1922* (Washington, D.C.: Government Printing Office, 1922).

————. Interior Department. Paul Gates, with a chapter by Robert W. Swenson. *History of Public Land Law Development.* Washington, D.C.: Government Printing Office, 1968.

————. Interior Department. Reports. Appropriate years.

————. Library of Congress. *Theodore Roosevelt Papers.* Microfilm, 1969.

————. Library of Congress. *George Sutherland Papers.*

————. Library of Congress. *William Howard Taft Papers.* Microfilm, 1969.

————. Legislative Reference Service. *Congress and the Monopoly Problem.* Washington, D.C.: Government Printing Office, 1966.

————. (Jerry A. O'Callaghan, "The Disposition of the Public Domain in Oregon," Ph.D. dissertation, Stanford University, 1951) published as *Memorandum of the Chairman to the Committee on Interior and Insular Affairs, United States Senate.* Washington: Government Printing Office, 1960.

————. *Official Register, 1901, Vol. 1.* Washington, D.C.: Government Printing Office, 1909.

————. Senate Reports. *Hearings before the Committee of Investigation of the Interior Department and Bureau of Forestry.* 61st Congress, 3rd Session. Sen. Doc. 719, Vol. 8.

————. Senate Reports. *Message from the President of the United States.* Doc, 644, Vol. 61. 61st Cong., 2d Sess. Washington, D.C.: Government Printing Office, 1910.

————. Senate Reports. *Joint Hearings Before the Committee on Public Lands and Surveys. February 11 and 12, 1926* (Washington, D.C.: Government Printing Office, 1926.

————. Statutes at Large. Appropriate years.

Utah. Territory of Utah. *Acts, Resolutions and Memorials Passed at the Several Annual Sessions of the Legislative Assembly.* Great Salt Lake City, 1855.

————. Committee to Study Operations of State Government, Works Progress Administration. *An Economic Study of the Development of Utah's Coal Resources.* Salt Lake City, 1936.

————. Department of Mines and Mining. *Report of the State Coal Mine Inspector,* 1896–1916.

————. Department of Mines and Mining. State Coal Mine Inspector's Correspondence.

————. "Joint Senate and House Committee of the Legislature of the State of Utah, to Investigate the Question of Coal Shortage, Said Hearings beginning on the 29th day of January, A.D. 1917."

————. Olson, Edmund T. *Coal Lands Report in Charge of Joseph Ririe, State Auditor.* Kaysville, Utah: Inland Printing, 1920.

————. *Report of the Industrial Commission,* 1917–1920.

————. Secretary of Utah Territory. Territorial Executive Papers. Microfilm.

————. State Land Board Records and Administrative Correspondence, 1896–1945.

MANUSCRIPT COLLECTIONS

Berkeley, California. Bancroft Library. Henry McAllister Jr. "Colorado Land and Improvement Companies, Colorado Springs, 1884." "Record—Sevier Railway Co." "San Pete Valley Railway Co. Minutes 1893–1910."

Bloomington, Indiana. Lilly Library, Indiana University Manuscripts Collection. A. T. Volwiler Papers.

Denver, Colorado. Colorado Historical Society. Denver and Rio Grande Western Collection, MSS. 513.

Price, Utah. College of Eastern Utah Library Special Collections. "Articles of Incorporation: Coal Companies."

Provo, Utah. Lee Library, Brigham Young University. Knight Investment Company Records, MSS 278; Oral History Collection, MSS 268; Peerless Coal Company Collection, MSS 277; Reed Smoot Papers, MSS 1187; Spring Canyon Area Coal Company Records, MSS 252; Utah Fuel Company Records, MSS 154.

Salt Lake City, Utah. Church of Jesus Christ of Latter-day Saints Historian's Office. Andrew Jenson's *History of Emery Stake;* Heber J. Grant Papers, MSS 1233; Joseph Fielding Smith Papers, MSS 4250.

————. Marriott Library, University of Utah Special Collections. Coal Legislative Hearings, Acc. 479; U.S.G.S. Coal Lands Survey (1905–1908), MSS 210; State Coal Mine Inspector's Correspondence.

San Marino, California. Huntington Library. Smith, Joseph F. "Another Plain Talk: Reasons Why the People of Utah Should Be Republicans."

Washington, D.C. National Archives. Record Group 49, "Homestead Papers"; Record Group 60, "Justice Department Straight Numerical Files"; Record Group 67, "Records of the Fuel Administration, Bureau of State Organizations"; Record Group 134, "Records of the Interstate Commerce Commission"; Record Group 267, "Supreme Court Appellate Cases."

UNPUBLISHED WORKS

Brown, Mildred E. "History: Justus Wellington Seeley II." Typescript, Castle Dale, Utah, 1970.

Grow, Stewart Lofgren. "A Study of the Utah Commission." Ph.D. dissertation, University of Utah, 1954.

Grundvig, Don Carlos. "The Evolution of the Mind of Man." Mimeograph. Loveland, Colo., 1965.

Jorgensen, John L. "A History of Castle Valley to 1890." Master's thesis, University of Utah, 1955.

Madsen, Charles H., ed. "Carbon County: A History." Typescript, 1947.

Remington, Newell C. "A History of the Gilsonite Industry," Master's thesis, University of Utah, 1959.

Smith, Jon Craig. "The Coal Industry and the Political Structure of Carbon County, Utah." Unpublished paper prepared for Dr. Edward Hart, English 315, Brigham Young University, winter 1980.

Strack, Don. "A History of the Development of Coal Mining and Railroads in Carbon County, Utah." Unpublished paper prepared for Dr. Merrill K. Ridd, Geography 335, Utah State University, 1983.

Teachers, pupils, and patrons of Carbon District. "A Brief History of Carbon County." c. 1933. Mimeograph.

Taniguchi, Nancy J. "Perceptions and Realities: Progressive Reform and Utah Coal," Ph.D. dissertation, University of Utah, 1985.

Winn, Eden Lorus. "Development of Utah's Coal Mining Industry, 1850–1900," Master's thesis, Brigham Young University, n.d.

PUBLISHED DECISIONS CITED

The Holladay Coal Company v. R. A. Kirker, Charles Kirker, and Frank Tidwell, 20 Utah 192; 57 Pac. 882 (1899).

School Land—Indemnity Selection—Mineral Character. Circular. 32 L.D. 39 (1903).

Highland Boy Gold Mining Company v. Strickley. 28 Utah 215 (1904).

Strickley v. Highland Boy Co. 200 U.S. 527 (1906).

United States v. Detroit Timber and Lumber Company. 200 U.S. 321 (1906).

United States v. Clark. 200 U.S. 601 (1906).

United States v. Keitel. 211 U.S. 370 (1908).

United States v. Union Pacific Railroad Co. 226 U.S. 470 (1913).

Diamond Coal and Coke Co. v. United States. 233 U.S. 236 (1914).

Los Angeles Switching Case. 234 U.S. 294 (1914).

Intermountain Rate Cases. 234 U.S. 476 (1914).

United States v. Sweet. 228 Fed. 421 (1915).

Milner et al. v. United States. 228 Fed. 431 (1915).

Ketchum v. Denver and Rio Grande Railroad. 248 Fed. 106 (1917).

Diamond Coal and Coke Company of Wyoming et al. 46 L.D. 101 (1917).
United States v. Sweet, Administrator of Sweet. 245 U.S. 563 (1918).
Ketchum v. Pleasant Valley Coal Co. 257 Fed. 274 (1919).
State of Utah v. Olson. 47 L.D. 58 (1919).
State of Utah, Pleasant Valley Coal Company, Intervener v. Braffet. 49 L.D. 212 (1922).
United States v. Diamond Coal and Coke Co. 34 Sup. Ct. 507 (1920).
Work, Secretary of the Interior v. Braffet. 275 U.S. 514 (1926).
Independent Coal and Coke Co. et al. v. United States et al. 274 U.S. 640 (1927).
Work, Secretary of the Interior v. Braffet, Administrator. 276 U.S. 560 (1928).
Shores v. State of Utah et al. 52 L.D. 503 (1928).
Utah et al. v. United States. 284 U.S. 534 (1932).
State of Utah. 71 L.D. 392 (1964).
Kadish v. State Land Department. 747 Pac. 2nd 1183 (1988).

NEWSPAPERS

Carbon County News, (Price), 1909–1932.
Deseret [Evening] News, (Salt Lake City), 1859–1942.
Eastern Utah Advocate, (Price), 1895–1915.
News-Advocate, (Price), 1918–1922.
Salt Lake Herald, 1881–1908.
Salt Lake Tribune, 1898–1936.
Sun, (Price), 1915–1928.
Sun-Advocate, (Price), 1932–33.
Valley Tan (Camp Floyd), 1859.

Index